NAMA-LAND

FRANK CONNOLLY

Gill Books

Gill Books
Hume Avenue
Park West
Dublin 12
www.gillbooks.ie

Gill Books is an imprint of M.H. Gill & Co.

978 07171 7547 5

Copy-edited by Matthew Parkinson-Bennett
Proofread by Jane Rogers
Indexed by Eileen O'Neill
Print origination by Carole Lynch
Printed by Clays Ltd, Suffolk

This book is typeset in Linotype Minion and
Neue Helvetica.

The paper used in this book comes from the
wood pulp of managed forests. For every tree
felled, at least one tree is planted, thereby
renewing natural resources.

A CIP catalogue record for this book is available
from the British Library.

5 4 3 2 1

For Madeleine, our much-loved mother, granny and friend to so many, whose departure left a huge absence in our lives. And for the beautiful twins, Rían and Alannah, whose arrival has brought so much joy in the wake of our loss.

Frank Connolly is one of Ireland's most distinguished investigative journalists and the author of the acclaimed bestseller *Tom Gilmartin: The Man Who Brought Down a Taoiseach.* He is currently Head of Communications at SIPTU, and is a regular contributor to print and broadcast media. He lives in Dublin.

ACKNOWLEDGEMENTS

Among the sources for this book are former NAMA staff and advisors to the agency, politicians, developers, journalists, economists, lawyers, real estate and other players in the property business in Ireland. Many of these are mentioned in *NAMA-land* and their names do not require repeating here. Given the sensitivities, commercial and otherwise, associated with the NAMA project, there are many people who assisted with the research for this book who do not wish to be publicly acknowledged. Others who have suffered as a consequence of the improper, unfair, illicit and unquestionably corrupt activities exposed in these pages have been generous with their time and in sharing their experience and plight.

NAMA-land could not have been completed without the assistance of Conor Nagle, commissioning editor in Gill Books, and other members of the publishing team, including Catherine Gough and Ellen Monnelly. Thanks are due to copy-editor, Matthew Parkinson-Bennett, proofreader, Jane Rogers, typesetter, Carole Lynch, and indexer, Eileen O'Neill. Solicitors, Kieran Kelly and Padraig Ferry, provided invaluable legal advice and assistance.

I greatly appreciate the support of my colleagues in SIPTU, in particular Karen Hackett, Deirdre Price, Sonia Slevin and Scott Millar in the union's communications department. I am also grateful for those who took time to read, correct and comment on earlier drafts, including David Connolly.

The onerous demands of a work such as this, and the tight deadlines involved, have consequences for my immediate family, especially my patient and loving partner, Mary Tracey, who carried so much of the burden imposed on our lives over the past year and more. Without her assistance and support, this work could not have been completed. My children, Oisín, Saoirse, Caomhán, Síomha and Liadh, as always are among my most ardent supporters – and critics. I am eternally grateful for their encouragement and love. I hope this work will assist in their quest, and that of their and future generations, for a better, more equal society in which their dreams can be fulfilled.

LIST OF ABBREVIATIONS

ADIA	Abu Dhabi Investment Authority
AIB	Allied Irish Bank
Anglo	Anglo Irish Bank
BHC	Belfast Harbour Commissioners
BNP	Paribas Banque Nationale de Paris Paribas
C&AG	Comptroller and Auditor General
C&W	Cushman & Wakefield
CBE	Commander of the Order of the British Empire
CBI	Confederation of British Industry
CEO	chief executive officer
CFO	chief financial officer
CPO	compulsory purchase order
DDDA	Dublin Docklands Development Authority
DUP	Democratic Unionist Party
EBS	Educational Building Society
ECB	European Central Bank
EIR	European (Access to Information on the Environment) Regulations
EPRA	European Public Real Estate Association
ESB	Electricity Supply Board
EU	European Union
FBI	Federal Bureau of Investigation
FOI	Freedom of Information
GBFI	Garda Bureau of Fraud Investigation
HSBC	Hong Kong and Shanghai Banking Corporation
ICAVs	Irish Collective Asset-management Vehicles
IBRC	Irish Bank Resolution Corporation
ICG	Longbow Intermediate Capital Group Longbow
IFSC	Irish Financial Services Centre
IMF	International Monetary Fund
IPUT	Irish Property Unit Trust
IRA	Irish Republican Army
JER Partners	JE Robert Companies
JLC	Jefferies LoanCore
JV	joint venture
KKR	Kohlberg Kravis Roberts
LIHAF	Local Infrastructure Housing Activation Fund

MLA	Member of the Legislative Assembly
MREG	Mack Real Estate Group
MSREF	Morgan Stanely Real Estate Funds
NAMA Act	National Asset Management Agency Act 2009
NAMA	National Asset Management Agency
NAMAIL	National Asset Management Agency Investment Ltd
NCA	National Crime Agency
NDA	non-disclosure agreement
NI	Northern Ireland
NIAC	Northern Ireland Advisory Committee
NIHE	Northern Ireland Housing Executive
NPRF	National Pensions Reserve Fund
NTMA	National Treasury Management Agency
NWL	NamaWinelake
OPW	Office of Public Works
PAC	Public Accounts Committee
PIMCO	Pacific Investment Management Company
PRSA	Property Services Regulatory Authority
PSNI	Police Service of Northern Ireland
PwC	PricewaterhouseCoopers
QIF	Qualified Investor Fund
REIT	Real Estate Investment Trust
REO	Real Estate Opportunities
RGSG	Rock Global Services Group Ltd
RUC	Royal Ulster Constabulary
SDLP	Social Democratic and Labour Party
SEC	Securities and Exchange Commission
SEM	search engine marketing
SIPO	Standards in Public Office
SIPTU	Services Industrial Professional and Technical Union
SPV	special purpose vehicle
TAIL	Treasury Asian Investments Ltd
TD	Teachta Dála
TH	Treasury Holdings
TUV	Traditional Unionist Voice
UUP	Ulster Unionist Party
ZCM	Zurich Capital Markets

PREFACE

When I first discussed a follow up to my book *Tom Gilmartin: The Man Who Brought Down a Taoiseach* (Gill Books 2014), I told Conor Nagle, commissioning editor in Gill Books, that I believed the next big story in Irish political and business life would centre on the disposal of vast quantities of public assets by the National Asset Management Agency (NAMA).

Like many others, I was sceptical of the prospect of its successful recovery of the billions of euro which had been given to the banks to restore their ability to lend and help generate economic growth, as well as of assurances that NAMA would not be a 'bail-out for developers'. However, I was prepared to give the executives of NAMA the benefit of the doubt when it came to their ability and experience in dealing with the scale of distressed property loans, which were transferred from the banks and which they were being asked to manage and prepare for disposal. It was clearly an immense undertaking and I believed it was fair to give those charged with this huge responsibility an opportunity to prove they were capable and confident of achieving the ambitious targets set by the then Fianna Fáil-led government when the agency was established in late 2009.

When we agreed in late summer of 2016 to try to write the story of NAMA, I was conscious that I would be unable to cover the entirety of the agency's activities over the past eight years given the scale of its operations. I would have to rely on my own ability to identify key sources and contacts who could help to pull together a narrative that would provide readers with an insight into the work of what has been described as the largest property management and disposal company in the world, and arguably the most secretive.

Among the very first people I contacted was the NAMA communications advisor, but my request for an interview with the senior executives of the agency, Frank Daly and Brendan McDonagh, was declined. Instead, I used the various announcements by NAMA on its website, in public speeches and statements, media interviews and releases, and in the appearance of the agency executives before various Oireachtas committees as a key source. I also had the benefit of the huge media coverage of the agency's work by Irish newspapers, radio, television and across social media.

Vital assistance was provided by the many public representatives who have taken an interest in the work of NAMA and who investigated its work in the

Dáil and at Stormont, including the public accounts and finance committees of the Oireachtas and the finance committee of the Northern Ireland assembly, which were particularly helpful in this regard. I spoke to many of those who are mentioned in the following pages and to others who prefer to remain anonymous. Among the latter are developers who felt constrained by the legal obligations they undertook when they signed non-disclosure agreements with NAMA as a condition of the agreements and settlements they made in respect of their hugely distressed loans, which were transferred to the agency.

Most were unhappy with their treatment by NAMA but were prepared to accept their responsibility for the reckless borrowing that characterised the final years of the so-called Celtic Tiger before the banking system and the economy collapsed. Others were unrepentant, blaming everyone but themselves for the quagmire of debt in which tens of thousands of Irish people found themselves when the recession hit, and the many more who took the brunt of the austerity measures that followed over several years.

Some developers clearly continue to enjoy many, if not all of the luxuries to which they were accustomed in the good times while others are struggling to recover their lost fortunes.

The anonymous NAMA Wine Lake provided interesting insights into the work of NAMA, while transcripts from various court battles involving the agency and numerous debtors in Ireland and other jurisdictions were also instructive. I spoke to a wide range of politicians, journalists, former NAMA staff and advisors, lawyers, estate agents and others with an insight into the work of the agency.

A veritable multi-billion euro industry has grown around the NAMA project with the arrival of global funds with deep pockets, which have swooped on the massive, multi-million-euro portfolios of distressed assets controlled by NAMA across several jurisdictions, including Britain, the US, France and Germany, as well as Ireland.

Asset managers, surveyors, solicitors, valuers, accountancy firms and receivers have made huge profits through their association with the vulture and other investors who have purchased the assets from NAMA at significant discounts. A number of these were associated with NAMA over the years either as direct employees or as consultants and advisors to the agency, a phenomenon which frequently raised questions in parliament and in public discourse over potential conflicts of interest.

There have been arrests and convictions of former NAMA staff while the Project Eagle sale of the Northern Ireland portfolio of assets by the agency to US fund, Cerberus, in 2014 led to allegations of corruption in relation to some agency staff and advisors.

There was always the prospect that the transfer of assets on the scale envisaged by NAMA's creators would offer an opportunity for self-gain and advancement to some of those involved, but the evidence would now suggest that the agency and its activities has made small and large fortunes for many real estate and other professionals, including a number of its former staff.

Then there are the international investors which purchased the assets in bundles so large and expensive that only a few, mainly US-based funds could afford, and were encouraged to do so by generous incentives provided by the Irish state in recent years. Some of these funds purchased assets at huge discounts before flipping them for significant profit in recent years, while others remain in the property business taking advantage of an acute housing shortage and soaring rents to maximise returns for their shareholders.

Finally, there are the tens of thousands who cannot afford to make the repayments on their mortgages in the wake of the crash and the employment crisis that followed, or to pay the excessive rents sought in a landlord-friendly market while the social housing list tops 100,000 and the homeless crisis continues unabated.

In seeking to cover these various aspects of the NAMA story, I have adopted a chronological approach which commences with the formation of the agency, its leadership and staffing. I have followed the progress or otherwise of some of the largest debtors whose excessive borrowing contributed so greatly to the property bubble and how they fared in their dealings with the agency.

I have tracked the inquiries made at the various Oireachtas committees and, in particular, the work of the Dáil Public Accounts Committee whose report, along with the Stormont inquiry into Project Eagle, helped to provide me with a road map to that complex and fascinating controversy. The thorough 'value for money' investigation by the Comptroller and Auditor General in 2016 offered an invaluable insight into the sale.

I have examined the progress of the agency as it moved from the acquisition to the accelerated disposal of its €32 billion distressed loan book and the political decisions and players who influenced its course. As controversies emerged over a number of these sales, there was clearly a resistance by those leading the agency, and the senior politicians and civil servants overseeing its work, to the establishment of an independent inquiry into the activities of NAMA. The details contained in these pages will hopefully be of relevance to the Commission of Investigation that has now been established to examine the Project Eagle sale and purchase, and other important aspects of the agency's activities.

This could not have been and certainly is not a complete account of the NAMA story. Such a detailed review was impossible in the timescale involved in producing this work, not least because of the commercial secrecy surrounding so much of the agency's operations and practices. In contrast with my book on Tom Gilmartin and the shocking culture of greed and abuse of power it exposed, involving a litany of illicit payments to corrupt politicians, *NAMA-land* involves the transfer of billions of euro in public assets in a manner which has, until now, largely avoided detailed scrutiny and control.

I hope this book will provide an insight into what has been one of the most ambitious, and costly, experiments by the Irish state following the economic and financial meltdown that has led to a lost decade of opportunity for the Irish people and which has left a huge debt mountain as its legacy to future generations. My objective has been to establish the facts of this immensely complex and politically sensitive subject, and to explain them in a fair and honest fashion to the reader. I hope I have succeeded and, if not, I bear sole responsibility for any short-comings.

Dublin, September 2017

CONTENTS

INTRODUCTION

In July 2015, the Irish political and corporate world was shocked when Wexford TD Mick Wallace claimed in parliament that a sum of £7 million had been lodged in an offshore bank account in connection with the sale of more than £1.24 billion (€1.5 billion) in publicly owned property assets.

The scandal over the sale of the Northern Ireland portfolio of assets controlled by the National Asset Management Agency (NAMA) continues to unfold and has damaged the reputations of leading politicians and business figures on both sides of the Irish border. It is to be investigated by a Commission of Investigation headed by a High Court judge, while many other aspects of NAMA operations have also come under scrutiny.

Over the last few years the largest transfer of property assets from public ownership to private interests in recent times has taken place in this small country on the edge of Europe. A total of €31.8 billion in distressed loans – with an original par value of €74 billion – transferred to NAMA following the banking collapse, have been sold in large bundles which only a handful of global funds can afford.

Hedge funds and other investment managers, many using Irish-registered subsidiaries, are sweating out the assets in order to multiply profits on commercial and residential properties they purchased at massive discounts. Thousands of Irish families and business people have lost homes or remain in permanent default on their mortgages and loans.

The Irish state, through NAMA, has facilitated the disposal of huge tracts of land and properties based on toxic loans which were transferred to the 'bad bank' after it was established in 2009. NAMA was set up to restore credit in the economy and to help the banks recover by removing their toxic loan debt. It was intended to sell off the hugely discounted loans over a ten-year period and make the maximum return for the exchequer and the Irish people. It has not worked out as planned.

By seeking to offload the properties as rapidly as possible NAMA may have failed to obtain the best return for the Irish people, and by appointing people to lead the massive property management project who had no experience in the real estate investment business it may have facilitated inappropriate decisions and mismanagement. Many people hired by NAMA have since left the agency to work for companies with a vested interest in the purchase of badly performing loans and debt. The agency is still embroiled in the massive political and financial scandal over the disposal, in 2014, of its Northern Ireland portfolio, Project Eagle, which contributed to the destabilisation and collapse of the power sharing executive at Stormont in early 2017.

The sale of Project Eagle resulted in critical reports from the Comptroller and Auditor General, which audits the NAMA accounts, and from the Public Accounts Committee (PAC). The Stormont Finance and Personnel Committee held public hearings in 2015 into the £1.2 billion (€1.5 billion) property portfolio sale from an original value of £4.5 billion (€5.1 billion) and heard details of alleged criminal behaviour and corruption at high levels of Northern Irish business and politics and at senior levels within NAMA. Questions have also been raised about other billion-euro sales of public assets by NAMA.

Former employees of the agency have been arrested and charged with leaking confidential information and other offences, while several others have been questioned. One man has been convicted; others are facing charges. Where did it all go wrong? Is it corruption, incompetence or both? How many of the controversial decisions on the disposal of billions of assets under the control of the Irish state are influenced by rich and powerful global funds and their locally connected, vested political and business interests? Why did some property developers get favourable treatment from NAMA while others were forced out of business? Have the interests of the Irish people been served by the manner in which their assets have been sold, at sharp discounts, to some of the richest funds in the world?

This work attempts to address these questions, beginning with the establishment of NAMA in 2009. *NAMA-land* chronologically examines the political debate surrounding the creation of the 'bad bank', the choice of its executive, board and other staff members and the agency's early work of transferring distressed loans from the main Irish banks. The book tracks the fate of NAMA's largest debtors, examining how the agency managed and then disposed of their loans. It traces the movement of staff out of the agency, the arrest of some former agency officials and the departure of others to the global funds and other firms swooping on the assets that were sold by NAMA. It also discusses how other firms swooped on the assets that were sold by NAMA. It details the background to the 2014 sale of Project Eagle, NAMA's Northern Ireland loan book, and looks at the political and business personalities who featured in the subsequent controversy. *NAMA-land* follows the various inquiries into the purchase and sale of Project Eagle and the extended debates in the Irish parliament over the proposal for a commission of investigation into it and other aspects of NAMA's activities. Inevitably, as in any project of this scale and complexity, many details will not be covered in this book. However, it will hopefully provide an insight into one of the most significant and far-reaching political and financial experiments in the history of the state, one which will have a profound impact on Irish society and its people for many years to come.

Chapter 1 ∿

GUARANTEED IRISH

B rendan McDonagh sat in a corridor in government buildings on Merrion Street where Taoiseach Brian Cowen, Minister for Finance Brian Lenihan, some other cabinet members, senior civil servants, bank executives, accountants, solicitors and other advisors convened on the night of the infamous 'bank guarantee' on 29 September 2008. 'Infamous' because the outcome of the crisis meetings, which followed the disclosure that Ireland's main banks were facing insolvency, was the decision to protect depositors for up to £100,000 and, controversially, all lenders, including unsecured bondholders – thus exposing the state to massive multi-billion-euro debts and inevitably forcing it into the arms of an EU Commission, European Central Bank and International Monetary Fund (EU/ECB/IMF) bailout programme.

McDonagh, a senior executive with the National Treasury Management Agency (NTMA), which is charged with handling the state's finances and ensuring access to the best bond yields and returns on the international markets, never received an invitation to the discussions that resulted in the bank guarantee, despite his patient vigil into the early hours of 30 September 2008. In the weeks and months that followed he was, however, central to the construction of the 'bad bank' established to transfer the distressed borrowings of the financial institutions in order to save what remained of a functioning banking sector. The objective, in particular, was to remove the toxic debt incurred by the main lenders – Bank of Ireland, Allied Irish Bank (AIB), Anglo Irish Bank ('Anglo'), Irish Nationwide Building Society and Permanent TSB – which were hugely exposed to a property market that had now completely collapsed. The other core objective was to restore liquidity in the banking system in order to allow it to resume its crucial function of lending to commercial and other borrowers as a key motor of the economy.

Most of the developers, builders and other investors who had borrowed freely and frivolously during the boom years were now broke. The value of their remaining assets was only a fraction of the monies which they had borrowed, and which had been lent so recklessly over the previous decade and more. A complete failure of state regulation, combined with an arrogant and greed-fuelled bonus culture in the banking sector, had brought down the entire economy as Ireland suffered the largest financial collapse of any developed country since the 1930s. The insistence by the EU and ECB that the debts owed to other reckless lenders in German, French, British and US financial institutions, including unsecured creditors, must be paid in full added billions to the debt mountain. It also contributed to the problems faced by the crisis-ridden Fianna Fáil-led coalition government with the Green Party as another turbulent new year approached at the end of 2008.

The finance minister, Brian Lenihan, turned to the NTMA to provide advice on how a new 'bad bank' could be formed and also consulted economist Dr Peter Bacon, who prepared a report and provided a detailed explanation of the role of NAMA when its birth was announced in early April 2009. At a press briefing in the NTMA offices in Dublin on 8 April, Lenihan unveiled the plan to transfer up to €90 billion of property- and land-related loans from the banks to NAMA, including unimpaired loans. Insisting that the initiative was not a bailout of the banks but of the economy, Lenihan said that it was about 'ensuring that business and individuals who cannot access credit, can access credit'. Dr Bacon, who had advised the government on land and housing policy during the boom years, added that the creation of the bad bank agency would involve bank shareholders taking considerable pain.

'We are cleaning the balance sheets of the organisations to ensure the institutions can resume their proper role as motors of credit in the Irish economy,' he stressed.

Inevitably, the announcement of the plan attracted criticism and scepticism at home and abroad with concerns expressed about the lack of detailed information on the extent of the bad loans, including from some of the developers whose debts were to be transferred to the new agency and for whom there was little public sympathy. However, there was some surprise when the chief executive of the NTMA, Dr Michael Somers, told the Public Accounts Committee (PAC) just weeks later that he had no idea how NAMA would operate. He was concerned at the haste with which the project was conceived, did not believe that the NTMA was the appropriate body to oversee the operation and insisted that it did not have sufficient staff to operate the new agency. Somers also disputed the extent of the state's exposure. He argued that at the end of 2008 the state's total gross debt was about €70 billion and it had about €20 billion in cash. The scale of his frustration about the manner in which NAMA was established emerged when it was revealed that Somers had sought to retire, with immediate effect, two months earlier. After 48 years in public service, including 18 as chief executive of the NTMA, Somers said that he was 'beyond normal retirement age'. In a letter to the finance minister, he wrote that his contract had been due to expire in December 2007 and had been extended by three years, but he was prepared to work 'in a non-pensionable capacity' until a successor was found.

His letter of 11 March 2009 came just one week after Lenihan had written to Somers asking him whether the NTMA could 'take steps to develop contingency plans for the provision of liquidity to the Irish banking system in the event of further liquidity pressures within that system'. Somers' expression of scepticism was an inauspicious start for the agency but one that did not deter its architects from preparing the necessary legislation, structures and recruitment of staff to take on the mammoth task of rescuing the banks and restoring some normality to the property market.

Born in Killorglin, County Kerry, Brendan McDonagh had worked as an accountant with the Electricity Supply Board (ESB) before he joined the NTMA in 1994. He became its financial controller four years later. In 2002, he was appointed as the agency's director of finance, technology and risk and was serving in that role when the challenge posed by the massive banking debt landed on his desk. With a Bachelor of Science degree in Business Management from the Dublin Institute of Technology, and having trained as a chartered accountant, the 41-year-old became managing director (later chief executive officer) of NAMA, which was soon to become the largest property management and disposal company in the world.

McDonagh, by his own admission, had never previously been involved in property development or finance, but he was charged with acquiring some €77 billion in distressed assets (discounted to €34 billion) and selling them off in a manner that yielded the highest return to the near-bankrupt state. These were best estimates as the real figures could only be confirmed on completion of detailed valuation of the loans. It was an awesome task and required McDonagh to surround himself with the best available talent, including many who were now struggling to find lucrative employment in the wake of a crash that had decimated the property and construction industry. That crash had affected members of an industry – including big developers, architects, surveyors, engineers, estate agents, auctioneers and valuers as well as the hundreds of thousands of people employed by building contractors, such as labourers, carpenters, electricians, plasterers and bricklayers – that made up the country's biggest employment sector during the good years and was a lucrative source of revenue for successive political administrations.

With Somers on his way out the door, McDonagh took much of the responsibility for the required preparations. He brought in a team of advisors, among them the estate agent John Mulcahy. Mulcahy had spent several years as a member of the property advisory committee of the National Pension Reserve Fund (another subsidiary of the NTMA), and had long experience of the Irish real estate market in his capacity as senior partner with Jones Lang LaSalle – one of the many auctioneers that prospered during the property bubble when house, apartment and office prices soared. Now he was to assist with acquiring, managing and disposing of many of the distressed assets moving to NAMA.

Also involved in the early days of NAMA was John Corrigan, who replaced Somers as chief executive of the NTMA in December 2009, just weeks after the legislation conferring immense powers on the new agency was narrowly passed in the Dáil. Operating under the direction of the NTMA, their task was to manage the loans and ensure that the original borrower repaid them or, if not, put the loans on the market or hold them until property prices began to recover. Optimising the return to the exchequer was the most important, if difficult, challenge. Soon the small NAMA team was facing challenges from banks who complained that the loans were being undervalued, and developers who believed they were being scapegoated by the process. There was also political criticism as the National Asset Management Agency Act 2009 (the 'NAMA Act'), conferring extraordinary and unprecedented powers on the new agency, made its way through parliament.

Unveiling the draft legislation in July 2009 just before the summer recess of the Oireachtas, finance minister Brian Lenihan recounted the background to the establishment of the new agency, in particular the need to restore the banking system.

> We must address the health and stability of our banking system – to ensure that the credit required by the economy is provided and that people's savings are protected.
>
> There is nothing in the proposed Bill that will provide a 'bail-out' for borrowers, whether builders, developers or otherwise. Anyone who owes money before NAMA continues to owe it, and is expected to repay the full amount of the debt.
>
> The Government has decided to adopt the proposed approach based on the advice it has received domestically, the advice of institutions such as the IMF, and also the example of other countries taking similar steps. The Government is convinced this response will ensure the safety, stability and capacity of the Irish banking system, all of which are key to supporting our economy.

Notwithstanding his assurances, the public and political debate which ensued revealed a deep scepticism about the project, not least given that its proponents were widely blamed for the policy and regulatory failures which caused the banking collapse in the first place. When he announced, on the resumption of parliament in September, the details of how NAMA would pay some €54 billion to the banks for distressed property loans with a face value of €77 billion, the reaction was even more hostile, with opposition parties and other prominent commentators expressing deep concern at the long-term implications of such a massive transfer of debt onto future generations of the Irish people.

While Lenihan assured the Dáil that the state would pay on average 30 per cent less than the face value of the bank loans, other experts claimed that AIB and Bank of Ireland would emerge with a significantly lower discount. Either way, the scale of the operation would involve NAMA purchasing an enormous €28 billion in loans from Anglo Irish Bank, €24 billion from AIB, €16 billion from Bank of Ireland, €8 billion from Irish Nationwide and €1 billion from the Educational Building Society (EBS).

The minister estimated the current market value of the loans to be €47 billion, representing an over-payment of €7 billion (to bring the amount up to €54 billion), which he described as an allowance to cover the long-term economic value of the assets. He claimed that NAMA would only require an increase in property prices of less than 10 per cent from current levels over 10 years to break even if property prices were still 45 per cent below what their value had been in late 2006.

The Oireachtas debate on the NAMA Act, which coincided with the run-in to the second referendum on the Lisbon Treaty, placed severe strains on the coalition government. The Green Party sought assurances and amendments from Fianna Fáil to satisfy its members that the government was not engaged, as Fine Gael leader Enda Kenny contended, in a 'daylight mugging' of the Irish people. Kenny complained that the government had 'been led by the nose by the banks and developers down this corridor of NAMA, and they have shifted a burden of €54 billion on to the backs of the Irish taxpayer'. Labour Party leader Eamon Gilmore called for a temporary nationalisation of the banks as an alternative to NAMA, saying:

Fianna Fáil fuelled a splurge of speculation and a property bubble in this country. They drove up the price of development land and they tax-incentivised a speculative property boom that was unsustainable. How did this Fianna Fáil Government turn around a good economy which was built on the back of the hard work of the very people who were buying those houses and turn it into the kind of economic depression we have now?

Gilmore told one of the several protests against government austerity measures outside Leinster House that the banking system had to be reformed in the interests of the public and not the developers, and the answer was not NAMA but a temporary nationalisation of the banks.

Inside the House, Gilmore's finance spokesperson Joan Burton asked whether the Irish people could trust Fianna Fáil and the minister for finance to head up what she described as 'the largest property firm on the planet'.

> Like one of the characters in *Alice in Wonderland*, this legislation requires the public to believe six impossible things before breakfast, all of which come down to a question of trust.
>
> Do we trust Fianna Fáil not to bail out the bankers and the borrowers? Do we trust the Minister who claimed that the blanket guarantee he introduced for the financial institutions last September would be the cheapest bank rescue in the world? Do we trust a Taoiseach who pleaded that Ireland's economic fundamentals were sound when it was plain to see we were teetering on the brink of disaster? Do we trust a Government that inflated a property bubble, ignored all advice to curtail property-based tax incentives and buried its head in the sand when the house of cards collapsed?

Sinn Féin called for a referendum on what its Dáil leader Caoimhghín Ó Caoláin described as 'this rotten Bill'. He said that a general election should be called to test public confidence in the government's strategy to deal with the fall-out from the financial crisis which had already resulted in a series of unpopular emergency budgets. His Dáil colleague Martin Ferris described NAMA as 'a bailout for the greediest and the most corrupt in Irish society: the bankers and the speculators whose boundless avarice has devastated the economy'. He said the government was robbing this generation and the next one after that, too.

> Sinn Féin has been calling all summer for a referendum on NAMA. You cannot put through a bill of this magnitude without asking the majority of people on the island if they support it. We all know why Fianna Fáil will not support a referendum: they know that asking people to vote Yes to NAMA is akin to asking turkeys to vote for Christmas.

The government was determined to push ahead and had only to surmount some internal dissension among its Green partners to ensure that the legislation would be passed in an October vote which took place just weeks after the Lisbon Treaty was endorsed. Its 'bad bank' proposal was supported by leading national and international finance and business interests, including some of the developers whose loans would soon be under the control of the new agency.

There were mixed messages from the Northern Ireland power sharing executive, with finance minister Sammy Wilson and enterprise minister Arlene Foster, both of the Democratic Unionist Party (DUP), expressing their concern about the potentially negative impact of NAMA on the local economy. The Sinn Féin Deputy First Minister, Martin McGuinness, expressed fears of a 'fire sale' of toxic Northern assets worth nearly €5 billion. McGuinness said the handling of the €4.8 billion of local assets, equivalent to one-quarter of the output of the North's economy, had considerable implications.

The cross-jurisdictional implications are significant in the absence of statements on the discount to be applied to the Irish bank loans and the precise length of time that NAMA will operate. A longer lifespan and larger discount would allow NAMA to pursue loans less aggressively as a short lifespan and small discount would appear to be disadvantageous from our viewpoint.

Trinity economist Brian Lucey, responding to academic support for NAMA from government advisor Alan Ahearne, said the project involved 'a conscious decision to use taxpayers' money to overpay banks for their toxic assets, thereby transferring billions of euro from the taxpayers to bank shareholders'.

On the eve of the Dáil vote, and with the Green Party onside with its Fianna Fáil partners, the NAMA enthusiasts received unwelcome and unexpected criticism from Nobel Prize-winning US economist Joseph Stiglitz. Speaking during a visit to Dublin, Stiglitz accused the government of 'squandering' public money: 'The Irish Government is squandering large amounts of money to bail out banks. There's a sort of a view that there's no alternative.' Stiglitz claimed that view was 'nonsense': 'The rule of capitalism says that when firms can't pay what they owe, they go bankrupt. It's a massive transfer of money from the public to bankers.'

The Columbia University professor argued that overpaying for loans was 'criminal', and NAMA was likely to 'burden this generation for 25–50 years or more. I am very uncomfortable with a government with such a minority support making such a decision.'

He said that the view that there was no alternative was 'just wrong': 'There is an alternative. Play by the rules of capitalism – if you can't pay back your debt, shareholders and bondholders lose.' Stiglitz claimed that 'countries which allow banks to go under by following the ordinary rules of capitalism have done fine. The US has let 100 banks go this year alone, as did Sweden and Norway in their crises.'

In contrast, the Irish bank bailout

is a simple transfer from taxpayers to bondholders, and it will saddle generations to come. The only thing that might give you solace is that, as chief economist of the World Bank, we see this type of thing happening in banana republics all over the world. Whenever a banking crisis happens, the financial sector uses the turmoil as a mechanism to transfer wealth from the general population to themselves. I've been very disappointed to see that it has happened, not only in banana republics, but in advanced industrialised countries.

Stiglitz's intervention prompted Fine Gael finance spokesperson Richard Bruton to repeat his party's call for an alternative approach to the bank debt transfer.

The approach outlined by Professor Stiglitz leaves the risk and responsibility for working out toxic developer loans with the bankers who made them, and the investors who funded them, while also ensuring that a cleansed and healthy banking system is ready to restart lending. There is still an opportunity to ditch the massive NAMA gamble and adopt Fine Gael's safer and more effective solution to fixing the banks by setting up a National Recovery Bank.

Ignoring the warnings from home and abroad, the government, with its slim Dáil majority, succeeded in getting the National Asset Management Agency Bill (2009) through on 15 October 2009, by 77 votes to 73, following a debate which involved an exhausting all-night sitting of the House.

Attorney General Paul Gallagher and his staff, with input from the Revenue Commissioners, assisted the parliamentary drafting necessary to protect the legislation from any future court challenge or the possibility of the Bill being referred to the Council of State by the president, as recommended by opposition parties, or the Supreme Court. President Mary McAleese, however, signed the Bill into law on 22 November 2009 without any such referral. Meanwhile, developer Paddy McKillen was already engaging in a High Court challenge against any transfer of his assets to NAMA, which was inevitably heading for the Supreme Court for adjudication.

Behind the scenes, the now acting managing director of NAMA, Brendan McDonagh, and his small team had been preparing the foundations for the new agency at the offices of the NTMA on Grand Canal Street in Dublin 2, in a building still owned by one of its subsequent clients and largest debtors, Johnny Ronan of Treasury Holdings. Along with John Corrigan, co-director of the NTMA, and two of its senior executives, legal advisor Aideen O'Reilly and deputy director Sean Ó Faoláin, an external group of senior finance department officials were involved in the policy steering group. They included Kevin Cardiff, Anne Nolan and William Beausang, all of whom had extensive tax and financial services expertise and they assisted with the unprecedented task of creating a durable structure to take over, manage and dispose of the largest single distressed property portfolio of any developed country in the wake of the 2008 crisis, or indeed for many decades.

External advisors included a team from leading solicitors firm Arthur Cox, led by managing director Padraig O'Riordain, accountants PricewaterhouseCoopers (PwC), and a London-based group from HSBC Investment Bank headed by Matt Webster, who provided expertise on the valuing of the loans to be transferred from the five banking institutions coming under the NAMA umbrella.

Within weeks of the legislation being passed NAMA had a chairman leading a nine-member board which was to oversee the complex operation. Former head of the Revenue Commissioners Frank Daly was appointed chairman for a five-year term on 22 December 2009. On the same day, he resigned from his position as public interest director of Anglo Irish Bank, which he had occupied for one year. Daly served as chairman of the Revenue Commissioners from 2002 until 2009. He first joined the Revenue in 1963 and had acted as a commissioner since 1996. During 2008 he also chaired the Commission on Taxation which reported in September 2009, just weeks after the draft legislation establishing NAMA was unveiled. Daly was an uncontroversial appointment and his experience in Revenue and more recently with Anglo Irish Bank, the largest distressed loan book coming into NAMA, was seen as providing solid expertise to the new board. Born in the seaside village of Abbeyside in Waterford in 1945, he was the son of a postman, while his mother's family were described in one profile as 'seafarers'. The *Irish Times* heard Daly describe his childhood as framed by activities on the beach, and he had been active in the scouts. He trained to be a teacher for three months before taking a job with customs and excise, which led to a public service career spanning six decades. His five-year term with NAMA was scheduled to end in December 2014, when he would turn 69.

Another potential nominee for the position of chairman, Michael McDowell, the former Minister for Justice, Progressive Democrat leader and Tánaiste in the Fianna Fáil-led government before he and most of his party colleagues lost their seats in their disastrous general election performance in 2007, would, if chosen, inevitably have raised political and media eyebrows. According to senior government sources at the time, McDowell's nomination by Brian Lenihan was rejected by Taoiseach Brian Cowen. Cowen was said to be dumbfounded when the finance minister proposed McDowell for the position and reacted with his familiar abrasiveness to the notion that he should support the nomination of the former politician and justice minister who had made such a significant contribution to the decline in popularity of the previous administration. McDowell had ingloriously resigned as leader of the Progressive Democrats, and from politics, when he failed to get elected in the 2007 general election and while many of his party colleagues were still on the battlefield and desperately struggling to hang on to their Dáil seats.

The board of NAMA, announced during Christmas week on 22 December 2009, attracted little or no media attention and the appointment of experienced financial consultants and accountants Éilish Finan, Michael Connolly, Peter Stewart and Brian McEnery to join Daly, McDonagh and Corrigan, now chief executive of the NTMA, disturbed no one's sleep. The choice of former county manager with Fingal County Council, William Soffe, may have prompted some queries, given the controversial history of the planning system in Dublin, but he had served on the Commission on Taxation with Daly and presumably already enjoyed a friendly and non-contentious relationship with the incoming chairman. The appointment of a leading International Monetary Fund (IMF) executive and US national, Stephen Seelig, to the board of NAMA did invite some comment, given his role as mission chief for the IMF in Estonia and Georgia and his work on debt restructuring in countries including Ireland and Uruguay over the years. His appointment did not come into effect for some months due to his outstanding commitments with the IMF, and he came on board initially in an advisory capacity.

If the board members did not exactly distract the commentariat from its end of year festivities, the appointment of the various heads of division six weeks later, in February 2010, did not go unnoticed by the growing number of people in the various professions with a potential interest in the work of NAMA, as well as some in the media.

Topping that list was the new head of portfolio management, John Mulcahy, who had already been on secondment from Jones Lang LaSalle on an interim basis with the agency since June 2009 and thus was among those most familiar with its origins, structures and strategies. Ronnie Hanna, a former senior executive with Ulster Bank and a graduate of Queens University in Belfast, was made head of credit and risk, while Aideen O'Reilly became head of legal and tax affairs – a reflection of the work she was already doing with the new agency and previously with the NTMA and its associated bodies, the State Claims Agency and the National Pensions Reserve Fund (NPRF). Another NTMA staffer, Sean Ó Faoláin, was made head of business services.

While ownership of the distressed loans was to be transferred to NAMA, which had ultimate control over key credit decisions, the banks would continue to manage them on behalf of the agency, and each of the five finance houses was to establish a specialised division to assess and value the loans to be transferred. However, the largest borrowers – up to 150 with assets which had been valued in billions at the height of the property bubble and a veritable who's who of the country's leading property developers during the boom years – were to have their portfolios of distressed assets managed directly by NAMA.

Expertise was sought from people with direct experience in the property industry and almost two thousand people sent in CVs based on their work as surveyors, architects, engineers and valuers during the good years, many of whom had now lost their jobs, for no more than 80–100 positions advertised by the new agency. Experts on loan valuations, with associated actuarial skills in securities and derivatives, interest swaps and other banking arrangements, were required. A panel of property valuation experts, with external assistance drawn from existing real estate companies, was also engaged during the recruitment process and the early bedding-in of the agency.

Inevitably, given his role as head of portfolio management and responsibility for negotiating with banks on the value of the loans to be transferred to NAMA and the timescale involved, John Mulcahy was the focus of both public and not-so-public attention; he had been among those professionals who had wrongly forecast a soft landing for the Irish economy before the 2008 crash. His role in pumping the property market in his capacity as managing director and chairman in Ireland of international real estate agents Jones Lang LaSalle was raised when he accompanied Lenihan and McDonagh for one of their regular briefings before the Oireachtas Committee on Finance and the Public Service in late August 2009. At this time, Mulcahy was on secondment to assist with the preparation of the valuation methodology to be employed by NAMA in assessing the value of distressed bank loans. At the hearing, Mulcahy stated:

> With regard to my experience, I am a chartered surveyor and have been in practice for 39 years. I do not know if longevity is a measure of success. I am chairman of Jones Lang LaSalle, although resigned at the moment. I have been seconded into NAMA in a personal capacity and have nothing to do with Jones Lang LaSalle at the moment. I have spent my working life mainly advising pension funds and others on investment in property. On the question of whether I called the market, while my natural humility gets in the way, I have been a bear for the past four years.

In fact, Mulcahy had been anything but a 'bear', for as recently as July 2007 he had observed that office take-up in the Republic was 10 per cent higher in the first six months of that year than in the same period the previous year. 'The prospects for the second half of 2007 and for next year looks [*sic*] equally promising, with a number of major space users … seeking proposals for suitable office accommodation,' he said, although he did warn of 'price corrections' in the residential market.

In 2008, he had warned that the economic downturn had taken the 'froth' off the commercial property market – a description which could be characterised as an understatement given the shock that had already hit the financial system since the St Patrick's Day collapse of Anglo shares and the solvency crisis that led to the infamous bank guarantee later in the year.

But Mulcahy had reason to err on the optimistic side given his role in some of the largest property transactions before the crash, including as advisor to South Wharf PLC in its sale of the Irish Glass Bottle site in the Ringsend area of Dublin for €412 million in October 2006. The purchase of the site by a consortium which included property developer Bernard McNamara, financier Derek Quinlan and the Dublin Docklands Development Authority (DDDA) proved a commercial disaster and contributed to the ultimate dismantlement of the state-run DDDA. Among its board members at the time was Seán FitzPatrick, chairman and former chief executive of Anglo, whose alleged conflict of interest in this and other land disposals by the DDDA led to a series of inquiries.

If NAMA wanted insider knowledge of the property game in Dublin, Mulcahy, a sixty-year-old chartered surveyor, certainly had form. He had rubbed shoulders with many of the leading businessmen and bankers who drove the so-called 'Celtic Tiger', including the likes of Larry Goodman and Sean Dunne, as well as acting for the agency in charge of state property, the Office of Public Works (OPW). He had also witnessed slumps in the market over the decades and was involved with major development companies, including British Land, in the construction of the Irish Financial Services Centre (IFSC) in the 1980s. He had for some years been an advisor on property to the NPRF and was familiar with a number of its senior personnel who helped to establish NAMA.

Following Mulcahy's appearance before the Oireachtas Committee, the Department of Finance defended his appointment on the basis that he would not be involved in the valuation of individual lands or properties. That would be handled by a panel of valuation companies, chosen by public tender. This panel, which invariably included real estate companies and surveyors, including Jones Lang LaSalle and other auctioneers, would use a template for valuation methodology devised by Mulcahy and others, the department said.

The choice of Mulcahy, it said, 'reflected his expertise in valuation' and the need to hire somebody with an understanding of the overall market.

In early May 2010, NAMA announced another set of executive appointments while confirming that it had completed the transfer of the first set of loans from Anglo at a discount of 55 per cent, bringing the total transferred to date from all five banking institutions under its remit to €7.7 billion, an overall discount of 50 per cent.

A graduate of Loughborough University and employee of Goldman Sachs and more recently Ernst & Young accountants in London, Graham Emmett was appointed head of lending, while Dublin City University graduate and former AIB trading executive Frank O'Connor was confirmed as head of treasury at the agency. Kevin Nowlan, a chartered surveyor who previously worked for AIB and Treasury Holdings, also joined NAMA in 2010 from his family property consultancy firm, WK Nowlan. WK Nowlan separately provided consultancy services to NAMA. Emmett was given responsibility for handling the distressed assets of Sean Dunne, one of the agency's largest debtors.

Financier Selina Dicker joined NAMA as head of lending and corporate finance, having previously worked on international real estate buyouts with global investors Rothschild and, more recently, Capmark.

The announcement on 13 May 2010 of a Northern Ireland Advisory Committee (NIAC) of NAMA inevitably received more attention north of the border, where the appointments of Frank Cushnahan and Brian Rowntree, from Belfast, received mixed reviews, given their sometimes controversial roles at senior levels in the public service. Rowntree had served as chairman of the Northern Ireland Housing Executive since May 2004, while Cushnahan was a senior figure in the Office of the First and Deputy First Minister of the Northern Ireland power sharing executive. The brief announcement by NAMA noted that Cushnahan was

Chairman of the Northern Ireland Department of Finance and Personnel Ministerial Panel of the Performance and Evaluation Delivery Unit; Chairman of the Audit Committee of the Office of the First and Deputy First Minister and Non-Executive Board Member of the Office of the First and Deputy First Minister.

It also confirmed that the NIAC would be chaired by NAMA board member Peter Stewart and would include his colleagues Brian McEnery, Éilish Finan and the NAMA head of credit and risk, Ronnie Hanna.

Within weeks of his appointment to the NIAC, Cushnahan invited Frank Daly to join the board of a company on which the Belfast man served as a director. Daly was registered as a director of Ciorani Ltd, a company associated with the Catholic Redemptorist religious order, in June 2010. The Redemptorists owned substantial lands across the country, including in Belfast and Dublin, and had been advised by Cushnahan in a number of their commercial transactions over a period of years.

That the chairman of NAMA had joined the board of a company made up in the main of members of the religious order was unusual, but the development went unnoticed at the time of his appointment. Cushnahan had a long history in business in the North that saw him perform as a management and financial consultant and board member of companies and agencies across both private and public sectors. He was equally comfortable advising the Catholic Redemptorists and providing his services to the Free Presbyterians, the DUP and others in the unionist community. In a deeply politically divided society, Cushnahan was able to cross the boundaries in a business community united in its pursuit of wealth. He had invited Daly to join him on the board of Ciorani, although the NAMA chairman never disclosed his reasons for accepting the offer, referring to it as a private matter.

Chapter 2 ~

CITY OF THE SPIRE

For a small country on the edge of Europe, Ireland has produced more than its fair share of globetrotting developers. The household names and masters of the universe in the property game during the boom years from the mid-1990s included Johnny Ronan and Richard Barrett of Treasury Holdings, Sean Mulryan of Ballymore Homes, Gerry Barrett, Paddy McKillen, Michael O'Flynn, David Daly, the Cosgrave brothers, Paddy Kelly, Liam Carroll and Sean Dunne, many of whom had expanded from their Irish core investments to places like London, New York, China, South Africa, the Czech Republic and the Caribbean in pursuit of even greater riches. Backing them were the Irish banks who were on a lending spree they thought would never end and with loan books that would have been unimaginable just a decade earlier. By December 2005, Anglo Irish Bank was exposed to no less than €6.4 billion in drawn loans to its 20 top borrowers.

For the sheer scale of his ambition, however, none could surpass the vision of Garrett Kelleher, of Shelbourne Development, to build the tallest building in the US. At 2,000 feet, with an estimated total cost of €2.1 billion, and designed by the globally renowned Spanish architect Santiago Calatrava, the foundation work and a seven-storey underground car park for the Chicago Spire commenced in May 2007. Located on a peninsula at the estuary of the Chicago River into Lake Michigan, and to include a People's Park in honour of the City's founder Jean Baptiste Point du Sable, the Spire would be the tallest residential building in the world and would put Chicago, the home of modern architecture, back at the forefront of cities boasting contemporary 'supertall' buildings.

Finance for the purchase of 2.2 acres of the seven-acre development site came from Anglo Irish Bank in Boston, which opened a Chicago office in July 2006. Anglo funded $54 million of the acquisition cost while Shelbourne and Kelleher invested over $200 million from their own resources during the two-year life span of the project.

Kelleher, who moved back to Chicago from Dublin after he bought the site in July 2006, had spent his younger years in the Windy City where, as an immigrant, he built up a successful contracting and residential loft development business in the 1980s and 1990s and where his first two children were born. He returned to Dublin in 1996 with his wife, Maeve, to try his hand at property development in Dublin. One of Kelleher's first developments in 1996 was the assemblage of a site on Parnell Street and Moore Street where he ultimately built a hotel and shopping centre following protracted litigation from the adjoining developers, Treasury Holdings.

It was not long before he came up against the culture of obstruction that infected planning in the city and was forced into expensive and time-consuming court action and other delays in order to achieve his development plans. Kelleher managed to assemble a strong team of professionals over the next few years and focused primarily on complex and strategic city centre development sites over the following decade.

After successfully emerging from a bitter battle with Keelgrove Ltd (a company owned by Treasury Holdings principals Johnny Ronan and Richard Barrett) over his plans to develop the hotel in Parnell Street, Kelleher went on to acquire properties at Burgh Quay, Aston Quay, Eden Quay, Sackville Place, O'Connell Street, Cathal Brugha Street, Parnell Street, Dawson Street, Tara Street, Poolbeg Street and Townsend Street, among others, in Dublin city centre. They included Apollo House and adjoining properties close to Tara Street. He had also acquired lands in Ranelagh and the former Cable and Wireless headquarters in Tallaght in west Dublin. Kelleher also developed a major residential and retail complex opposite The Square in Tallaght and completed a major office block on St Stephen's Green. By early 2004, Kelleher had become a major player in the city's property market and had purchased a number of prime office buildings in central Brussels and Paris. He had walked away from the £240 million purchase of the Richard Rogers-designed Lloyd's of London in the British capital because of structural defects.

In discussions with the OPW, which owned Hawkins House, where the Department of Health was located, Kelleher outlined his vision for a 600,000 square foot scheme on the adjoining lands, including office and residential development and a large plaza, with underground pedestrian links to the nearby DART station at Tara Street and the planned Luas link between the existing red and green lines to south and west Dublin, respectively.

Large corporates, including Bank of Ireland, Arthur Cox and KPMG, had been seeking proposals to replace their then redundant premises and were approached as prospective tenants in the rejuvenated quarter while the Department of Health would move to new offices following the demolition of the sick Hawkins House building. For some years, Kelleher discussed the scheme with the OPW property executive, David Byers. John Mulcahy, then managing partner at Jones Lang LaSalle's Dublin office, advised the OPW on the proposal.

With several banks, including Anglo Irish, Ulster Bank and Bank of Scotland Ireland, and other funders offering to finance this and other planned schemes in Dublin, and his Chicago project at the early design and planning stage, Kelleher was on the cusp of a major breakthrough as a global property player. He had put much of his own money into the Spire and by late 2007 had refinanced his various Dublin assets with an assortment of lenders.

Then the wheels came off the wagon, first in the US and soon after at home. Construction of the Spire began in May 2007, with permits obtained and up to 100 people employed on foundation work on the site and in offices in Dublin, London and Chicago. The end value of the scheme on completion was projected by Savills, London, at $3.5 billion. Kelleher needed to raise an additional $1.6 billion. He had equity of $500 million in the project from cash investments and the site's land value, he claimed. The development with the benefit of zoning for 2.75 million square feet and approved building permits, and the additional land Kelleher had assembled, was valued by Deloitte in 2007 at $350 million and by CBRE at some $370 million. Local contractors were committed to partnering with the China State Construction company in the completion of the Calatrava-designed project.

Just as Kelleher publicly launched the Spire in January 2008 in Chicago with an elaborate roadshow of the scheme to potential buyers in more than 12 cities and important financial centres across the world, and having sold over 30% of the 1,200 condominiums off the plans in less than six months, contractors got nervous as Kelleher's resources dried up. His plan was criticised publicly as un-American by none other than US billionaire and rival property developer Donald Trump, but a major crisis emerged closer to home when one of his major funders, Anglo Irish Bank, effectively ran out of money on St Patrick's Day 2008.

A perfect storm engulfed Kelleher and the project as Anglo could not advance the funds necessary for completion and contractors called in monies owed before Kelleher was able to pay them. Under Illinois law, contractors who work on a project, including his own company Shelbourne, were potentially entitled to payment before the bank in the event of foreclosure, and a line of consultants, contractors, suppliers and the expensive architect and designers were queuing for their monies as the Spire hit the wall. Kelleher was unable to raise the money necessary to complete the project as there was no development finance available anywhere. Kelleher searched the globe. As the dramatic global financial and property crash followed the collapse of Lehman Brothers Bank in the US in September 2008, Kelleher was looking at the disintegration of his nascent development empire on both sides of the Atlantic. His outstanding debt from the Spire project to Anglo US rose from $54 million to $92 million, including interest and penalties, but it was not insurmountable in the context of his overall borrowings.

When Garrett Kelleher arrived back in Ireland in 2009 he made contact with John Mulcahy, one of the architects of NAMA and a man he had known professionally from a number of transactions. Mulcahy explained how NAMA would work, what the agency's expectations of developers would be, and he purportedly gave Kelleher assurances regarding his assets and his business.

Over several months of negotiations with NAMA, Kelleher proposed a solution which would involve the agency advancing him funds so that he could negotiate with outstanding creditors and preserve value. With the US economic recovery under way, he insisted that if trade creditors were dealt with he could raise sufficient funds in Chicago to repay NAMA entirely and in time resurrect his stalled Dublin city centre office and residential projects, in particular the ambitious co-development with the OPW of the site off Tara Street. It soon dawned on him that the agency was not amenable to following his business plan and projections but was keenly interested in fire selling his assets in Dublin and the US.

The developer also found that some of his own staff at Shelbourne were looking for other opportunities, given the transformation of the property market and the financial difficulties the company faced on both sides of the Atlantic. Among the young executives who cut their teeth in the industry working for Kelleher were Brian Berg and Richard Moyles, two graduates in property economics from the Bolton Street College of Technology in Dublin. Berg went to work for Irish businessman Ronan McNamee before joining the Australian-based real estate investor Pepper Group. In 2009, Moyles joined forces with a former senior Anglo Irish Bank official, Robert Kehoe, to set up a new company called Arrow Asset Management. Kehoe was one of the founders of Newlyn Developments, which had offices in the Shelbourne headquarters at Hume Street, off St Stephen's Green. Newlyn had built houses and commercial developments across Dublin and County Wicklow, as well as in the UK and Portugal, during the boom years before its loans of just over €20 million were transferred to NAMA.

Among the other principals of Arrow were Newlyn directors George McGarry and Christy Dowling. Real estate specialist Adam McCormack, who had done extensive valuation work for NAMA while previously employed by Kelly Walsh Property Advisors, also joined the Arrow team. Arrow set up offices in Herbert Street in Dublin, where Newlyn and Kelly Walsh also relocated.

Another of Kelleher's team, Tom Hamilton, left Shelbourne to head up the Irish arm of the UK investment company Development Securities, while Emmett O'Reilly, the firm's finance director, went on to become CFO of Argentum, a joint venture between Newlyn and Australian investors Anchorage.

Kelleher was forced to quit the high-rent and exclusive offices near St Stephen's Green, as the bills continued to mount while his construction projects were stalled. He did not, however, consider himself down and out of the property game, and insisted that he would do his utmost to prove that his treatment by NAMA was unfair, in breach of his previous agreements and the NAMA Act.

Chapter 3 ∾

FAIR GAME OR FOUL

Like a number of his colleagues in the NTMA and the NPRF, where Enda Farrell worked, the arrival of NAMA below their offices in the Treasury Building, on Grand Canal Street in Dublin, offered an opportunity and a fresh challenge for him. In 2009, he joined a small team of people who took over the lower floors of the building for the new agency. While some in the NTMA saw their role as defenders of Ireland's financial position in the global bond markets compromised by their association with what they perceived as a glorified debt collection and toxic loan agency, Farrell decided that he could usefully offer his skill set as a market valuation specialist to NAMA. Besides, the NPRF was being wound down, as its €20 billion in reserves was being used by government to shore up other expenditure in the midst of the crisis in the public finances.

Raised in Castleknock, west Dublin, Farrell attended the Catholic University School in Leeson Street, from where he went on to study property economics and real estate at Bolton Street College of Technology and later at Oxford Polytechnic in England. After graduation, Farrell took a position with the giant UK property investment group Hammersons in Paris, where he met his future wife, Belgian-born Alice Kramer. From 2002 to 2004 he worked with Prudential in London before returning to Dublin to join Hypo Real Estate, a large German-owned real estate lender with offices in the IFSC in the city. Farrell worked for six months on property loan restructuring in the firm's London offices. Some years after Farrell left the company it suffered financial meltdown following the 2008 crash and was subsequently nationalised by the German government. Farrell also spent two years in the UK working for US Prudential.

In 2005, he learned that the NPRF was looking for people with expertise in alternative asset management and he was offered a position in the Treasury Building. That year his wife secured employment with Ernst & Young in Dublin. Within three years, they had two children and he took the decision to move to NAMA.

During the formative months of the agency, Farrell worked closely with Mulcahy, whom he knew from the auctioneer's role as property advisor to the

NPRF, McDonagh and, before his retirement in late 2009, Michael Somers. Farrell also knew the incoming NTMA chief executive John Corrigan, a former AIB executive who had been his immediate superior in the NPRF. Farrell had an influential role in the early engagement with the banks over the transfer of their loans as the new organisation grew from a handful of people to over three times the anticipated number of about 100 over the following years. His responsibility was to ensure that the valuations of the properties on which the loans were based were accurate by current standards at the time and that they were verified by credible third parties. It meant regular engagement with bank officials, in particular the units in the main banks dealing with NAMA, and, quite often, disputes and arguments over whether he and his colleagues were undervaluing the assets in order to ensure that the new agency could 'turn a profit'. When developer Paddy McKillen questioned why his loans were being transferred to NAMA, and took legal action to prevent it, a discussion took place within the agency during which it became clear to Farrell that some of his colleagues believed that developers, including McKillen, whose loans were still performing, were fair game. Indeed, he was informed that the agency could not achieve its objectives of getting the maximum return for the exchequer from the €31.8 billion it paid for the distressed loan books without screwing either the banks or the developers, or both.

'How is NAMA supposed to make a profit if we don't get assets like McKillen's?' he was asked by one senior official in November 2009.

By mid-2010, Farrell's important role in the agency was underlined by the fact that he controlled the entire spreadsheet of NAMA loans and the property assets underlying them, and was in constant negotiations with banks and with prospective buyers of the distressed assets which were now being released onto the market. He was also facing countless and constant queries about property portfolios from the external valuers hired by the agency, from internal staff handling NAMA clients and from members of the public calling the agency for information, which led him to refer to himself as the 'Joe Duffy for distressed debtors', after the well-known RTÉ radio presenter. On occasion, he was approached by colleagues, including senior executives, about individual properties in which they expressed an interest, including for their own family members or friends. The information was invaluable to those seeking to pick up sites or larger bundles of residential and commercial lands that were now under NAMA control. There was no shortage of international vultures beginning to circle the distressed Irish property market. Given the inability of the banks to lend until they were adequately recapitalised, and the bankruptcy or near collapse of the majority of Irish developers and builders, there were few people or companies in the country with sufficient funds to purchase the property portfolios, including billion-euro bundles of commercial, residential and zoned land, being put out to tender by NAMA. As the agency received instructions from government to maximise the return to the exchequer in as short a timescale as possible in order to relieve the enormous national debt, the agency focused on selling off the most valuable assets, including tranches in the US, Britain and Europe.

Among them were the London properties controlled by McKillen and his companies, including the iconic Claridge's, Connaught and Berkeley hotels, over which the developer was separately fighting the wealthy UK-based Barclay brothers for control. Farrell found himself clashing with Mulcahy and others over the discounts applied to the distressed loans that were transferring from the banks. The higher the discount applied, the more NAMA could profit from the subsequent sale and the better deal the vulture funds and other potential purchasers could obtain in a 'buyer's market'. He also noticed that while some developers were being chased 'to all quarters of the planet', as one executive noted during their daily 6.00 p.m. conferences, others were treated more leniently. On one occasion he was asked to provide the entire NAMA spreadsheet, with its detailed breakdown of all commercial and residential lands and properties under its remit, to the Department of Environment. He suggested that this could be in breach of the NAMA Act provisions covering confidential disclosure of commercially sensitive information, but was instructed to do what he was told. He was aware that some banks which had records of the data they had provided to NAMA were also providing information to prospective buyers. He was conscious that some of his colleagues had handed over spreadsheets on tranches of NAMA-controlled properties in Ireland and abroad to investment companies hunting for profitable information and deals. The key to unlocking profitable acquisitions was the ability to distinguish between the potentially lucrative assets and the bad debts on the €25 billion loan book transferring to NAMA. While NAMA had posted huge amounts of information on the assets it had acquired across various jurisdictions on its well-constructed and informative website, and was attracting increasing traffic from interested parties, for obvious reasons it did not disclose the underlying value of the properties under its control.

In July 2010, NAMA released its first annual statement and updated business plan for the coming year, which included a stinging rebuke by chairman Frank Daly of the participating institutions which, he said, 'had not disclosed or had been unaware of the financial crisis afflicting their borrowers'.

To say the least we are extremely disappointed and disturbed to find that, only months after being led to believe that 40 per cent of loans were income-producing, the real figure is actually 25 per cent. We are equally taken aback to learn that the banks were not even using the full range of legal options available to them in order to secure income in respect of troubled loans. The banks displayed a remarkable generosity towards their borrowers. NAMA has no intention of maintaining that approach. We will pursue all avenues to ensure the fullest possible repayment of all outstanding monies from relevant borrowers and we will work towards increasing the income stream for NAMA as soon as possible as part of the Debtor Business Plan review process.

Behind the scenes, as far as Farrell was concerned, there was an unhealthy rush to complete valuations, many of which, he felt, were inadequately costed by some of the external agencies employed to provide a second opinion of his work and that of his colleagues. Farrell was under immense pressure to complete valuations and was working 12- to 14-hour days, bringing tens of thousands of certificates for signature by more senior personnel, before they were passed on to external loan valuers. When he complained that the process was not sufficiently thorough or professional he was told: 'I am the bishop and you are the altar boy. Just get on with it.'

The message was that he could not possibly know how to value a semi-detached bungalow in Mullingar or a suite of offices in the IFSC as professionally as the experienced people in the real estate business. Under pressure from bankers telling him that his valuations of assets were too low and from colleagues complaining that they could not sell properties because the values were too high, Farrell unsuccessfully sought a less stressful role within the agency, preferably in capital markets. Unable to take any more and temperamentally unsuited to the work he was being asked to do, Farrell pressed the self-destruct button. He began to share information he had gathered over the previous 18 months and which he retained on spreadsheets containing the addresses and values of all NAMA properties. He provided a colleague with a valuation sought by one borrower, who was disputing the NAMA assessment of one property. He claims that he assisted a senior executive in accessing information on the value of a property in the south-west in which a relative of his colleague was interested. He retained copies of the tracker spreadsheets he had built up over his period with NAMA and sent them by email to his wife. He used his NTMA email address to forward information to various people inside and outside NAMA, which he believed was not confidential given that the banks were providing similar information to clients, although they were not, unlike him, subject to the provisions of the NAMA Act. He heard that another figure associated with NAMA had provided information on NAMA's 20 top borrowers to a leading global investment company. He learned of 'off-market', below-value sales to investors which appeared to conflict with a requirement that all properties sold by the agency were to be subject to rigorous and transparent tender procedures. In late 2010, having made a decision to leave the agency, he obtained information on a NAMA property at Strawberry Beds in Lucan which he subsequently purchased at some 10 per cent of its value at the peak of the property market.

Before he departed, he shared confidential NAMA information concerning its entire US portfolio with a Dutch pension firm, one of whose directors, Barden Gale, he knew as a property advisor to the NPRF.

He also provided extremely sensitive data relating to the assets of developer Garrett Kelleher, including the Spire project in Chicago, to a New York invest-ment fund. He gave information to a third party on valuations of the Jervis Street Shopping Centre in Dublin, owned by Paddy McKillen. He also knew that another colleague had shared confidential information with the Barclay brothers in London concerning McKillen's 'Coroin' investment vehicle, which included the developer's hotels in the city and which were the subject of litigation in the English High Court. He believed that certain borrowers and potential investors were being allowed significant information which gave them an advantage over others. Most, if not all, of the valuations circulated by Farrell in breach of NAMA confidentiality rules were based on 2009 valuations which were now two years out of date, given the further drop in the property markets.

Large multi-million asset portfolios sold in bundles by NAMA were given various names. One was Project Nantes, which comprised some €300 million of personal loans to the directors of the Avestus investment group led by a group of accountants and property experts who previously worked for financier and former Revenue Commissioner Derek Quinlan at his company Quinlan Private. Quinlan, like NAMA chairman Frank Daly, had served for many years with the Revenue Commissioners before he moved into property finance and acquisition.

The properties were being offloaded by NAMA at some 10 per cent of their original value. Among the properties was Sunday's Well, a large house near Lucan close to land owned by Farrell's father. It had been owned by Avestus director Thomas Dowd. With the assistance of the NAMA colleague who handled the portfolio, Farrell and his wife purchased the house from AIB, which was managing the loan on behalf of NAMA, for €410,000 in August 2011. Farrell had informed NAMA two months earlier that he intended to resign from the organisation but agreed to spend some months completing valuation work until he finally parted company with the agency in February 2012. He took up a position in the Dublin office of London-based investment management firm Forum Partners.

Chapter 4 ~

POLITICAL ARRIVALS

In November 2010, the flailing Fianna Fáil-led coalition, with Brian Lenihan as finance minister, was forced into a bailout programme run by the troika of the ECB, the EU Commission and the IMF. They demanded that monies lent by European banks, and by all bondholders, including unsecured investors, be repaid in full in exchange for the finance required to keep public services and the Irish state functioning.

The crash had prompted the decision by the non-Irish Bank of Scotland Ireland to pull out of the Irish market, leaving its owners, Lloyds, with distressed loans of some €350 million. These were subsequently acquired by US fund Kennedy Wilson. Other British and European banks soon followed, leaving a massive €200 billion in distressed assets across the island, including those from the five main Irish banks, which were transferred to NAMA, or later to the Irish Bank Resolution Corporation (IBRC).

The decision not to allow at least some of these institutions – in particular Anglo Irish and Irish Nationwide – to fail, and let the bondholders, investors and the near-bankrupt developers fight over the carcass rather than place the burden on the public and the tax payer, was in hindsight a major factor underlining the magnitude of the task facing NAMA. The infamous bank guarantee, the controversial setting up of NAMA and the arrival of the troika in Dublin as tens of thousands of working people marched against the disastrous mishandling of the economy and the imposition of harsh austerity measures sounded the final death knell for the Fianna Fáil-led government.

The general election of early 2011 resulted in a seismic shift in the Irish political scene and saw Fine Gael replace Fianna Fáil, whose share of the vote collapsed to 17 per cent, with a loss of 51 seats, as the largest political party. A resurgent Labour Party, with 37 seats in the Dáil, its highest ever number, went into coalition with Fine Gael, which won 76 seats and 36.1 per cent of the popular vote. The new Taoiseach, Enda Kenny, appointed former leader and veteran politician Michael Noonan as finance minister. From the outset Noonan established a close and supportive relationship with the NAMA executive, in sharp contrast with the critical views expressed by the party leader and senior figures when they opposed the manner in which the agency was established two years previous.

In February 2011, NAMA suffered its first major legal setback when the Supreme Court ruled that the agency's decision, in December 2009, to acquire loans of €2.1 billion held by companies owned by Paddy McKillen was invalid. The court ruled that the decision made by the agency's interim management team on 11–14 December 2009 was taken before NAMA came into existence on 21 December of that year. The court was ruling in an appeal brought by McKillen against an earlier High Court decision that had rejected his claims that the agency had acted improperly in its pursuit of his loans. Among those who gave evidence in his unsuccessful High Court action was economist and NAMA critic Joseph Stiglitz, who claimed on affidavit that there were 'compelling arguments' against the transfer of McKillen's loans to NAMA.

'For the Government's process to work well, it is crucial it focuses on identifying loans for which principal and interest is not being repaid,' Stiglitz argued. The Nobel Prize winner said that NAMA should be confined to paying for bad loans and that its incentive and ability to underpay banks for good assets was 'highly problematic'. He warned that the economic benefit of moving performing loans to NAMA was 'questionable at best' and would leave the banks weaker and the taxpayer no better off.

In a further judgment in the case issued two months later, in April 2011, the Supreme Court unanimously ruled that McKillen should have been given an opportunity to make representations to the agency before it decided to acquire his loans. While it rejected a claim by McKillen's legal team, led by Michael Cush SC, that a section of the NAMA Act was unconstitutional, the court ruled that the agency did not have an arbitrary right of untrammelled discretion to acquire assets.

It said that the general principles of fairness and due process derived from the Irish constitution meant that McKillen had a right to be informed by NAMA of its intention to acquire his loans and to make appropriate representations. The court suggested that the property and contractual rights of the developer could have been affected by any proposed loans acquisition.

In Dellway Investments v. NAMA, the Supreme Court unanimously held that McKillen had a right to be heard before NAMA moved on his assets. Judge Adrian Hardiman was particularly trenchant in his criticism of NAMA. During the hearing Attorney General Paul Gallagher, speaking for the agency, submitted that in circumstances of such a deep financial and banking crisis the state did not have an obligation to comply with fair procedure or to hear McKillen's objections before NAMA moved on the developer's assets.

Hardiman said, 'But it is the business of the law to identify such circumstances: otherwise the cry of "emergency" would be sufficient to set all rights aside at the whim of the Executive. The cry of "emergency" is an intoxicating one, producing an exhilarating freedom from the need to consider the rights of others and productive of a desire to repeat it again and again.'

It was a significant defeat for NAMA less than two years into its operations. At the time, McKillen was still battling to maintain control over his London assets, including the luxury hotels, and was concerned that NAMA would move on his assets while he was engaged in his dispute with the UK-based Barclay brothers, notwithstanding the Supreme Court ruling in Dublin.

His fears appeared to be justified in this respect following comments made by Brendan McDonagh, now re-branded as Chief Executive Officer of NAMA, to the Joint Oireachtas Committee on Finance, Public Expenditure and Reform in early September 2011 about the agency's plans to dispose of lucrative UK assets under its control.

Insisting that the agency was committed to a 'competitive sales process', McDonagh confirmed that 'some substantial transactions currently in the pipeline will proceed to sale and that the proceeds will help to reduce our debt and that of some of our debtors'. He said that NAMA was 'preparing to dispose of valuable assets' and that a 'significant proportion of the underlying property is located in the south-east of England and this is attracting strong interest from international investors'. By this time, NAMA had approved property asset sales of some €4.6 billion and this would rise to over €6 billion by the end of the year, he said.

Within three weeks of the committee hearing, NAMA confirmed that it had completed the sale of loans attached to the three luxury hotels in London. It said that

> the loans had been provided to the Maybourne Hotel Group by two Irish banks to fund the acquisition of the hotels in 2005. NAMA acquired the loans at the end of June 2010 from the banks. The loans were sold for in excess of €800 million with NAMA recovering 100% of the original value of the loans plus interest. The loans were acquired by Maybourne Finance Limited, which is a company controlled by Sir David and Sir Frederick Barclay.

Relations between McKillen and NAMA, already fraught as a result of the High Court and Supreme Court actions, were now openly hostile and it was evident that the agency had a formidable and well-financed opponent who would obstruct any further move against him that he perceived might damage his business interests.

In October, board member and chair of the NIAC Peter Stewart resigned due to the 'onerous' demands of the work he had been doing for the agency since he was first appointed in 2009. On his departure, he said that a recent review of the structures of NAMA should be 'fully implemented'.

The review had been carried out, at NAMA's request, by retired banker Michael Geoghegan and was published in early December 2011. It acknowledged that 'an enormous amount of work has been done and a lot achieved [by NAMA] in a very short time [since the agency was set up]' and that 'NAMA is pretty much at a point where I would have expected it to be at this juncture'.

Geoghegan recommended changes to the operation of the agency and said that 'its ability to make this transition effectively will define its ability to realise the kind of financial return for the Irish taxpayer which must be achieved from the assets it has purchased.' He noted that 'the Chief Executive [Brendan McDonagh] is respected by all for his ability to absorb a very intense workload' but said that he must be 'liberated to focus on the more strategic or entrepreneurial aspects of the role'.

Geoghegan recommended a 'greater delegation of authorities from the Board to the Executive'.

The review proposed the restructuring of the portfolio management, credit and risk, lending and legal departments, recommended that 600 smaller debtors 'currently managed by the banks themselves [under NAMA authority] be brought back into the agency proper' and, in order to facilitate this, that the agency 'recruit an additional 200 staff at a maximum cost of €25m'.

Finally, the review recommended the appointment of a number of senior executives including a chief financial officer, a head of strategic planning and a head of audit. Within months, John Mulcahy was appointed as an executive director of NAMA.

Chapter 5 ～

THE VULTURES CIRCLE

Michael Noonan ensured that NAMA was given free rein to pursue its objective of maximising the return of its sales to the exchequer, and indeed to do so in advance of the originally intended deadline of 2020. His newly installed secretary general of the Department of Finance, and fellow Limerick man, John Moran, appeared comfortable with the acquisition of billions in distressed assets by the so-called vulture funds landing in Ireland, including NAMA-held assets.

Mainly US funds including Cerberus, Goldman Sachs, CarVal, LoneStar, Oaktree, Blackstone, Pacific Investment Management Company (PIMCO), Davidson Kempner, Apollo and others were eyeing the vast quantity of residential and commercial loans which were now in default. Invariably, the hedge and equity funds hid behind a veil of secrecy and myriad Irish-registered subsidiaries, sometimes just brass-plate operations working from the offices of some of the bigger Dublin law firms. They began to sweat out the debts of the estimated 90,000 home and small-business owners facing default on their mortgages, many of them unaware exactly which financial entity had acquired the deeds and control of their property from their former lenders.

The ultimate owners were, of course, those like Blackstone, which once boasted that it 'likes to invest in countries with blood on the streets', or Goldman Sachs, once famously described in the US *Rolling Stone* magazine as 'a great vampire squid wrapped around the face of humanity, relentlessly jamming its blood funnel into anything that smells like money', or indeed Cerberus, named after the legendary three-headed dog in Greek mythology that guarded the entrance of the Underworld, allowing the dead to enter but letting none out. Apart from his three heads, he also had a serpent's tail, a mane of snakes and the claws of a lion.

The funds needed local partners to identify the best-quality assets from the bundles of distressed loans in default across the island and to maximise the returns from their acquisitions and disposals. A new breed of ambitious and informed, largely Dublin-based asset managers, valuers and estate agents emerged to assist the global sharks, while the large accountancy firms and solicitors identified long-existing loopholes to minimise, indeed almost eliminate, any tax liability from their operations.

NAMA had appointed over sixty law practices across the country which, along with property valuation and accountancy firms, would share in the estimated €2.6 billion in professional fees which the agency expected to spend over the following years. Among the legal firms selected were big hitters such as Dublin-based Arthur Cox, Matheson Ormsby Prentice and William Fry. Other Dublin firms appointed to the legal panel included Ivor Fitzpatrick, BCM Hanby Wallace, Beauchamps, Eugene F Collins, Mason Hayes & Curran, LK Shields and Eversheds O'Donnell Sweeney. Outside Dublin, prominent solicitors were appointed in every major city and town, giving rise to potentially serious conflicts of interest down the road as NAMA dealt with distressed borrowers whose interests were or had been represented by the same legal firms.

Following a long pattern of poor corporate and financial regulation and enforcement, which had contributed to the crash in the first place, senior officials in the Department of Finance and the Revenue Commissioners ignored early warnings that the vulture funds were availing of obscure tax exemptions. These included Section 110 provisions in the Taxes Consolidation Act 1997, which allowed companies set up to hold distressed loans and mortgages to avoid paying tax on Irish property-related transactions. Section 110 companies were also using charitable trusts in order to achieve significant write-offs on property acquistions.

NAMA was fighting a battle on a number of fronts, including defections and leaks from its own ranks, the swarming vulture funds and their local partners (some of whom were also acting as consultants to the agency), growing political and media scrutiny and increasing suspicion of criminal activity by some of its former staff. One story which began to spread around town was of a NAMA official who had pocketed a substantial cash sum from a debtor in return for a promise to assist with an early exit for the developer from the agency's control. Despite its earlier promise of greater transparency and accountability, the agency's response was to pull down the hatches and indeed limit access to information which it believed might hinder its ability to complete its mandate, using legislation to deter prying investigators if necessary.

However, its main focus was to acquire the assets of the leading developers and to dispose of them for the highest price – inevitably pitting its extensive legal powers and resources against some of the wealthiest men (for they were almost all men) in the country. Some followed McKillen into the courts, using their financial muscle to challenge the best efforts of NAMA to gain control of the assets behind their huge loans.

Treasury Holdings, with debts of €1.7 billion transferred to NAMA, enjoyed a tempestuous relationship with NAMA executives from the start, notwithstanding the irony that the agency was working out of a property owned by its co-director Johnny Ronan. Ronan had developed the Treasury Building on Grand Canal Street with McKillen during his early years in the property business in Dublin in the 1990s, before he formed Treasury Holdings with lawyer Richard Barrett. The building, an office block, featured on its outside wall a sculpture of a naked woman climbing the façade. It had originally been male but Ronan objected to the notion of a nude man trying to reach his top-floor office.

Ronan became the poster playboy of the Celtic Tiger, with his glamorous and extravagant lifestyle the subject of regular features in the gossip pages, not least when a weekend trip to Morocco with leading model Rosanna Davison sparked a public street brawl with his then girlfriend and fashion celebrity Glenda Gilson at the height of the boom.

Away from the headlines, Ronan and Barrett built a property portfolio of offices, apartments and hotels across Dublin and County Wicklow before expanding globally in the years before the crash.

Barrett, a qualified barrister, and Ronan, an accountant, formed Treasury Holdings in 1989 and in less than a decade had developed real estate projects with a combined value in excess of €4.6 billion, expanding the residential and commercial portfolio it built in Celtic Tiger Ireland to a property empire that stretched to the UK, Russia and China.

NAMA vigorously pursued Treasury and its property vehicles, including Real Estate Opportunities (REO), which controlled the company's Chinese assets and the very lucrative site of the former power station in Battersea in London which Ronan and Barrett planned to develop for prime office and residential use. They argued that a rapid-fire sale of this and other valuable assets in their extensive global portfolio would be counter-productive and costly for the Irish exchequer and public, but their appeals fell on deaf ears. Treasury owed another €1 billion to non-NAMA banks – reinforcing the agency's argument that the company could not trade its way out of its financial difficulties. Ronan and Barrett, on the other hand, believed that they were capable of recovering from their indebtedness if the valuable assets under their control were allowed to realise their full potential. In particular, they believed that the successful development of Battersea Power Station, the largest single urban regeneration site in central London, which REO had purchased for £400 million in 2006, could yield a multiple of that sum.

In January 2012, NAMA moved to appoint receivers Ernst & Young and PwC to the assets built over two decades by Treasury – provoking yet another legal response from Ronan and Barrett, who sought an injunction from the High

Court to prevent the hostile transfer of their loans. Treasury also declared its intention to launch judicial review proceedings to halt the NAMA action on the grounds that two global investors, Macquarie and Hines, had made an offer to buy out the loans for a sum in excess of the amount the agency had paid the banks for them. The distressed Treasury loans had a par value of some €2 billion when NAMA took them over for a reported €900 million, or just 45 cents in the euro, a 55% discount. The agency responded in a statement that it had

> engaged rigorously with Treasury Holdings since 2010. Unfortunately, it has not been possible to achieve a mutually acceptable agreement on the way forward with respect to the group's NAMA loans ... NAMA analysed the two proposals made and they were not commercially acceptable. The NAMA board decided to proceed with the appointment of Receivers at the end of today's standstill period.

The agency said it had not engaged in negotiation with the two third-party investors, but had merely sought clarification of offers.

According to a report the following day on the informative NAMA Wine Lake (NWL) website, established anonymously to monitor the progress of the agency and its clients, relations between NAMA and Treasury appeared to deteriorate in December 2011 when the agency and other lenders appointed administrators to the Battersea Power Station. There were also reports of the agency seeking to have receivers appointed to other Treasury properties, including the PwC building in the Docklands (a tenancy which prompted questions over the appointment of the accountancy firm as receivers), the Central Park complex in Leopardstown in south Dublin and the Ballymun Shopping Centre on the north side of the city.

Subsequently it was reported that the receivers were also appointed to the sky-scraping Alto Vetro apartment building on Grand Canal Dock. It was close to Montevetro, also built by Treasury and acquired by NAMA, which sold it to the US technology giant Google for €99 million in February 2011. In total, 22 companies controlled by Treasury were the subject of the orders sought by NAMA, although PwC declared that it would not be involved in the proceedings regarding its own headquarters in the Treasury-built complex at Spencer Dock. REO, the property vehicle controlled by Treasury, immediately announced that it was suspending share dealings on the London Stock Exchange and confirmed that NAMA was seeking amounts totalling over €560,000 from it and an associated company, Montevetro II Limited. In affidavits provided before the opening of the case in February 2012, NAMA confirmed that it had acquired €1.7 billion of Treasury loans at par value while the debtor owed another

€1 billion to non-NAMA banks. The Treasury Group's financial statements at 28 February 2010 showed it to be 'balance sheet' insolvent to the tune of €859 million, according to the agency. NAMA had since provided €103 million of new advances to the group. In July 2011 Treasury said that it was going to run out of cash by September.

Central to the heated discussions between the Treasury boys and NAMA was portfolio manager Graham Emmett, who was responsible for negotiating with Ronan, Barrett, their accountants and other managers in relation to their debt and reporting back to Mulcahy and Ronnie Hanna on the progress or otherwise of the discussions.

Emmett also handled the debts of another major player in the global property market, Sean Mulryan, and his company, the Ballymore Group. Mulryan had started his mainly house-building business in Kildare and Wicklow in the 1980s before expanding to Britain and some European cities, including Prague, over the next 20 years. His residential development with another high-profile property player, Sean Dunne, at Charlesland near Greystones in Wicklow in the early 2000s was the largest of its kind in the country at the time. It led to persistent allegations of malfeasance on the part of some officials and elected members of Wicklow County Council. The claims centred on the manner in which public lands were acquired by the developers from the council through an 'exchange of easements' which involved disposals of valuable public assets, for little or no money, and without a vote by elected members of the local authority.

Gabriel Dooley, an estate agent who acted for Mulryan in the assembly of the site at Charlesland, alleged that political influence was used to ensure that the scheme obtained the strategic tracts of public land to ensure access to the 1,800-home residential development. Dooley also claimed that he was owed over €4 million by Mulryan in relation to a retail venture they had sought to develop at Florentine in the centre of Bray before the crash and the subsequent acquisition of the lands by Bray Urban Council. Dooley also made serious allegations around the management of his own debt to Anglo Irish Bank and in a detailed complaint to the Garda Bureau of Fraud Investigation claimed that a NAMA unit working on loans at a branch of Anglo in London had improperly shared information on his loans and financial situation with a senior executive of Ballymore while he was pursuing his claim for damages against the property company in 2010. The unit in Anglo also informed a Ballymore executive of Dooley's threat of legal action against the company. Dooley had obtained detailed information under data protection legislation to confirm the exchange of correspondence between the Anglo officials and a senior Ballymore executive. In his statement to the Garda Bureau of Fraud Investigation (GBFI), Dooley said:

On 8th December 2010, I received a call from Barry Hickey of Ballymore stating that he had received a call and an email regarding the €4 million owed to me. He was furious on the phone as I had showed an intention to issue legal proceedings against Ballymore … He stated to me that Ballymore always regarded me as a long-standing close friend of Ballymore Group going back many years. No one else was aware of my plan to sue Ballymore except myself, the Anglo people and my legal team. There is no reason … that Ballymore should have been aware of this very sensitive information.

In January 2011, Dooley refused an offer of a six-figure sum from Ballymore to settle the outstanding debt. The auctioneer also complained to NAMA about the actions of the unit handling his distressed loans in the London office of Anglo. The agency said in response that the officials in the unit in London were employed by Anglo, not by NAMA. The GBFI informed Dooley in January 2016 that his allegations did 'not constitute a criminal offence in this jurisdiction'.

Along with the successful Charlesland development and other lucrative projects in Dublin and Kildare, Mulryan concentrated on expanding his property ownership in London. He was fortunate to have accumulated tens of millions in property in the Canary Wharf area and close to the stadia and other facilities in east London required for the 2012 Olympics hosted by the city. In a particularly astute investment, Ballymore Properties bought 60 acres in the Lower Lea Valley 'wastelands' close to where the £2.3 billion Olympic Park was constructed in Stratford and where he planned to build 18,000 homes and 5 million square feet of commercial property. At one point before the financial crash his investments in Britain were estimated at €18 billion, although his exposure to NAMA, when the dust settled from the banking crisis and his loans to Anglo and Irish Nationwide were transferred to the agency, was just under €2 billion. Mulryan, originally from Oran in County Roscommon, was one of a handful of developers to receive €200,000 per annum from the agency to help it manage the disposal of his property portfolio on top of an unspecified bonus if he helped to obtain more than NAMA paid his former banks for the assets.

While Treasury continued to battle with NAMA over the management of its debt, Mulryan adopted a strategy, and advised other developers to do likewise, of co-operating in the management and disposal of his bad debts. The outcome for the two competitors in their dealings with the bad bank agency could not have been more different. Graham Emmett was central to the negotiations with both, along with his superiors Mulcahy and Hanna, and all three would no doubt deny that there was any favouritism involved in their dealings with any of the high-profile developers who had accumulated so much bad debt and distressed assets.

It was a matter of some embarrassment for the agency, however, when it emerged that Emmett had been offered a position as chief executive of Ballymore's British operations before he resigned from the agency in January 2012. It was made clear to him that to take up such an offer would feed a perception, put about by a number of disgruntled NAMA debtors, that some of the agency's clients were favoured above others.

Emmett left NAMA a month after the decision to call in the Treasury loans was made and before the High Court action taken by the company against the appointment of the receivers commenced. He joined the London-based ICG-Longbow Real Estate Capital, specialists in commercial real estate debt in the UK, before becoming a partner in debt restructuring firm Cheyne Capital Management a year later. There was public controversy when it emerged that ICG-Longbow purchased property assets from NAMA several months after Emmett left the agency.

Explaining the reasons for his departure, Emmett told the *Sunday Independent*: 'I have no problem with the board of NAMA. My issue was the interference by Government in the employment contracts that had been signed. It's the minimum salary and the requests for [pay] reductions and the long-term incentive plan, the whole gamut. It's not just to do with bonuses.'

Meanwhile, Donal Mulryan, who worked with his brother Sean at Ballymore Properties for several years before branching out to build his own property portfolio, much of it in the UK, also found the going rough in the wake of the crash. In October 2011, assets of some £220 million (€257 million) which had been transferred from Donal Mulryan's company, West Properties, and others he controlled in the UK to the bad debt agency were put on the market, including commercial schemes around Manchester and London. It was confirmed at the time, in November 2011, that Donal Mulryan had been appointed following the sale to advise Morgan Stanley, which purchased his assets for a reported knock-down price of £65 million (€76 million).

The fortunes of the 20 top developers now under the auspices of NAMA were varied, with some, like the Grehan brothers, Ray and Danny, who had €1 billion in debts with the agency, and John Fleming and Bernard McNamara, opting for bankruptcy in England. Ray Grehan was declared bankrupt in the UK in December 2011, with total debts of £417 million (€523 million), in the expectation that he would be freed of his debt mountain within the two years available under British bankruptcy rules. However, because he failed to declare significant transfers of assets in the months prior to his bankruptcy, a restriction order was imposed on Grehan, preventing him from acting as a company director in Britain or from borrowing more than £500 without disclosing his status as a restricted bankrupt. With an address in Abuja, Nigeria, Grehan's attempt to restore his former glory as one of Ireland's most prolific spenders and borrowers of the boom years, including his lavish payment of €171.5 million (an extraordinary €84 million an acre) in 2005 for the former Veterinary College in Ballsbridge, was not an easy ride. His filing for bankruptcy followed the appointment of receivers by NAMA over his company and the personal assets of himself and his brother, Danny, just over six months earlier in April 2011. As well as the Veterinary College site, the assets included the Grange apartment complex in Stillorgan, south Dublin, and the Glenroyal Hotel in Maynooth, County Kildare. In London the brothers owned the valuable One Hyde Park building and a tower in Canary Wharf, among other properties. NAMA was pursuing the pair and their company Glenkerrin Group for over €600 million. Danny Grehan filed for bankruptcy in London just weeks after his brother, in January 2012.

Ray Grehan made life considerably more difficult for himself when he was forced to admit that he had failed to disclose four bank accounts as well as his transfers of an apartment, substantial monies and other assets to his wife and daughters after his loans were taken into NAMA, and further had made an inaccurate statement of his affairs to the High Court in London in December 2011. He admitted that he had sold his interest in a suite in the Ritz Carlton Hotel in Toronto, Canada, in November 2011, and a quarter share of a casino in the Netherlands valued at €50 million to his daughter for just €1.

When questioned in court in London in March 2012, Grehan confirmed that in August 2011 he had transferred his 26 per cent share in the Dutch casino in August to Subiaco, a company registered in the British Virgin Islands. He gifted his daughter 75 per cent of the shares in Subiaco, granting her a 19 per cent interest in the casino while Grehan retained the remaining stake. Subiaco was established by Mossack Fonseca, a Panama law firm which specialises in providing offshore services to companies and individuals seeking to disguise the true ownership and origin of particular assets. In March 2012, as the court proceedings in London were under way, Mossack Fonseca informed British Virgin Islands regulators that the beneficial owner of Subiaco was a Spanish resident, Marcelino Alvarez Garcia.

Prominent Cork developer John Fleming was among the first to avail of the relatively lax UK bankruptcy system after his property company collapsed in 2010 with debts of €1 billion. Fleming had developed major housing projects in Cork city and county during the good years. In comparison with the then 12-year waiting period in Ireland, Fleming was discharged from his bankruptcy in November 2011, after just 12 months, following which he returned to his home and business base in Bandon, west Cork. Worth an estimated €138 million at the height of the construction boom, his company JJ Fleming Holdings built housing estates, hotels and windfarms before going into liquidation in 2010. However, NAMA and other creditors continued to pursue Fleming after his exit from bankruptcy and demanded that any income in excess of his living expenses, including his pension, should be surrendered. Another company, JJ Fleming (Bandon), in which three of his daughters became directors, was formed in 2009 to carry on a construction business while his son-in-law and former employee, John O'Brien, purchased John Fleming's family home in February 2011. Christy Hayes, previously a foreman for John Fleming, opened another building company, Donban, at the former headquarters of the Fleming Group in Bandon.

Another well-known developer, Bernard McNamara, moved to England in early 2011 to obtain a speedy bankruptcy from his debts of €1.2 billion. His firm, Michael McNamara Ltd, had once owned Dublin's iconic Shelbourne and Burlington hotels, which for years hosted political conventions and celebrity-filled gala events, and Parknasilla Hotel in County Kerry. The Clare-born developer and former Fianna Fáil councillor was known as a ruthless operator and was embroiled in countless rows with competitors and creditors alike as he blazed a trail across the capital city and the country with his large commercial and residential developments. His particular empire came crashing down with the disastrous investment in the former 24-acre derelict Irish Glass Bottle site in Ringsend at the mouth of the Liffey in Dublin. Once again, the fingerprints of Seán FitzPatrick and Anglo Irish Bank were all over the deal, which ultimately brought down the state-controlled DDDA at massive cost to the public purse and to the people in the surrounding communities. They had long been promised a dividend in terms of employment and training from the commercial developments in the heart of the north and south inner city, which was never delivered. Expensive and prolonged investigations and reports into the internal conflicts of interest and the political interference of senior political figures in the work of the DDDA never saw the light of day.

Other long-abandoned working-class estates across the city were similarly deprived when in 2008 Bernard McNamara withdrew from a number of schemes in which he was committed to redevelop run-down, council-owned flat complexes through public–private partnerships. He was not deterred, however, from expanding his business empire through the purchase of hotels, office blocks and retail developments, some in partnership with Jerry O'Reilly and David Courtney and their company, Select Retail Holdings, and other joint ventures. After the shambles of the Irish Glass Bottle property investment, their company, Radora Developments, forked out more than €300 million in late 2006 for a large residential and office scheme at Elm Park on the Merrion Road in Dublin, mainly funded by Anglo but with minimum exposure of just over €60 million to the three investors. McNamara's close associations with Fianna Fáil saw him elevated over the years to a number of state boards, including the National Roads Authority and the Great Southern Hotels group. This provided him with access to useful information on future government infrastructure projects. Meanwhile his annual knees-up at the Galway Races (in his Radisson SAS hotel in the city, more discreet than the Fianna Fáil tent at the raceground) allowed him to entertain those in business, finance and politics whose assistance he required to maintain his growing property investment and construction empire – not least in the form of tax incentives, for which he lobbied his powerful political contacts.

By early 2010 McNamara was insolvent, with debts of €1.4 billion, and fighting off creditors and former partners, including his new, powerful adversaries in NAMA, in various law suits. His departure a year later to England to avail of its light bankruptcy regulations saw him finally discharged of much of his debt mountain and within a few years his name was gracing the hoardings of major construction projects in Dublin, including a development by telecoms billionaire Denis O'Brien on St Stephen's Green, much to the chagrin of an angry and disgruntled citizenry forced in their hundreds of thousands into deep indebtedness and increasing impoverishment. Not to mention the 200,000 or more employed during the boom years in the construction industry, from labourers, craftspeople, engineers and architects to suppliers of essential products and materials.

Other developers, including Gerry Gannon, Joe O'Reilly, and other members of the so-called 'Maple 10', who had purchased shares in Anglo to prevent its collapse in 2008, had their huge loan books transferred to NAMA, with no certainty that any of their businesses, or their fortunes, would survive. The Maple 10 was the name given to ten of the largest Anglo borrowers who agreed in July 2008 to secretly purchase one per cent of bank shares owned by businessman Sean Quinn in order to reduce the bank's exposure to him. By mid-2008, Quinn had built a 28 per cent stake in Anglo and the bank executives panicked. The other members of the Maple 10 were builders Seamus Ross, John McCabe and Sean Reilly; developers Paddy McKillen, Gerry Conlan, Gerry McGuire, Brian O'Farrell and Paddy Kearney made up the rest of the list. Kearney was in Nice in the south of France when he received an early morning visit from Anglo executives David Drumm and Pat Whelan, and he agreed to sign up to the scheme. Kearney owned shopping centres and other commercial properties in the North and in England through his company PBN, which he had established with Neil Adair, who ran Anglo's operations in Belfast for several years. Sean Quinn ended up losing control of his multi-billion-euro property, hotel, insurance and cement business and went from the richest man in Ireland to one of the most despised as he entered years of litigation over the whereabouts of his various assets across the globe.

Similarly, Sean Dunne was pursued, as Brian Lenihan had threatened, to the end of the earth. Chris Lehane, the administrator appointed over his assets, took legal action in the US and other jurisdictions in an effort to chase down funds, including art, properties and monies. Lehane suspected that Dunne had transferred assets to his wife, the former gossip columnist Gayle Killilea. The builder from Tullow, County Carlow started off as a quantity surveyor before forming Mountbrook Homes, a housebuilding company, in 1983. Over the years he emerged as one of the leading developers of offices, hotels, large-scale residential projects and shopping centres while also making a name for himself as another extravagant spender in both his private and business life. In the 1990s he built a mansion for then Fianna Fáil finance minister Charlie McCreevy in County Kildare and he later developed Whitewater shopping centre, the largest in the country outside Dublin, and the Riverside IV building in the Dublin Docklands. He spent a record €379 million (€54 million per acre) in 2005 for the Jury's and Berkeley Court hotel sites in Ballsbridge and bought nearby Hume House for €130 million. A year later he bought the AIB bank centre in Ballsbridge for €207 million, which added to his exposure when the crash hit just two years later. His main lenders for these purchases were Ulster Bank, owned by Royal Bank of Scotland, and other overseas banks including the Kaupthing Bank of Iceland, although his debts to Anglo and other Irish banks forced him into the grip of NAMA in 2011. Just as his plan for a €1 billion retail, office and residential scheme on the Jury's site (modelled on London's Knightsbridge shopping quarter and including a 37-storey diamond-shaped apartment block) was granted planning permission, the agency appointed receivers over his business interests in relation to debts outstanding to the Irish banks, including loans backed by Dunne's personal guarantee. After a series of planning appeals the Ballsbridge development was scaled back, and by September 2011 a development costing just €300 million, with the tower reduced to 12 storeys, received planning approval.

By then the site was worth just €50 million, a drop of almost 90 per cent from its pre-crash value, while another property at Walford on the exclusive Shrewsbury Road in Dublin 4 was put on the market for €15 million just six years after Dunne and his wife paid €58 million for the property.

NAMA and other creditors were forced to cross the Atlantic after the Dunnes moved to the US. In March 2012 the Commercial Court in Dublin granted a summary judgment order to NAMA for repayment of €185 million to the agency, of which some €150 million was backed by personal guarantee.

The combined debts of these and many other developers to various banks amounted to well over €100 billion – a staggering hangover from the years of hubris, helicopters and luxury homes, particularly given the relatively small size of the country and economy. Inevitably, it also had significant repercussions for the political, regulatory and banking system and spawned NAMA as well as several inquiries into the banking collapse.

As the agency called in the loans, the valuers, accountants, solicitors and surveyors it had recruited included some of the very companies that had pumped the property bubble in the first place. They were now picking up lucrative contracts for the professional fees offered by NAMA. Familiar names from the property market included Jones Lang LaSalle, in which John Mulcahy continued to hold shares worth over €2 million when he joined NAMA as head of portfolio management.

Donal Kellegher, another executive recruited by NAMA, held shares in Savills – an auctioneer which won lucrative valuation contracts from NAMA. DTZ Fitzgerald, Lisneys and CBRE, all of which had benefited from hyping the property boom, propitiously gained a slice of the action from NAMA at a time when their incomes from property sales had melted, while on the legal and accountancy side, Arthur Cox, KPMG and PwC benefited, notwithstanding their roles as advisors to the banks over the period when they brought the economy to its knees. Ernst & Young was also providing consultancy services to the agency, despite the controversy over its audit of Anglo-Irish Bank in 2009. Auditors from the accountancy firm gave evidence in the criminal trial of former Anglo chairman, Seán FitzPatrick, who hid over €120 million in loans from the bank's annual audit through the infamous end of year 'bed and breakfast' arrangement with Irish Nationwide in 2009. FitzPatrick made regular appearances in the Dublin courts as he fought off attempts by the state to prosecute him on various charges relating to his role in the crash.

NAMA board member Michael Connolly held a substantial, although seriously depleted, shareholding in Bank of Ireland, where he previously worked, and which was of course one of the largest banks forced to transfer billions in toxic debt to the agency. As NAMA did not come under the provisions of the Freedom of Information Acts (1997 and 2003), an exemption which was the subject of public criticism by then Ombudsman Emily O'Reilly in her 2009 annual report, it proved difficult for inquiring journalists, politicians or indeed many whose loans were taken over by the agency to get accurate information on the valuation processes involved and the manner with which they were dealt. Indeed, some NAMA insiders suggested that how you emerged from your dealings with the agency depended significantly on which portfolio manager was handling your debt. NAMA insisted that valuations were based on 2009 figures and that its methodology was agreed with the European Union in 2010. The most detailed information available was contained in the annual report of the

Comptroller and Auditor General (C&AG) in his audit of the agency while news bulletins, policy statements and other information was published on NAMA's website. On occasion, information was provided to selected journalists by NAMA executives or their public relations advisors on a confidential basis.

Following the 2011 general election, NAMA came under scrutiny from the new forces that entered the Dáil following the routing of the outgoing Fianna Fáil-led government. While the agency undoubtedly benefited from the outspoken and generous encouragement of the new Minister for Finance, Michael Noonan, to whom it was ultimately answerable, it was not so pleased when a fresh crop of more radical politicians began to question how the agency was functioning and the secrecy surrounding much of its activities. With the Labour Party now in government as a minority partner with Fine Gael, its previously more critical approach to NAMA, by former finance spokesperson Joan Burton among others, was muted. However, the Minister for Public Expenditure and Reform, Brendan Howlin, committed to the introduction of legislation that would make NAMA amenable to Freedom of Information (FOI) requests from which it had previously been excluded.

The arrival of a cohort of left-wing TDs from Sinn Féin, independents such as Mick Wallace and Clare Daly and elected representatives from the People before Profit and Anti-Austerity Alliance groupings added a colourful and challenging approach to long-established parliamentary procedures and also led to greater transparency across a range of public bodies, including NAMA.

A former builder and property developer, Wallace first raised his concerns about NAMA in the Dáil in May 2011 when he claimed that the agency was 'liable to flood the market' and that it would sell properties 'at a good deal less than [their] real value'. He said that 'as much as possible of NAMA-controlled property should be retained in the hands of the state for sports, cultural or residential purposes'.

During a Dáil debate on the future of Dublin's Moore Street, the historic site where the leaders of the 1916 Easter Rising made their final stand before surrender, Wallace argued that the area should be turned into a cultural quarter. He said that the site had full planning permission, with some conditions, and that the developer in question, Joe O'Reilly, owner of Chartered Land, 'is in NAMA which gives the State more power than usual'.

Many of the buildings on the street were built after 1916 but the whole street should be preserved as a cultural quarter, with the buildings rebuilt as they were before the Rising. It would be money well spent.

Arguing for the development of a new cultural quarter, similar to the one he developed along the Liffey quays, Wallace continued:

For those Members interested in checking it out I recommend the Italian Quarter along the quay which has worked well. The place was packed today in the sunshine and it has a lovely atmosphere. Preservation and commerce can go together. We preserved the old facade and we worked in co-operation with Dublin City Council.

The following month Wallace raised the issue of salaries of people employed at NAMA, and addressing Brendan Howlin, he also asked who decided which people were most suited to work in the agency.

Who decided who would get the jobs? I have encountered many people who worked for banks and in real estate who have moved into NAMA. It seems they are getting more money now than they ever got in their previous jobs. I do not understand that, given that they are doing much the same type of work. It is questionable whether they should have got the work when one considers that they were part of this mess in the first instance.

In reply, Howlin, a TD representing the same Wexford constituency as Wallace, said that it was his view that nobody in the public service should earn more than €200,000, or €250,000 in the commercial semi-state sector, but that the NTMA and NAMA were an exception to this rule.

The government, with its overwhelming majority of Fine Gael and Labour TDs, concentrated its efforts on recovering the economy, reducing unemployment and public spending and sorting out the banking problem, but it was operating under the supervision of a troika which was demanding increasing levels of austerity, labour reforms and other unpalatable remedies to the country's debt problem. When it came to NAMA, Noonan insisted that it should speed up its disposal of assets, ostensibly to honour commitments to the troika. John Moran, the new secretary general at the Department of Finance, had a background in the US corporate banking sector. He took a keen interest in the workings of NAMA and in the landing of the vulture funds who were eager to take advantage of the heavily discounted residential and commercial asset sales in Ireland, which was fast becoming the most attractive place in the world to make substantial and quick profits from real estate.

In July 2011, in its first published annual report, NAMA confirmed that it had by now acquired 11,500 loans of 850 debtors, with loans of €71.2 billion transferred from the five institutions for which it paid €30.2 billion, a discount of 58 per cent.

NAMA estimated that 61 per cent of the property assets securing NAMA loans were in Ireland, 32 per cent in the UK and Northern Ireland and 7 per cent in the rest of the world. An estimated 59 per cent of the assets comprised investment property and 41 per cent comprised land or property under development.

Twelve NAMA debtors had par debt in excess of €1 billion each, not including any debt they had with non-NAMA institutions.

In his presentation to the Oireachtas Joint Committee on Finance, Public Expenditure and Reform on 9 September 2011, NAMA chairman and senior executive Frank Daly dealt with the criticism of excessive secrecy surrounding the work of the agency. He informed members of the inherent conflict between NAMA's role as a debt management and disposal agency and its public responsibility of openness and transparency.

> It is regularly suggested that we are secretive and lacking transparency, notwithstanding the fact that the law, under sections 99 and 202 of the NAMA Act, prohibits us from disclosing confidential information, including information relating to debtors. We have, however, a clear policy of being as transparent as we can within these legal constraints and we try to be as accessible as possible to public representatives, the media, interest groups and representative organisations. The legislature has handed us an ambitious commercial mandate which is to realise the best achievable financial return by reference to the value of acquired assets so that, at the very least, we are expected to break even over time.

Addressing the widespread and understandable concern that an agency handling billions of euro of public monies should be shrouded in secrecy, and was not covered under the already restrictive provisions of FOI legislation, Daly explained that transparency was incompatible with the objective of achieving the best return:

> it is necessary to point out that this objective is in conflict with calls for greater transparency. Greater transparency means that we would have to reveal our hand to the very people who are in negotiation with us – potential purchasers of NAMA loans and underlying property. This would be commercially foolhardy – a bit like showing your hand to an opposing player in a card game … I wish to make it very clear, however, that NAMA is and will always be a fully accountable public body. We are subject to regular scrutiny by this Committee and by the Public Accounts Committee. We report on a quarterly basis to the Minister and to the Oireachtas.

In his opening remarks, and reflecting the proposals of the earlier Geoghegan review of the agency, NAMA CEO Brendan McDonagh told the Finance Committee that it had 'recruited over 190 staff with the specialist skills and experience required to manage a portfolio of property loans with balances in excess of €72 billion.'

He said:

our attention is now increasingly focused on dealing with the 850 debtors whose loans we have already acquired. Our intention is to manage the largest 180 of these debtors directly (their debts total about €62 billion). The other debtors – accounting for about €10 billion in loans – are being managed, under delegated authority from NAMA, by some 500 staff in the participating institutions.

So far so good – but then came the questions from the committee members, some of whom had only been elected for the first time seven months previous and were still finding their bearings in the arcane world of parliamentary procedure.

First up was Fianna Fáil finance spokesman Michael McGrath from Cork, who had taken over that role in June 2011 following the death of former finance minister Brian Lenihan in the same month. First elected to the Dáil in 2007, McGrath was first appointed opposition spokesman on public expenditure and reform after his party lost office in its disastrous performance in the February 2011 election. He reminded McDonagh of the commitment he had made at a previous committee hearing and when the agency was first unveiled that NAMA would not be 'a bail out for developers'. He said that he gleaned from comments made by Daly that this commitment had not been kept. He asked about the practice of some of the agency's more prominent, and reluctant, clients to transfer assets to family members or opaque locations to put them out of reach of the agency.

McGrath said:

However, there appears to be a theme running through Mr Daly's remarks that the objective is to recoup the €30 billion the State has paid through NAMA, plus costs. He referred to Section 10 of the National Asset Management Agency Act in that regard. I have a different interpretation of that. I believe NAMA is obliged to pursue developers for the full amount owed, but there appears to be back-tracking by NAMA in that regard.

He claimed that, far from pursuing developers 'for every cent they owe', Daly appeared to 'be satisfied to pursue developers only to the extent of securing the amount that NAMA paid for the original loan'. McGrath also queried the pair on the type of salaries the agency had approved for developers who were assisting with the winding down of their debts owed to it.

Daly replied that salary ranges were between €75,000 and €100,000, and in a small number of exceptional cases up to €200,000 per annum in return for 'typically' a 75 per cent reduction in the overheads of the company or business involved. Daly explained:

It is a hard decision over which we agonise, but, ultimately, it is a realistic commercial decision. In many of these cases the alternative would be to employ receivers at exorbitant rates of €180 per hour or something similar who might take a very long time and may not have the same interest in getting out of this as would the debtor. We are trying to align the interests of the taxpayer with those of NAMA and the debtor who wishes to get out of this and to repay his or her debts. That is the overarching question.

In response to the question of the emergence of white knights from foreign lands landing in town to refinance the distressed developers, McDonagh would not rule it out in principle, but only if NAMA achieved a return that was in the taxpayers' interest.

The common and not incredible perception was raised that developers and other property investors who had gorged on, and subsequently rolled over, gigantic loans ranging from €100 million to almost €400 million for individual projects in some of the more excessive cases had surely put away a slice of their banker's generosity for a rainy day. McDonagh told Deputy McGrath that having studied the business plans related to about €22 billion of the €30 billion in loans paid for by NAMA there was no evidence of any such 'pot of gold'. McDonagh continued:

As I said when we spoke to the committee previously, some of the major debtors transferred substantial assets to family members. As part of our agreement with them, a number of those debtors have brought the assets back to the table. That is one of the first things to be done and it must happen before we will sit down and agree a deal with a debtor. In other cases, however, debtors are refusing to bring the assets back. As it is in the public domain, members will know that we are involved in a number of actions against such debtors in terms of the pursuance of personal guarantees.

Sinn Féin TD Pearse Doherty, one of the new influx of left-wing deputies in the Dáil, described as 'appalling' the level of debt forgiveness for developers and speculators revealed by the NAMA executives, compared to the treatment of debt-ridden homeowners following the recession.

It is appalling that this is happening. It goes beyond the remit of NAMA and runs contrary to the spirit in which the agency was established. How many developers have been offered the 10% model of forgiveness? What is the total value of the debt that has already been or which may be extended by NAMA – that is, the State – to these developers? Do our guests have a view on an arm of the State providing for such debt forgiveness when 95,000 people are in mortgage arrears as a result of buying homes from the developers in question?

Doherty also raised the sensitive question of the appointment, without any tendering procedure, of a number of people to senior positions within the agency and the bonuses in excess of €50,000 paid to some of its employees.

He cited a reference in the agency's annual report to one of its directors, Stephen Seelig, a former board member of the IMF, running up expenses of €35,915 in 2010 for attending meetings and asked whether it was essential that Seelig travelled to Ireland to attend some 35 board, audit committee and risk management meetings when teleconferencing facilities could have been used.

Doherty sought clarification on whether NAMA was willing to allow developers to buy back assets at reduced costs, even if it involved a higher offer than other bidders – despite its stated position that it would not do so. He then brought up the recent decision by the Supreme Court in favour of developer Paddy McKillen, which was a severe embarrassment to the agency.

What was the legal bill picked up by NAMA in the Paddy McKillen case? How much did that case cost NAMA? I want the cost involved including the amounts paid to advisers and experts, the division of employee time, and the amount that NAMA contributed to Paddy McKillen's costs. Who is responsible in the delegates' view for NAMA losing the case? Who was responsible for taking the view that a decision had been made validly at NAMA on the transfer to NAMA of Mr. Paddy McKillen's loans before the agency had even been incorporated? Has anyone at NAMA or any of its advisers faced penalties as a result of the losses incurred in the Mr. Paddy McKillen case which it has been speculated cost between €2 million and €4 million?

A new arrival into politics, former banker Peter Mathews, Fine Gael TD for Dublin South, followed up with some questions surrounding the McKillen case, including the role of former Attorney General Paul Gallagher, who represented

NAMA in the legal action and who was among those who provided legal advice on the establishment of the agency, now the largest property management company in the world.

Members have seen the purpose of this entire project was to enable the banks to be stabilised. The former Attorney General, Mr. Paul Gallagher, stated that this was the overarching objective at the Paddy McKillen case. I know this because I attended the hearings. Moreover, as Mr. Paul Gallagher was an architect of NAMA, there was professional skin in the game in that High Court hearing, which subsequently was heard by the Supreme Court.

I understand the investment by people, professionally and otherwise, in the current policy position. However, we can question it. Even at this stage we can ask whether it would be more efficient and effective for the collection of loans to be carried out by the banks for their own account.

Mathews further raised the situation whereby a small group of individuals, including US financier Wilbur Ross and other US investors, had acquired a 35 per cent stake in Bank of Ireland in 2011 'for a meagre sum of €1 billion', yet the bank was still on life support from the state. The state provided, he said, 'the safety net for the liabilities of the bank', but only held a 15 per cent interest.

Chapter 6 ～

THE EAGLE IS LANDING

The business of NAMA north of the border was becoming an important focus of the agency's activities and involved direct dealings with the power sharing administration at Stormont as well as members of the Belfast business community.

Addressing the Northern Ireland Chamber of Commerce in October 2011, Frank Daly said that the Northern Ireland (NI) loan book accounted for just 5 per cent of the value of NAMA's total loan portfolio and that the nominal value of the loans acquired was approximately £3.35 billion (€4 billion) and was accounted for by 55 debtors in Northern Ireland.

While the scale of distressed borrowings in the North, which included assets held by various developers in the UK and other overseas locations, was small compared to the overall value of assets under its control, its disposal had the potential to embroil the agency in major political controversy.

Daly said that NAMA would seek to stabilise the North's property market, generate transactions, provide liquidity and encourage phased disposals. He said that the agency could take a longer-term approach where necessary and was not interested in disposals at fire sale prices.

Daly told his audience at the luncheon in Hillsborough Castle – attended by NI secretary of state Owen Patterson, Frank Cushnahan and other members of the NIAC, prominent business and political figures and a number of developers already under the agency's remit – that NAMA was committed to listening to stakeholders in Northern Ireland with a view to devising tailored solutions for the local marketplace.

'We want to ensure that our approach is appropriately tuned for the Northern Ireland market. We have developed good relationships with policy makers in Northern Ireland,' Daly told his audience.

Little did he know of the nature of those 'good relationships', although there were certainly more than a few people in the room who had an inkling of what their prospects might be if plans being prepared by Cushnahan and his associates, David Watters and Andrew Creighton, along with a number of senior politicians, were to come to fruition. Watters was a partner in Belfast accountancy firm RSM McClure Watters, which was on the panel of advisors to NAMA on property values, while Creighton was a well-known property developer in the North, and a director of William Ewart Properties Ltd (the loans of which were in NAMA), among other firms.

Since 2010, not long after he was appointed to the NIAC, Cushnahan had embarked on a global roadshow during which he paraded the potential rewards for investors interested in purchasing the NI portfolio of NAMA-controlled assets.

One of those Cushnahan alerted was a long-time contact and businessman, Barry Lloyd, who was based in the Far East and always on the lookout for a potential deal. When Cushnahan informed him that a substantial portion of the NI portfolio was coming on to the market in the near future, Lloyd got his contacts book out.

Lloyd was chief executive of Microchannel Technologies Ltd, which was first registered at an address in Clogher, County Tyrone, in 2000. Starting out as a search engine marketing (SEM) brand, the company evolved to become 'a technology provider of advanced bid management analytics and internet marketing software'. In 2010 he sold the company, but Lloyd continued to provide SEM consultancy services worldwide, including to many wishing to take advantage of the emerging markets of China, South-East Asia and the Middle East, where he claimed to have developed good relations with senior government officials.

Lloyd said that Cushnahan first told him about his engagement with NAMA and its role in acquiring distressed assets from the Irish banks in December 2010. Lloyd claimed that he was advised by Cushnahan in an email of the 'substantial opportunities for major returns to be made for anyone who could access international/institutional funds to acquire blocks of development assets from either developer and/or NAMA'. Cushnahan intimated that Lloyd's connections in China could be vital to securing a slice of the NAMA action in the North. Lloyd later recalled that Cushnahan said, 'my connections to certain senior persons in China could be "key" to potential opportunities emanating from NAMA'. During a trip to Belfast in 2010, Lloyd was introduced to a number of property developers at the offices of Tughans solicitors, where Cushnahan was based.

In April 2011, Cushnahan wrote an email to Lloyd's wife, Hillary, describing the model for the acquisition of the distressed assets whereby investors could 'acquire particular assets at significant discounts so as to allow the banks to shrink their balance sheets as quickly as possible'. In the email, Cushnahan described Andrew Creighton as one of 'the most substantive players' in the business and that he was in a position to put together property deals for potential investors yielding a substantive 'upturn for the related counter-parties who have an acceptable formalised arrangement'.

Lloyd and his business partner, Peter Banks, then sought out potentially suitable investors in the Far East, including at Nomura bank of Japan. He wrote to Cushnahan by email in April 2011 advising that he had also received a positive response from a 'Chinese Business Associate' who indicated that he could bring several wealthy investors to Northern Ireland 'to discuss an initial investment of over $250 million'. In order to advance this possible deal, Lloyd requested that Cushnahan provide him with a draft agreement

> to demonstrate that we were empowered to open discussions on behalf of the various relevant UK and Irish parties (including NAMA) and we would all (the Chinese Business Associate, Dr Cushnahan and I) sign said agreement, which would also include detail of how each of us would be remunerated.

Between April and August 2011, Lloyd discussed with Cushnahan the investor interest he and Banks had secured from business people in China and Thailand and from other contacts in Malaysia, Singapore and Indonesia. However, something had happened that appeared to sour the investor's interest after their initial enthusiasm. Lloyd explained: 'In each of the said discussions, we were met with enthusiasm only to be met a few days later with a complete about turn in attitude from said individuals and with no explanation for their emerging concern.'

In November, just weeks after Frank Daly's address to the NI Chamber of Commerce in Belfast, Lloyd told Cushnahan that the 'Chinese Business Associate' had come back with an expression of interest from some 'high net worth' investors from China. Lloyd sought further legal agreement documents which had been drafted by Tughans solicitors and asked about arrangements for a possible visit by the investors to Northern Ireland. The documents prepared by Tughans included, according to Lloyd, a non-circumvention and introducers agreement and a confidentiality agreement.

Cushnahan replied in an email of 17 November to say that he was delighted to hear of the Chinese interest and that the portfolio of distressed assets in other banks not under the control of NAMA, including Ulster Bank, Northern Bank, Santander and Barclays, could also become available to potential investors.

'Up to that point my recollection is that Dr Cushnahan was proposing that only NAMA assets and portfolios would be the subject of our dealings,' Lloyd later said on affidavit. By this stage, according to Lloyd in an email of 30 November 2011, the potential investment pot on offer from the Chinese funds had grown to £1 billion on condition that any deal would depend on the portfolios put forward and 'if potential investors would be able to obtain permanent resident status or a UK or Irish passport'.

Between November and December, Lloyd and Banks continued their discussions with potential investors through their 'Chinese Business Associate' and another Chinese businessman on the various options put forward by Cushnahan in relation to the NAMA and other asset disposals ostensibly under his control. Lloyd later explained:

We discussed matters such as the interested parties from Northern Ireland (including banks and developers), the potential fee structure, the very serious and sensitive nature of the dealings and the importance of maintaining strict confidentiality around all matters as we would be liable to serious implications if said confidentiality was breached.

Lloyd assured his investor clients that the assets available were offering high yield returns and that they were dealing with 'the most reputable organisations' which had 'solid development and property management credentials'. The majority of the properties, he told his Chinese contacts, were leased by 'leading British companies in both retail and commercial sectors or by government backed bodies' or were 'otherwise in a position to offer solid revenues' over the investment term.

Lloyd and Banks were obviously keen to ensure that they would be recognised as the only route for global investors to this potentially lucrative portfolio spread across Northern Ireland and the UK and insisted that they could only reveal the details of the properties in question after the various confidentiality agreements were signed. Lloyd recalled

I advised all three [Banks, the Chinese Business Associate and the Chinese businessman] that no developer knew about the other developers we were talking to and that no bank knew about any other bank with whom we were discussing matters.

Lloyd asked Cushnahan to set up meetings with the relevant NAMA personnel and politicians and the banks in order to obtain written authority to engage in negotiations and to reassure his Chinese and other potential investors that he had the endorsement of the agency and others.

Cushnahan replied with an email stating that 'we don't want to get politicians involved because they are too greedy', and that he, Cushnahan, was the key person.

Following a meeting on 22 December 2011 with Cushnahan and certain developers and lawyers from Tughans, Lloyd advised the Chinese businessman that Cushnahan had selected six proposals as examples of the potential portfolios and distressed assets, including NAMA-controlled properties, which were available to potential investors. Among them were 'developments in central London, England, Scotland, Wales, Northern Ireland and Dublin'.

Lloyd also obtained a letter signed by John George Willis of Tughans solicitors which confirmed that Lloyd and Cushnahan were seeking to introduce Chinese investors to properties in the UK and Ireland. Willis suggested in the letter that Tughans could engage with law firms retained by any Chinese investors and said that potential investors should enter into a detailed and specific confidentiality agreement in relation to the property assets and any discussion relating to them. By the end of January 2012, Lloyd told Cushnahan that he was ready to visit China and get confirmation of the availability of funds from the Chinese investors and their willingness to sign up to the confidentiality arrangements.

On 20 February 2012, Lloyd wrote to Willis to inform him that Nomura, the bank acting for one of the investors, had requested more detailed information about the property portfolios. He said he had advised Nomura that they must sign the confidentiality agreement and the introducers agreement before any introductions to the properties could take place. He sent an edited confidentiality agreement received from Nomura to Willis for his review and approval.

In March 2012, he discussed possible arrangements for permanent residency status in the UK for potential Chinese investors with his Chinese middlemen and Banks. He described how UK resident status had been obtained by people in return for a minimum investment of $3 million. He said that they could secure a minimum return of 10 per cent per annum on any investment, not including the revenue from the sale of any of the properties in question.

Lloyd also referred in his discussions to a requirement which Cushnahan had mentioned regarding payments to certain Northern Ireland political parties arising from their investment and applications for UK resident status. Lloyd said that the name of Gareth Robinson, son of the first minister, Peter Robinson, was mentioned 'in that regard'.

On 13 March, he sent a final confidentiality agreement from Nomura to Ian Coulter of Tughans to review and approve so that he could send it on to the Japanese bank for signing. Along with the non-disclosure documents, he also sent two sample portfolios to Richard Moore of Nomura to indicate the quality and type of the portfolios available. The portfolios were a property bundle known as Project Swan and another called William Ewart Group which Cushnahan had described as a very safe investment opportunity.

On 14 March 2012, confidentiality and introducer agreements between the special purpose vehicle (SPV) set up for the investment, Lloyd's Microchannel

Far East Company Ltd, and Nomura International PLC were signed. On 24 April, Cushnahan sought an update from Lloyd asking about progress with the Chinese investors and reminded him that he had spent a considerable amount of time on the various developer proposals and meetings with government sources in relation to the requests for UK residency. 'He asked me to send him an email (addressed only to Cushnahan) as to what was happening in order to avoid losing credibility with some very "heavy hitters" who may be of particular interest to us in the period ahead,' Lloyd wrote in a subsequent affidavit detailing his correspondence with Cushnahan.

On the same day, Banks received an email from Moore of Nomura stating that pursuing the property portfolios was 'not something Nomura as a bank would look at'.

Two days later Lloyd told Cushnahan that progress with the Chinese investors had slowed, possibly due to 'recent negative publicity about alleged movement of funds for property investments from China to Hong Kong'. He also complained that he had not yet received from Cushnahan any 'formal written authority from NAMA' in relation to the portfolios and distressed assets and that this was a contributory factor to the delay in advancing a deal.

Lloyd and Banks and their business associates believed that the end of the road for this particular venture had arrived, given that both the Chinese investors and Nomura had pulled back from the negotiations. They moved on with their lives and chased other business opportunities.

Chapter 7 ~

CORPORATE INSIDERS

B y the end of 2011, Daly, McDonagh and other NAMA executives had too much on their plates to follow every single phone call or email involved in the multitude of transactions under their supervision. They had completed the acquisition of bad loans from the banks and had paid €31.8 billion for the acquired loans of €74.2 billion with an overall discount of about 58 per cent on the property portfolios. They had also, with the encouragement of Noonan and the Department of Finance, sold off some of the cream of the assets and raised €4.6 billon. Eighty per cent of these were abroad, in healthy real estate locations including London, Miami, Florida and New York. There was concern that NAMA was selling its best assets too quickly and would end up with a portfolio of bad loans that would be difficult to offload, particularly given the difficult circumstances and slow recovery of the Irish property market. Asked about this by members of the Dáil Public Accounts Committee (PAC) in October 2011, McDonagh said that the NAMA board

> has always held the view that we should have an orderly and phased disposal of assets. The game changed with regard to the board having a free discretion in terms of the timing of the disposal of assets when the obligation arose under the Troika programme with regard to generating cash. ... we are constantly trading off, in terms of whether it is the right time to sell the asset and whether the asset price is as good as it is going to be.

McDonagh confirmed that NAMA controlled approximately $600 million worth of assets in the US, the majority (by value) in New York. The main assets in continental Europe, he said, were in Germany, France and Portugal, with smaller pockets of assets, ranging from €10 million to €20 million, in Malta, the Czech Republic and Poland. 'Collectively, these add up to €120 million so it is not a huge amount,' he said.

He confirmed that just two developers who were assisting with the disposal of multi-billion euro portfolios were being paid €200,000 per annum for their work.

McDonagh also told the PAC that of the 188 debtors which were under the direct management of the agency some 143 business plans had been assessed and the rest were near completion while good progress was also being 'made on business plans by debtors whose loans are being managed by the participating institutions on our behalf.'

He also told the PAC that while NAMA was chasing debtors for the full repayment of their distressed loans it was not a likely outcome for many, given the poor state of the property market. While debtors remained legally obliged to repay all of their debt, some of the properties securing loans had fallen in value by about 60 per cent from the peak of the market, he said.

Frankly, in the case of some debtors, this is all we can ever hope to recover and, in some of these cases, we have initiated, or expect to initiate, enforcement. Members can rest assured that we will pursue every penny where it makes economic sense to do so.

McDonagh also revealed the differing approaches by NAMA to individual debtors. Many debtors were bust, 'did not hoard a huge amount of money for the rainy day' and wanted to cooperate with the agency. He said, 'There are two types of people who do not want to co-operate with us.'

One is the type who probably should never have been in the property business. They got into it because they thought they would make money but they were never property people. The second type are people who potentially might have assets and do not want to bring them back and therefore we have to initiate enforcement action against them. There is no pot of gold out there ... but I would say, across the portfolio, the maximum amount all the debtors combined would have would be somewhere between €400 million and €500 million.

Questioned by Sinn Féin deputy Mary Lou McDonald about the salaries paid to NAMA employees, McDonagh revealed that he was paid €430,000 per annum but had declined a bonus for the year, which he said equated to 30 per cent of his annual salary.

Frank Daly explained that the salaries for NAMA personnel were the responsibility of the NTMA, which paid them. He confirmed that 'across the NTMA family, there are 17 people earning in excess of €200,000, 14 of whom earn in excess of €250,000'.

Contrasting the rates of pay with the austerity measures being imposed by government on large sections of the population, McDonald asked whether the agency was giving value for money. 'I do not believe NAMA is a good creation,' McDonald said.

Daly pointed out that NAMA had to put 'a first team' on the pitch 'against everybody else who is engaging with us, whether they be investors, debtors, bankers or whatever. That is why those salaries are needed.' The total cost of the 200 staff now employed by NAMA was about €20 million per annum, all on individually negotiated contracts, he said.

McDonagh confirmed that a sum of €7.5 million had been spent on legal fees up to September 2011, anticipating a cost of €10 million by the end of December. He said that it would cost the agency some €50 million in the required due diligence on the loans acquired from the banks for about 25,000 properties now under its control. There was no question that a relatively small number of legal, accountancy, real estate and valuation providers were to make serious money from their work for NAMA. There was a new generation of millionaires in the making from the NAMA project, including a few of its own staff.

Notwithstanding the scepticism of some Oireachtas members, mainly of the political left, and a small number of media commentators, the work of NAMA in managing and selling off the billions worth of assets under its control continued without much criticism and the voices of those economists who questioned the bad bank model were muted. It was evident that by the end of 2011, NAMA was allowed to get on with its challenging work without much interference or negative comment, except from some of those who were forced to engage with the agency: the builders, developers, speculators and property owners who had extended themselves during the bubble.

The resignation of Michael Connolly from the board of NAMA in late November 2011 would have hardly been noticed were it not for the brief and understated comment by the finance minister praising his 'important contribution to the work of the agency, especially in his role as chairperson of the credit committee.'

The reasons for the resignation were not explained, nor were they sought, although rumours abounded within NAMA. The agency continued with its work, the scale of which ensured that while there would be bumps along the road, the rapid disposal of its assets would see it past the finish line before any real scrutiny of its work commenced. At least, that was the fervent hope of those at the top of the organisation, who no doubt were aware that, under the surface, confrontation and crisis were emerging on a number of fronts.

Only the anonymous website NWL and the usual suspects on the opposition benches of the Oireachtas took any great interest in the workings of the agency, and it was, by and large, left to its own devices. The fact that it was not at that point covered under FOI legislation also deterred any academic or journalistic investigation into the inner workings of what had now grown into an immense and powerful institution which influenced the lives of many tens of thousands of Irish people, for better or worse.

Unaware of the activities of Frank Cushnahan and his Asian contacts, Frank Daly met with the Northern Ireland finance minister Sammy Wilson in December 2011 to update him and the media on the agency's plans for its distressed Northern Ireland assets. He explained that the loans held by NAMA covered £2 billion of undeveloped land, a further £1 billion of investment property, and £350 million of property and land undergoing development. The loans were linked to properties across the North, with 32 per cent linked to property in Belfast, 19 per cent in County Antrim (excluding Belfast), and the remainder in counties Derry, Tyrone and Armagh.

Notwithstanding the optimistic and positive assessments they were providing to the various Oireachtas committees they attended, Daly and McDonagh were coming under increasing pressure to reveal more than they would have wished about the internal workings of NAMA and were also dealing with increasingly negative media comment over some of its commercial decisions.

In early March 2012, finance minister Michael Noonan announced that Daly would become a member of the new group to advise him on the progress of the agency, governance and other matters relating to it. During a speech in December 2012, the minister had flagged that Michael Geoghegan, who had published what Noonan described as the 'generally positive' review of the agency, would be appointed as chairman of the three-man advisory group. He said the chairman would bring to the task almost 40 years of experience with global banker HSBC (the Hong Kong and Shanghai Banking Corporation), where he had served as chief executive from 2006 until he stepped down in December 2010.

Geoghegan left the bank just over a year later when it was the subject of an inquiry into claims that it had been involved in money laundering on a global scale. A US Senate investigations subcommittee had discovered that the bank had allowed Mexican drug proceeds, Iranian funds and suspicious Russian money to enter the US and gain access to US dollar liquidity over several years. In its year-long inquiry during 2011, the subcommittee found that HSBC violated several rules and exposed the US financial system to a 'wide array of money laundering, drug trafficking and terrorist financing'. According to the report, HSBC's Mexican affiliate channelled $7 billion into the US between 2007 and 2008, which possibly included 'proceeds from illegal drug sales in the United States'. HSBC was forced to pay a $1.9 billion fine to the US Department of Justice in 2012 following publication of the report. There was no suggestion that Geoghegan was involved in any way with the illegal operations investigated by the Senate committee and he continued in his role with NAMA after the scandal was exposed in the US.

The appointment of Denis Rooney, a quantity surveyor and former head of the International Fund for Ireland, as a member of the new group to advise the minister was also announced and reflected the importance of its asset management task in Northern Ireland, even though it formed less than 5 per cent of the total NAMA portfolio. It also reflected the unease that had been expressed by the members of the Northern Ireland executive, including Sammy Wilson and Peter Robinson, about the potentially negative influence of NAMA over the North's struggling property sector.

Rooney had previously served as chairman of two prestigious bodies in the North – the Institute of Directors and the Royal Institution of Chartered Surveyors. He established the surveying and project management practice DRA in 1984, which he sold in 2003, and also worked as chief executive of a planning and engineering consultancy, White Young Green Ireland.

Noonan said that the advisory group would provide him with advice on strategy for the agency, the appointment of directors and senior executive pay, and noted that all three members had agreed to work for free. What was not clear was how Frank Daly, as chairman of NAMA, could also be part of an independent advisory group overseeing the agency. He was on an annual salary of some €150,000 at this point.

Once again, Pearse Doherty posed an awkward question to Daly at a hearing of the Finance Committee in March 2012 into the role and functions of NAMA. Referring to the recent appointments to the advisory group, he said: 'I was surprised by the appointments that were made. I do not understand the role of the advisory board. Perhaps the chairperson can explain it? I understood its role was to give the Minister independent advice on the operation and functioning of NAMA and to help direct NAMA.'

Daly replied that

the role of the advisory group is confined to advising the Minister on NAMA strategy, as proposed by the board ... advising the Minister on appointments to the board ... advising the Minister on the remuneration of senior executives ... and advising the Minister on any other matters as he considers appropriate.

So there was no conflict and none arose at the first meetings of the advisory group, Daly said. On the same day as he named the members of the advisory group, Noonan announced the appointment of the head of asset management, John Mulcahy, as an executive director of NAMA, in line with a recommendation of the Geoghegan review. The review had argued for the inclusion of more executive directors on the board, which was somewhat depleted, given that Michael Connolly and Peter Stewart had both resigned during 2011.

'I believe that Mr Mulcahy has significant property management skills which will make him an asset to the board of NAMA as it concentrates fully on the active management of its asset portfolio,' Noonan said. Daly also welcomed the appointment, saying that 'together with the wider team at NAMA, John has made a very significant contribution to our work since the agency was created and I am very confident that he'll make a very valuable contribution at board level.'

Mulcahy's elevation reflected the significance of his role as head of asset management, in which capacity he had worked extensively with developers, receivers and joint venture partners who were able to identify the most suitable properties and developments that could be managed by NAMA to boost their value and the agency's cash flow. The new appointments were not universally welcomed as they appeared to confirm a view that NAMA was a tightly controlled and centralised body stacked with corporate insiders. Mulcahy's promotion to the board came as it emerged that the real estate firm he previously chaired, Jones Lang LaSalle, was paid more than any other firm for valuation work by NAMA, earning fees of €1.24 million over the previous two years.

Allegations of a conflict of interest in relation to Mulcahy were aired in the Dáil by Sinn Féin leader Gerry Adams, who had obtained the figures from the Department of Finance. 'The fact that a firm with close links to NAMA management is the top recipient of these fees highlights again the need for closer scrutiny of the work of NAMA,' Adams said. 'I am concerned that NAMA is not properly managing conflicts of interest.' He said Fine Gael had promised before the previous election to expose NAMA to greater public scrutiny but progress on this had been 'negligible'.

NAMA replied by insisting that it had clear procedures for managing potential conflicts of interest involving staff members. The agency also pointed out that the property valuation work was awarded following a competitive tender process. However, both within and outside NAMA there were serious questions about the manner in which Mulcahy, in particular, was deciding on property valuations, with the banks complaining that his imposition of 2009 values was unrealistic and inaccurate given that prices had continued on a downward curve over the following years.

The matter was also raised by Pearse Doherty at a meeting of the Finance Committee in early 2012:

Advice was given to the late Minister for Finance in 2009 that the property sector had reached rock bottom. I believe this advice was given by someone who is now involved with NAMA but who at the time was involved with Jones Lang LaSalle. However, the value of commercial property has fallen by 20% since that advice was given.

Once again Mulcahy, though unnamed, was brought into the frame as the key decision maker in relation to NAMA valuation policy.

Replying to Adams in the Dáil, Noonan said that of the €13.3 million spent by the agency on property valuations, €12.4 million related to once-off property valuations carried out as part of due diligence on acquired loans. The rest related to valuation required as part of the agency's ongoing management of the portfolio it had acquired, he said. He also said that valuation fees incurred by the agency are recovered from financial institutions through a reduction in the acquisition price of property.

The other valuation firms on the list of earners from NAMA over the previous two years included Donal O'Buachalla & Co., which earned €1.2 million since 2010, followed by Colliers International (€978,000), Lisney (€861,000) and Knight Frank (€756,000). Other well-known firms on the top 10 list were WK Nowlan, Cushman & Wakefield, Lambert Smith Hampton, HWBC and Savills Commercial.

The appointment of WK Nowlan Associates was also interesting in that one of its former executives was by then a senior executive with NAMA. The firm had been associated with valuation work for NAMA from the outset in 2009, so it came as no surprise that it was chosen for the valuation panel three years later. Bill Nowlan, the company founder, was well known in Dublin's property game, having worked from the early 1980s with Irish Life. He had been associated with John Mulcahy for a long time, since Jones Lang LaSalle had provided real estate services to Irish Life over many years. His son Kevin Nowlan joined NAMA in 2010 as a property advisor and ended up as senior portfolio manager for the agency before his departure in early 2013.

A former Irish international rugby player and chartered surveyor, Kevin Nowlan had worked with Anglo Irish Bank before he joined Treasury Holdings and then became managing director of the family firm. With NAMA, he acted as portfolio manager for, among others, the transferred loans of Sean Dunne, who was less than cooperative with NAMA after he moved to the USA.

Before he joined NAMA, Kevin Nowlan placed his 30 per cent shareholding in WK Nowlan into a trust. When he left NAMA he set up Hibernia Real Estate Investment Trust (Hibernia REIT) with US-based Irish businessman Frank Kenny, which focused on the purchase of Irish property and loans. Hibernia REIT was registered in October 2013 and was among the first such trusts established in the country.

His father, Bill Nowlan, had advised NAMA and lobbied the Department of Finance to introduce the necessary legislation to allow for the operation of REITs in the Irish market. The trusts operated on the basis that investors could avail of tax reliefs which encouraged them to invest savings through professional property firms with a promise of a guaranteed income, in contrast to speculative property investments that were not as safe a bet.

Hibernia was among the first REITs to be formed in Ireland, copying a model developed in the US after the sub-prime scandal which contributed to the property collapse in 2008. 'Go REIT or Go Broke' was the slogan used in the US to entice small and large investors to take shares through the new real estate trust schemes.

Nowlan was joined at Hibernia REIT by Mark Pollard, another former NAMA employee, who was involved in managing the property portfolio of Sean Mulryan's Ballymore Group while he was with the agency.

Among those who recognised and wrote internal NAMA reports on the potential of the REIT model was Enda Farrell. Farrell gave advice to Department of Finance officials on the value of REITs to the distressed property market. Farrell claims that before he left NAMA, he received a phone call from Frank Kenny, who was interested in his plans for the future. During the phone call they discussed the proposal for the establishment of a REIT in Ireland. Kenny said that he had obtained Farrell's phone number from his NAMA colleague Kevin Nowlan.

The other real estate firms selected for the NAMA panel for valuations were equally well-known players in the Dublin property market, including Knight Frank and Cushman & Wakefield, and they would benefit hugely from their association with the agency over the coming months and years.

NAMA was now defending the manner in which it chose professional advisors, including valuers, lawyers and accountants, and was openly accused of ignoring potential conflicts of interest involving its staff. The agency employed Gordon & Associates as an external public relations consultant. The company was headed by Ray Gordon, a former advisor to the Progressive Democrats when they were politically influential in a number of coalition governments, and was now earning his money handling media and other queries about NAMA, among other corporate clients. Internally, Martin Whelan dealt with the task of communicating the complex activities and decisions of NAMA to a public audience that was beginning to question the agency's role and its relationship with the people who were blamed for causing the financial and property collapse that had ruined the lives of so many citizens. As NAMA came under the increasing gaze of various Dáil committees and a more sceptical media it responded aggressively to criticism.

At a meeting with the Finance, Public Expenditure and Reform Committee on 13 March 2012, Daly was robust in his response to some media reports which he described as inaccurate and influenced by developers who had a grudge against the agency over its handling of their loans, saying: 'I am sometimes surprised at the readiness of a small number of commentators to accept often deliberately misleading stories about NAMA without showing the scepticism that might be due given the obvious interests of many of those promoting these stories.'

Responding to a query from Fianna Fáil finance spokesperson Michael McGrath, Daly told the committee that NAMA expected to recover the almost €32 billion it had paid the banks for the distressed loans, although it would be 'a huge challenge', but added that prospects of recouping their €74 billion face value was 'pretty weak'.

McDonagh told committee members that a further €4 billion in asset sales would have to be approved over the next two years, bringing total sales to €9 billion, if the agency was to repay the troika's target of €7.5 billion – a quarter of its debts – by the end of 2013.

This statement ought to have prompted the question of whether the EU/ECB/IMF troika had insisted on NAMA achieving certain targets as part of its requirements in return for the Irish bailout, but it was not asked or answered on this occasion.

McDonagh said that the agency had agreed business plans with 530 debtors, taken enforcement action against over 180 more and had yet to assess the business plans for another 60. Two-thirds of the 790 debtors in NAMA were working 'constructively' with the agency, he said.

Daly said that NAMA had decided not to bring 600 smaller debtors into the agency under its direct management, as recommended in the Geoghegan review, but instead had sent five of its staff on rotation to work in each of three banks from which it had acquired loans – IBRC (formerly Anglo Irish Bank and Irish Nationwide Building Society), AIB and Bank of Ireland.

On the same day that his party leader was raising the conflict of interest allegations in NAMA in the Dáil chamber, Pearse Doherty told the hearing that he had introduced legislation to bring NAMA under the Freedom of Information Act 1997 in order to improve transparency at the agency.

Chapter 8 ～

WINNER, LOSER, SURVIVOR

Mick Wallace was elected to the Dáil for the Wexford constituency in February 2001, but his path into politics was not a conventional one. He announced his intention to stand for election on TV3's *Vincent Browne Show* and left himself just 16 days to canvass. He managed to top the poll, thanks largely to his involvement in football in Wexford, having managed the county's under-18 soccer team for over 20 years and the under-16 side for 16 years. In 2006, he established a new club, Wexford Youths FC, which entered the League of Ireland in 2007.

Never far from controversy, he became the subject of much criticism in December 2011 when he was reported in the media as having failed to pay all the pension contributions of the workers in his construction company M&J Wallace Ltd. He insisted that all the pension contributions were eventually paid in full, but he was fined over €7,000 for late payment. He ran into another political and media storm in 2012 when it transpired that three years earlier the company had underdeclared its VAT liability by €1.4 million. Wallace accepted that his company had withheld VAT but said that he did so in order to save it from collapse as, like many others in the business, it was struggling to pay wages and debts. He said that he hoped to make all outstanding VAT payments when trading improved. He agreed a repayment arrangement with the Revenue Commissioners, but within a year ACC Bank called in his loans, obtained a court order and placed M&J Wallace into receivership.

Already under media attack for his unrepentant left-wing views and actions, Wallace rejected calls for him to leave politics and insisted on continuing to raise issues he believed to be of national importance, including Garda mis-behaviour, the use of Shannon airport by the US military, mental health, the treatment of prisoners and the impact of government austerity policies on low-income families.

With his background in construction, he was better equipped than most TDs to recognise the impact of NAMA on the industry, the provision of housing and the wider economy. He was among the first politicians to raise the issue of salaries paid by the agency to its staff and to a small number of developers who were earning as much as €200,000 a year from NAMA to manage and dispose of their assets.

What concerned Wallace and others was the apparent selective treatment of some NAMA clients while others, in his view, were thrown to the wolves.

He told the Dáil that he did not support 'people bashing the pay of public servants on low and middle incomes', but neither did he support the high salaries being earned by some NAMA employees or the payments to a small number of developers (including Bernard McNamara).

> I know some people who worked in banking and real estate and when they moved to NAMA they got an increase in salary. That is not very impressive. There has not been much accountability or transparency in how NAMA has done its business in that regard. I do not know how much control the Minister has over it but it leaves much to be desired. In the current climate and given all the cuts endured by people who are hurt most by the austerity to give this individual more than €200,000 is not good enough.

In June 2012, NAMA announced that, following consultations with finance minister Michael Noonan and his counterpart in the North's executive, Sammy Wilson, it was to reappoint Frank Cushnahan and Brian Rowntree to the NIAC for another two-year term. Commenting on the reappointments, Noonan said:

> I would like to thank Frank Cushnahan and Brian Rowntree for agreeing to continue serving on NAMA's Northern Ireland Advisory Committee. I see this Committee as having a very important role in assisting NAMA to meet its objectives on both sides of the border. It is very important that NAMA, like other agencies, acts on an all-island basis.

Indeed, Cushnahan and Rowntree were seen by the NAMA executive as crucial to its work of disposing of the property portfolio it controlled in the North. As Daly said earlier in the year to the Joint Committee on the Implementation of the Good Friday Agreement, which included politicians from both parts of the island, its strategy in Northern Ireland was 'informed by the expertise of local professional advisors', and in particular the NIAC.

> The committee's contribution to our understanding of the issues and the market is very important and I refer in particular to the contribution of two external members of that committee from Northern Ireland, Frank

Cushnahan and Brian Rowntree, two highly respected business leaders in Northern Ireland and they are very generous with their time and with their advice to us.

Daly was accompanied to the committee hearing by Ronnie Hanna, the now head of asset recovery at NAMA and a former senior executive of Ulster Bank, based in Belfast. Hanna would, no doubt, have agreed with his chairman in the praise lavished on Cushnahan in particular, as they were well known to each other as members of the relatively small elite of the city's business and banking community. Also present on behalf of NAMA at the hearing was Jonathan Milligan, who worked with the NIAC.

Whether or not any of those who so readily endorsed Cushnahan were aware of the activities of the NIAC member which were taking place under the radar of public attention, the reality was that he was already engaged in a series of arrangements, consultancies and contacts directly relating to his work for NAMA, some of it flowing directly from his correspondence and dealings with Barry Lloyd in the Far East and others closer to home. Cushnahan had made a declaration of his interests to the NIAC, informing it that he provided financial consultancy services to a number of clients whose loans were in NAMA. In 2011 and 2012, he disclosed that he provided services to five debtors, which rose to seven by 2013. The debtors involved accounted for some 50 per cent of the entire Northern Ireland portfolio in value terms. He said that he was not paid by all of these clients but he was certainly rewarded handsomely by at least one of them.

These NAMA debtors were deeply concerned as to how they could save their businesses and property portfolios, which were now under the control of an agency acting on behalf of the government of the Republic, a different jurisdiction.

A number of developers lobbied senior politicians in the NI executive, including Peter Robinson and Sammy Wilson. The politicians had already managed to ensure that Cushnahan was appointed to the NIAC, along with Brian Rowntree, who was also chairman of the Northern Ireland Housing Executive (NIHE).

Wearing his two hats – as a consultant to seven NAMA debtors and as a member of the NIAC – as well as his long relationship with Peter Robinson and his son, public relations practitioner Gareth, Cushnahan was in a position of influence and he was not afraid to use it.

Among his debtor clients was a County Down property developer, John Miskelly, who was concerned that he would suffer huge financial loss if NAMA were to sell off his commercial properties in Belfast and other parts of the UK. Miskelly was further distressed because of a serious illness which required regular treatment in a Belfast hospital.

He was also wary of Cushnahan and some of his political and other associates and took the precaution of carrying a hidden tape recorder to meetings with the property consultant, including a number which took place in the car park of the Belfast City Hospital and in the Royal Victoria Hospital.

During one discussion in August 2012, Cushnahan told Miskelly that he was going to help him with a refinancing deal which would get his assets out of the clutches of NAMA. Cushnahan was concerned that nobody else was aware of the cash payment of £40,000 'in bundles of two' which he was to receive from the developer.

'Nobody else knows now?' Cushnahan is heard saying on tape as the pair sat in the front seats of his car. 'Nobody?' he repeats as the cash is handed over. Miskelly confirms that their arrangement is not known to anyone else. Promising that he can help Miskelly to escape the clutches of NAMA, Cushnahan name-checks Ronnie Hanna: 'Don't worry, I'll work with Ronnie. See, the great thing is we have Ronnie.'

During the conversation, Cushnahan also names Gareth Robinson as someone who was of assistance in relation to his work for NAMA debtors. He had mentioned the help he was receiving from the son of the first minister in correspondence with Barry Lloyd in Bangkok earlier that year. In February 2012, Cushnahan said that Gareth Robinson had assisted with 'progressing the possibility of entrance visas' for Chinese or other Asian clients prepared to purchase the Northern Ireland loan book from NAMA.

Cushnahan wrote to Lloyd: 'I have approached Gareth Robinson, the son of the First Minister, to research and compile the application(s) … Could you let me have an update on what, if any, progress you have made?'

All of this was taking place during the period when the NAMA chairman and chief executive, and the finance minister Michael Noonan, were praising Cushnahan for his important work for the agency. If any of them, or their myriad advisors, had taken a look at Cushnahan's various business activities and other public roles over the previous two decades in Belfast, they may not have so readily accepted his nomination by Robinson and Wilson as a member of the NIAC in 2010.

Among those he was also advising was Belfast businessman Paddy Kearney, the largest property developer in the North before his loans were transferred to NAMA, and a member of the Maple 10.

During 2012, Cushnahan and some of his business associates were preparing plans to sell off the entire NI loan book to a single buyer and were meeting with US law firm Brown Rudnick and Belfast solicitors Tughans with a view to putting together proposals that could attract a major investment fund, or funds, to purchase the NAMA-controlled portfolio of properties in the North. Apparently none of this was known to the senior executives of NAMA, Daly and McDonagh.

Chapter 9 ~

THE TITANIC QUARTER

When it came to doing business during the 30 years of political and military conflict in Northern Ireland, bookmakers were largely a safe bet. Many betting shops were damaged during the ruthless IRA bombing campaign against commercial targets in cities and towns across the North during the 1970s and '80s, while some witnessed atrocious sectarian attacks by the UDA, UVF and other loyalist groups. However, even in the toughest of the working-class neighbourhoods that bore the brunt of the conflict, bookmakers and publicans continued to prosper as punters took refuge in gambling and drink.

SP Graham enjoyed a good reputation in both communities and managed to maintain a thriving business that expanded over the darkest of times when many other commercial enterprises went to the wall, victims of various recessions as well as the reluctance of people to venture too far from their homes in a heavily militarised and threatening environment.

Graham's bookmakers hit the headlines in February 1992 when UDA gunmen shot dead five innocent customers and wounded seven others at their shop in the nationalist Lower Ormeau Road in Belfast, a particularly gruesome mass killing.

After its founder, Sean Graham, died in 1986, his wife Brenda took over the running of the chain while raising a young family. Almost 20 years later, the business had expanded into property development and management in Belfast alongside the core betting operation, and employed over 170 people.

By 2005, as other bookie chains, including Eastwoods and William Hill, became targets for buyouts by the larger corporates such as Ladbrokes and Paddy Power, the Graham family sought advice as to how to maximise the family enterprise. The ageing Mrs Graham was advised by her long-serving accountant, Brian Tanney, to get in touch with a well-connected professional advisor who could steer the company's fortunes at a time of intense rationalisation and competition in the betting market. His name was Frank Cushnahan, and he had been known to her late husband.

Cushnahan was appointed as company chairman and director with the task of recommending to Brenda Graham the best way forward for the betting chain, and was soon installed in an office in the company headquarters in King Street in Belfast. The arrangement was that Cushnahan would work for two or three days a week for a salary of over £60,000 per annum as well as a 5 per cent share of the total income from the various family enterprises. These included Lehill Properties and its subsidiaries AD Enterprises, Fernhill Properties and STH 500 Ltd.

Eighteen months into his chairmanship, Cushnahan approached the elderly Mrs Graham with a business plan which involved the disposal of some of the more lucrative parts of the betting operation. During the period, one of Ireland's leading bookmaking firms had been sold for an extraordinary £135 million and another smaller operation for £25 million. Wherever you looked, the gaming business, with its growing focus on the multi-billon online betting market, was a gilt-edged investment and the Grahams were sitting on a potential goldmine.

At least that is what the man known by some as 'Superman Frank' and the canny auditor, Brian Tanney, tried to convince the family matriarch. Without the knowledge of his employers, Cushnahan engaged in behind-the-scenes discussions with betting giant Paddy Power and other potential investors. By 2008, it became apparent that Cushnahan was actively engaged in selling the business instead of developing it as he was contracted to do. An increasingly anxious Mrs Graham complained to her son Gareth that she was being pressurised into disposing of key parts of the betting empire by Cushnahan and Tanney. She was being harassed and bullied by the pair who were 'aggressive to her', the octogenarian claimed. She felt she couldn't talk to them and they had ignored her appeals not to pursue their strategy of seeking offers for valuable slices of the betting operation. When Gareth Graham told Cushnahan that his mother was not interested in selling the company piecemeal and to let any offers he had solicited from potential bidders expire, the chairman reacted badly. He responded that it was a huge mistake to reject his proposals and that he would not be hanging around to help the company if other shareholders did not accept his advice.

Graham was aware that Cushnahan, with his 5 per cent shareholding, had a vested interest in disposing of the most valuable assets in the chain, and was not displeased when the chairman left the company in October 2008. For months, their relationship had been deteriorating and little had been achieved in their planned exercise to improve the management and the fortunes of the Graham enterprise. With Cushnahan out of the way, the Grahams concentrated on running the betting and other side of their operations as the greatest banking and property crisis since the Wall Street crash came to town.

Gareth Graham would be the first to admit to a certain innocence when it comes to politics and its interaction with the banking and business world. The family was from a Catholic and nationalist background and had been brought up in the middle-class suburbs of Belfast, shielded from the people and places most affected by the political conflict. Of course, the presence of armed British soldiers and police at every street corner, the armoured cars and checkpoints, the daily disruption of normal civil and commercial life could not be ignored, but the family managed to come through the decades of the Troubles largely unscathed. Politically, they managed to maintain a neutral stance and were not identified with any camp in a bitterly divided city, a position that was essential if they were to successfully operate across the communities.

Frank Cushnahan was also from a Catholic background but over the years he had become more closely identified with the Protestant- and unionist-dominated business elite in the city. By the time he arrived at Graham's, he had served on several company boards and was a 'go-to guy' for prominent unionist politicians. Following secondary education at the Catholic-run St Malachy's College in north Belfast he went into banking and worked his way up to serve in senior positions in Ireland and the UK, including as managing director of Chase Bank Ireland (previously owned by Bank of Ireland) and Western Savings Ltd.

By the late 1990s Cushnahan had set up his own financial consultancy specialising in corporate finance and management buyouts and acquisitions, and had served on several corporate boards including the publicly listed Lamont Holdings, Delta Print and Packaging and off-licence group Wineflair.

In the late 1980s Cushnahan also served on the board of the Belfast Harbour Commissioners (BHC), and it was this role which first brought him into public focus, and controversy, as the independent statutory corporation grappled with the challenge of rejuvenating the docks area in the east of the city.

Comprising almost 20 per cent of the Belfast city area, the 2,000-acre Harbour Estate is home to the traditional shipbuilding enterprise Harland & Wolff, whose two massive cranes shadow the skyline, and which provided employment for thousands of almost exclusively Protestant workers since first established in 1861.

In 2000, when Cushnahan was chair of the Harbour Commissioners, he led negotiations with Harland & Wolff for a lease and development deal for a planned Titanic Quarter (named after the Belfast-built ship which sank in the Atlantic Ocean during its maiden voyage in 1912), on 105 acres of land within the Harbour Estate. The following year the deal became the subject of an inquiry by the Regional Development committee of the Northern Ireland parliament. The political controversy centred on the failure of the BHC to advise the committee and the Minister for Regional Development, Gregory Campbell, of the details of a leasing agreement made in December 2000 between the BHC and Harland & Wolff which effectively opened up the harbour lands for massively lucrative commercial and residential development.

The deal was soon followed by the purchase of two Harland & Wolff subsidiaries – Harland & Wolff Properties and Titanic Quarter – by Swedish giant Fred Olsen Energy, in February 2001, which to say the least came as something of a surprise to some senior department officials.

In his evidence to the committee's inquiry in May 2001, Cushnahan conceded that while he understood the 'consternation' surrounding the deal and his failure to advise Gregory Campbell about it in advance, he insisted that he and BHC chief executive Gordon Irwin had acted with 'full integrity, full accountability, openness and impartiality' and were guided by the best interests of 'our users and all of the stakeholders in Northern Ireland'.

He said that he wished 'to dispel any misconceptions that material benefit or personal gain have arisen for individuals on the board or in the management team from any transaction initiated by the BHC. That suggestion is misleading and disingenuous to the integrity of all those concerned.'

When they did inform the minister, after the deal was signed on 20 December 2000, Campbell complained that he should have been given the courtesy of advance notice concerning the disposal of valuable public lands.

Cushnahan explained:

I can understand the consternation. In all sincerity, we had been advancing this transaction for two years and we published what we were going to do for public representatives. All that was going to happen on 20th December was the signing. We did not know that it was to be signed on that day. ...

Mr Irwin and I met the Minister who said that we should have done him the courtesy (of advising him in advance of the deal). The point I made to Minister Campbell was that, in all sincerity, we believed we were applying the best interests of the port to get the deal done and we had the approval, wrongly you might say, in the public interest to get it completed. Therefore, I told the Minister that I did not believe that I should have to come back to tell him that I had signed it. The Minister acknowledged that he knew what we were doing.

The Regional Committee was not impressed by Cushnahan's argument and in its findings concluded that the BHC 'should have been proactive in seeking to publicise the deal in the interests of public openness and accountability, as well as the significant potential benefits that the deal would bring to the Northern Ireland economy'. Notwithstanding the admonishment in the final committee report into the controversial lease agreement, Cushnahan was awarded a CBE (Commander of the Order of the British Empire) in the UK honours system in 2001 for services to the economy.

Within two years, the Titanic Quarter site was sold by Fred Olsen Energy for £47 million to Dublin-based Harcourt Developments, led by Donegal man Pat Doherty, who had a successful history of property development in the Republic, the UK and the US. Included on the board of Harcourt Developments was Andrew Parker Bowles, the ex-husband of Camilla Parker Bowles who subsequently married Prince Charles. Parker Bowles was a former British army officer who served in Northern Ireland in the early 1970s. His associations undoubtedly helped Harcourt Developments ease any tensions when it took control of a landbank so symbolically significant to the unionist-dominated political and business, as well as the working-class Protestant communities in the city.

Cushnahan's role brought him into close contact with another rising star in the political firmament. The Harbour Estate sat at one end of the East Belfast constituency of local MP and assembly member Peter Robinson. Robinson served as Minister for Regional Development on two occasions between November 1999 and October 2002 (during which time Gregory Campbell also served as minister for a period) and was in regular contact with Cushnahan and the BHC as it planned the regeneration of the Belfast waterfront along the banks of the River Lagan. It was a relationship which was to deepen in the ensuing years as both men climbed the ladder of their respective careers in politics and business. Robinson was no stranger to commercial controversy himself, with a history of involvement with builders and property developers on his home turf of Castlereagh, where he was a long-time member of the local borough council and a former estate agent.

Among the reasons advanced by Cushnahan during committee hearings for the urgency of the lease agreement with Harland & Wolff was the need to build on the success of other projects along the river Lagan, and in particular the Odyssey Arena.

Developed by businessman Peter Curistan and his Sheridan Group (named after his wife, Ann Sheridan), the Odyssey was 50 per cent funded by a £45 million government grant from the UK Millennium Commission and was intended as a landmark project to mark the turn of the century. Curistan raised the balance of the £100 million cost from his own resources and contributions from the Department of Education and the Sports Council of Northern Ireland. He had a track record as he had successfully developed the first multiplex cinema and shopping mall in Belfast in the late 1980s and had also opened the IMAX cinema complex on Parnell Street in Dublin.

A native of Andersonstown in west Belfast, Curistan partnered with a US leisure firm for the Odyssey Arena, which hosted major sports and entertainment events and was soon earning annual profits of £4 million following its opening in

2000. In 2003, he was named entrepreneur of the year by the Northern Irish Institute of Directors for his contribution to the city, and he had an ambitious £60 million plan to extend his riverside operations with a scheme of apartments, a hotel and visitor attractions on a tract of land adjoining the Odyssey at Queen's Quay which was owned by the Laganside Development Corporation.

Unfortunately for Curistan, other business interests had their eyes on the site and despite his emergence as preferred bidder in a tender competition, a series of events contributed to the sudden and dramatic collapse of his growing business empire.

As he awaited confirmation that his bid had secured the contract from Laganside, Curistan was warned by accountant David Watters, a former colleague in accountancy firm PwC, where Curistan once worked, that he should 'watch out for due diligence'. He had encountered Watters at the Cutters restaurant in Belfast where the accountant was lunching with developer Kevin Lagan and Belfast businessman Andrew Creighton. The underbidder for the contract was the Lagan Group, a prominent construction firm with powerful political and financial connections in the city and headed by Kevin Lagan.

Just as his company was awarded the contract in June 2005, Curistan was astonished to read an article by business journalist Shane Ross in the *Sunday Independent* which alleged that he was connected to the IRA. The article was based on information, which was available in the Companies Office in Dublin, that a co-director of the company which ran the IMAX operation on Parnell Street was a senior official of Sinn Féin.

Dessie Mackin had handled the party's finances from its offices in Parnell Square in Dublin for several years and also ran a security firm. He had been introduced to Curistan as someone who could assist with his accounts as well as providing services for an apartment block he owned in the city centre.

Curistan needed a resident of the Republic of Ireland as a director of his registered company and a new financial advisor after his long-time accountant died following a stroke in March 2005. In August of that year the Northern Ireland edition of the *Sunday World* tabloid, which like the *Sunday Independent* is also owned by Independent News and Media, published a two-page spread repeating much of the same material. Curistan sued both newspapers for defamation.

As the decision on the contract for the Queen's Quay site approached, Curistan received a phone call from a BBC journalist to ask him whether he was aware of comments concerning him which had just been made in the House of Commons by Peter Robinson MP.

Using parliamentary privilege, Robinson alleged on Wednesday 8 February 2006 that Curistan and his businesses were linked to the IRA and called on the

Northern Ireland secretary Peter Hain to 'ensure the activities of the Sheridan Group and its association with the IRA's dirty money are fully investigated, and will you guarantee that no further public money is channelled in their direction until, if ever, they get a clean bill of health'.

Robinson continued:

It has now been revealed that over several years senior IRA figures have accumulated massive wealth. Their finance director, Des Mackin, now owns property worth more than £1.75 million. He has a conviction for IRA membership in the mid-1980s and served as Sinn Féin's treasurer.

He, along with the Belfast tycoon Peter Curistan, are the two co-directors of numerous companies, seven of which were prosecuted in the District Court in Dublin recently for failing to keep proper accounts.

The government, instead of rewarding republicans for criminality, should address the involvement of men such as these in government initiatives. For Curistan is the key private sector investor behind Belfast's flagship £100 million Odyssey centre in my east Belfast constituency. Many of us have been aware of Mr Curistan and his business activities and until recently I believe those people believed that they were legitimate.

Over recent reports they now, I believe, will consider that is not the case. His Sheridan Group was awarded a massive development contract in June 2005 by the Laganside Corporation which is a public body, for residential provision, offices, a hotel, niche retail, waterfront cafes, and other leisure facilities together with parking.

Curistan, understandably, said he was 'shocked' by the remarks which were widely reported and which he said had endangered himself and his family. He challenged the politician to make the allegations outside the privilege of Westminster where he could be sued. He invited Robinson to bring in auditors to inspect the previous ten years of accounts of the Sheridan Group which would confirm that his business was completely above board.

If the object of the parliamentary exercise was to remove Curistan from the lucrative Laganside contract it was immediately successful. The vendor company withdrew its offer. He still owned the Odyssey, but soon found himself accused of bringing the Trust which had been set up to oversee its development 'into disrepute'. The board of the Odyssey Trust was made up of voluntary members from the city's business elite and was chaired by a senior partner in PwC, Alan Gibson. It could not force Curistan to relinquish his financial control of the Odyssey but it could make life difficult for him.

The Police Service of Northern Ireland (PSNI) chief constable, Hugh Orde, stated publicly that the businessman had never been a subject of any investigation by the force and Curistan took judicial review proceedings against Laganside over its threat to pull out of the Queen's Quay transaction.

Only a few years earlier Curistan had been among 25 key clients of Anglo Irish Bank who were whisked off, with their wives, to a luxury hotel in Paris, before being brought on the Orient Express to Venice for an all-expenses-paid trip. Now he was struggling to convince the bank's chief executive in Belfast, Neil Adair, that he could ride the political storm following Robinson's extraordinary attack on his reputation in the British parliament and continue to develop the successful Odyssey operations.

At this time, there was something of a hiatus in the North with political institutions in suspension and direct rule in place for over three years. An agreement reached in October 2006 opened the way to elections for a new assembly and the formation of a new executive in May 2007.

When Robinson became finance minister of this administration he brought in Cushnahan to advise on the North's capital assets, which involved a review of the public property portfolio controlled by the NI executive.

Cushnahan was also continuing his consultancy work for the Graham family and with a number of other corporate and public bodies in Belfast, including as a non-executive member of the audit committee of the NIHE, an authority with an annual budget of £750 million. In 2007 he resigned his position on the audit committee and within months was appointed chairman of the Red Sky Group, a company which held maintenance contracts worth many millions with the NIHE.

An investigation by the Northern Ireland Audit Office into the housing executive and the contracts it awarded found guideline breaches within the NIHE in the conduct of at least 27 land deals, with its executive being given wrong information in relation to property sales, and land deals being transacted below market value.

Subsequently, the Public Accounts Committee at Stormont found serious discrepancies in its dealings with Red Sky, and singled out Cushnahan for his 'totally unethical behaviour' during negotiations between NIHE and the company over its alleged overcharging for maintenance work on public housing developments.

The committee is ... concerned about the involvement of a former non-executive member of the housing executive's audit committee [Cushnahan] – who resigned from the audit committee prior to its March 2007 meeting and became chairman of the Red Sky Group in April 2007 – in negotiations

with Red Sky to recover sums which had been paid to the company as a result
of it overcharging for work.

While it is unclear as to which side he was representing at these negotiations,
in the committee's view, his involvement was totally unethical and could and
should have been avoided. It also highlights a fundamental breakdown of
governance and proper accountability in that his involvement was not
discussed by senior management at any stage with the audit committee, board
or the department.

Despite the controversy he sometimes invited, Cushnahan continued to attract
lucrative corporate clients, particularly in a property market that was enjoying
spectacular growth at the height of boom years boosted by the bedding in of the
peace process and the advance of several billon euro in loans by Irish- and British-
based lenders, not to mention EU grant aid. Anglo Irish was an aggressive lender
to the NI market, while Bank of Ireland and AIB were also active in providing
loans to investors from both sides of the border and further afield.

The £1 billion Titanic Quarter and the promotion by the Laganside
Corporation of the largest waterfront development in Europe was an important
catalyst for investor interest and Cushnahan's long experience and access to
influential business and political figures made him a significant player in the
corporate life of the city. As Gareth Graham and others were to discover, he was
also a man who could be ruthless and more than willing to make full use of his
influence to damage those perceived to be a threat to his ambition.

Chapter 10 ~

CHECKING FOR LEAKS

In early August 2012, the NAMA press officer received a phone call from the *Sunday Times* over the purchase by Enda Farrell and his wife, Alice Kramer, of the property in Lucan called Sunday's Well. The newspaper had learned that Farrell had purchased the property from NAMA in August 2011 while he still worked for the agency and it planned to publish the story the following Sunday.

Farrell missed a call on his mobile from *Sunday Times* journalist John Mooney, but when he contacted the newspaper he was informed that the journalist was away from his desk. No sooner had he put the phone down than he received a call from a former colleague in NAMA, Paul Hennigan, to say that all hell was about to break loose. Brendan McDonagh was on a family holiday in the south of France when he was contacted by his press people, who gave him details of the house purchase by Farrell, of which he was completely unaware. Hennigan also asked Farrell to 'keep him out of' any ensuing controversy even though he was involved in handling the Avestus portfolio, which included the Sunday's Well property, and was involved in authorising its sale to his former colleague. Farrell agreed not to land him in the proverbial 'dung heap' and warned Hennigan that there was 'big trouble' ahead.

Although Farrell had informed Hennigan about his purchase of the Lucan property, he had not formally disclosed it in writing to his superiors at the agency, including Brendan McDonagh and John Mulcahy. When Forum Partners learned about the growing scandal surrounding Farrell, they asked him to leave quietly and paid him a month's salary.

Alice Kramer also left her employment at Ernst & Young even though she was completely oblivious to the significance or detail of the NAMA valuation files she had received from Farrell months previous. She was also pregnant with their third child when her world was thrown into chaos by the unfolding crisis.

NAMA quickly contacted its auditors, Deloitte, to investigate whether there had been any breach by Farrell of NAMA guidelines or legislation and to prepare a report on the matter. Within days a search of Farrell's email records at the agency by Colm McDonnell and David Kinsella of Deloitte uncovered suspicious communications with his wife at the Dublin office of Ernst & Young where she worked. The emails were unrelated to the house purchase but included multiple attachments which were sent over a period of months from late 2011 to early 2012, just before Farrell sent his letter of resignation to McDonagh in mid-February 2012.

The files sent to Kramer included financial information relating to properties acquired by NAMA. While of limited commercial use, given that they related to valuations done three years earlier in 2009, they were of potential benefit to third parties as they identified properties controlled by the agency, their historic valuation and whether they were likely to be sold.

By early September 2012, an application was brought by NAMA before Judge Peter Charleton, in a private hearing of the High Court, who granted the agency permission to enter and search the home of Farrell and Kramer at The Motte, Knockudder in Dunboyne, County Meath. The 'Anton Piller' court order gave NAMA, or its agents, the right to search and seize evidence without prior warning. It also prohibited publication of the details of the order.

Later that month, the couple and their two small children were disturbed as they prepared dinner one evening by a team from Deloitte bearing a court order which gave them permission to search their property and seize any material of relevance to their investigation.

The team left some hours later with memory sticks, mobile phones, laptops and computers and any paperwork they could get their hands on that related to Farrell's work for NAMA.

Deloitte continued its inquiries on behalf of the agency, which took another ten weeks from the raid on Farrell's home before it informed the Garda of his alleged criminal behaviour. With his wife in an advanced stage of pregnancy, Farrell was concerned with ensuring she would not be implicated in any criminal proceedings and they made plans to leave the country as soon as their new baby was born. She was understandably shocked and upset by developments which had the potential to destroy her career as well as his, although there was no evidence that she had done anything other than receive his emails at her place of employment.

Kramer had received from her husband some 33 separate emails with attachments between 18 October 2011 and 28 February 2012 containing what John Mulcahy described to the Garda as 'highly confidential and commercially sensitive information' belonging to NAMA.

There was a possibility that under the NAMA Act (sections 7 and 202), the National Treasury Management Agency Acts 1990 and 2000 (in particular section 14 of the 1990 Act), and the Official Secrets Act 1963 (sections 4, 5 and 6) she could also face prosecution for assisting her husband's unauthorised dissemination of NAMA files.

On 12 September 2012, High Court judge Mary Finlay Geoghegan ordered that any future proceedings should be held in open court and lifted the prohibition on publication of details of the order. However, she prohibited publication of the affidavits made by Farrell and John Mulcahy in the previous week. The agency was given until 8 October to confirm whether it intended to pursue a claim for damages against Farrell and Kramer. After two adjournments to allow NAMA to complete its investigation and assess the damage caused by the disclosure of its confidential information, Judge Peter Kelly in the High Court made an order preventing the couple from distributing any confidential information 'relating to loans, security and any other assets' acquired by the agency and 'relating to any debtor or other person' dealing with it and 'any proposals of a commercial nature' submitted to NAMA. Judge Kelly also gave leave to NAMA to provide 'information and documentation' to the Garda obtained under the search and seize order granted to it by Judge Charleton in early September.

Farrell had already made a statement to Deloitte confirming the details surrounding the acquisition of the Sunday's Well house in Lucan. It had been put up as security for the loans of Thomas Dowd and his company Avestus. The property was purchased by Dowd for €4.1 million during the boom years but he accepted an offer of just €410,000 from Farrell and Kramer in August 2011 and the sale was closed the following November. While the sale was arranged through AIB, which was managing the loan on behalf of the agency, it was approved by a senior NAMA portfolio manager, Paul Hennigan, and a senior credit manager, as required by agency policy. Hennigan told Deloitte that when he saw the name of the purchaser of the property he had confronted Enda Farrell and asked him whether he was the person named in the conveyancing documents.

Deloitte reported that there was no evidence that 'the sale had taken place at undervalue'. Deloitte found that Farrell failed to inform the CEO of NAMA of the purchase, as required under the agency's 'conflict of interest' code of practice. Farrell disputed this and insisted there was no requirement at the time of the purchase for properties sold by NAMA to be openly marketed.

Such a requirement was introduced in October 2011 and a new policy was implemented whereby the NAMA executive had to be notified prior to any decision on an 'off-market' disposal. In a report following its investigation into the Farrell house purchase, Deloitte recommended that every purchaser of a NAMA property must confirm whether they or any person with a beneficial interest in the transaction was a NAMA officer.

There was no mention in that report by Deloitte, which was released in November 2011, of the distribution by Farrell to other parties of confidential information on NAMA debtors and properties.

By the time it had completed its report, Deloitte had clocked up costs of some €236,159 for its forensic investigation, while legal fees of €335,640 were due to solicitors Arthur Cox. After successful civil proceedings against them by NAMA in late 2012, Farrell and his wife were hit with the bill for both and were forced to sell the Lucan property and other assets, including an apartment in Paris, to cover the debt. They sold the property for €475,000, which was €65,000 more than Farrell paid for it, to help cover the costs.

On 26 September 2012, soon after they received their first complaint from NAMA, a team from the GBFI, led by Detective Sergeant Martin Griffin and Detective Garda Gareth Lynch, arrived at Farrell's home at Knockudder with a search warrant. After their search, the fraud bureau officers took away mobile phones, a laptop, CDs, notebooks and other documents from the house. Farrell informed them that Deloitte, instructed by NAMA, also had possession of USB keys, computers and other material which had been seized from the house earlier in the month.

On 2 October, at a meeting at the Deloitte offices in Dublin, the electronic devices, phones and other material the accountancy firm had taken from Farrell's home in September were returned to him. He handed them over on the same day to the GBFI officers.

A week later, Farrell voluntarily provided a taped interview with Lynch and Griffin at Blanchardstown Garda station in Dublin, where he admitted in detail what he had done. In his first voluntary statement, Farrell described how he had sent confidential NAMA documents on Sean Mulryan's Ballymore loans to Canadian asset management firm Brookfield. He sent Richard Liao of Brookfield the valuation reports, the NAMA business plan and an independent review of the €1.3 billion Ballymore portfolio.

However, nothing came of Brookfield's effort to negotiate a joint venture with Mulryan, as the developer was not interested in the proposal. In 2010, Farrell sent a valuation report to Liao relating to a property in London known as the BMW site. He also sent Liao the business plan review for the Galliard portfolio, which owned sites adjacent to Ballymore's in London, but this time by post, as he was concerned that an email contact could be traced back to him.

In December 2010, Liao asked him to meet with executives from a Canadian firm, Fairfax Financial Holdings, which was keen to invest in Ireland. Again, he used the post to send the business plan review for Harcourt Developments, owned by Pat Doherty, who had developed the Titanic Quarter in Belfast but whose debts were now with NAMA. By his own admission, Farrell was not authorised to send this material to third parties, but he had convinced himself that by identifying possible international partners for the agency, McDonagh might move him from the tortuous due diligence and valuation work he was doing under Mulcahy's supervision into a more interesting sales or capital markets position.

In January 2012, Liao asked him for a copy of the marketing presentation on Ballymore prepared for NAMA by international investment bank Lazard. Liao had left Brookfield but said that he knew investors who might be interested in a joint venture partnership with the agency. On this occasion, Farrell sent the document from his work email but he told the gardaí that he did not think the information was confidential and that his action could help NAMA attract potential investors.

His wife, Alice, was not taken in for questioning and the couple continued to make plans to leave Ireland as soon as their baby was born the following April. During his interview, Farrell told the detectives that a senior NAMA portfolio manager, Paul Hennigan, knew of the Sunday's Well house purchase and had authorised it as he handled the disposal of the distressed loans of developer Thomas Dowd and other directors of Avestus.

Before their departure to Belgium, Farrell gave another voluntary, and detailed, interview to the GBFI officers in June 2013 at Leixlip Garda station. The Farrells subsequently left to make a new life in Brussels, where Kramer's family lived. Farrell informed the gardaí of his intentions and told them that if they wanted to arrest and charge him they should do it before he left the country as he could not be forced to return home given that there was no similar offence under Belgian law that would make him liable to extradition proceedings.

At a meeting of the Oireachtas Committee on Finance, Public Expenditure and Reform on 24 October 2012, the story of the leaked files and Farrell's property acquisition was the main item for the TDs and senators present. McDonagh, Daly, Hanna and Mulcahy were present for the session, which focused first on the property transaction, the subject of the as yet unpublished Deloitte report, before it moved onto the allegation that Farrell had taken and distributed confidential information belonging to the agency.

Daly told the committee members that while he had not been authorised to purchase the property, Farrell had not 'enjoyed any benefit from the transaction' and that the Deloitte investigation had found that the price paid was in line with market value. He insisted that Farrell had failed to disclose the purchase to NAMA, 'as he was required to do'. The fact that Farrell had dealt with Paul Hennigan in relation to the Sunday's Well property – Farrell claimed Hennigan had informed him about it in the first place – was not mentioned by Daly, and clearly was not sufficient to meet the NAMA approval requirements in relation to such transactions. In his interview with Deloitte, Hennigan denied that he knew of Farrell's involvement in the Sunday's Well transaction until he asked his colleague about the names on the conveyancing document. He did not admit that he authorised the sale, as Farrell contended.

Daly insisted that the 'commercially sensitive and confidential information', as it was described in Mulcahy's statement to the Garda, 'would be of limited value' to any third parties to whom it was sent and was 'unlikely to prove commercially damaging to the agency at any point in the future'. Nor was it 'prejudicial to any of our debtors', Daly told PAC members. He said that the agency was 'encouraged by the level of active co-operation' from parties who received the information. He also confirmed that there was one other investigation into another employee of NAMA but that he was precluded from commenting further due to the continuing inquiries.

Committee chairman Ciarán Lynch of Labour got straight to the nub of the issue by asking a series of direct questions. To whom was the information leaked? What was the full extent of the information and did it include 'the detail of every NAMA property'? Was it a master spreadsheet of all loans acquired by NAMA? What was the public loss to third parties? What procedures are in place to highlight a potential conflict of interest or the transfer of information?

Daly explained that Farrell had escaped normal IT security procedures of NAMA by sending the 33 emails in question to his wife's corporate account at her office in Ernst & Young. As the accountancy firm had daily and confidential dealings and communications with NAMA the information transfer evaded the security net. Farrell, Daly explained, would have been unable to send the data to a personal email account or transfer it to a memory or USB stick, such was the level of internal NAMA and NTMA security.

'His wife appears to have forwarded those 33 e-mails to Mr. Farrell's personal account. Beyond that, we believe Mr. Farrell would have sent information to fewer than ten parties, which we have identified to date,' Daly said. He insisted that no sensitive financial data was released and that Farrell may have sent 'extracts' to a number of people rather than the full documentation he had transferred to his wife, and from her to his personal email address. He said that the information concerned 2009 property valuations and loans and the value for which they were acquired by NAMA.

Again, in contrast to the description of the information by Mulcahy, he said it was 'sensitive information because it was confidential under sections 99 and 202 of the NAMA Act but ... it was historic'. The other questions – to whom the information was sent by Farrell and whether it was the entire NAMA spreadsheet – went unanswered.

Fianna Fáil TD Michael McGrath asked why the agency did not call in the Garda rather than commission Deloitte to undertake a review. Why go to the

High Court and seek an Anton Piller order to secure documents, communications and materials from Farrell rather than involve gardaí? McGrath asked. He said he hoped that any Garda investigation would not be compromised by the way NAMA reacted to the *Sunday Times* query in relation to Farrell's purchase of the Sunday's Well property in 2011 and the removal of its confidential files.

Daly reminded the committee members that it was only through the Deloitte investigation that the agency discovered that confidential files might have been removed. Deloitte had retrieved 93,000 emails sent by or to Farrell between 2009 and 2012, when he worked for NAMA, and of these 'only 33 were of concern'.

Sinn Féin TD Pearse Doherty asked why NAMA did not ban those parties who received confidential information from Farrell but failed to disclose to the agency that they had received it. Doherty asked whether any other employee of NAMA could have provided sensitive information 'by other means, orally, for a period'. In reply, Daly insisted that he did not believe any other members of staff were involved in leaking sensitive information and that he was satisfied about 'the probity and integrity of NAMA staff in general'. He continued:

All I can say to the Deputy is, at this stage of the investigation, we do not believe there has been commercial damage to NAMA and we do not believe that there is prejudicial damage to our debtors. I acknowledge that there is reputational damage and none of us wants to be here today explaining it away. As far as I can see at this stage, this is a one-off incident where somebody very deliberately set out to circumvent the controls in place at NAMA.

Daly confirmed that there was another ongoing investigation into one member of staff and insisted: 'If the Deputy is hinting in any way that there are widespread suspensions or investigations in NAMA, that is absolutely not the case.'

Doherty then pressed Daly on the sale of loans to UK investment firm ICG-Longbow, which had recruited former NAMA head of lending Graham Emmett following his departure from the agency in early 2012. Seven months later he joined ICG, which had recently purchased part of the multi-million debt used to finance the acquisition of the Ramada Docklands hotel in London from NAMA. Daly insisted that 'the former staff member of NAMA had absolutely nothing to do with ICG-Longbow at the time the transaction was carried out'. Daly said later that the former NAMA employee had joined ICG-Longbow some nine months after the transaction was completed.

Doherty replied: 'There is a practice of former members of NAMA at a very senior level moving on. I am talking about the head of lending who now works for a company that bought loans off NAMA in the past. Now we know that the company approached NAMA.'

Asked by People before Profit TD Richard Boyd Barrett whether there should be a cooling-off period for former NAMA employees before they go to work for companies that engage with the agency, Daly said:

> Cooling off periods cost money. The reality is we have no reason to believe that the small number of people who have left NAMA since its foundation have in any way compromised NAMA or used their knowledge to disadvantage NAMA. In an ideal world one might introduce a two year cooling off period but the reality is that, for a start, we would have to pay such people for the two years. Is that what the Deputy wants? Does he want people who leave to be paid by NAMA for one or two years after they go? I think we should be proportionate.

By this time, Daly, McDonagh and Mulcahy had been informed in detail by the Deloitte investigators of the number and content of emails sent by Farrell to various parties and the identity of the recipients. Among them was a full list of all residential properties held by NAMA which he was instructed by a senior NAMA official to send to the Department of the Environment in mid-2011. This was done at the request of the junior minister of the department, Jan O'Sullivan, who was looking into the prospect of acquiring NAMA-controlled properties for the provision of badly needed social housing.

The 33 emails sent by Farrell to Kramer between October 2011 and February 2012 included financial information about properties held by NAMA, their locations and details of ownership. The documents included asset disposal strategies in relation to some NAMA debtors and valuation spreadsheets. It was to be some time, however, before the detailed information which Farrell had removed from NAMA before his departure from the agency was revealed to the public. Despite their cautious replies at the meeting of the finance committee the agency knew that Farrell had taken the entire tracker spreadsheets containing details of addresses and valuations for all NAMA-held properties.

The information contained details of property portfolios previously controlled by some of Ireland's leading developers including Derek Quinlan, Sean Mulryan, Paddy McKillen, Garrett Kelleher of Shelbourne Developments, Michael and John O'Flynn of O'Flynn Construction, Michael Cotter of Park Developments and Joe O'Reilly, owner of Castlethorn Construction and Chartered Land, one of NAMA's biggest debtors. For the NAMA executives, this was a potential disaster for the agency as Farrell was not some junior employee but a key member of the original team, across whose desk had flowed all the addresses and valuations for all NAMA-held properties. He was also privy to sensitive information concerning the inner workings of NAMA and its personnel from the very establishment of the agency. In short, he knew where quite a large number of bodies were buried.

It was not long before he told the GBFI everything else he knew about leaks of NAMA material and other misbehaviour in which some of his former colleagues were also implicated.

During more than 12 hours of questioning at Leixlip Garda station between 19 and 24 June 2013, Farrell provided detailed information about his leaking of confidential information from NAMA. Farrell described the pressure he was under in the agency and how some senior executives were unhappy about the large 'haircuts' he applied to the value of bank loans transferred to NAMA. He claimed that McDonagh had told him how the late finance minister Brian Lenihan had said, 'we are fucking the banks and the country', and how the head of the NTMA, John Corrigan, had met Farrell in the building and referred to 'you and your fucking haircuts'. The banks were complaining that the valuations were too low, while 'many of my colleagues in NAMA told me they couldn't sell property because the valuations were too high', Farrell told Detective Sergeant Griffin and Detective Garda Lynch.

The then 37-year-old explained that Forum Partners, which he had joined soon after leaving NAMA the previous year, paid him a basic salary of €98,000 plus a discretionary bonus if certain targets were hit, including if he successfully identified investment opportunities for the company or other investors and helped with its existing investments in France.

He denied that his possession of confidential NAMA material helped him to land the well-remunerated job with Forum and insisted that he made no suggestion to his new employers that his insider knowledge would give him any competitive advantage in acquiring NAMA-controlled property. He accepted that he had sent the 33 emails containing the spreadsheets he had developed to track the property valuations and due diligence he had completed while with NAMA. One batch of 20 attachments contained 11,000 valuation reports submitted to NAMA by the banks and some 900 second-opinion valuations he had commissioned in line with NAMA policy. The emails included par values, which were the loans given by the banks to developers, and the loan acquisition value, which was the price paid by NAMA for the loans. Farrell accepted that the information was confidential to the agency and that he had sent them to his wife's email account in order to bypass the NAMA security system, but claimed that he did not 'use the information for advantage to myself'.

'I sent it to my wife to bypass the firewall but I did not seek to make any advantage,' he said. In relation to one attachment he sent to Alice Kramer, referring to properties in the Ballymore Group which had transferred to NAMA, he said that he did not make any use of it. 'Ballymore would be one of the more interesting clients of NAMA,' Farrell told the detectives during one interview.

Farrell said that he had become 'desensitised' to the confidentiality of the documents he had taken, some of which he had sent to himself through Kramer on more than one occasion. Asked why he would send them if he already had the information, he replied, 'They represented all my work and I was very proud of the work I had done.'

The information, he repeated more than once, had no commercial value because it was over two years old, but it was useful for potential investors to know the existence and location of NAMA-controlled properties that might come up for sale. Among those to whom he sent information were his new employer, Forum, and other third parties including IFSC-based company QED Equity, securities firm Canaccord Genuity, also in Dublin, and property investors NewRiver and InWest. He also provided some information to friends but did not accept any reward and had rejected offers where 'there would be something in it for me'.

He insisted that NAMA did not own the valuation files and other information he passed on. He cited legal advice he had received while in NAMA to the effect that the banks from which the loans were transferred were still the owners of the files.

Among others to whom he sent confidential information while he worked with the agency were Peter Reilly and David Jackson of UK Prudential. According to Farrell, the two employees of UK Prudential wanted information on properties in Germany controlled by NAMA, and he obliged by sending the William Ewart portfolio, but he did so after consulting with the portfolio manager who was responsible for the loans involved. William Ewart was among the property companies in Belfast whose distressed loans were taken in by NAMA.

He also sent confidential information to Jos Short, chairman of London-based global property investors Internos. He sent some to his friends in acts of what he described as 'pure bravado', and in the case of one, 'to flatter him and his ego'.

Farrell had tried to establish his own business, which he called the Irish Property Recovery Company. He said this was his 'roadmap' out of NAMA, but he failed to get it off the ground, due to a lack of interest from potential backers. In his presentation to global corporations, Canadian-based Fairfax Financial Holdings and the Abu Dhabi Investment Authority (ADIA), Farrell used a case study based on the confidential information that NAMA held on Ireland's most successful retail venture, the Dundrum Shopping Centre, which was developed by Joe O'Reilly and his company, Chartered Land.

What sparked his decision to purchase the Sunday's Well property and to take the NAMA spreadsheets, however, was an encounter Farrell claims he had with Brendan McDonagh. At the time he was having difficulties with Mulcahy and was seeking to ingratiate himself with McDonagh. According to Farrell, he was approached by the chief executive, who was seeking information about a house in Kerry which was in NAMA and which, McDonagh said, his niece was interested in buying.

> He had asked me to get a valuation on a NAMA property in Kerry his niece was interested in buying. He said a developer was playing hardball with his niece and that she wanted to know what the NAMA valuation was. He told me his niece was pregnant. Without hesitation, I found an adjacent property and gave out the valuation to Brendan McDonagh.

Farrell also asked a colleague, Breifne Brennan, whether she knew anything about the property and she replied that McDonagh had just sent her an email asking about it.

'It was at this point I decided to purchase Sunday's Well and to take the tracker spreadsheets. These spreadsheets were the ones I had worked on for years and contained all addresses, valuations for all NAMA properties.'

He described how another colleague asked him for all the valuations relating to one of his borrowers who was complaining that there was a huge difference between his opinion of the value of certain assets and the NAMA valuation. His colleague said that he was sending the valuations on to the borrower. Farrell claimed that this 'indicated to me that the information was not confidential'.

'It was also known that the banks shared the valuations with borrowers, as was their right.' He repeated that he was given legal advice within the agency which confirmed that the banks, not NAMA, owned the valuations.

This perception was rejected by Mulcahy, who told the fraud bureau investigators that the information sent by Farrell was 'of a confidential nature and key to the day to day business of NAMA'.

Mulcahy told the gardaí:

> The information includes information acquired in confidence by NAMA as to various lists of properties, their locations and details of ownership. Among the documents misappropriated are a number of NAMA tranche valuation spreadsheets.
>
> These are control documents for property valuations and give some property details, but more particularly give initial property valuation figures

showing the name of the original valuer and the reviewing valuer. The actual valuation of the property in 2009 is of limited commercial use now, but it is of some benefit to know the existence of the property, the historic valuation and that it is likely to be sold.

Farrell replied that he accepted Mulcahy's statement 'in its entirety' but that he had only sent to third parties 'information limited to the valuations', which Mulcahy had acknowledged is 'of limited commercial value'.

Farrell insisted that 'the information was out of date, inaccurate, manipulated and was the first part of a process in which I had no influence'. The information was two years old, Farrell said, and since then 'the market had fallen considerably'. He claimed that he told another portfolio manager that he had sent spreadsheets to his wife, and the colleague confirmed to him that he also sent out similar material to potential purchasers. Farrell also suggested to the gardaí that a former senior figure in the agency had provided confidential information to a global property company, Hines, which was interested in purchasing a property previously owned by the Ballymore Group in Birmingham, England. Hines was also bidding for the property portfolio previously controlled by Treasury Holdings and they had 'done extensive due diligence on the top 20 borrowers in NAMA'. The interest by Hines in their portfolio was mentioned in the unsuccessful High Court action taken by Johnny Ronan and Richard Barrett of Treasury against NAMA in early 2012. Paul Hennigan confirmed to Farrell that he had shared a confidential bid letter with the Barclay brothers, who were engaged in an intense battle for control over the Maybourne group of luxury hotels in London with Paddy McKillen. McKillen's lawyers had come across the information leaked by the NAMA official in the discovery process of the developer's High Court action against the agency in 2010. Farrell said that he had also provided Hennigan with information about the hotels and golf courses under NAMA's control.

He claimed that before he left the agency he had spoken to Hennigan about the distressed Avestus loans. Farrell had been asked to get an updated valuation on an office block in the Avestus portfolio which was located at 2 Kingdom Street, Paddington, in central London. He discovered that Avestus had signed a very large lease with the communications giant Nokia UK, which had significantly increased the value of the property but of which Hennigan was unaware. The borrower, Avestus, was seeking an updated valuation that would not exceed £80 million in order to secure refinancing. The value, in Farrell's view, exceeded £95 million, with the increase due to the lucrative Nokia lease. Farrell claimed that he asked Hennigan whether he had 'gone native' in relation to his favourable treatment for the borrower. Hennigan said that he was acting in NAMA's best interests and that he intended to press ahead with the sale of the Avestus loans, excluding the Paddington property, in an off-market transaction called Project Nantes. When Farrell joined Forum Partners in April 2012, he contacted Hennigan in NAMA to seek a copy of the Avestus business plan and he was informed that the company was out of NAMA.

He told gardaí that Hennigan 'forwarded to me an email which confirmed that Project Nantes had completed and Avestus were out of NAMA and I believe that NAMA were at a substantial loss due to a breach of his duty to the tax payer to obtain the highest possible price for the loans'.

Farrell said that he had received from Hennigan an email written by US investors Clairview, which was a partner with Avestus in acquiring the loans back from NAMA. In the email a Clairview executive is seeking permission to issue a press release confirming that Avestus was out of NAMA. The reply from NAMA was that no press release could be issued as the loans 'were not openly marketed', according to Farrell. A subsequent response to Clairview from NAMA states that the company 'should be satisfied they acquired the loans at arguably below market value'.

Farrell said that he obtained the confidential Avestus business plan from Hennigan when they met on the banks of the Grand Canal near the headquarters of NAMA in the Treasury Building. According to Mulcahy's affidavit to the Garda in the preparation of a file on Farrell's activities within NAMA, the business plan document was confidential to NAMA.

'Paul Hennigan handed me this document outside the Treasury Building along the canal, around July 2012, months after I left NAMA,' Farrell said. During his final interview in June 2013, Farrell said that Hennigan knew everything about his purchase of the Sunday's Well property in Lucan and that he had personally informed McDonagh about Hennigan's knowledge of the sale. In the course of the Deloitte inquiry into the house purchase, Hennigan professed to have had no prior knowledge of it.

Before Farrell signed his lengthy and voluntary statement to the Garda, he accepted that he had taken confidential information belonging to NAMA but denied that he used it to 'provide any advantage to third parties or myself and there was no disadvantage to NAMA'.

In the following weeks the managing director of QED Stewart Doyle and the firm's financial analyst Ken Rouse, as well as Ray McMahon of Canaccord, confirmed to gardaí that they had received documents from Farrell including attachments detailing information from NAMA, which they handed over to the investigation team.

Chapter 11 ∾

LETTERS AND DEFECTIONS

As the Farrell controversy faded from public view and the inevitably tedious investigation by the fraud squad continued, the agency executives concentrated on their main task of bringing more loans under its wing, working with the 500 staff in the units in Bank of Ireland, AIB and Anglo Irish Bank and preparing to bring billions worth of assets to the market for disposal.

In October 2012 Ronnie Hanna had assured the Chartered Accountants Ulster Society at a meeting in Belfast that the agency would 'not engage in so-called "fire sales" in Northern Ireland or indeed any other jurisdiction'.

Our role is to make sure that sales take place on a phased basis over a measured timeframe. NAMA will continue to play its part in bringing stability to the Northern Ireland property market and our track record to date shows that our actions have been matching our words.

Hanna also said that NAMA had provided liquidity of £100 million to debtors in the North and was working well with those who 'are willing and able to co-operate with it'. He pointed to the 'strong working relationships with key stakeholders in Northern Ireland, including the Minister for Finance and Personnel and his Department; the Northern Ireland Assembly and Business Trust; and a range of public sector bodies'.

He told the gathering of accountants that the agency relied 'heavily on the local input and experience that is available to it through its dedicated Northern Ireland Advisory Committee'.

Hanna's presentation was timely as a number of interested parties in the room were already considering the merits of bundling the entire portfolio into a package that could be sold to a single buyer. While the 2009 valuation was used as a reference point by NAMA for future sales, the par value of the North's loan portfolio at the time of its acquisition by NAMA in 2010 and 2011 was €5.38 billion and it was acquired by the agency for €2.65 billion.

Unknown to the other members of the NIAC, Frank Cushnahan had engaged in meetings in late 2012 with US-based international law firm Brown Rudnick and Tughans solicitors in Belfast on the concept of single loan-book disposal of the entire NI portfolio. Cushnahan had set up offices in Tughans, where he worked closely with senior partner Ian Coulter and held meetings with his debtor clients who were in NAMA and other business associates.

A key figure in Brown Rudnick's London office was Tuvi Keinan, who had previous dealings with NAMA and was known to some of its executives in Dublin as someone who could help find investors for big portfolios that only a small number of global funds could afford to purchase. However, Daly and McDonagh were not aware of the meeting in late 2012 between Cushnahan, Tughans and the US law firm, or of its subsequent approach to PIMCO, which expressed an interest in NAMA's loan portfolio in the North.

As NAMA entered the third year of its existence the two senior executives were instead focused on their successful generation of some €10.5 billion cash flows, with €6.9 billion accounted for through asset disposals and the remaining €3.6 billion from mainly rental income derived from properties controlled by debtors or receivers the agency had appointed.

Launching their results for 2012, McDonagh said that 'the generation of €10.5 billion in cash in the 33 months since the first loans transferred to NAMA reflects a strong performance in terms of asset disposals and also shows the importance for NAMA of capturing the rental income from assets under the control of debtors'.

Daly was equally upbeat about prospects for the agency and the property market, remarking that the agency was on target to meet the senior bond redemption of €7.5 billion by the end of 2013 and of completing its work by 2020.

The legal battles fought by the agency were listed in the annual statement and included the challenge by Treasury Holdings to the agency's appointment of receivers over some of its assets and its proceedings against Treasury seeking to reverse the so-called Treasury Asian Investments Ltd (TAIL) transaction. This involved undervalued share transfers by Ronan and Barrett of €20 million, which NAMA claims put some €46 million beyond the reach of the agency and other creditors. There were the High Court and Supreme Court cases brought by Paddy McKillen over NAMA's move to acquire €1.4 billion loans associated with the developer which eventually resulted in some €7 million incurred costs for the agency. NAMA also took asset recovery proceedings in a number of foreign jurisdictions. Among the places where NAMA engaged legal services were the Czech Republic, Portugal, Malta, France, Germany, Belgium, the Isle of Man, Spain, the British Virgin Islands, Poland and Jersey.

In figures released to Sinn Féin TD Mary Lou McDonald, the agency confirmed that since its inception it had spent almost €40 million in legal fees. Arthur Cox received the highest fees of the Irish-based law firms with earnings of over €4 million, followed by A&L Goodbody (€2.5 million), McCann Fitzgerald (€2.4 million), Matheson (€2.1 million), William Fry (€1.89 million), Byrne Wallace (€1.72 million) and Eversheds O'Donnell Sweeney (€1.51 million). Earnings by international firms working for NAMA overseas were led by Hogan Lovells, which made fees of €4.06 million, with Maples and Calder and Allen & Overy each taking over €2.5 million since 2010.

One of the more bizarre legal actions was taken by NAMA against Mary McCabe, whom the agency pursued to get its hands on an 8.38 carat diamond ring, a necklace and a bracelet after winning judgments against her for €21 million. Her husband, John McCabe, and his company built the Abington development in Malahide, County Dublin, where houses sold for more than €1 million before the property crash. His companies owed NAMA over €235 million arising from a series of loans and guarantees, most of which were advanced by Anglo Irish Bank and others by Bank of Ireland and AIB. He was also one of the Maple 10 who controversially bought shares to shore up Anglo in July 2008. The couple lived in Rath Stud in Ashbourne, County Meath, whose previous owners included former Taoiseach Charles Haughey. In late January 2013 the agency appointed a receiver, Jim Hamilton, over the three items of jewellery. The agency believed that the ring alone was worth over €150,000. The receiver was appointed after NAMA executives learned that the ring had been sold at auction in Florida in the US and Hamilton was granted an order in the courts in Dublin to retrieve the $205,000 proceeds from the sale.

If all seemed relatively smooth on the surface, the agency and its executives were experiencing turbulence underneath, particularly given the number of high-profile staff who were jumping ship – including to some of the large funds who were eyeing up NAMA assets for heavily discounted purchases.

Among the early leavers, in February 2013, was Kevin Nowlan, who was a key figure in the agency and had been portfolio manager over the distressed loans of the elusive Sean Dunne among others.

Nowlan left NAMA soon after his father, Bill, addressed the REIT Forum conference in Dublin, a gathering of 500 investors, property owners and auctioneers eager to learn of the opportunities provided by the promised new legislation to allow for REITs.

Writing about the conference in the *Irish Times* on 6 February 2013, Bill Nowlan defined an REIT as 'a tax efficient way to enjoy the benefits of owning investment properties without the hassles of being a landlord'.

The conference was also addressed by the secretary general of the Department of Finance, John Moran, who, according to Nowlan, 'spoke about his ambitions to make Ireland a base for international REITs in much the same way as Dublin is now an international centre for aircraft leasing'.

Nowlan described how the NAMA head of asset recovery, John Mulcahy, addressed the conference 'about the potential role of the agency and its borrowers in providing a significant supply of quality property for REITs'. Nowlan wrote:

According to the European Public Real Estate Association (EPRA), the potential in the Irish market could reach €5 billion within five years, supporting earlier estimates from NCB of a potential market in three to five years in excess of €2.5 billion. So how do we get from here to there? The first thing is the legislation which should be enacted by early April in the Finance Act. Then there will be the work by the Stock Exchange in preparing listing rules. After that it is over to the market to make it all happen. In Ireland, with the exception of NAMA there are probably only one or two existing property businesses that could get to the minimum €250 million threshold, so the assembly of portfolios to reach this size will be the first challenge. The second challenge will be in attracting international investors to Irish REITs.

Bill Nowlan quoted Philip Charls, the chief executive of the EPRA, as telling the conference that over 'the past five years REITs have significantly outperformed income yield on equities and bonds around the globe'.

With asset manager Nowlan, Mulcahy and Moran all singing off the same hymn sheet it was only a matter of time before the REIT legislation was enacted and a new injection of funds availing of its measures to improve 'tax efficiency' for investors landed into the Irish property game.

Among the others to depart NAMA and go back into the real estate business was Ronan Fox, who spent two and a half years with the agency before joining the ADIA in September 2012. Nicknamed 'the desert fox' by his NAMA colleagues, he was head of a team that included Enda Farrell, Paul Pugh and Paul Hennigan and had led the disposal of €6 billion in distressed assets while he worked with the agency, including the loans of the two largest debtors, Joe O'Reilly and Bernard McNamara, who had combined debts of €4.2 billion.

Up to 80 per cent of the assets sold by NAMA were in the UK, where market conditions were more favourable and where property investors such as ADIA were seeking out bargains, among them the 42 hotels owned by Marriott in the UK which were in administration. These had been previously owned by Avestus Capital Partners in partnership with two Israeli investors.

Another former NAMA manager and expert in corporate finance, Selina Dicker, left the agency after two years to join Europa Capital Mezzanine, a subsidiary of the US Rockefeller corporation. Portfolio manager Colm Lundy also left in 2012 to form his own property consultancy, CL Asset Management. He joined the agency after several years with Newlyn Developments. Lundy fell out with the company over an €8 million payment he claimed he was owed as part of a profit share agreement, but settled the case in 2008.

In November 2011, the *Irish Times* reported that Lundy was the subject of an internal NAMA inquiry over his involvement with Newlyn – the debts of which had transferred to the agency. It was reported that the agency was 'examining whether Mr Lundy has any personal exposure to Newlyn's debts or connected borrowings and, if so, whether this has been disclosed to the agency'. When its loans were transferred to NAMA, Newlyn had debts of €22 million owed to various banks. At the time, the directors of Newlyn included Robert Kehoe, Christy Dowling and George McGarry. The company had been active in a number of upmarket residential developments in Dublin and Wicklow and had property investments in Portugal.

Portfolio manager Michael Hynes left the agency in early 2013 to join Hudson Advisors Ireland, an asset management division of US investment vehicle Lone Star. Before he went into NAMA, Hynes had worked with Bernard McNamara. John Grayken, the sole owner of the $45 billion Lone Star, took out Irish citizenship in the 1990s and after the banking collapse purchased Project Kildare, a €650 million loan book from AIB, and a large slice of Anglo's £8 billion US distressed property assets, at heavily discounted prices. Grayken made a fortune buying up distressed banks and loans in Japan and South Korea as well as the US, where he swooped on the properties of tens of thousands of home owners after the sub-prime lending collapse.

The slew of departures from NAMA did not dampen the enthusiasm of chairman Frank Daly when he told the Association of European Journalists in late February 2013 of agency plans to invest €2 billion in commercial and residential developments, including office accommodation in the Dublin Docklands, which had just been designated a Strategic Development Zone by the government.

He said that NAMA had approved sales with a total value of €11 billion since inception, completed asset disposals of €7 billion and was close to completing a further €2 billion. He confirmed that 80 per cent of sales to date were in Britain, 'reflecting favourable conditions and strong demand in that market'. He also announced that NAMA was to provide €1 billion in funding to the special liquidators of the IBRC. This followed a government direction to the agency to acquire the unsold residual element of the IBRC loan portfolio which, Daly said, would 'significantly increase NAMA's workload'. 'Potentially, depending on the scale of loan transfers, the size of our balance sheet could increase by close to 50%.'

A former non-executive director of the IBRC, Oliver Ellingham was appointed to the board of NAMA a few weeks later. Ellingham was a director of over 150 companies, mainly in England, and was a former head of corporate finance (Europe) at BNP Paribas and a senior executive with BNP Paribas (UK). Among the connections he listed on his published profile was the Fine Gael party.

While NAMA was extending its remit in the Republic and preparing more massive property bundles for sale in the slowly recovering market, it was also active in Northern Ireland with an announcement in April that it was to provide funding for a 95-unit housing development in Millmount, Dundonald, near Belfast. The site, Daly said 'was to be developed by Baker Tilly Ryan Glennon, the court-appointed administrator to the site, and a subsidiary of the Northern Ireland-headquartered Lagan Group'.

This foray into the Belfast property market followed direct discussions involving the NI finance minister, Sammy Wilson, and NAMA. The Millmount site was previously owned by Belfast developers Noel Murphy and Adam Armstrong before they sold it to brothers Michael and John Taggart for £96 million, borrowed from Anglo Irish Bank, in 2007. A year later the Taggarts were forced into administration by Anglo, with the loan eventually ending up in NAMA. Wilson contacted the agency in 2012 seeking finance to rescue the Millmount development, which was now under the control of Lagan Homes, the Belfast property firm owned by Kevin Lagan and his family. Kevin Lagan had been a partner with Noel Murphy in another company, Lagmar, and both were on good terms with senior members of the DUP, including Wilson and Peter Robinson. In April 2013, NAMA confirmed that it was to put €9 million into the Millmount development, which would allow Lagan Homes to kick-start an ambitious build of 700 homes on the 90-acre site. Central to the political lobbying which resulted in the NAMA investment was Gareth Robinson.

Within weeks of the announcement, a meeting was arranged to discuss the potential sale of the entirety of the NAMA portfolio in Northern Ireland. It was attended by Wilson and Robinson and representatives of Brown Rudnick, Tughans and the giant US investment fund, California-based PIMCO, with funds of up to $1.5 trillion. Present at the discussion with the two senior DUP politicians on 22 May 2013 was Tuvi Keinan of Brown Rudnick, Ian Coulter of Tughans, Frank Cushnahan of the NIAC and a PIMCO executive.

The PIMCO executive believed that the politicians he was meeting were there as representatives of the Northern Ireland power sharing government. Indeed, the firm had been informed that the NI executive needed to meet with its representatives in order to assess its suitability as a purchaser of NAMA's NI loan book. PIMCO was also informed that the government in the North did not want 'a fire sale of homes and businesses' and that it was seeking a 'longer term approach to investment and development of the assets' by the purchaser. The company was not aware that it was only meeting one half of the power sharing executive and that the DUP's government partner Sinn Féin had not been informed of the discussions.

What emerged was a proposal that Brown Rudnick would make an approach to NAMA to purchase, in one bundle, the total portfolio of distressed assets in the North, which involved over 850 properties, including a sizeable number in England. Arising from this initial meeting, Keinan wrote to Wilson on 24 June, saying that Brown Rudnick had identified two clients who had each 'confirmed that they would, independently, be committed to a process of a potential outright purchase' of NAMA's Northern Ireland loan book.

Keinan was a senior partner with Brown Rudnick, specialising in property transactions exceeding $200 million in value and head of the firm's 'special situations team'. He said in the letter that of the two interested investors 'one in particular is highly committed and will be well known to NAMA as highly competent'.

Although not identified at the time, one of the two clients was PIMCO, which eventually became the opening bidder for NAMA's Northern Ireland portfolio. Keinan's letter said that Brown Rudnick's clients wanted to move as fast as possible, on a 'cash only' basis, and with a 'short 4 week due diligence process' for the top 20 loans. The letter said that if the entire NAMA Northern Ireland stock could be bought in a single transaction, local suppliers – tradespeople and professionals – would be used by the purchasing fund to maximise the value of the deal for the Northern Ireland economy.

Perhaps crucially, the letter also said that

all contingent liabilities and/or personal guarantees from the Borrower Connections would be capable of being released. Consequently, the underlying assets, which are the principal subject of the underlying debt, would be retained as security and the existing guarantees will no longer be impeding borrowers from undertaking new business ventures.

This was music to the ears of Wilson and his boss, Robinson, who had been expressing his concerns about the prospect of several high-profile debtors, including a number close to him, having their personal guarantees on their loans called in.

One of them, Paddy Kearney, yet another of the Maple 10, was exposed to more than £300 million in distressed loans in NAMA. According to Kearney, NAMA was threatening and intimidating him in relation to the distressed loans of his company, PBN, and he appealed to Robinson for help at a private meeting on 17 May, days before the first minister's meeting with PIMCO, Brown Rudnick, Tughans and Cushnahan.

In response to Kearney's pleas, Robinson wrote to NAMA chief executive Brendan McDonagh on 24 May seeking clarity in relation to Kearney's debt. He wrote on paper with the official letter head of the Office of the First Minister and asked McDonagh to help 'find a solution to bring both NAMA and PBN forward'.

Following the 22 May meeting, a senior member of the European real estate practice of Brown Rudnick was confident enough to inform PIMCO by letter that NAMA was 'now in the loop' in relation to a potential purchase of the NI portfolio and had appointed a named individual to look after the transaction. The letter mistakenly named Northern Ireland businessman Denis Rooney, who was a member of a ministerial advisory group on NAMA and had no direct involvement with the sale of the NI portfolio.

The Brown Rudnick letter, dated 24 June 2013, also set out a number of principles in relation to the management of the portfolio following a successful purchase, including the adoption of a long-term strategy and a release from personal guarantees for cooperative borrowers. It suggested that incumbent borrowers would continue in the day-to-day operation and development of relevant assets and that Northern Ireland supply lines would be utilised as far as possible.

On the same day, Sammy Wilson wrote to finance minister Michael Noonan, enclosing a copy of the Brown Rudnick letter, and told his counterpart in Dublin that there were two clients interested in acquiring the entire NI portfolio in a single sale. Wilson said that Brown Rudnick had introduced him to the investors referred to in the letter from the solicitors. A month later, Noonan wrote to Wilson advising him to contact NAMA in relation to the approach from Brown Rudnick and passed on the letter from the NI finance minister to the agency, which received it on 4 July. It appears that the letters sent to Noonan were intended to influence NAMA to ensure that preferential access was provided to a client or clients of Brown Rudnick with whom the firm, and others involved in the various meetings over previous weeks and months, had a commercial relationship. The reference to the release from personal guarantees for certain borrowers who cooperated also echoed the pleas of developer Paddy Kearney to Peter Robinson. Robinson had publicly expressed his concern about the threat to the NI property market and, more importantly, to certain developers if NAMA or any other investor called in their loans and personal guarantees, including some who were supporters of the DUP or, as in Kearney's case, of himself.

Chapter 12 ~

COMFORTING THE AFFLICTED

To coincide with the publication of NAMA's 2012 annual report in late May 2013, Daly and McDonagh made themselves available for some media interviews armed with impressive statistics to show that the agency was not just meeting its targets but exceeding them and defying the scepticism of some critics surrounding the work of NAMA.

Daly claimed that about 4,000 residential properties had been identified for social housing, although he did not reveal the disappointing uptake from local authorities around the country who were not impressed by the quality of houses and apartments, many unfinished and in unsuitable locations, on offer from the agency.

He mentioned some 'big-ticket transactions' that the agency had recently closed, including, Ciaran Hancock wrote in the *Irish Times*, 'the sale of its one-third interest in the landmark Citi Tower in London's Canary Wharf for about £333 million; and the €195 million for its Project Aspen portfolio in Ireland to a joint venture vehicle in which NAMA will hold a 20 per cent share'.

Project Aspen comprised loans relating to developer David Courtney which was sold earlier that month for a reported €200 million to a consortium led by US fund Starwood Capital and including Dublin firm Key Capital and UK-based Catalyst Capital. NAMA was to retain a 20 per cent share in the project, which included the Garda offices on Harcourt Street in Dublin, a building used by Davy Stockbrokers in Dawson Street, four Superquinn stores, including in the upmarket city suburbs of Ranelagh and Rathgar, sites in the IFSC, and Carrickmines Retail Park in south Dublin.

The portfolio had a par value of €810 million and was the largest sale in Ireland by the agency since its formation, with the new owners paying under 25 cents in the euro according to media reports, although this return to NAMA was stretched over five years. Announcing the deal through Gordon PR, the agency said:

Under the terms of the agreement, NAMA will sell the loan portfolio to the new joint venture entity, which will be 20% owned by NAMA and 80% owned by a consortium led by Starwood. … NAMA will provide a senior secured loan (vendor finance) to the joint venture, with an initial loan to value of less than 60%. The loan will carry a commercial rate of interest, and is expected to be repaid within five years.

Controversially, the consortium retained Courtney to assist with the 'period around the transition of ownership' although, the agency insisted, he would not be participating in the sale. This led to further questions concerning the involvement of borrowers in loan sales, which was expressly forbidden under NAMA rules of engagement.

One sceptic writing on the NWL blog questioned the methodology employed by the agency, asking

> why NAMA is actually disposing of these loans. It is providing most of the funding and retaining a 20% interest. Why doesn't the National Asset Management Agency act like an agency and manage its own assets. Why should a US investment group be able to generate a better return than NAMA? Of course, it is joined by local asset managers, Key Capital, but is this transaction an admission by NAMA that its asset management skills are inferior to those of a relatively small Dublin asset manager? There will also be some questioning as to the involvement of David Courtney himself in the sale.

In the Dáil, finance minister Michael Noonan was indeed questioned on this very point, with Sinn Féin's Pearse Doherty arguing that the NAMA rules state that while borrowers may cooperate with potential buyers, they can only do so as long as it is not 'during the sales process'. Doherty asked Noonan whether he was 'concerned that the borrower may derive a benefit from providing pre-sale advice to certain bidders'.

The minister replied that he was

> advised by NAMA that it cannot preclude market participants from approaching debtors to discuss their property assets or to indicate potential interest in acquiring either properties or loans. Nor can NAMA preclude debtors from engaging with such potential purchasers. To do either would be counter-productive and could stifle normal commercial discussions in the property market and in particular could discourage international investors from exploring acquisition possibilities in Ireland. However, NAMA has very clear rules regarding the open marketing of loans or of properties on which it holds security.

The exchange was significant in that Noonan was ensuring how NAMA, at least under his watch, would interpret its own rules and the definition of what constituted the boundaries of the 'sales process', and laying down a marker on behalf of the government and the agency that he would not put up unnecessary obstacles that might 'discourage international investors from exploring acquisition possibilities in Ireland'. As more vulture funds circled the distressed but now slowly recovering property market, this first major sale of loans in Ireland paved the way for even bigger disposals of asset bundles that only the wealthiest of global investors could afford.

Explaining the logic of this approach, Daly told the *Irish Times* that the joint venture approach, with NAMA putting up the vendor finance and retaining a stake in the process, was likely to be repeated in the future. He also declined to confirm the amount of public money involved in either the €1 billion Citi Tower deal or Project Aspen, insisting that NAMA did not intend to 'reveal its hand' in these transactions, despite the clamour that the agency should be more transparent. 'Everybody thinks NAMA should reveal its hand. I can understand this ... it is taxpayers' money we're dealing with and we are a public entity. But we are a public body that is required to deal commercially for the best return of taxpayers.'

While earlier disposals of loan portfolios had included the cream of agency-controlled assets in the UK, Daly did not accept the suggestion that the agency was left with bundles of distressed assets in Ireland that would be offloaded at any price. He was not going to be sucked in by big funds claiming to have billions at their disposal and ready to do quick deals which would not be to the benefit of the Irish people. 'We're well used to people telling us that they have billions and they want to come in and buy this, that and the other from us. The reality is that they want to buy it at a price that would be simply a huge and unforgivable loss to the Irish taxpayer.'

Daly argued that the NAMA portfolio in Ireland was a lot better than many people thought and cited its holdings in the Dublin Docklands as a prime example.

The agency, he said, had approved €800 million in investment with €500 million already drawn down, including for the expansion of shopping centres in Drogheda and north Dublin and residential apartment blocks in south Dublin. And, of course, the agency was to take on any residual loans from the €26 billion IBRC loan book that the special liquidator, Kieran Wallace, could not sell by the end of 2013. The latest data showed that 36 per cent of the remaining NAMA portfolio was based in Dublin with 21 per cent in London, 18 per cent in the rest of the Republic, 12 per cent in other parts of Britain, 3 per cent in Northern Ireland, and 10 per cent in other parts of the world.

McDonagh told the media that NAMA had approved €11.7 billion of asset sales including €4 billion during 2012, with another €2 billion in the pipeline. Eighty per cent of the sales had taken place in Britain, with almost two-thirds in London, including the estimated £1 billion secured recently for Citi Tower in Canary Wharf from an investor based in the Middle East. NAMA had retained a one-third share in the sale, which related to loans previously held by Derek Quinlan and English lawyer, Glenn Maud.

The annual report said that the agency was paying particular attention to the Dublin Docklands, where it held significant holdings and was attracting the interest of tech giants such as Google and Facebook.

Daly rejected the suggestion that NAMA was sitting on a lot of dud properties and noted that it would make €4 billion available in Ireland for capital investment and vendor finance to help stimulate the market out to 2016.

> As recovery comes, and NAMA contributes to that recovery, the prospects for our Irish assets will be much, much brighter. They will become quite quickly the low-hanging fruits of the future.

Within weeks NAMA announced its intention to invest £15 million to complete an office and leisure complex development in Lanyon Place in Belfast, close to the Waterfront Hall conference and entertainment venue. The agency was also providing £9 million to fund the 95-unit housing development in Millmount, in Dundonald, close to Belfast, Daly told a delegation of the Northern Ireland Assembly and Business Trust at a meeting in Dublin in June 2013. He said that the agency had already approved £87 million in asset sales in Northern Ireland.

Meanwhile, the agency was chasing some of the bigger fish in the Republic whom, its executives believed, were not playing by its rulebook. These included Sean Dunne, who had flown to the US in 2010 to avoid his multiple debt repayments – including €250 million to NAMA – and where he had sought bankruptcy. In early June 2013, NAMA joined the efforts of Ulster Bank, also owed €250 million by Dunne since it backed his outlandish purchase of the Jury's site in Ballsbridge before the crash, and which was seeking to have the former developer declared bankrupt in Ireland as well as in the US. The US court-appointed trustee Richard Coan accused Dunne of failing to produce documents as required by law, including details of payments he or his wife, Gayle Killilea, had received in the two months before he filed for bankruptcy.

Dunne had also failed to turn up at a recent meeting of his creditors who travelled to the US to meet him, Coan told the bankruptcy court in Bridgeport, Connecticut, over which Judge Alan Shiff presided, and was refusing to cooperate until the court in Dublin ruled on the application by Ulster Bank to make him bankrupt in Ireland. With characteristic defiance, Dunne claimed that he had sought the US bankruptcy as a 'shield' and not a 'sword', as Ulster Bank claimed, and that NAMA's attempt to reverse what it claimed were fraudulent asset transfers to his wife was 'ill-conceived'. He told the court that he looked forward to facing NAMA chief executive Brendan McDonagh in a US court. He said that it would be unfair and a 'manifest error' if he were to be declared bankrupt in Ireland, where it would take him 12 years to have the bankruptcy discharged.

Ulster Bank had begun Irish bankruptcy proceedings against the developer in February 2013, six weeks before he filed for the same process in the US in a move his main creditors believed was an attempt to evade legal action in Dublin. They were seeking to recover assets which he was believed to have in Ireland, South Africa, Switzerland and possibly in England. Dunne claimed that he had $15 in his bank account and less than $1,000 in cash and was facing claims against him for £1 billion by his Irish creditors. After hearing more than two hours of opposing arguments, Judge Shiff granted the motion allowing Ulster Bank to continue with its legal bid to make Dunne bankrupt in Ireland.

At the lower end of the debt league table, NAMA also pursued Galway developer and hotelier Michael Finn and his wife Claire, whom it accused of investing some €600,000 in a car resale business and transferring assets to their children while they were insolvent with debts to the agency of €108 million. Finn, who was involved in the Spanish Arch and House hotels in Galway City, had loans from Anglo and AIB transferred to NAMA in 2010. He had failed to hand over title deeds to property which had been transferred or to give the agency rental monies from properties it now controlled to pay down their debt. An application by NAMA to have the case fast-tracked in the Commercial Court was granted by Judge Peter Kelly in mid-June 2013.

While NAMA was chasing some debtors 'to the ends of the earth', or at least as far as the US in the case of the 'Dunner', it was also facilitating the massive transfer of property ownership from Irish borrowers to private equity, mainly US investors with vast funds at their disposal. Among the larger investors were Kennedy Wilson, which was purchasing land and buildings in Dublin, including the State Street building in the Docklands for €108 million, the Gasworks complex in Dublin 4 and the huge Clancy Barracks site on the edge of the Liffey near Kilmainham in Dublin 8. While Kennedy Wilson insisted it was in for the long haul, others from the US, Israel, Malaysia, Singapore, Germany, Russia and China were eyeing up office buildings, hotels, retail and apartment blocks, in search of bargains that could be flipped for a healthy return within a few years, or months in some cases. The Burlington Hotel, purchased by Bernard McNamara for €288 million in 2007, was acquired by the giant US Blackstone Group for just €67 million less than five years later, while South African investor Beatrice Tollman of the Red Carnation Hotels group took over the historic Ashford Castle in Cong, County Mayo, for a steal at €20 million in May 2013. This was less than half the €50 million paid out by Galway developer Gerry Barrett for the castle in 2007 before some of his loans were transferred to NAMA. The Bank of Scotland (Ireland) appointed a receiver over the property in 2011.

Not everyone was elated at what the *Irish Times* benignly described in an editorial as the 'globalisation of Irish property assets', but for real estate and other property agents and managers it proved something of a bonanza after years of doom and gloom in the market, among them Jones Lang LaSalle.

'What's interesting is that this is really the first time that there has been serious international buying in the Irish market,' Jones Lang LaSalle managing director John Moran told the *Irish Times*. Moran continued:

> The Irish market traditionally was left to the Irish institutions, developers or property companies, and it is probably the first time we've seen a real significant sea change of ownership in the market. ... The way the market tends to work is the private equity guys come in first. They inject liquidity into the market by starting to trade as is happening at the moment and then, as that evolves, you tend to get a second wave of investors come in which would be the institutional investors, people with slightly lower return requirements than private equity and they tend to buy up what the private equity guys create.

The extent to which this property dealing enriched a new elite of asset managers and surveyors, valuers and auctioneers obtaining lucrative work from NAMA was also evident from the emergence of new companies exclusively built around the servicing needs of foreign investment capital. The outsourcing of this work by NAMA also meant that the agency was not always in a position to monitor transactions of properties it put on the market for sale across the country or abroad. The scale of the property transfers over a relatively short space of time inevitably generated controversy and allegations of conflicts of interest involving NAMA staff and also the agents they hired to dispose of assets.

Frank Daly's upbeat comments at the launch of the annual report about the prospects for the Dublin Docklands were confirmed when the agency announced its first major transaction using its Qualified Investor Fund (QIF) vehicle authorised by the Central Bank in early July. Oaktree Capital Management, based in Los Angeles in the US, joined up with Irish construction firm Bennett and

NAMA in the development of lands in the south docks. 'The South Docks Fund,' said NAMA, 'is a sub-fund of Targeted Investment Opportunities PLC, an umbrella fund with segregated limited liability between sub-funds of which Oaktree is the investment manager and Bennett Property Limited is the property manager. NAMA will be a minority shareholder in the sub-fund.' With $78 billion in assets under its management, Oaktree was the first global fund to avail of the QIF investment vehicle announced by NAMA executives earlier in the year.

QIFs had been the subject of some debate when first identified as suited to the NAMA investment strategy by agency executives over preceding months, not least because they can be authorised by the Central Bank within 24 hours and 'are exempt from Irish tax on its income and gains, irrespective of where its investors reside', as explained by investment advisors SEI. 'No withholding taxes apply on income distributions of redemption payments made by a QIF to non-Irish resident investors.'

This tax-efficient and speedy process allowed NAMA to enter agreements with global hedge funds that wished to move on distressed real estate assets in Ireland in a speedy and tax-efficient fashion once the minimum funding capabilities were established. Explaining how amendments to legislation since 2010 had made the Irish QIFs more flexible and attractive to hedge funds interested in the 'redomiciliation of previously unregulated funds to Ireland', law firm Mathesons described how the 'new provisions facilitate a straightforward migration process to Ireland for investment funds from the Cayman Islands, British Virgin Islands, Jersey, Guernsey, Bermuda and the Isle of Man'.

Unsurprisingly, the new scheme aimed at global investors was not without its critics. A five-year exemption from withholding tax was availed of by the so-called vulture funds who placed the billions of Irish property assets they were acquiring into tax-friendly QIFs or their 'first cousin', the Irish Collective Asset-management Vehicles. The generous exemptions for the funds were spearheaded by the Department of Finance and its secretary general John Moran, who along with finance minister Noonan was keen to ensure that every possible obstacle to wholesale acquisition by the global investment community of distressed assets was removed. The NAMA executives were keen to avail of the legislation as it meant that their task of clearing their books of billions in bad loans would be made easier. However, it would be some time before the full implications of these tax exemptions would emerge.

Chapter 13 ～

THE DEPARTURE LOUNGE

The haemorrhage of staff disclosed by the agency in its spring annual report continued into the autumn and became the subject of some discussion when its senior executives met with the Public Accounts Committee (PAC) in late September 2013. By then the list from the departure lounge had lengthened and even the figure of a 10 per cent annual turnover since 2010 was looking somewhat hopeful as the resignation letters piled up. Of 250 people hired since its formation, some 25 had left in the months leading up to the drafting of the report, and what concerned management was not only the number but the seniority, experience and acquired knowledge of those jumping ship into the willing arms of the global property and asset management funds looking for deals in a recovering domestic market. Ostensibly, the cuts in pay and pension entitlements in the public service and the fixed-term contract arrangements under which they worked, for average annual salaries of €100,000, were the reasons for the exodus but it was evident that a number of recent defectors were headhunted.

Senior asset recovery manager Paul Hennigan joined Prime London Partners, a UK firm that was seeking attractive property investments in Ireland. A minor political stir erupted when a Labour Party senator, Lorraine Higgins, complained that the UK fund Hennigan was joining had paid close to £150 million (€172.3 million) to NAMA only two years earlier when it purchased luxury office buildings at 11–12 St James Square in London. The buildings were transferred to the agency as part of the property portfolio of Dublin firm D2 Private. The revelation by the *Sunday Independent* that Hennigan had been managing the D2 assets when they were sold to Prime London Partners, acting for a Malaysian wealth fund, prompted the remarks by Galway-based Senator Higgins.

Higgins complained to finance minister Michael Noonan that Hennigan had left a threatening message on her constituency office phone demanding that she remove offensive comments about him on her website. She claimed he had tried to 'silence' her with his message. 'Would you please arrange for the removal of the highly offensive statement you have on your website? Unfortunately, you obviously have no understanding of the background to this. I might have to take legal matters [*sic*] into the insinuations you are making,' Mr Hennigan's voicemail said. Higgins said that she had concerns over the movement of former NAMA officials to firms that could have an interest in acquiring assets and loans under the control of the agency.

Noonan reminded her that all past and present employees of NAMA were subject to the provisions of the Official Secrets Act and the NTMA and NAMA Acts, which prohibited them from disclosing any of the confidential information they had handled at the agency. He said that the 'best defence against such possible abuse or misuse of information is to ensure, as NAMA does, that assets are openly marketed and subject to competitive sales processes.'

Hennigan later responded to Higgins with an angry rebuttal in the *Sunday Independent*:

> Having dedicated myself to NAMA and the taxpayer for three years, despite the personal and financial cost to me and my family, it is grossly unfair, insulting and deeply offensive that a member of our Oireachtas, albeit unelected, attributes scandal to my ongoing contractual obligations to NAMA and my current employment – both of which she quite clearly knows nothing about. In my view, it is this type of manufactured and false hysteria that is preventing NAMA retaining or attracting staff, ultimately to the detriment of the taxpayer.

Hennigan did not mention a number of other factors which may have prompted his departure, including the controversy he sparked when he took to the witness box a year previous in the ongoing and intense legal battle between Paddy McKillen and identical twins David and Frederick Barclay over control of the Maybourne Hotel Group in London. Hennigan had been accused of providing information he had acquired through his work with NAMA to the Barclays, much to the annoyance of McKillen, who believed that the agency had sought to undermine him at every turn in order to grab the cream of his performing assets. Hennigan strongly defended his relationship and correspondence with the Barclays and their executive, Richard Faber, arguing in court that his and NAMA's behaviour was justified by the need to ensure that the agency could recover the full amount of the debt owed to it by Coroin, the property vehicle originally established to take over the London hotel group.

'NAMA believed with justification that the Barclay brothers' offer would be the only time that it could reasonably expect to be offered the full amount for the Coroin debt,' Hennigan told the court in May 2012. The Barclays bought the Coroin debts of more than €600 million in September 2011. As portfolio manager over the AIB loans of Avestus and one of its directors, Thomas Dowd, Hennigan had also been involved with the now disgraced Enda Farrell in the acquisition of Sunday's Well, the house in Lucan purchased for 10 per cent of its original price. Farrell had also named Hennigan as one of the NAMA officials who had passed information to third parties, and while this had not yet emerged publicly due to the continuing Garda investigation, Hennigan was aware that his role in the house purchase had been outlined in an early admission by his former colleague.

Hennigan was followed out the door by Alison Rohan, who departed in September 2013, just as McDonagh, Daly and her immediate boss, John Mulcahy, briefed the PAC on the annual report.

Rohan was seen as close to Mulcahy, who was friendly with her father, the successful businessman and developer Ken Rohan. She left to join Kennedy Wilson, which had emerged as the largest single purchaser of Irish real estate assets in the recent past. In May 2013, it paid out just over €300 million for the former Treasury-owned Opera House portfolio including the Stillorgan Shopping Centre, KPMG's offices on St Stephen's Green and the Bank of Ireland building on Mespil Road in Dublin 4. At NAMA, Rohan had worked on the property portfolio of the Ballymore Group. Before NAMA, she worked for D2 Private, the property firm established by Deirdre Foley and David Arnold.

Addressing the PAC on the issue of the numbers quitting the agency, McDonagh confirmed that 50 staff had left in the previous two years, including to international property and equity firms setting up in Ireland, and to London. Responding to Labour TD Derek Nolan, who asked about potential conflicts of interest of staff with insider information joining private investors, McDonagh repeated the standard line that the 'best way of ensuring no one can steal a march on anybody else is to ensure that all the assets are openly marketed, in so far as it is practicable'. He said that anyone leaving NAMA had to give three months' notice and that appropriate mechanisms were in place to deal with anyone 'using information inappropriately'. However, McDonagh confirmed that it was planned to increase the notice period which NAMA staff were required to give before leaving the agency from three to six months.

McDonagh insisted that only one of 'the senior executive team' agency had left NAMA since its inception. He was referring to Graham Emmett, who had left the agency in 2012 and joined Longbow in London amid some controversy. The NAMA chief executive declined to get into further discussion about former staff, including more recent, high-profile departures. Pressed by Mary Lou McDonald on whether a 12-month cooling off period should be introduced for departing staff before they take up new jobs in the wider property industry, Daly intervened: 'It is almost as if there were evidence that people had abused their positions. That is not the case,' he said, repeating the point made by the chief executive about the consequences of breaching the Official Secrets, NTMA or NAMA legislation. Daly continued:

> I do not believe they are being poached for any so-called insider knowledge they might have or any use they might make of information relating to debtors that they gained in NAMA. ...
>
> If there were a cooling-off period of 12 months, for example, one could not interfere with somebody's right to work without actually paying him during the period in question.

He said that tax payers might not appreciate the agency rewarding people for sitting at home for 12 months. In a wide-ranging session, the NAMA executives were challenged on two other questions that had considerable significance for its work and which motivated its conduct. The first concerned the role of the troika in directing the work of the agency and setting targets for it, including the task of selling its most valuable overseas assets, in order to achieve a requirement of paying off 25 per cent of its debt, or €7.5 billion, by the end of 2013.

McDonagh said in reply to Labour's Derek Nolan:

> Within a few months of setting that target, the troika arrived here [late 2010] and adopted that target. It said we had to meet that and had to generate the amount of money required to pay off 25% of the debt by end 2013, whether we were on target towards achieving that or not. The question was where we could get that money and the best place to get it was from the overseas markets where we had assets.

Pursued by Fine Gael TD Eoghan Murphy, McDonagh clarified the exact role of the troika in directing or influencing the targets for debt repayment by the agency, with a plan to clear 50 per cent by 2016 and 80 per cent by 2018. Murphy asked if the troika set those targets.

'It is aware of them,' replied McDonagh

'Did the troika set them?' asked Murphy, again.

'No. It is like the Government dealing with the troika. The conditionality is up to the end of 2013. If there is to be future conditionality, I am sure it will form part of that,' replied McDonagh.

Going to the heart of the matter which had been central to the government's and NAMA's explanation for its rapid disposal of its most valuable assets over the previous three years, Murphy asked whether the troika was dictating the sale by NAMA of overseas assets ahead of Irish assets.

McDonagh replied: 'No, that was set by the NAMA board. Part of the troika's mission over the last three years has been to examine whether NAMA has been following the correct strategy and it has been satisfied that we have been following the correct strategy because we are generating the cash to pay back the debt.'

'Was it directing the board in any way?' asked Murphy.

'No,' said McDonagh.

'Not at all?' asked Murphy.

'No. I am sure if the board was not pursuing the correct strategy and generating cash quickly enough it would have words with the Minister,' McDonagh explained.

'So it reserves the right to try to direct the board but has not done so?' asked Murphy, still uncertain about the relationship between NAMA and the troika.

McDonagh explained that the minister can issue directions to the board of NAMA and that the Department of Finance reports back to the troika. The CEO said that he had quarterly meetings with the troika to discuss 'strategies and whether we are generating cash sufficiently quickly' and 'to update it on our progress towards meeting the target'. This explanation of NAMA's autonomy when it came to its targets for disposal may have come as a surprise to those who had interpreted previous comments in this regard by both the minister and the agency as implying that it was under the cosh of the troika. Many may also have been taken aback by McDonagh's explanation to the PAC that NAMA, as a state body, also includes a special purpose vehicle (SPV) which keeps the 'organisation off-balance sheet for Government debt purposes'.

National Asset Management Agency Investment Ltd (NAMAIL), he said, was capitalised with equity of €100 million, of which €51 million came from private investors and €49 million from NAMA. Asked by Fine Gael TD Kieran O'Donnell for the identity of the private investors, McDonagh explained: 'The three private investors are New Ireland Assurance, Prescient Investors – formerly AIB Investment Managers – and Walbrook Investments which bought Irish Life's shareholding last year.'

New Ireland was a member of the Bank of Ireland Group while Walbrook was a subsidiary of UK investment firm Walbrook Capital. The company, which in October 2012 acquired the 17 per cent share in NAMAIL previously held by Irish Life, was formed by former Barclay's bankers Michael Keeley, Geoff Broomhead and Simon Haworth. Before setting up Walbrook in 2011, Keeley ran a controversial Cayman Islands based scheme called Protium, which Barclay's used to take $12.3 billion of toxic assets from its balance sheet. After the scheme was criticised for 'pushing the envelope too far' by UK bank supervisor Andrew Bailey, the bank dissolved the company and brought back the distressed assets onto its balance sheet in 2011. Keeley had also been a member of Barclay's 'structured capital markets' team, which specialised in 'tax arbitrage and mitigation', criticised by Bailey for its 'buccaneering culture' before it too was dissolved in the wake of the Libor scandal in the UK in early 2013. The other shareholder, Prescient Investors, was formerly AIB Investment Managers before it was taken over by a South African-based firm in mid-2012. Two months after the PAC discussed NAMAIL, Prescient was acquired by Davy, Ireland's largest stockbrokers. Prescient continued to operate in Ireland through its subsidiary, Stadia Fund Managers.

McDonagh also confirmed to the PAC that the agency had offered 4,000 homes to local authorities for social housing, although campaigners had complained that less than half that number had been accepted as suitable by councils across the country, that even fewer had been completed and made available to families in need and that the number offered was minuscule compared to the housing and homeless crisis facing the country.

The bottom line, however, was that the agency had generated €9.2 billon from the sale of assets, with 80 per cent made from UK, mainly London, asset disposals, and €4 billion in cash from lettings. It was on course, said the executives, to raise the €30 billion it was expected to deliver by the time it wrapped up in 2020 or thereabouts.

The session may have been tougher than previous occasions as the agency faced more difficult and mounting challenges on a number of fronts, not least the loss of senior and experienced staff. Addressing the International Corporate Restructuring Summit in Dublin's Convention Centre the day after the Oireachtas exchanges, the head of asset management, John Mulcahy, referred to some of the challenges faced by the agency, among them what it had done with the unfinished headquarters of the defunct Anglo Irish bank on the north side of the Liffey quays in the Docklands.

'We sold the old Anglo headquarters to the Central Bank on the basis that every film crew that came to Dublin wanted to shoot the Anglo building. It was like a burnt-out tank on the road to Kuwait as a symbol of our failure,' said Mulcahy to his bemused audience of financiers, bankers and property suits. 'We decided we had to get this bloody thing off our stocks. So we sold it to the Central Bank and I thought they would have started work by now but they seem to have got a puncture somewhere along the way.'

Only days earlier he had bemoaned, again, what he described as the 'unbelievable challenge' of retaining staff at the agency.

The only thing I would worry about for NAMA will be how difficult it will be for us, over the next couple of years, to retain the fantastic people that work for NAMA. That's an unbelievable challenge for us and I don't have the answer to it.

He obviously had one answer in mind when he announced, unexpectedly, less than three weeks after the speech that he was to retire as a board member and head of asset management with effect from the end of February, in just over four months' time.

If anyone was leaving with a wealth of knowledge and inside information from NAMA it was the chartered surveyor who was among its architects and whose influence had marked the progress of the agency since its formation in December 2009. He was appointed its first head of portfolio management in the same month, having been for over a year an advisor on secondment from Jones Lang LaSalle. In March 2012, he was appointed to the NAMA board and a month later was made head of asset management at the agency, powerful roles that placed him at the very centre of the operation, familiar with its complex property portfolios, their value and disposal strategies. His departure was a major blow to the executives he was leaving behind, even if the public tributes were less than detailed about his role.

'John has made an enormous contribution to the development of NAMA over the past four years. On behalf of the Board, I wish to thank him for his contribution and for the insight, expertise and sound judgement that he brought to his work. We will very much miss him, both personally and professionally,' said the chairman, Frank Daly. Brendan McDonagh was a little more effusive about his right-hand man:

John was a pivotal presence both before and since the establishment of NAMA. It would have been very much more difficult to deal with the scale of the challenge that we faced four years ago without the undoubted expertise of John who was, and is, widely respected in the property business. His deep understanding of the property markets, domestically and internationally, coupled with his innate calmness, wit, wisdom and guidance were immense assets to NAMA and to me personally. We wish him a long and fulfilling retirement.

He was replaced by long-time agency executive, Mary Birmingham. She had previously worked as a surveyor for Irish Life and then as Project Manager with Pizarro Developments, which was planning a €2 billion town centre in Bray before the crash scuppered the project.

Within weeks of the announcement, Mulcahy was offering his advice on the challenges facing the residential and commercial property markets, and in late

October told the Society of Chartered Surveyors that a housing shortage was imminent unless 20,000 homes were delivered each year to meet demand in urban areas. He blamed a regulatory system which 'contrives to make it a slow process', while suggesting that NAMA had up to 10,000 units in its portfolio that could potentially help to ease the building pressures. He warned that price 'peaks and bubbles' emerging in some parts of the city meant that it could be too late for 'evasive action' to regain stability in the Dublin housing market. He blamed delays in getting house-building programmes underway on the public planning and zoning process, a claim that was quickly rejected by housing minister Jan O'Sullivan as a 'partial analysis'. It was also one which appeared to remove responsibility from NAMA for its abject failure to provide a significant number of affordable and suitable homes from its huge property bank. Many of those offered for social housing to local authorities were deemed to be in need of thorough refurbishment and in the wrong locations while large swathes of finished residential bundles on its distressed loan book were being sold to private funds at knock-down values.

According to Mulcahy, NAMA would prefer to sell assets to Irish investors who were in for the long haul rather than to foreign wholesalers whose only interest was to turn a quick profit, and he welcomed the emergence of the REIT model since amendments had been made in the budget for 2013 a year previous. He cited the establishment of Green REIT as an example of the private sector seizing the opportunity which, he said, NAMA would otherwise have done.

REITs, he said, are 'a terrific idea because they raise capital and that capital can invest in Ireland'. Turning to the chairman of the REITs Forum, Bill Nowlan of WK Nowlan, Mulcahy mischievously asked how plans for a second Irish REIT were coming along. Only three months earlier, Nowlan had welcomed the flotation of the first Irish REIT by Green Property, describing it as 'great news for the Irish property industry as it marks the continuing re-professionalisation of the commercial property sector following its invasion (and destruction) during the era of loose money from Anglo Bank and so on'.

Writing in the *Irish Times*, Nowlan explained:

To date, NAMA and IPUT (Irish Property Unit Trust) are the only companies with an existing portfolio suitable for a REIT – and they don't seem to be rushing into this space. Green is taking a sensible course in the circumstances.

IPUT, with a portfolio of over €250 million in commercial properties, was a major owner of rental commercial property in the city and, with Green, was aiming to attract long-term equity investment from overseas.

Chapter 14 ⌁

THE CLOCKWORK CASH MACHINE

It did not take long for the new kid on the block to emerge: it was announced in late November 2013 that Hibernia REIT was to float on the Dublin and London stock exchanges and hoped to raise up to €350 million with which to purchase and rent out properties. Neither did it come as a total surprise that its main drivers included Kevin Nowlan, the senior portfolio manager at NAMA who had left the agency the previous February to re-join WK Nowlan.

For several months, Kevin Nowlan and US-based Frank Kenny, founder of the Willett Group, had been seeking potential investors for the new REIT. Among the first to come on board was George Soros, who took an 8.22 per cent stake in Hibernia REIT through his Quantum Fund. Others included Moore Capital, owned by Wall Street investor Louis Bacon, while another giant US fund, CREF, also took a share in the new property vehicle.

Another stakeholder, with some $125 billion in assets under its management, Putnam Investments was not unfamiliar with the Irish property market, having managed property investments for the NPRF since the early 2000s. Among those who advised the NPRF on its property portfolio from that period was John Mulcahy, who was on the fund's property advisory committee for many years. During his tenure from 2004 to 2014 the NPRF dramatically increased exposure to global property investments from €50 million to over €1 billion.

It was during his years on the advisory group that Mulcahy came in contact with Enda Farrell, who worked with the NPRF until the formation of NAMA in 2009. Mulcahy then became his boss as head of asset management. Another long-time member of the NPRF's property advisory group was US banker Barden Gale, who was among those to whom Farrell provided confidential NAMA information after he resigned from the agency in early 2012.

Nowlan and Kenny invited some of Ireland's most prominent business figures to join the board of Hibernia as non-executive directors, including former Aer Lingus chairman Colm Barrington, and Stewart Harrington, an experienced property consultant, a former partner in Jones Lang Wooton and founding partner of Harrington Bannon surveyors as well as non-executive director of Argentum Homes. Former KPMG chief executive and *Irish Times* non-executive director Terence O'Rourke was also appointed a non-executive director. Danny Kitchen, the man appointed by the late Brian Lenihan to chair the dysfunctional Irish Nationwide Building Society in 2009, following the banking collapse, became the chairman of Hibernia REIT.

Within four months of announcing his decision to leave NAMA, in April 2014 John Mulcahy became chairman of IPUT, the property company that Bill Nowlan had, just weeks earlier, suggested was ideally placed to develop the REIT model in Ireland, given the portfolio of rental commercial properties under its ownership. Mulcahy's return to the private sector was not universally welcomed, given his previous and highly sensitive position in NAMA, but it followed a pattern that was all too familiar to critics and supporters of the agency alike.

Belfast man Kitchen, who had previously worked with Green Property chief Stephen Vernon, was an experienced player in banking and property and had participated in some 60 investor meetings with Kevin and Bill Nowlan and Frank Kenny in the promotion of Hibernia REIT before it launched.

He described to the *Irish Times* how international funds saw Ireland as the 'golden child of the recovery'.

They are saying, 'How can I play this?' And there is not that many ways. They can buy Bank of Ireland but, other than that, the two REITs [Green and Hibernia REITs] are the obvious way to do it. The first sell was to convince them on the Irish property story. The second thing was the credibility of the management team. The third thing was how quickly can you get the money out. Those guys can deploy that cash elsewhere, so they need you to be convinced that money can be deployed pretty quickly. Really, what you want though, is a long-term income play that is going to deliver 6, 7, 8 per cent per annum, a clockwork cash machine. Initially, the idea is to build up a reasonably well-balanced portfolio between offices, retail and distribution sheds.

If the model was reasonably simple, it depended, according to Kitchen, on knowing when the property market was going to recover sufficiently to attract new investment in building offices and apartment blocks. In the meantime, he said, 'the vast majority of property in Dublin is owned or controlled by people who don't really want it – NAMA, the banks. That gives you a great pool of potential assets to buy.'

I have never seen a market where so many people are trying to get out of real estate. It gives you a great opportunity to buy a really good property portfolio. The big challenge will be deployment of the money we raised.

Hibernia was firmly focused on the Dublin office market. 'The rest of the country is going to struggle,' said Kitchen. 'When is the earliest you can conceivably see a new building coming out of the ground? It is probably [20]17. It is straightforward: if there is more demand than supply, then rents are going to go up.'

The biggest player in the market, was of course, NAMA, which was in the business of offloading billions of euro in property loans and assets from its balance sheet, and whose operations and strategies were familiar to the Hibernia REIT founders and to Kevin Nowlan in particular. As the portfolio manager overseeing the distressed property portfolio of Sean Dunne while at NAMA, Nowlan was called to give evidence in a US court during the long-running litigation between the developer and the agency and other creditors, on both sides of the Atlantic. During hearings in Connecticut in February 2013, Nowlan denied that he had leaked information to the media concerning NAMA's hiring of a private detective agency, Kroll, to investigate Dunne and his alleged hidden assets around the world, as reported by journalist Tom Lyons in the *Sunday Times* in July 2011. Nowlan also denied he was the source of a story in the same newspaper in March 2011 about the expected appointment of Grant Thornton as receiver over Dunne's assets. Nowlan insisted that the decision on which debtor was to be put into receivership was one for the credit committee of NAMA, which included at the time Graham Emmett, Ronnie Hanna, John Mulcahy and Brendan McDonagh, as well as board members Michael Connolly and Peter Stewart. He said that the committee made the ultimate decision about Dunne's receivership on foot of the recommendation by the portfolio management team, which he headed. He said that the chairman of the credit committee did not call for a vote but read the 'feel of the room' when it came to its decision.

In a subsequent complaint to the GBFI in 2014, Dunne alleged that Nowlan and his US-based partner in Hibernia REIT, Frank Kenny, had discussed Dunne's business activities in the US over a year prior to the launch of Hibernia REIT. This was evident in an email from Kenny to Nowlan which was provided to Dunne's lawyers by NAMA during the discovery process in the US litigation. In the correspondence, Kenny wrote to Nowlan to say that he had heard that Dunne had bid for a $12 million site in Rye, New York, and that the former developer was running a $20–30 million business in the US. Both claims were untrue, Dunne insisted. Immediately after the email exchange, in July 2011, NAMA moved on Dunne's assets and appointed Grant Thornton as receivers.

In December 2013, Nowlan told *Property Week* magazine that Hibernia REIT was interested in purchasing the NAMA portfolios Project Holly, comprising a loan book worth €300 million built by developer Sean Reilly, and Project Platinum, which included city centre office blocks previously owned by Sean Dunne.

'There are no restrictions on me [bidding for NAMA assets],' Nowlan said. 'NAMA competitively tenders everything, so I am at no advantage.'

Frank Kenny emigrated to the US in the early 1980s to head up the interests of the Irish builders, Durkans, having previously worked with Bill Nowlan in Irish Life. He formed the Willett Companies LLC in Rye, New York, in the early 1990s. The chartered surveyor was made a senior advisor of Hibernia while maintaining his office and retail property company in the US.

As demand for office accommodation grew in Dublin along with signs of corporate economic recovery, the REITs were ideally placed and sufficiently financed to take over commercial assets coming on the market, including from NAMA and the IBRC, before construction activity resumed to anything like pre-crisis levels in the city or across the country.

The decision by the government in February 2013 to appoint a special liquidator to the IBRC, which had taken over the distressed loan books of Anglo Irish Bank and the Irish Nationwide Building Society, had considerable implications for NAMA. The agency had been asked to acquire any loans which were unsold by the liquidator Kieran Wallace following a loan valuation and sales process due for completion before the end of the year.

In preparation for this task, which would add up to 50 per cent to NAMA's distressed loan book, the agency appointed two service providers to manage the loan portfolios due to be acquired from the special liquidator.

In September, NAMA announced that it had selected Certus as the preferred bidder to manage the billions in commercial loan portfolios due to be transferred. It also announced that a consortium of Pepper Asset Servicing and Serco was selected as preferred bidder to provide services on the portfolio of personal, mainly residential, mortgages which it was to acquire from the special liquidator with an estimated par value of €1.8 billion. The Sydney-based Pepper group had set up in Ireland as Pepper Finance Corporation (Ireland), trading as Pepper Asset Servicing, in September 2012, and was managing distressed and other mortgages and loans across the country.

NAMA estimated that the IBRC commercial loan portfolio could have a par debt value of up to €22 billion in addition to the personal mortgages. It was a considerable increase in the workload for the agency and it involved setting up another SPV, National Asset Resolution Ltd, as well as taking on about 180 staff, who were familiar with the loan books, under the NTMA umbrella from the former IBRC to help manage their acquisition and disposal.

NAMA was forced to drop the plan to contract Serco when it emerged that the company was under investigation by the UK justice ministry and police following an audit of government contracts obtained by the outsourcing firm. The Serco Group, based in Hook, Hampshire in the UK, had contracts to operate public transport and traffic control, aviation, weapons sales, prisons and schools for the British government and other public and private clients. The controversy erupted in May 2013 when a report by the UK Prison Inspectorate found that up to 60 per cent of inmates in the newly built Thameside jail, which Serco managed near London, were locked up for 24 hours each day.

A report by the *Guardian* newspaper found deep flaws, including the falsification of data and a failure to meet minimum national standards, in Serco's management of an out-of-hours GP service in Cornwall. An official inquiry found that there was a culture of lying and cheating at the company. If that was not bad enough, the UK justice ministry found it had been overcharged by Serco and another contractor by up to £50 million on contracts for the tagging of offenders. Investigators found that one in six tags paid for by the state did not exist, which was a matter of some embarrassment to the department responsible for law and order and to the company.

Following the Thameside prison controversy the company embarked on what it described as 'a series of initiatives' including a 'gangs strategy' and measures to help prisoners with mental health issues. Some people, Serco said, in July 2013, would now be permitted outside their cells 'during the core part of the day'. In relation to the overcharging for their tagging contract Serco said it 'will not tolerate poor practice and behaviour and wherever it is found we will put it right'. It added that UK justice secretary Chris Grayling had said that he had 'no information to confirm dishonesty had taken place' on the part of Serco.

NAMA announced a board decision not to proceed with a planned contract with Serco and said it had 'decided to launch a new tender process for the provision of primary and special services on the residential loans portfolio'.

Capita Asset Services was appointed to assist with the recruitment of staff for NAMA in relation to the loans to be transferred from the IBRC. However, the transfer of the IBRC loans did not proceed. In April 2014, Noonan announced that there was no longer a requirement for NAMA to take on any IBRC loans. He said that the IBRC was expected to repay the agency the €12.9 billion it owed from a promissory note transaction financed by NAMA in early 2013.

Chapter 15 ⌒

TURNING THE CORNER

A s NAMA entered its fifth year of operations, its executives were pleased to pass what they described as their first major milestone with the redemption of €7.5 billion of senior bonds by the end of 2013, leaving some €22 billion outstanding.

'The NAMA Board has set a target of redeeming another €7.5 billion in Senior Bonds by the end of 2016 and its expectation is that all senior debt will be redeemed by 2020,' the agency announced in its end of year statement.

While it was upbeat about its prospects of meeting its target over the next five years or more, the agency was also heading into stormy waters on a number of fronts, some of which were the subject of tense exchanges at a hearing of the PAC on 20 December 2013.

The hearing was precipitated by the emergence of a so-called 'dossier' of information relating to the leak of confidential information by Enda Farrell, which was circulated to certain members of the Oireachtas and raised by Senator Darragh O'Brien in the upper house and by his Fianna Fáil leader, Micheál Martin, in the Dáil just days before Christmas.

The dossier contained information suggesting that details of the financial affairs of Paddy McKillen, among others, had been distributed by Farrell to various commercial interests before and after he left NAMA in early 2012. It was compiled by a private detective, Denis O'Sullivan, who spoke to Farrell, first by telephone in early December 2013 and then at his home in Brussels, and had taken extensive notes of their conversations. Just before O'Sullivan contacted him in Brussels, Farrell had received an unsolicited call from former Fianna Fáil junior minister Conor Lenihan. Lenihan asked Farrell if he would speak to a representative of Paddy McKillen. The former TD for Dublin South-West had worked for a Russian oligarch in Moscow after he retired from politics following the loss of his Dáil seat in 2011, but had since returned home and lived in London and Dublin. He described McKillen as someone badly done by and, according to Farrell, said that the developer was fighting to save 2,000 jobs and deserved every assistance he could get in his battle against powerful corporate and state enemies, including NAMA. Farrell knew Lenihan and his late brother and former finance minister, Brian, from their days growing up in Castleknock and agreed to talk to O'Sullivan. O'Sullivan knew nothing of Lenihan's intervention and said that he had been given Farrell's phone number by Liam Cunningham, a senior executive at McKillen's company, who had received it directly from Farrell several months earlier, in July 2013, after the former NAMA official contacted him.

Denis O'Sulllivan was a retired garda from Fenit in north Kerry who was now working as a private detective advising corporate and other clients. He joined the Garda in 1983 and was among a number of young recruits sent to Ballinamore, County Leitrim, later that year to assist in the search for supermarket executive Don Tidey, who had been kidnapped by members of the IRA. The deaths of a young soldier, Private Patrick Kelly, and a garda, Garry Sheehan, during a rescue operation had a profound effect on O'Sullivan; the two young men were killed close to where he was standing in the Leitrim woods. O'Sullivan went on to work for the Garda fraud bureau until he resigned from the force to pursue his interest in the less constrained and more lucrative world of commercial private investigation. Working out of a small office close to Merrion Street and government buildings in Dublin, O'Sullivan built a reputation as something of a specialist in finding hidden assets and enjoyed a wide range of contacts with security agencies across various jurisdictions.

O'Sullivan travelled to meet Farrell in Brussels in December 2013 and sought out any information he had that could be of use to his client. McKillen was continuing to pursue what he felt were unfair and inappropriate invasions of his private business and personal financial affairs, including by some officials of NAMA. He had openly accused former NAMA official Paul Hennigan of providing information about his commercial affairs to representatives of the Barclay brothers during his battle over control of the Maybourne group of hotels in London. Hennigan had given evidence disputing this which had been accepted in the UK High Court, but McKillen and O'Sullivan clearly felt that Farrell might have more relevant information on those responsible for leaking information from NAMA to commercial rivals and others.

O'Sullivan was particularly interested in any information Farrell might have in relation to Hennigan. Farrell had previously told the officers from the GBFI that Hennigan met him when they worked together in NAMA and admitted that he had just been interviewed by legal and compliance officers of the agency 'because he had shared a confidential bid letter, which had been addressed to Brendan McDonagh, with the Barclay brothers'. He knew a lot more about Hennigan, which he had already discussed at length with the GBFI.

O'Sullivan spent several hours talking to Farrell, who at that point was a shattered individual, and took detailed notes of their conversations. On his return to Dublin, the private detective provided transcripts of his interviews with Farrell to Cunningham. He also handed them over to members of the GBFI, which he believed he was obliged to do as a citizen who had come across evidence of possible criminal activity.

Within a week of the Brussels meeting the 'dossier' was circulated to Darragh O' Brien, who raised issues concerning leaks from NAMA in the Seanad on 16 December, as did Fianna Fáil leader Micheál Martin in the Dáil, which in turn prompted the PAC appearance by Daly and McDonagh. Some media organisations had obtained snippets of the dossier's contents which were published in the days before the hearing. During the same period, Independent Newspapers' security reporter, Paul Williams, left several messages on Farrell's mobile phone seeking an urgent interview and informing the former NAMA employee that he had photographs of him in his Brussels 'hideaway'. In fact, Farrell was living openly in his wife's home town and close to her family. Farrell was more annoyed when he read contents of the 'dossier' in some media reports which attributed statements to him that he claimed he had not made. One newspaper said that Farrell had admitted to 'destroying the lives' of people, which he believed was not a complete or accurate reflection of what he told O'Sullivan. O'Sullivan was also uncomfortable with the release of the dossier to politicians and the media and was concerned at the effect it might have on Farrell's already vulnerable condition.

O'Brien was the first to raise the sensitive issue of confidential leaks from NAMA when he asked whether the Garda Commissioner was going to investigate the serious allegations brought to him over recent days. O'Brien said in his address to the Seanad on 16 December:

> Information is being leaked from NAMA and is being given to vulture funds and other investors in order to confer financial advantage on them. This will ensure that these entities will profit off the backs of taxpayers and that viable businesses will be shut down as a result. I need to know today whether the Garda Commissioner has been requested to carry out a detailed investigation into corruption and impropriety in NAMA.

Two days later, Martin raised the political temperature with further details from the dossier.

> One of the allegations being made which requires urgent clarification from NAMA is that an entire file on a person whose loan book was with NAMA was sent to a partner in a major global property company who was acting on behalf of that person's rival in advance of a major and high-profile court case.

That would be a shocking revelation if proved true; therefore, the issue cannot be left hanging; it needs an urgent response. Did this happen and if it did, is it just an isolated case or are there others like it? It has also been asserted that property valuations have been manipulated, which is extremely serious. A person quoted in the material states: 'There were perfectly good loans written down in the banks so as to keep the NAMA dream alive. I was the one they relied on to get the massive low valuations. I destroyed people with these valuations.' That is extremely serious and cannot be left unanswered for any period.

While the Taoiseach sought to fend off the question with reference to various Garda investigations into leaks from NAMA and in respect of unanswered FOI requests to the finance department by the Fianna Fáil leader, the pressure was mounting on the NAMA executive to dampen the fire ignited by the leaked dossier at the PAC.

Accompanied by Frank Daly, secretary general of the Department of Finance, John Moran, and his officials, McDonagh opened his contribution at the PAC with a vigorous attack on unnamed people who had made 'serious allegations' against NAMA in documents circulated to 'certain media outlets and members of the Oireachtas over the past week'.

'There has been a carefully orchestrated operation targeted at a small number of media outlets and Oireachtas Members and its intended purpose is clear: to damage NAMA and thereby undermine the financial interests of the State,' McDonagh claimed. The allegations, he said, had been made by ex-employee Enda Farrell, and among documents which had been circulated 'were [some] provided by NAMA during the legal discovery process as part of English High Court litigation in 2012.' According to McDonagh, Farrell had provided a 'full file' of personal information on Paddy McKillen to a third party, a disclosure which 'contradicts his previous sworn statements'. He said that NAMA never retained a file detailing information about McKillen and normally held in a business plan submitted by debtors to the agency including details of his personal finances, assets and liabilities. It no longer required such information because of the decision by the NAMA board in July 2011 not to acquire McKillen's loans. This followed the decision of the Supreme Court to grant the developer's appeal against an earlier High Court decision which would have forced him into NAMA.

McDonagh continued: 'Before I move on from the allegations regarding disclosure of information, a second case was referred to the Garda by NAMA in February of this year [2013]. It relates to a complaint made to NAMA of a possible unauthorised disclosure of a single document by another ex-employee.' He said that the earlier complaint against Farrell and this 'second case' of possible unauthorised disclosures of agency information were under investigation by the GBFI. The information recently circulated to the media included a claim, apparently emanating from Farrell, that NAMA had engaged 'in a deliberate process of manipulating the valuation of property which was collateral for its acquired loans', according to McDonagh. Refuting the claim, he said that a key element in the valuation of the loans acquired by the agency from the five banking institutions in 2010 and 2011 'was the current market value of the property or other collateral securing the loans'. The valuations were set by valuers commissioned by the banks in the first instance and were conducted under the 'Red Book' standard of the Royal Institution of Chartered Surveyors. Explaining the process, McDonagh said that these valuations were then reviewed by a second firm of valuers appointed by NAMA, and in the event of disagreement between the two, an independent third valuation was carried out. McDonagh said:

At no stage in this process did NAMA itself determine property valuations. Mr. Farrell, who is believed to be the source of the new allegations, had an administrative role in the property valuation process as a conduit between the banks and the loan valuers. He had no valuation role whatsoever.

The suggestion that he had no valuation role was news to Farrell, who spent all his time on such work and had claimed that he was constantly under pressure from the banks, who claimed his valuations were too low, and from colleagues in NAMA, who claimed they were too high and made assets difficult to offload.

Moving on to fresh allegations made concerning McKillen over recent weeks, McDonagh told the committee that the developer had served a statement of claim on NAMA in April 2013, which included an allegation that the agency 'had provided confidential information and assistance for the Barclay brothers during 2011 when Mr. McKillen and the Barclays were in dispute about their respective shareholdings in the Coroin company which owns three London hotels'.

The statement of claim from solicitors Lyons Kenny included copies of emails and other correspondence between NAMA and representatives of the Barclay brothers. The solicitors maintained that the emails suggest that NAMA had 'improperly offered to assist the Barclay interests' by supplying it with confidential information about Coroin and McKillen. They included details of a memo compiled by Aidan Barclay, son of David Barclay, which suggested that NAMA officials and the Barclays had discussed a strategy on how best to deal with McKillen. The emails, it was claimed, suggested that the Barclays were 'lobbying' NAMA officials, a potential breach of the legislation governing the agency.

McKillen claimed that he had 'suffered loss, damage, inconvenience, and expense' as a result of the actions of NAMA.

After NAMA responded that McKillen had unlawfully used privileged information from documents obtained under discovery in his English High Court proceedings, the developer withdrew his claim and submitted an amended statement in July 2013. McDonagh said that in October 2013 NAMA filed a full defence to all claims made by McKillen which 'would continue to trial in the High Court'.

McDonagh said that NAMA is involved

in a very difficult business with a lot at stake for the taxpayer and others. In seeking to do its job professionally it inevitably finds itself in dispute with various parties. Some of these will inevitably seek to intimidate or discredit NAMA for their own purposes. Presumably, the strategy is that if enough mud is thrown, some of it will stick.

He said that his staff were 'of a very high calibre and carry out their difficult duties with great commitment and diligence. We have every confidence in their integrity and professionalism. Unfortunately, in every walk of life there are bad eggs, but, thankfully, in our case, they have been few.'

Daly entered the fray to tell the PAC members that the agency had

referred two complaints about former employees of the agency to An Garda Síochána pursuant to section 202 of the National Asset Management Agency Act which deals with unauthorised disclosure of confidential information. We have also referred two complaints under section 7 of the Act against NAMA debtors to An Garda Síochána for failing to provide accurate statements of affairs. All of these matters are under active investigation by the Garda.

He accused unnamed elements of carrying out 'an organised campaign of misinformation'.

In this agency we have learned not to believe everything all of our debtors tell us. We verify what is presented to us. It would be very foolish of us not to do so. This week's events suggest others, unfortunately, do not take the same basic precautions. It seems extraordinary to me that such unquestioning credibility has been given to a series of allegations about NAMA advanced, apparently, by an individual who is under investigation as a consequence of a formal complaint made about him by NAMA to the Garda Síochána.

The presence and contribution of John Moran helped to throw some light on the substance of the allegations that were being irresponsibly aired by some media organisations, as Daly claimed. Moran, it turned out, was there to defend not just his department in relation to its cautious response to FOI queries concerning certain loans held by IBRC, but also to address accusations which, he said, were 'possibly defamatory in respect of officials in the Department and myself'. He was referring to reports that he had wrongly communicated with Richard Faber, the representative of the Barclay brothers, during their very public and bitter dispute with McKillen over control of the London hotel group.

When asked by committee chairman John McGuinness whether he could clarify the suggestion that there was inappropriate contact by him with people wishing to purchase properties, Moran replied that

despite suggestions to the contrary, I have never met the Barclay brothers and I have never spoken to Mr. Faber. All I received was one e-mail which I passed on to officials in the Department, which then described this, correctly, as a commercial matter largely to be dealt with by the bank [IBRC].

Moran was referring to an email he sent to Faber in October 2012 in relation to the Barclays' attempt to buy out €300 million in personal debt owed by McKillen to IBRC. Replying to an email from Faber, Moran said he would copy the communication to two of his colleagues who were more involved in the wind-down of IBRC. In the email, Moran said

I leave it to them [to determine] if it is appropriate to contact you or the bank in the first instance. In any event, I would mention that should you feel you are not making the right progress for whatever reason with IBRC, they remain at your disposal (as of course do I if you are unable to reach them).

In March 2013, McKillen complained to finance minister Michael Noonan about what the developer described as 'an inappropriate informality and familiarity between senior officials in your department' and a Barclay brothers executive. In his letter, McKillen referred to a 'stark contrast in tone and content' between the department's correspondence with Mr Faber and its correspondence with him, 'which has been conducted on a strictly formal basis as normally expected of correspondence emanating from senior Government officials'. McKillen claimed that there was 'an open door to your senior officials for Mr Faber', while his requests for meetings had been routinely refused.

Out of 19 FOI requests to the department requesting further details on the relationship between Moran and his officials with the Barclays, only six were granted, but the secretary general indicated that the unreleased emails would suggest that the department's only concern was that IBRC would, in its disposal of assets, ensure best value for the taxpayer from competing bidders. It was the first opportunity for Moran to explain his role in the controversy since it had erupted earlier in the year and it was evident that he and his colleagues in NAMA, as well as the minister, were determined to present a united front when it came to criticism or attack from any quarter. When he finished his opening remarks, the PAC chairman asked Moran to consider whether he should provide the committee with the material refused under the FOI request in order to 'allay any speculation or fears that the public have with regard to the Department of Finance'.

Moran also explained his role in relation to NAMA, with which he was in contact 'almost daily on one issue or another' and 'more formally on a monthly basis reviewing NAMA's progress, strategy, update on cashflow generation and sales processes'. Asked how often he would meet Daly and McDonagh, Moran said that relations with NAMA were handled by senior department officials Declan Reid and Ann Nolan, who had 'primary responsibility' for dealing with the agency. Asked by Fine Gael deputy Eoghan Murphy how frequently the minister would be involved in discussing NAMA, Moran replied: 'Certainly there is an intense engagement quarterly. If any specific issue is raised, effectively, there is an open door policy if Mr Brendan McDonagh or Mr Frank Daly or anybody else wants to have a conversation with the Minister ... our officials would support that discussion.'

Responding to a question from Fine Gael deputy John Deasy, McDonagh clarified Farrell's role in the valuation process, and appeared to dilute his earlier insistence that the former official had no involvement with it. He said that Farrell reported to John Mulcahy, 'who has more than 40 years' experience in the property valuation industry'. He said that Mulcahy had to sign off on the valuations prepared by Farrell before they went out to the external loan valuation firm.

Probing Farrell's motives further, independent deputy Shane Ross asked Daly why he had felt it so necessary and urgent to come before the PAC in response to a 'dossier' of allegations which the NAMA executives had not read but which was circulating in certain media and political circles. Referring to his chief executive's earlier statement, Ross asked Daly whether he believed that the people behind the allegations were, as McDonagh had claimed, setting out to damage the financial interests of the state.

'If one damages NAMA, one damages the financial interests of the State,' answered Daly.

Ross insisted that criticising NAMA for any reason did not mean the critics 'are trying to damage the interests of the State. Mr. Daly is making the interests of the State synonymous with the interests of NAMA.'

Daly replied:

I do so because NAMA is owned by the taxpayer. The agency paid €32 billion to the banks, of which €30 billion is a contingent liability on the State. We have repaid €7.5 billion of that so the figure is no longer €30 billion but the balance is still a contingent liability on the State. If, therefore, one damages NAMA, one damages the State.

Ross stated that 'because NAMA is owned by the taxpayer does not mean it is acting in the interests of the taxpayer', adding that 'it is very dangerous for an organisation such as NAMA to identify itself with the State in that manner. This is partly related to the fact that the agency is in a monopoly position that it views itself in that way.'

He accused Daly of making 'a good job of demolishing the accuser and he may be right to do so', but asked how Daly could be so certain of Farrell's motives if he had not read the document circulated by persons unknown to NAMA. Daly insisted that he had it from several very good sources that the views in the documents came from Farrell.

From very good sources, and the same thing has been said to us from several sources, Mr. Farrell would seem to have had views. By the way, Mr. McDonagh acknowledged that Mr. Farrell was a very hard-working individual who worked in a very stressful situation. He now seems to be articulating personal views about NAMA, which is fine. If, however, we knew what they were, I would deal with them on a case by case basis.

During the exchanges, McDonagh confirmed that of the 63 staff who had left the agency since inception, 29 had departed in 2013. He confirmed that it was unclear how much of its €18 billion in unsold loans would be transferred from the IBRC over the coming months. He added that the liquidator had indicated that 'there are only likely to be three individual debtor loans which he would possibly transfer to NAMA out of that book, which total about €500 million in empowered debt terms'. There was no mention of whether McKillen's debts to the IBRC, now the liquidator, would be included in any such transfer.

Ross pursued McDonagh on the cost to NAMA of litigation between the agency and the developer from his successful Supreme Court challenge. He also asked whether NAMA was conscious of the hurt caused to McKillen by the agency selling his loans to the Barclay brothers with whom he was 'at odds' and that the sale could be seen as 'insensitive or even malicious' given that the developer was engaged in a commercial battle with the purchasers. Insisting that it was a business transaction and that the loans were sold at par value, McDonagh cited a similar occasion when 'we sold a loan which had a share charge over another debtor's shareholding to a Malaysian sovereign debt'. This was in reference to the sale of the Treasury-owned Battersea Power Station in London, which NAMA sold against the determined resistance of the debtors. McDonagh said that it was 'a pure coincidence' that the McKillen loans were sold to the Barclay brothers and that whatever grievances the developer had 'are simply his views. My view is that I am running a business and I take business decisions.' He told Ross that he would be prepared to meet McKillen, as he previously had at the developer's request in February 2011.

In reply to the same question, Moran said he had no problem meeting McKillen, who at any rate had since been in Moran's 'department meeting officials'.

When it came to her turn, Sinn Féin deputy Mary Lou McDonald said she felt she was 'on the set of an Agatha Christie drama', in terms of the complaints made to the Garda by NAMA and the long exchange over the allegations made by McKillen against NAMA and Moran. She referred to the case of John Fraher, who, she said, had made a very serious complaint to the Data Protection Commissioner over NAMA's handling of his personal and business information. Despite the earlier comments by the executives about the oversight and accountability of the agency, McDonald suggested that many people viewed NAMA as 'virtually impenetrable'.

Fraher's complaint followed a judgment against him and in favour of NAMA for €5.5 million in April 2013. The judgment against the Tipperary businessman was in respect of various debts incurred by him and his business partners in relation to properties he owned, mainly in Munster. His co-borrowers included Jack Ronan, who was the principal in Cork company Vita Cortex, which hit the news after 50 members of the trade union SIPTU staged an occupation of the furniture factory for almost six months in late 2011 and early 2012 after they were denied their redundancy entitlements. During the dispute, the workers picketed the Poppyfield Retail Park in Clonmel, County Tipperary, owned jointly by Fraher and Ronan, which Fraher claimed had caused him financial loss, even though he was not connected to the Vita Cortex business. The issue raised by McDonald at the PAC concerned a claim by Fraher that in the course of his dealings with NAMA his financial advisors had been sent details of loans owed by other people, including former business associates. He also claimed that the details of loans owed by people unconnected to him but who had dealings with his former business partners had been improperly distributed by the agency. Included in the information sent to his financial advisors by NAMA official Padraig Reidy was detail on the par value of the loans but also the value at which they were acquired by the agency.

Fraher told the Commercial Court that he sought to settle his own loans to NAMA in July 2012 and that his offer would have produced a surplus for the agency, based on the acquisition values revealed to his advisors by Reidy, but his offer was rejected. He said the 'offer was refused out of hand and without any negotiation as it did not deal with his co-borrowings'. He sought bankruptcy in the UK some weeks after the court appearance and judgment against him.

McDonald did not go into further detail on the Fraher case, but accused the NAMA executives of undue secrecy in its operations, saying, 'You are immune to freedom of information legislation and that creates a ready perception not of wrongdoing but of secrecy which lends itself to the unfolding of situations such as the one we are dealing with here.' She said that the agency was 'out of the reach of democratically elected persons such as us', and noted that 'your fortunes and the financial fortunes of the State are joined at the hip'.

Daly reminded McDonald that NAMA was operating in the commercial arena and so could not put its 'cards on the table and indicate what we paid for individual loans or assets we are trying to sell. If we did so, we would be telling people about our pricing.' Agreeing to differ on the matter, McDonald revisited the issue of 'cooling off periods' for departing NAMA staff given the high turnover and asked about the 'level of contact between NAMA or NAMA developers and former employees of the agency wishing to acquire NAMA properties? Have former employees acquired such properties and, if so, how often have they done so?'

McDonagh confirmed that 'there are certain firms which are buying assets in the Irish market and which [former NAMA] people have joined. Those people might not be directly involved but the firms they have joined might be bidding for assets.' After further exchanges, McDonagh conceded that some former staff were working for firms that were dealing with agents appointed by NAMA.

We appoint agents to sell the loans or we get debtors or receivers to appoint agents to sell the underlying properties. So they would be working for firms which might be in contact with those agents in terms of buying the assets. However, our *modus operandi* is that agents provide full information to all potential bidders for the assets in order that nobody has an undue advantage.

Asked whether this would allow for access to insider knowledge, McDonagh replied that the issue has been 'completely overblown', given that the values acquired by NAMA were based on property prices of 20 November 2009, when the agency was established. McDonagh said:

Everybody knows that the Irish market has declined by 25% since November 2009, so there is no proprietary information as far as I can see. The market is the market. I would love it if some of these people were able to pay us what we paid for the assets in November 2009. We would not be carrying €3.6 billion worth of impairment if we could orchestrate that. However, we cannot do so.

Responding, McDonald said:

Mr. McDonagh might not view people leaving NAMA, not serving proper cooling off periods, going to work for wealth funds or whatever and then, by some other means, being involved with going back to NAMA and acquiring properties as being problematic. However, in terms of the credibility and standing of the organisation, I strongly suggest to him it is a problem for members of the public and for the uninitiated who are not familiar with the finer details relating to how NAMA operates.

Referring to the recently circulated dossier of allegations, McDonald summarised the NAMA position:

Their proposition is as follows: a disgruntled Mr. Enda Farrell is the source of these allegations. Reference has been made to a complete file or a full file in respect of Mr. McKillen, and no such file actually existed or was in the possession of NAMA. Nonetheless, somebody has gone to great lengths to put together a dossier of sorts and that somebody has drip-fed it into the political system and into the media. Presumably, they are referring to Independent Newspapers. When they talk about certain media outlets, I presume it is the *Sunday Independent*. That is quite a scenario, is it not? That is shocking, is it not?

On the day before the PAC meeting, the *Irish Independent* had published a story claiming that an unnamed former employee had alleged that NAMA had deliberately undervalued property loans and that he personally had 'destroyed people with these valuations'. It went on to report that Enda Farrell had admitted to leaking information from NAMA and that 'he was just one of a number of people to do so'. Farrell was quoted as stating that he met with an unnamed woman and 'gave her everything' on developer Paddy McKillen. The report claimed that the developer had written to the Garda Commissioner, Martin Callinan, to complain of the 'inexplicable behaviour' of NAMA officials which had 'seriously jeopardised' his business.

Addressing what he said was a reference in recent media reports to a request for information he had allegedly made to Farrell about a 'property in Wexford', Daly said that he had no recollection of making any such inquiry. According to Farrell, he had been asked by a colleague to get information about a property in which Daly expressed an interest.

'What does inquiring about a property mean? There are people who come to me to ask me whether we have properties in Cork or Dublin,' said Daly. 'Let us be clear – I have no recollection of ever inquiring about a property in Wexford.'

McDonagh intervened to tell the PAC that it had also been suggested that his niece had bought a NAMA property in Kerry:

> I do not think it has been written, but it has been mentioned to me that one of the allegations is that my niece bought a NAMA property. I have three nieces living in County Kerry and can assure the committee that none of them has bought a property.

What Farrell had said in his early statements to the Garda was that he had heard of a query by Daly in respect of a property in Wexford. He said that John Mulcahy had an email in relation to Daly's request for information but he, Farrell, knew nothing else about it. He also described how he was asked to get information about a specific property in County Kerry where McDonagh's niece was interested in buying a house. Farrell said that he discussed the request with a colleague in NAMA, Breifne Brennan, and that he had assembled the information as requested.

In June 2013, Farrell had recounted to the GBFI how he had 'bumped into' McDonagh earlier in the year and during their brief conversation mentioned the request concerning the house in Kerry.

Farrell recalled the meeting and the earlier request for information from McDonagh because it had contributed to his disastrous, and life-changing, decision to purchase the house in Lucan which had led to the destruction of his career and, almost, of his marriage. He told gardaí:

> It was at that point I decided to purchase Sunday's Well in Lucan and to take the tracker spread sheets. These spread sheets were the ones I had worked on for years and contained all addresses, valuations for all NAMA properties. It also indicated to me that the information was not confidential.

In the course of the same interview, Farrell mentioned the passing of NAMA information by his former colleague Padraig Reidy to one of his 'borrower connections' in reference to the John Fraher case.

While I was in NAMA, a colleague Padraig Reidy asked me to send him all the valuations relating to one of his borrower connections. I asked how he was getting on with the borrower. He told me there was a huge difference between the borrower's opinion of the value and the NAMA valuation. He told me he was sending the valuations to the borrower to demonstrate the difference. Hence, I didn't believe the valuations were confidential.

Asked whether Reidy had attempted to gain anything from this disclosure of NAMA information, Farrell replied, 'No but it was raised in a civil case between NAMA and John Fraher, I think.' Farrell went on to claim that the banks shared valuations with their borrowers and that he had been advised by the NAMA head of legal Aideen O'Reilly that they were the property of the banks whose loans had been transferred and not of the agency. This was disputed by NAMA, which insisted in its statements to the GBFI in the Farrell case that the information was confidential to the agency and it was in breach of various laws to impart it.

The heat was turning up on the agency in the Oireachtas, in the courts and in the media, some of it fuelled by disgruntled but still well-endowed borrowers. Sensitive issues the agency was furiously attempting to dampen in private were set to publicly erupt as the fifth year of NAMA-land dawned.

Chapter 16

CLOSING THE DEAL

W hen Michael Noonan spoke before 400 members of the business community in Belfast in late September 2013, he sought to address concerns about plans by NAMA to dispose of its Northern Ireland portfolio of loans with an estimated value of £3.35 billion, including properties in Britain and elsewhere. He told the Northern Ireland section of the Confederation of British Industry (CBI) that it had always been the intention of NAMA to make phased asset sales in the North, and when 'the economy is right', the agency could increase the pace of those sales.

> We have a Northern Ireland Advisory Committee who advise the [NAMA] board, who are very aware of the situation in Northern Ireland and who represent Northern Ireland's best interests. No one should have any concerns about how Northern Ireland is represented. I am very confident that NAMA will make the right decisions.

Noonan did not alert his audience to the actual pace of 'behind the scenes' activity in relation to the NI loan book held by NAMA, or indeed of the communication he had received three months earlier from finance minister Sammy Wilson informing him that US law firm Brown Rudnick had two clients interested in acquiring the entire portfolio in a single sale and of commitments it contained in relation to the personal guarantees of debtors.

Neither was Noonan's CBI audience informed that only two weeks earlier, on 9 September, NAMA received a letter from PIMCO expressing its non-binding interest in purchasing the agency's €5.38 billion (£4.61 billion) par value NI loan book in a short and exclusive sales process for €1.1 billion. The NAMA board heard the proposals when it met three days later and noted in the minutes that 'there is an issue about open marketing, and the chairman advised that such an initiative is highly politically sensitive and should be treated as very confidential'.

The extreme sensitivity involved explained, perhaps, why the assembly of the rich and powerful at the CBI lunch in Belfast later in September did not get any inkling of what was going on behind the scenes even though two speakers, Noonan and Ian Coulter, who was chair of the Northern Ireland section of the business confederation, had knowledge of events taking place privately in rooms in Belfast and Dublin. There was also the added dimension that the letter sent by Wilson to Noonan could have been seen as political interference in the process and an attempt to gain preferential access to a sales process for clients of Brown Rudnick with whom it had a commercial relationship. This added to the delicate nature of the whole business and also raised issues about NAMA's policy of ensuring an open sales marketing process, which McDonagh and Daly had so often insisted was fundamental to ensure that conflicts of interest based on insider information could not take place.

Noonan did not know of the details discussed at the 22 May meeting between PIMCO representatives from the US, Tuvi Keinan, Coulter and Frank Cushnahan and Robinson and Wilson. He was equally unaware that another major US fund, the New York-based Fortress Investment Group LLC, had also met with Cushnahan and accountant David Watters in Belfast in December 2012. The chief executive of Fortress, Michael George, and another Irish representative of the firm, Brendan McGinn, were introduced to Wilson after their initial discussion with Cushnahan and Watters about the potential purchase of NAMA's Northern Ireland loan book. Belfast-born George was displeased that he was not subsequently invited for further discussions with the North's businessmen and politicians on a possible role for Fortress in the purchase given that it was one of the world's largest investment management companies, with funds approaching $60 billion by 2013. McGinn was a long-time associate of Cushnahan. In 2008 they were involved in seeking Irish American and other investment into projects they were promoting in the North. McGinn was also a director of the charity Co-operation North, which supported cross-community initiatives in Ireland. In 2013 he was a director of Fortress Credit Ventures (Europe) Ltd with a registered address in Clonee, County Meath.

Neither were Cushnahan's colleagues in NAMA to know that the NIAC member was engaged in some unusual business dealings with at least one of the borrowers whose debts were under the control of the agency. John Miskelly was one of a number of NAMA debtors who hired Cushnahan for advice and assistance on how to best escape the clutches of NAMA without being forced into bankruptcy or worse. Miskelly had developed hotels and other commercial properties in Belfast and other centres in counties Antrim and Down and knew that Cushnahan enjoyed good relationships with Peter Robinson and his son Gareth.

Miskelly was also a shrewd operator and took the precaution of recording some of his meetings with Cushnahan, including one in the car park of Belfast's

City Hospital, where he was receiving treatment for a serious medical condition, in August 2012. During their discussion in a car, Cushnahan said that Gareth Robinson was providing him with useful assistance and needed to be 'looked after', and that he was confident that Miskelly's difficulties with NAMA could be resolved with the help of the senior politicians and others. Miskelly handed Cushnahan a bag containing £40,000 in cash before their meeting concluded.

Cushnahan had, of course, been touting his contacts and abilities and his role as a member of the NIAC as far back as 2010, and had used his friendship with Barry Lloyd to make approaches to potential investors from the Far East, including China and Japan, where the powerful Nomura bank was based. The bank had expressed an interest in the Northern Ireland portfolio at the time.

Cushnahan had informed the NIAC on a number of occasions in 2011 and 2012 that he was advising business people whose debts were with the agency, but this did not appear to be a matter of any concern to other members of the committee or indeed of the NAMA board, which was heavily represented on the NIAC. Frank Daly, who had taken over as NIAC chairman in October 2011 following the resignation of Peter Stewart, met committee members in offices Cushnahan used at Tughans. The other members of the NIAC at this time were NAMA directors Brian McEnery, Éilish Finan and Willie Soffe, as well as 'external members' Cushnahan and Brian Rowntree and head of asset recovery at the agency, Ronnie Hanna. Even when it emerged by December 2012 that the six debtors to whom Cushnahan provided financial advice represented approximately 50 per cent of the entire NI loan book of NAMA in value, no one in authority appeared to blink.

The office in Tughans' Belfast headquarters at Marlborough House on Victoria Street was clearly the epicentre of the ambitious plans hatched by Cushnahan and the firm's managing partner, Ian Coulter. Coulter acted for many of the North's leading developers as well as for the DUP and Peter Robinson, a former estate agent and property owner with homes in Belfast and Florida. Coulter was chairman of the influential CBI in the North from early 2013 to 2014. He and a number of other businessmen in Belfast, including Cushnahan and Watters, had developed the idea of a single sale of NAMA's Northern Ireland portfolio. In late 2012, Coulter called Keinan of Brown Rudnick to discuss their proposal for a 'potential real estate transaction involving the loan book'. Keinan had been a partner in Brown Rudnick's office for less than a year, but the law firm had dealt with clients of Tughans, including in relation to NAMA loans, in the past. With extensive experience in structuring property transactions and loan sales, Keinan had previously worked on Project Saturn, which involved one of the early sales of a NAMA non-performing loan portfolio for Morgan Stanley in 2012.

On the Brown Rudnick website, Keinan claimed to have engaged in 'sourcing and executing an off-market discounted UK loan portfolio sale from NAMA'. The agency later disputed this claim and asserted that the sale of the UK portfolio to Morgan Stanley was 'fully openly marketed'. Keinan also worked on Project Aspen, the largest NAMA sale of non-performing loans since its inception. Coulter explained that a single-sale transaction could help business and NAMA debtors in the North, as well as NAMA and potential investors, and asked Keinan whether he could identify and recruit institutional clients who might be interested in getting involved. Coulter had not been involved when Tughans served as local counsel for Brown Rudnick in relation to two non-NAMA real estate transactions earlier in 2012, but he was familiar with the London office of the US law firm and how it structured its fee arrangements.

In many of the projects on which he had worked for the firm, Keinan was paid, like many in the business, on a success fee basis rather than an hourly rate for work done. Clients benefit under this structure as it transfers the transaction risk with respect to legal fees to the law firm, which is not paid unless the deal is closed. Fees under this structure are usually substantially larger than fees paid on an hourly basis as compensation for the law firm for taking the risk that it would not be paid if the client did not succeed in the case or close the deal. Keinan, Coulter and Cushnahan spent much time discussing the potential fee they might receive if they managed to attract an institutional investor to buy the NAMA loan book in the North.

At the meeting in late November 2012 at the Tughans office in Belfast, Cushnahan explained to Keinan that he held an unpaid voluntary position as an external member of the NIAC. According to Keinan, Cushnahan insisted that he had no conflicts of interest in advising on the proposed sale of the NAMA loan book. During the discussion, Coulter told Keinan that he and Brown Rudnick were the only parties with whom they were discussing the proposal. It was at this first encounter that the two Belfast men raised the issue of an unspecified success fee and their preference for it to be split three ways between Brown Rudnick, Tughans and Cushnahan.

On 14 February 2013, Keinan, Coulter and Cushnahan met with Sammy Wilson to get an idea of how the proposed transaction would go down with the Northern Ireland executive in which the DUP and Sinn Féin were the two largest parties but which also included ministers from the UUP, SDLP and Alliance parties.

Keinan arranged a further meeting with representatives of PIMCO at its London offices on 30 April 2013, where they were briefed on the respective roles of Cushnahan and Tughans. Cushnahan was introduced by Coulter as a senior business figure and former CEO of Chase Bank Northern Ireland, chairman of the Belfast Harbour Commissioners and a member of the NIAC. There were some discussions with other potential investors over the following weeks, including one who asked to be kept informed of progress in relation to the proposal and opportunity.

On 8 May 2013 PIMCO signed a confidentiality agreement with Brown Rudnick in which the US fund was named a 'potential investor' and Brown Rudnick named as its advisor in relation to a possible purchase of NAMA-controlled loans in the North. Meetings were set up for PIMCO and the other interested bidder with representatives of the Northern Ireland executive for later in the month. On 22 May, Andrew Balls, the PIMCO managing director as well as its head of European portfolio management, Laurent Luccioni, executive vice-president and head of commercial real estate, and James Gilbert, senior vice-president of real estate portfolio management, met Peter Robinson and Wilson for talks in which Keinan, Coulter and Cushnahan also participated. Cushnahan's advisory role on behalf of PIMCO was explained to the politicians at the meeting and no objections were raised. This was unsurprising as the politicians had recommended him for the role on the NIAC in the first place. His membership of the NIAC was also discussed and assurances given, and accepted, that there were no conflicts of interest involved. His unorthodox dealings with at least one NAMA debtor, Miskelly, and his paid consultancy work for five others representing over 50 per cent of the loan book at the centre of the deliberations was not mentioned in any subsequent records of the meetings kept by Brown Rudnick or PIMCO.

Following the meeting, Robinson and Wilson asked Coulter to get a letter from Brown Rudnick which could be forwarded to NAMA setting out the details of a proposed loan portfolio acquisition. This was provided after the law firm consulted with PIMCO to obtain any information or observations it wished to include. The letter was addressed to Michael Noonan and sent to Wilson, who passed it to his counterpart in Dublin with his own cover note. As the process took shape and progressed, Cushnahan, Coulter and Keinan again met with PIMCO on 29 August 2013 and discussed the success fee arrangements to be put in place in the event that the proposal and loan purchase was completed. Cushnahan was to work on a 'fully contingent basis' and prior to any payment full disclosure of his role and remuneration would be made to all stakeholders involved in the sale, including NAMA and the NIAC. PIMCO recognised the significance Cushnahan could bring to the table given his local knowledge and 'personal and extensive track record' in credit, real estate and 'individual developers' dynamics in the North and wanted him to continue in a consultancy role 'post-acquisition'. The fund managers appreciated that his insight into the local property market would assist its underwriting process and on the other side of a successful purchase he would also be useful when it came to dealing with individual debtors, some of whom he was clearly familiar with. For Cushnahan, this was not only a lucrative potential pay day, it also provided him with extraordinary leverage over the debtors to whom he was providing consultancy services and indeed over others who were desperate to have their distressed loans, and the personal guarantees held by NAMA over them, resolved without losing businesses, homes and other assets. With Coulter, he was now going to emerge as one of the most powerful players in the North's business community, with influential friends at the head of government and in its largest political party, the DUP.

For its part, Brown Rudnick signed a confidentiality agreement committing the law firm to provide services including: advising PIMCO; accompanying the funds representatives to meetings with NAMA, the Stormont executive and others; assisting in the structuring of the purchase; and consulting on high-level strategy. In relation to NAMA, Keinan and his colleagues in the law firm dealt in the first instance with Ronnie Hanna and his assistant, Cian Kealy. John Collison, head of residential delivery with the agency, was also involved in the discussion with Keinan. During September and October 2013 there were frequent communications between the Brown Rudnick and NAMA teams, with James Gilbert of PIMCO also included in the conversations and correspondence.

The first conversation between arguably the two most significant players in this high-stakes game, Keinan and Hanna, took place on 9 September 2013, the day the non-binding expression of interest in the purchase of NAMA's Northern Irish loan portfolio was received by the agency from PIMCO.

On 18 September Keinan and Gilbert met with Hanna, Collison and Cathal Durkin of NAMA regarding PIMCO's formal and non-binding indication of interest. They discussed the logistics of any such transaction. Noonan, who had travelled to Belfast for the CBI lunch, met with Robinson and his recently appointed finance minister, Simon Hamilton, on 27 September at Stormont, where they discussed the notion of an exclusive sale. The Deputy First Minister Martin McGuinness was not informed about this high-level meeting. A note taken by Robinson's principal private secretary Jeremy Gardner recorded Noonan as stating that while NAMA had social obligations to meet, its commercial mandate meant that it could not impose conditions on any buyer following the sale. He also 'indicated that whilst there would be no exclusivity clause there was in his view only one potential buyer. Mr Noonan undertook to discuss the situation with the CEO of NAMA and was confident that both administrations could work together with the potential buyer to overcome any difficulties.' Clearly, the DUP politicians were keen to ensure that debtors, including prominent party supporters, would not suffer undue financial pain if the sale process to a single purchaser proceeded, and in particular that there would be some alleviation of their exposure to the huge personal guarantees on their loans. Noonan explained to the Dáil the following week, on 3 October, that his reference to 'working together' meant that 'both sides shared an understanding of the importance of NAMA to the economy of Northern Ireland and the care needed in dealings in Northern Ireland regarding NAMA's management of the portfolio'. He said that he did not mean to imply in his remarks to Robinson and Hamilton that the Irish government would work with PIMCO or any other potential buyers but that he 'would have expressed confidence that NAMA would be able to work with potential buyers to overcome any difficulties and that [he] would have committed to maintaining an open dialogue between administrations to the extent that was helpful'.

On the day before the meeting between Noonan, Robinson and Hamilton, on 26 September, PIMCO wrote to Brown Rudnick acknowledging an earlier confirmation by the law firm that its success fee would 'be split into three equal parts between yourselves, Tughans Solicitors and Frank Cushnahan CBE'. This was the latest communication in a series exchanged between PIMCO and Brown Rudnick over July and August 2013 on the issue of the success fee and was not the first time that there was a reference to the three-way split.

According to Brown Rudnick's records, PIMCO and its legal team, including compliance officer Hugh Mildred, met on 5 September to review the success fee proposal. The legal team requested that PIMCO pay the fee to Brown Rudnick, which could then distribute it 'at its own discretion'. It also suggested capping total compensation at a level of £16 million. Four days later, on 9 September, PIMCO sought curriculum vitae details for Coulter and Cushnahan, which confirmed that the fund was fully informed of the intended recipients and the nature and scale of the success fee arrangement envisaged, even if its structure had not been finalised.

At its meeting of 7 October, attended by Cushnahan, the NIAC was informed of the PIMCO bid and that the NAMA board would decide on its response and possible further engagement with the offer when it met three days later. Daly explained to his colleagues 'what a NAMA sales process would entail with value and open marketing key considerations for the agency'. The minutes referred to 'external member feedback' on the proposed approach to support the board's consideration of the matter at its meeting on 10 October. One of the two external members, Cushnahan made no disclosure of interest at the meeting even though he must have been privately elated that a deal he had helped to engineer and from which he stood to gain enormously was coming closer to fruition. His support and that of the other external NIAC member, Brian Rowntree, was brought to the attention of the board at the meeting along with other issues they had raised including concerns about price, marketing and the likely discount that would be sought by PIMCO if the 'strategic purchase' was to proceed. The board heard that PIMCO's interest in the portfolio was based on its view that the NI property market had bottomed out, on the underlying value of the UK assets in the portfolio and on the size of the NI loan book. It received an opinion from the executive members involved, which set out potential risks and mentioned the 'politically sensitive' nature of the proposal and the need for confidentiality.

The executive recommended that great care should be exercised 'with regard to debtor selection/exclusion' and that debtor cooperation was 'important to ensure a successful outcome'.

Although PIMCO had sought an exclusive and off-market transaction, the board insisted that the sale must be in line with the agency's policy that transactions were openly marketed. Ronnie Hanna was tasked with signing a non-disclosure agreement (NDA) with PIMCO with a view to 'further due diligence towards the completion, ultimately, of an openly marketed loan sale in accordance with board policy in respect of the portfolio – the request for which will be brought back to board for formal approval at a later date'. The board agreed that access to the virtual data room should be no less than that provided in any other sales process and that any final offer would have to be formally approved with its members.

After PIMCO signed the NDA on 16 October 2013, it was given access to the data room in order to 'prepare an informed bid based on the top 55 assets' in the loan book. The sale process was given the title Project Eagle, which would be used from then on by Hanna and the asset recovery team in any correspondence or exchanges with potential buyers and advisors. The data included the NAMA valuation reports from 2009, locations and up-to-date tenancy schedules for the 55 largest assets, and addresses for the remaining ones.

PIMCO was also advised by estate agents Cushman & Wakefield and UK-based REIT, NewRiver, which were given access to the data room.

On 7 November 2013, Frank Cushnahan resigned as a member of the NIAC, citing personal reasons for his departure. There was no formal statement by NAMA or any media release about his decision to step down. He was not a member of the board, so presumably his departure did not warrant any such mention. In contrast, when accountant Éilish Finan ended her four-year term on the NAMA board some weeks later, there was the ritual expression of the agency's gratitude for her work as chair of its finance and operations and member of the audit committee and the NIAC.

On 4 December 2013 PIMCO presented another bid to NAMA with a price range of between £1.1 billion and £1.3 billion, subject to ongoing due diligence, and repeated that it would prefer a closed transaction for the portfolio. It was clear that PIMCO was making the running with regard to the price of Project Eagle and was maintaining strong pressure to ensure an exclusive bidding process in its correspondence to NAMA sent through Brown Rudnick. On the day before the NAMA board convened to discuss the latest PIMCO bid, asset recovery official Cian Kealy sent a message to Keinan mentioning his 'big day tomorrow' and wishing him 'good luck' with the outcome. Keinan replied with equal enthusiasm. Both had previously worked on NAMA disposals in the UK. The message underlined the relationship which Keinan had developed with Hanna and Kealy, who were now almost at one with PIMCO and Brown Rudnick when it came to an exclusive sale process and the best achievable price range.

At its meeting on 12 December, the NAMA board considered the offer and PIMCO's request for exclusivity. Hanna prepared a briefing note for the board seeking guidance on the 'appropriate response to PIMCO to enter into a closed transaction with no formal open marketing campaign of the Project Eagle portfolio of loans'. He also recommended a minimum sale price for Project Eagle of £1.3 billion (€1.57 billion). After its examination of the top 55 assets in the portfolio, PIMCO had valued them at £950 million while NAMA had valued them at £891 million, or £59 million less. However, applying a discount rate of 5.5 per cent, a net current value of £766 million was forecast, which was £184 million below the PIMCO bid. In contrast, the bid by PIMCO in relation to several hundred other, less valuable assets in the portfolio came in below the NAMA valuation by £128 million after the 5.5 per cent discount was applied.

In its cost–benefit analysis of an open market or closed sale process, the executive briefing paper suggested that it would take between three and six months to gather the necessary underlying and property information and a further six weeks to complete other preparatory work for the open sale option.

The board agreed at its first meeting of 2014, on 8 January, that the minimum reserve price should be set at £1.3 billion (€1.57 billion). However, in its assessment of the PIMCO proposal and its valuation NAMA relied largely on its existing cash flow projections and did not obtain current market valuations of all the property assets from loan sale advisors, as was normally the case prior to portfolio sales. At the time NAMA had intended to sell off the NI loan book in individual or smaller lots up to 2020 and the cash flow projections were based on potential rental income from the properties over that time after maintenance and disposal costs were deducted. It was during this process that a discount rate of 5.5 per cent was applied over the lifespan of 2013 to 2020. The 12 December board meeting had heard a range of estimates of the value of the Project Eagle portfolio which were based on different assumptions about the timing and actual value of the cash flows to be realised at the 5.5 per cent discount rate applied. The board warned that alternative net present value discount rates should be used in evaluating potential transactions and that they should be based on 'qualitative information'.

After its discussion of the merits of an off-market sale and its potential for sparking requests from other NAMA debtors for similar treatment, against an open market sale which could provoke a hostile political reaction in the North, the board agreed to a 'limited, focused and time bound open market process' as the prudent course of action. It requested Hanna, the author of the proposal which appeared to favour an off-market approach, to prepare another paper on price and the limited, open process on which it had just agreed. Hanna had failed to persuade the board of the 'off-market' strategy which would have suited PIMCO and the other players in Northern Ireland with whom he was in contact. Until then, it appeared that the strategy employed, including in regard to price, had been heavily influenced, if not dictated, by PIMCO and its advisors.

Frank Daly also informed the meeting about a contact from the NI finance minister Simon Hamilton, who was seeking an assurance that the sales process 'undertaken by NAMA should not be seen as publicly "auctioning" the NI portfolio'. Daly also told the meeting that the priority for NAMA was to have an open marketing approach which was 'appropriate, focused, time bound (given sensitivities and confidentiality concerns) while of course being sensitive to the NI position'. The minutes of the meeting on 8 January did not record any suggestion that the reserve price of £1.3 billion would result in any loss on the transaction.

The board appointed Lazard, which had been among the firms on its panel of loan sale advisors since early 2012, to advise on the appropriate marketing approach 'which will balance market requirement with the need for confidentiality'. It cited the reason for not putting this task out to tender as due to 'sensitivities' over the Project Eagle sale process. The board also agreed to approach at least two other major international investors and provide them access to the data room for two weeks to prepare their bids while PIMCO was permitted the same timeframe to complete its due diligence on the so-called 'tail of the portfolio', the portion that did not include the 55 largest and most valuable assets.

The board asked Hanna and his team to 'meet with PIMCO to advise them of the intended approach regarding the other short-listed investors noting that this would be as much to protect PIMCO's interests with regard to the integrity of the disposal process'. It also agreed that Lazard should 'submit a recommendation within an appropriate timeframe'.

The sale was to be carried out in a single rather than two-stage bidding process which would have allowed for more bidders to be approached to carry out initial pricing analysis and establish their interest without committing to the more expensive, full due diligence process which would be required at the second stage.

On 13 January Lazard was provided with a 'verbal briefing', having signed an NDA on 9 January, the day after the decision was made to appoint the firm as advisors. There are no documents or minutes to outline what the briefing entailed. A meeting of the board on 16 January agreed that 'PIMCO should be advised, post Lazard's appointment, of the intended approach regarding the marketing to a limited number of potential investors', and that the board would meet again the following week, if necessary, to discuss Lazard's response and proposals. Within days, Lazard was provided access to the virtual data room for Project Eagle and a day later, on 22 January, gave its 'pitch book' presentation, setting out its understanding of the assignment to members of the NAMA executive.

The pitch book* (see p. 163) provided a detailed breakdown of the portfolio and the proposed sales and transaction processes, and outlined a preferred timetable and list of suitable bidders without jeopardising confidentiality with 'the overriding objective' to maximise the recovery for the Irish taxpayer.

Lazard added Oaktree to the shortlist of possible bidders, with US fund Cerberus switched to the reserve list. By early February 2013 it had approached three investment firms, Blackstone, Starwood and Oaktree, to join the bidding process. Only Oaktree agreed. Lazard then invited three other potential bidders, including Cerberus and Lone Star, both of which signed up. By mid-February, there were four investment funds lined up for the sales process: PIMCO, Oaktree, Cerberus and Lone Star.

On 13 February, the board was informed of the list of potential bidders and of the progress being made on the responses from each investor. It agreed that the data room would contain redacted valuations for the top 55 properties or 85 per cent of the loan book by value and full valuations of the balance of 800 properties (15 per cent by value).

The confidential nature of the process was breached when media reports emerged, also on 13 February, suggesting that PIMCO was 'understood to have made it known to senior politicians in the North' that it was interested in acquiring 'outright NAMA's northern portfolio'. The board noted that the 'confidentiality agreement was no longer relevant' given the press reports and said that Lazard would now be given the 'flexibility to increase the number of bidders involved in the process if genuine, credible interest arose'.

The secrecy breach had the immediate effect of reawakening the interest of Fortress, which had not heard anything of consequence in relation to the proposed sale from NAMA since its principal, Michael George, and his advisor, Brendan McGinn, had held their meeting in December 2012 in Belfast with

Cushnahan and Watters. George wrote to Taoiseach Enda Kenny and to NAMA CEO Brendan McDonagh about his firm's desire to enter the process to acquire Project Eagle and indicated that he was somewhat frustrated not to have been given an earlier opportunity to make a bid.

In an email sent from his office in New York to Kenny's most senior advisor, Andrew McDowell, on 13 February 2014, George wrote: 'We've heard that NAMA/ Dept of Finance is running a "process" for the loans to Northern Irish borrowers. Being from the North I've taken a keen interest in this €4 billion portfolio and would like to throw our hat in the ring. Might you have any insight as to how we can get involved?'

McDowell replied that he had passed on his request to NAMA, to which George responded that had 'also reached out to Brendan' (McDonagh). When McDonagh heard that Fortress was seeking to discuss the Project Eagle sale with NAMA, he told Hanna to direct George to Lazard for any information he required.

Goldman Sachs contacted NAMA to indicate that it would be interested in participating in 'any process that seeks to maximise proceeds for NAMA and the State'.

Several other firms expressed an interest but only two, Fortress and Goldman Sachs, were permitted to join the Project Eagle sales process. Lazard told NAMA that it believed that the six remaining bidders could generate sufficient competitive tension for the process and that it did not intend to permit any more participants. It was now PIMCO, Cerberus, Oaktree, Lone Star, Fortress and Goldman Sachs in the race, all huge US investment funds blessed with many billions of dollars at their disposal with which to purchase distressed assets in various countries across the globe in the wake of the banking and financial crisis. On 14 February another fund, Apollo, withdrew its interest in a letter to NAMA expressing its disappointment that PIMCO had already enjoyed extensive access to the agency in advance of the start of the process, which gave it a material advantage. It said that it did not have sufficient time to complete the necessary due diligence under the proposed timeline as it had only signed an NDA three days earlier.

Lazard gave the six bidders a deadline of 14 March to submit their tenders and provided them with the minimum price range it expected. Lone Star was the most active player of the six in terms of the percentage share of the European commercial real estate loans they each held. Including performing loans, it had acquired in excess of €1 billion by 2014, a 40 per cent share. Cerberus was close behind at 36 per cent and Goldman Sachs was at 16 per cent. Fortress and PIMCO purchased no such loans, while Oaktree was not listed in the survey published by real estate firm Cushman & Wakefield. On 4 March, due to the amount of legal due diligence required, the period for bids was extended to 25 March.

By this time, there was no formal agreement between PIMCO and Brown Rudnick on any success fee arrangement for Frank Cushnahan, although, in late February, there had been an exchange of correspondence on the matter and the Belfast-based consultant had continued to work on the purchase of Project Eagle on behalf of the US fund and the law firm – clearly without the knowledge of the NAMA board.

On 27 February Brown Rudnick responded to a request from PIMCO that the 'compensation structure' take the form of an asset management agreement rather than a success fee. This meant that any fee would be based on Cushnahan's contribution to the management of the portfolio after its acquisition from NAMA. The law firm proposed the creation of an SPV and what it described in its letter of offer as a 'put option' along with management fees for assisting with the management and disposal of the loan book. According to Brown Rudnick, PIMCO also discussed with Ian Coulter whether he would play a similar role following the transaction 'as distinct from Mr Coulter's role within Tughans, pre-closing'.

Under this proposal, neither Coulter nor Cushnahan would be compensated based on their work on a successful PIMCO bid, as suggested in earlier discussions and correspondence during 2013, but on work they did for the US fund after it purchased the loan book. Until then, according to Brown Rudnick, and presumably as far as Cushnahan understood, he was to be part of a success fee or asset management arrangement, although there was no binding agreement on this with PIMCO. His compensation package would be disclosed to NAMA at a time mutually agreed between PIMCO and Brown Rudnick. Whatever payment Coulter was to get was, at least until this point, to be agreed with his partners at Tughans, which would receive any fee payment intended for him as well as other legal costs it incurred.

On 10 March PIMCO head of legal and compliance, Hugh Mildred, who had six months earlier negotiated Brown Rudnick's £16 million success fee and discussed Cushnahan's involvement in the 'three way split', contacted NAMA to inform the agency of information it had 'discovered' in relation to the fee arrangement. Also involved in the conference call were PIMCO's external legal counsel and Ronnie Hanna.

Mildred informed the NAMA head of asset recovery that it had planned to compensate Brown Rudnick in a success fee which was, he said, 'not unusual'. However, PIMCO legal had discovered, through its own inquiries, that the fee was to be 'split three ways between Brown Rudnick, Tughans and Mr Frank Cushnahan'.

Mildred asked Hanna if NAMA was aware that Cushnahan stood to benefit if PIMCO acquired the Project Eagle loans. Hanna said the agency was not aware of the fee arrangement and it would need to consider the matter further.

Mildred told Hanna that the fund was 'still investigating the matter but wanted to be transparent'. Clearly, no final agreement had been reached on the alternative arrangement of management fees to be paid after the deal was closed between PIMCO and NAMA, leading to the fund's legal team picking up the phone to NAMA. Brown Rudnick did not know about PIMCO's decision to alert NAMA to its concerns over the fee arrangements. During the conference call with Hanna on 10 March, PIMCO legal had indicated that the fund would consider whether the transaction could proceed without payments to the proposed success fee recipients.

Unsurprisingly, there was much hand-wringing within the Treasury Building and other offices around Dublin when it emerged that PIMCO and Brown Rudnick had been involved in discussions relating to the payment of success fees for many months leading up to the phone call on 10 March. It must have been a matter of even greater shock for many NAMA executives and directors to learn, for the first time, that Cushnahan was in line for a fee payment along with Brown Rudnick and Tughans. At a meeting convened the following day, 11 March, the board was informed of a 'potential issue which had arisen [the previous day] in relation to Project Eagle during a conference call between the head of asset recovery and senior divisional manager, NAMA legal and legal counsel for PIMCO'.

The board noted that Cushnahan had not disclosed any conflict of interest in relation to the Project Eagle/PIMCO discussions while a member of the NIAC or since his resignation in November 2013. It acknowledged that while no member of the NIAC had access to confidential debtor information, Cushnahan 'would be knowledgeable about NAMA's strategy with respect to NI'. It said that 'the involvement of Frank Cushnahan with PIMCO raised a significant reputational risk to NAMA'. It also noted that there were 'reservations' about a success fee being paid to Tughans, which could have come as no surprise given that Cushnahan had offices in their Belfast headquarters where a number of meetings of the NIAC were held since 2012.

Finally, the board discussed whether the PIMCO bid was now 'fatally flawed' as a result of a 'potential perception that PIMCO might have benefited from insider information as a result of Cushnahan's involvement'.

As the board meeting came to a close, Hanna said he would advise PIMCO of the board's concerns and views, which he did soon after the meeting. He called the fund and said that the proposed success fee arrangement of between £15 million and £16 million was considered by the board to be a very serious issue. He asked PIMCO to reflect on the matter and revert to NAMA. In a later call to Hanna, PIMCO expressed its disappointment at the failure of some parties to disclose their interest to the agency. PIMCO explained that it did not wish to remain in a process that could be associated with impropriety for either PIMCO or NAMA and that it was willing to withdraw completely.

Hanna asked whether there were any 'other options' and if the deal could 'be shaped differently for the arrangement fee to come out'. Hanna said that the main concern for NAMA was the proposed success fee to Cushnahan, although the agency was aware that one-third of the fee was to go to Tughans. Indeed, it was payable to one individual in Tughans – its managing partner, Ian Coulter – as was noted during this conversation between Hanna and PIMCO legal.

In the early evening of 12 March 2014, PIMCO called NAMA to say that it 'had no option but to leave the process' given the absence of disclosures that should have been made to NAMA concerning the success fee and its scale of up to £16 million. In response to Hanna's earlier question about proceeding with a deal that could be shaped differently and excluding the arrangement fee, the PIMCO representative said that he could not see how any 'change' would allow his company to continue with the transaction. The head of legal at NAMA expressed her appreciation of PIMCO's position and the fact that it had considered alternatives before deciding to withdraw. She thanked PIMCO for bringing the matter to NAMA's attention and expressed disappointment that what it had disclosed about success fees had effectively made its withdrawal inevitable. In return, PIMCO said that it would confirm its withdrawal in writing while its external legal representative, who was also involved in the discussion, noted that it was clear that NAMA had not been aware of the 'finder's fee'. If this exchange between lawyers was heavily loaded with cautious and legalistic terminology, it was because both organisations knew that there was a prospect of extremely expensive and damaging litigation if the controversy over fee payments was not extinguished quickly and in private.

They said that they would adopt an agreed approach to media and other communications and would consult with each other in any further responses or comments. PIMCO also confirmed that it had not informed Brown Rudnick of its decision to withdraw, while NAMA decided it had no reporting obligations in regard to Lazard and 'no need to take positive action'. Finally, they agreed to discuss their communication of the message the next day, including to PIMCO's other 'advisors'.

At the NAMA board meeting on 13 March, members noted that PIMCO had withdrawn after NAMA indicated its difficulty with the £16 million, three-way split fee arrangement and had declined to accept it. It also noted that the discussions involving the payments to Cushnahan, in particular, stretched back to April 2013. It recorded that 'the board noted that PIMCO had advised that the negotiations had commenced in April 2013 and noted further that Frank

Cushnahan had not resigned as a member of the NIAC until 7 November 2013 nor had he made any disclosure of his involvement'. PIMCO formally notified the agency of its withdrawal on the same day, leaving two bidders in the sales process for Project Eagle: Fortress and Cerberus. The board was informed that 'based on indications arising from their limited data room activity, Fortress appeared to be less actively engaged in the process than Cerberus to date'.

Immediately after the board meeting, Daly informed finance minister Michael Noonan of PIMCO's withdrawal and its reasons for doing so at a critical stage of the sales process. Although the minister had made certain directions and requests to the agency in the past, he did not have the power under the NAMA Act to instruct what course it should take in relation to its commercial transactions. The minister could not interfere in commercial decision-making but could only give written directions to NAMA towards the achievement of its objectives, according to his interpretation of the Act. This reading of his influence also contrasted with the assertion by McDonagh to the PAC in December 2013 that the minister had the power to direct NAMA, and on occasion, used it.

Of course, it would be expected that his advice and that of his legal officials would be heeded. When he learned of this extraordinary development in the highly sensitive and confidential Project Eagle sales process, he certainly did not suggest that it be 'put on ice' until all the facts became clear. It might have been expected that NAMA would have interviewed some of the key players implicated in this potential political controversy, including Cushnahan, and its loan sales advisor, Lazard, among others, before proceeding with the competition. Indeed, Lazard might well have appreciated being informed of the relationships between PIMCO, Brown Rudnick, Tughans and Cushnahan, and Cushnahan's association with several NAMA debtors in the North, given its professional and supervisory role – but this did not happen either. A formal interview with Cushnahan, who had responsibilities arising from his membership of the NIAC, including under ethics and disclosure rules, could have been arranged in order for the agency to gather further useful information about the 'behind the scenes' dealings in which he was involved over many months and years. A phone call or more to some of the NAMA debtors to whom he had provided advice or indeed to others with whom Cushnahan was professionally and politically connected might have revealed useful information in advance of any decision to proceed with the Project Eagle sale. However, it appeared one conversation with the finance minister in Dublin was enough to give the green light to the largest single sale of public assets in the history of the Irish state and its transfer, at a significant discount, to an international investment or 'vulture' fund. At any rate, Noonan and his secretary general John Moran were committed to supporting, indeed encouraging, an accelerated disposal strategy of public assets to only those few global funds who could afford to purchase them, given the huge bundles of loans involved – despite the very obvious opportunity such vast multi-billion transactions could offer unscrupulous elements offering various services in the globalised asset procurement and property management business.

As recently as 5 February 2013 Noonan had given advice to NAMA when he suggested that the agency should accelerate its asset disposals in order to help the government reduce its debt ratio from 120 per cent to 94 per cent of GDP. At a strategy 'away day' meeting in Dublin's Herbert Park Hotel, Noonan asked the agency to 'consider whether it could advance the repayment schedule of senior bonds through accelerating asset disposals with a view to making bank assets more saleable'. His decision not to intervene in the Project Eagle sales fiasco may well have been influenced by his earlier direction to the agency to accelerate its disposal of assets as quickly as possible. Either way, the Project Eagle process continued, and the players still in the race lined up to seize the ultimate prize. The stakes were very high and there were some very influential political and corporate figures ready to provide their assistance to their favoured bidder, whenever and wherever needed, on both sides of the Atlantic. On 14 March Lazard reported that Fortress and Cerberus were seeking an extension to the revised bid date of 25 March. Approval was granted by McDonagh and Daly to extend it to 31 March 2014, as suggested by the sale advisors. On 27 March they agreed to a further extension to 1 April for both parties, a reflection of the intense activity involving both bidders as the deadline approached for their final tender proposal.

Having considered its options following the withdrawal of PIMCO, Tuvi Keinan and his colleagues at Brown Rudnick decided that they had put too much hard work and resources into its effort to secure the Project Eagle portfolio and would not let their efforts go to waste. They were unhappy that PIMCO had not informed it of the fact of, or reasons for, its withdrawal from the process and concluded that they had no conflict of interest in assisting another bidder. Brown Rudnick could only surmise from informal discussions with the fund that PIMCO had withdrawn due to

the transaction shifting from an 'off-market' opportunity to an open bidding structure, internal discord within its own organisation more generally, and/or NAMA's negative perception of Mr Cushnahan's proposed advisory role on behalf of PIMCO, given his prior membership on [sic] NIAC.

As PIMCO had never executed a letter of engagement with Brown Rudnick and was no longer in the bidding process, Keinan and his superiors assessed that having spent considerable time and expertise advising the US fund, it could 'leverage its pre-existing work product for the benefit of another potential bidder'. It received assurances from Coulter that none of the materials and information his firm had gathered over preceding months 'derived from PIMCO or any inappropriate source' and that its former client expressed no objection to it approaching other potential bidders.

Brown Rudnick also knew that NewRiver and Cushman & Wakefield, who had also advised PIMCO on the bid, were offering their services to other funds that remained in the race.

As Cushnahan's role was a contributory factor to PIMCO's withdrawal, Keinan and Coulter resolved that the former NIAC member would have no involvement in any contractual arrangement they agreed with any other party seeking to use their services in connection with the Project Eagle sales process. Keinan and senior executives at the firm also insisted that neither he nor anyone else in Brown Rudnick would speak or correspond with Cushnahan in any manner following PIMCO's withdrawal on 12 March 2014.

Having reassured themselves that they had no outstanding professional conflicts in continuing engagement with the NAMA sale, Brown Rudnick executives approached Cerberus, an existing client of the law firm, to offer its strategic advice and support for the bid and also the local knowledge and expertise of Tughans in Belfast.

Keinan was on good terms with Robert Falls in Cerberus, having previously worked with him at Morgan Stanley, and informed the US fund of the opportunity presented by the sale of Project Eagle. Falls served as managing director before he left the bank in 2012 to lead the European operations of Cerberus with Ranald Coggle, who was also employed by Morgan Stanley in the mid-1990s.

During his time with Morgan Stanley, Keinan, from London, was involved in the purchase from NAMA of a property in the dockland area of the city. The property was part of the distressed loan portfolio (known as Project Neptune) of Donal Mulryan, brother of Sean Mulryan of the Ballymore Group. NAMA also wanted to dispose of another retail business in Manchester from the portfolio, but Morgan Stanley was not interested in purchasing it. The circumstances surrounding the sale of the Manchester property was subsequently the subject of Garda inquiries resulting from claims made to the GBFI by Enda Farrell, but nothing emerged from the investigation. Morgan Stanley also invested on behalf of the NPRF over the years through its property arm, Morgan Stanley Real Estate Funds (MSREF). Keinan was a central figure in the Project Eagle purchase and had relocated to Dublin for Brown Rudnick for several months prior to its completion, working out of the offices owned by solicitor Bernard McEvoy in Fitzwilliam Square.

The ink was not dry on the letter of withdrawal received from PIMCO on 14 March when Keinan met with Falls, managing director of Cerberus European Servicing Ltd, and Ron Rawald, its managing director and head of European real estate. Keinan explained to the Cerberus executives that he was initially approached by Tughans regarding Project Eagle and had been engaged in the months of discussions with NAMA on behalf of PIMCO before the latter's withdrawal. Keinan explained that Brown Rudnick would seek to retain Tughans, and that the Belfast firm had worked with Cushnahan as part of their advisory services on Project Eagle. Confirming that Cushnahan's previous role with the NIAC and the plan for him to 'perform post-closing work' may have been a factor in PIMCO's sudden withdrawal from the process, Keinan made clear that his firm would not be communicating with the Belfast consultant while providing legal services to Cerberus. The US fund retained Brown Rudnick to advise on its bid for Project Eagle but only after receiving assurances in relation to the law firm's compliance with 'applicable anti-corruption and conflicts of interest laws' which are in any case normal features of such an engagement letter. The contract provided for a success fee for Brown Rudnick of £15 million if the transaction negotiations with NAMA were successful, and it was acknowledged that this would be split with Tughans after any sale of Project Eagle to Cerberus. Again, the success fee was, according to Brown Rudnick, 'within the typical range for a transaction of this nature' given its size and complexity and the contingent nature of the fee. Tughans also confirmed its compliance with the applicable anti-corruption and conflict of interest laws and in early April 2014 the detail of the agreements between all three were disclosed to NAMA by Cerberus. However, this was communicated to NAMA only after Cerberus made its final bid for the Project Eagle loan book.

On 3 April, two days after it submitted its final bid, Cerberus was asked by NAMA whether success fees were payable under the terms of its agreement with legal and other advisors. Rawald replied that it had engaged NewRiver, which had also advised PIMCO, and Brown Rudnick for the Project Eagle purchase.

After consulting with his internal legal team, Rawald wrote to Ronnie Hanna later that day to confirm that Brown Rudnick had sub-contracted work to Tughans with which it intended to share 50 per cent of its success fee. He also assured Hanna that Cerberus would obtain from Brown Rudnick written certification from Tughans that it was acting in conformity with the US Foreign Corrupt Practices Act 1977 and the UK Bribery Act 2010.

When NAMA heard from Cerberus that it was using the same law firms which acted for PIMCO, it sought assurances that no fee would be paid by Brown Rudnick and Tughans to any other party, in particular to 'any current or former member of the NAMA board or current or former members of a NAMA advisory committee in connection with Project Eagle'. Cerberus 'provided both oral and written confirmation to NAMA that neither firm would share their part of the fee with any current or former member of NAMA or a NAMA advisory committee'. From this exchange, it was evident that it was very late in the day when Cerberus confirmed to NAMA that it had hired Brown Rudnick and Tughans to provide legal services. The information could have provided NAMA with another reason to halt, or at least suspend the sale, as it was in breach of its non-disclosure agreement, which required Cerberus to inform the agency of any appointment of advisors, but no such action was taken.

Cerberus also failed to disclose to NAMA other breaches of their NDA, including that it had passed details of the adjusted reserve price to Brown Rudnick on 21 March, shared a letter received from Lazard with Brown Rudnick on 25 March which it believed was then shared with Tughans, and informed Brown Rudnick on 27 March that its request for an extension to the bid deadline had been accepted.

Meanwhile Cerberus was engaging in its own diplomatic offensive and on 25 March wrote to the NI finance minister Simon Hamilton regarding the acquisition of Project Eagle. It promised that it would employ a long-term asset investment strategy, utilisation of local supply chains and the release of corporate and personal guarantees attached to the loans – almost a carbon copy of assurances provided to Robinson and Hamilton by PIMCO in the autumn of 2013. It also echoed a letter sent to NAMA by Jeremy Gardner on Robinson's behalf in January 2014. The letter contained a proposed memorandum of understanding of how the borrowers should be treated by the purchaser of the NI loan book. It was dismissed by Daly as a 'debtors' charter' at the time.

The Cerberus plans for cooperative borrowers involved debt for equity swaps and the availability of further debt funding. In what had to be a choreographed arrangement in advance of the detailed letter from Cerberus outlining its plans, Robinson and Hamilton met former US vice-president and Cerberus chairman, Dan Quayle, at a meeting in Stormont also attended by Ian Coulter on 23 March 2014.

A trained lawyer, Quayle served as US vice-president from 1989 to 1993 under President George HW Bush and was previously congressman and senator for Indiana. Famous for his malapropisms, Quayle told the *Wall Street Journal* in 1989: 'I believe we are on an irreversible trend towards more freedom and democracy, but that could change.' When he joined Cerberus after his term as vice-president, Quayle could hardly have imagined that his new role would involve him travelling to a small country on the other side of the Atlantic promoting the benefits of the multi-billion investment fund to its senior politicians or inviting significant controversy in doing so.

On this occasion, Cerberus assumed that their meeting was an official one with the first minister, but this was disputed by Deputy First Minister Martin McGuinness when he learned of it. McGuinness insisted that such a meeting can only be 'official' if the Office of the First and Deputy First Minister is informed and the meeting is included in its timetable of formal events. On the contrary, his office, which carried equal weight to Robinson's, was not so informed. It probably did not come as a huge surprise to McGuinness and his advisors at Stormont that they were 'kept out of the loop' by their government partners on certain matters, including sensitive commercial decisions and actions. Relations between Sinn Féin and the DUP were, as McGuinness said, 'appalling' over many months during 2013 and 2014, often threatening to collapse the political institutions. One senior Sinn Féin figure recalled that there appeared to be a pattern that relations deteriorated or crises erupted in and around the times when certain sensitive business dealings involving Robinson and his associates were taking place and contact between the two government parties was at a minimum.

McGuinness had been involved in a conference call in January 2014 with Robinson and Michael Noonan, during which the finance minister announced Irish government support for NAMA to proceed with the sale of Project Eagle as a single bundle. During the call, Robinson expressed his support for proposals put forward by PIMCO in relation to absolving cooperative debtors of their personal guarantees, among other commitments close to his heart. However, when he met McGuinness at a political event just hours after his meeting with Quayle at Stormont in late March, the first minister never mentioned that he had just had discussions on the North's distressed property loan book with the former US vice-president.

If the local furore which followed his visit was wearisome, it was nothing compared to the reaction of the US Department of Justice when it discovered that Quayle, still referred to by its agents and other administration officials as 'Mr Vice-President', discovered that he had taken an unscheduled trip to Ireland which purportedly had not been cleared by the senior officials responsible for his personal security. It is also understood that Quayle met prominent banking and legal figures in Dublin during his short trip to Ireland.

On the same day as the Cerberus letter to Hamilton was delivered, 25 March, a senior executive of Fortress met with Hanna and his deputy head of asset recovery, but the NAMA executives insisted afterwards that there was no discussion of Project Eagle at what was described as an 'introductory' meeting.

Cerberus representatives met with finance department officials in Dublin on 28 March, when they discussed, among other matters, the fund's recent acquisition

of waste management company Greenstar, its interest in the Permanent Trustee
Savings bank and Project Eagle. In contrast, when Fortress managing director
Michael George wrote to NAMA on 31 March, seeking guidance in relation to
Fortress's bid, McDonagh told Hanna to send back a message that all
communications should go through Lazard.

On the same day, and almost 24 hours before the bidding process was to close,
Noonan and his senior department officials received a delegation from Cerberus,
including its chairman and former US treasury secretary under George W Bush
until 2006, John Snow. They discussed the fund's interest in Project Eagle and
their plans to meet senior NAMA executives for a courtesy visit later in the day.
Snow expressed some concerns over the bidding process for Project Eagle but the
detail of the discussion remained confidential. When the US delegation later met
Daly and others, the NAMA chairman advised that they could not talk about
their planned bid for Project Eagle.

An experienced politician, lawyer, economist and businessman, Snow was a
former head of the giant US railway corporation CSX before he was appointed
treasury secretary by Bush in February 2003. Under his direction the rail company
failed to pay its due taxes in 1998 and 2001, which Snow attributed to operating
losses and its joint purchase of the government-owned rail line Conrail. He was
pursued by the US media in relation to reported multi-million dollar personal
loans he accumulated from the company while head of CSX. The debts were
wiped out when its share values plummeted.

The NAMA board was not informed of the meeting between Snow and other
senior Cerberus figures with its own executives on the day before the closing date
for bids. No one from the Department of Finance or the government press office
disclosed, until months later, that Noonan had met with a former US treasury
secretary or the content of their discussions on the day before bids for Project
Eagle closed, at 1.00 p.m. on 1 April 2014.

When its board met at short notice on 3 April to discuss the bidding process
and the issue of success fees, only Brendan McDonagh was present in the room
in the Treasury Building, with four members joining him by conference call. It
was reminiscent of the night of the bank guarantee in September 2008, when a
fateful cabinet meeting was held to discuss the proposed and controversial
blanket bank guarantee. The late-night 'incorporeal' meeting of cabinet
involved Taoiseach Brian Cowen contacting his ministers by telephone to
discuss the issue and approve decisions. On that occasion, McDonagh was left
outside the room while the meetings between government and bankers were
taking place through the night of 29–30 September. This time he was the only
one present in what was arguably the most important meeting of the NAMA

board and certainly its largest and most fraught commercial decision since its inception.

The board meeting heard that Brown Rudnick and Tughans were to share a success fee if Cerberus was the successful bidder and no others were to receive any portion of the fee. Aideen O'Reilly, head of NAMA legal, said that Tughans was to receive the fee rather than any named individual partner of the solicitor's firm. A report from Hanna's asset recovery team was presented, which included the information that the minimum reserve price had been reduced to £1.23 billion (from £1.3 billion) due to sales of some £83.6 million in assets from the portfolio by NAMA over recent months. The Fortress bid totalled £1.075 billion, or £155 million below the minimum reserve price, and did not include as much detail as the Cerberus tender documents, including a requirement to allocate their offer to individual assets within the portfolio. It was also conditional on being an exclusive offer to Fortress with a further 30-day extension to allow it to gather further information on the assets involved.

On the other hand, Cerberus made an offer which was well over the reserve price, had allocated prices to individual assets, did not seek exclusivity and had a more robust business plan than that put forward by Fortress. The board once again agreed to get a written assurance that no payments were intended for any former director or advisory committee member in connection with the Cerberus bid. Aideen O'Reilly prepared the draft for Cerberus in which the assurance was provided.

NAMA then decided to continue negotiations with Cerberus as the lead bidder based on its £1.24 billion offer for Project Eagle and with the intention of closing the sale by 31 May 2014. McDonagh and Hanna were delegated the authority to approve a revised minimum reserve price of £1.2 billion, depending on diligence issues, and to negotiate the final terms and conditions of the sale. The sale was finally agreed in June 2014 for £1.137 billion following an adjustment to take account of property sold by NAMA from the portfolio while the sale to Cerberus was under way. This amounted to £76 million, comprising a group of properties and loans sold under the perhaps unfortunately codenamed Project Shift. In its completion letter signing off on the deal on 25 June, Lazard said that 'having regard to the information available to us and NAMA's objectives, the sell-side process of the transaction was appropriate for the sale of a loan portfolio of this nature'. In a less than fulsome endorsement of the decision to dispose of the portfolio, the sale advisors said they 'would not express an opinion on the relative merits of the transaction as compared to alternative transactions, timing or strategies that might be available to NAMA'.

On 31 July, Cerberus paid Brown Rudnick its success fee of £15 million and the 50 per cent share to Tughans was passed on once the Belfast firm had confirmed that it was in compliance with the required and relevant anti-corruption, anti-money laundering and conflicts of interest laws. Assurances provided by Tughans on 13 August confirmed its understanding that the fee would not be shared by any third party, including Cushnahan, and that the fee was payable to the law firm and not to Coulter as an individual. With that in mind, the fee was to be paid to an official Tughans bank account after appropriate invoicing and under the direction of the firm's finance director.

While the biggest transaction in corporate history in the North was playing out beyond the glare of media or public scrutiny, the NAMA executives were busy with challenges, large and small, on many other fronts. Their attempt to close down the allegations made in the media, in the Dáil and at the PAC in December 2013 was not as effective as they might have wished and indeed some statements made in their defence were about to come back to haunt them. Enda Farrell was particularly aggrieved as he languished in exile in Brussels, his reputation seriously damaged, unemployable and minding his small children while his wife, Alice, tried to make a living in her home town.

Farrell was unhappy not because he believed he had done nothing wrong but because he knew that others, including some more senior than him in NAMA, had similarly passed on documents and other information from the agency to outside parties. He was also annoyed by the manner and tone with which McDonagh had trounced him at the PAC on 20 December and at the way in which the 'dodgy dossier', as he called it, had been compiled and distributed to certain politicians and the media. When he read the media reports and watched the Dáil and PAC proceedings, he was incensed at how information he had, somewhat naively, given voluntarily, was now being spun against him. In particular, he felt that McDonagh had sneered at the suggestion that he might have asked Farrell for information on a property in County Kerry on behalf of his niece. Frank Daly had been asked by PAC chairman John McGuinness to comment on requests they made to Farrell about the valuations on certain properties to which he had access. Daly responded:

I have not seen it, but I am told that somewhere in this dossier there is one line that reads, 'I think Frank Daly enquired about a property in Wexford'. That is all. I never knew Mr. Farrell and, to my knowledge, never met him. I certainly have no recollection of ever inquiring about a property in Wexford.

It was surprising that they had never met as Farrell was one of the first people to be employed by NAMA and had addressed its management and board meetings.

When Farrell next met detectives by arrangement in Dublin two months later in February 2013, he realised that his discussions with Denis O'Sullivan had been made available to the Garda investigation team.

The dossier compiled by O'Sullivan formed the basis of a number of additional questions the fraud squad officers put to Farrell when they met at Clontarf Garda station on 22 February 2014.

The GBFI officers interviewing Farrell first asked how he came to meet Denis O'Sullivan, to which he responded that they had met in Brussels and that he had sent him a document relating to work done by Paul Hennigan in NAMA, in whom the private investigator had showed a particular interest.

'He told me he works for Paddy McKillen,' Farrell told the gardaí. They then asked about Liam Cunningham, who worked for McKillen and with whom Farrell had spoken on one occasion. Cunningham had provided Farrell's contact details to O'Sullivan and the detective had handed over the dossier to McKillen's man. Asked about Hennigan, Farrell recounted his former colleague's alleged involvement with the Barclay brothers and said that he had spoken to him several months previous.

I rang him over the summer in 2013 and I apologised for dragging him into my mess. He was in Dublin airport heading to his job in London … in Prime Properties. Paul bent backwards to help certain borrowers. Among them were Avestus over Project Nantes and Deirdre Foley from D2.

Farrell said that Hennigan knew about his purchase of Sunday's Well and had left the decision document concerning the sale, which named him and his wife, on Hennigan's desk at NAMA at the time. Farrell said that Hennigan had asked him to 'keep his name out of it' if he was queried about the purchase. Complying with the request, Farrell had lied to the *Sunday Times* journalist in August 2012 when he said that no one in NAMA knew about the purchase before the newspaper discovered details of the transaction. He also said he paid market price for the property, that no inducement was requested, or offered, in connection with the purchase and that if it had been sold as part of the wider Project Nantes portfolio the agency would have received just 10 cents in the euro in value. He said the estimated €300 million in personal loans of Avestus directors were sold off for between €20 million and €30 million, from what he had learned within the agency. He confirmed that Hennigan had provided him with the Avestus business plan which was attached to the Anton Pillar order granted against Farrell by Judge Peter Charleton in September 2012. Farrell confirmed that he had supplied Elaine Tooke of auctioneers Knight Frank with valuation details of the Jervis Street Shopping Centre, developed by McKillen, but that he had not provided any information on the developer's personal finances as had been claimed in some recent newspaper reports. He denied a suggestion by the gardaí that he had secured a job with Forum Partners based on confidential information he disclosed and that this represented a corrupt act.

'I don't accept that. Was it not the function of NAMA and the Irish state to attract foreign capital into the Irish market? I accept that I used confidential information in the presentation I prepared [for Forum],' he said, including valuations relating to the Dundrum Shopping Centre. He accepted that his actions were 'reckless' and that he had apologised to NAMA over his 'error in judgement'. He responded to questions about other named individuals in NAMA who had sought valuations from him or supplied him with agency documents or about whom he had heard allegations that they had leaked confidential information, including a since-departed senior figure within the organisation. Farrell told the gardaí that another NAMA official, Paul Pugh, was under investigation for alleged leaking of information or other improprieties and that he had heard this from his own solicitor, Robert Dore. Asked about the request by Frank Daly about a property in Wexford, and whether the chairman was not entitled to inquire about any property in NAMA, Farrell replied: 'No, I don't have further information about it. There is an email from [John] Mulcahy about it.'

Shown notes of his telephone calls and meeting with O'Sullivan, he agreed that they reflected the conversations they had had but contained some inaccuracies and a word, 'bollix', which he said he did not believe he would use. He said that O'Sullivan was 'colourful in his words' and he denied telling the private investigator that NAMA was 'hell bent on destroying the banks'. However, he agreed that the notes of his discussions with the private detective shown to him by the GBFI officers were largely 'accurate'.

Farrell confirmed that when he was interviewed by Richard Willis of Arthur Cox and Michael Moriarty from NAMA in late 2012, he volunteered to them that he had shared confidential agency information with two individuals, including Barden Gale, to whom he supplied 'all of the US portfolio' of NAMA by email to his office at Dutch pension firm ABP. Farrell said that he also sent confidential NAMA information to Lee Neibart from Apollo Real Estate in New York, with whom the NPRF invested during Farrell's time at the state pension fund. The information contained valuation reports of the Chicago Spire, which was then on hold as its developer, Garrett Kelleher, struggled to clear his debts with NAMA.

Farrell also said that he had confirmed to *Sunday Independent* reporter Ronald Quinlan the request made by McDonagh concerning the house in Kerry on behalf of his niece, in response to a phone call from the newspaper.

O'Sullivan had met with the GBFI team at the Clarence Hotel and its offices some weeks prior to their interview with Farrell where the former garda explained the motivation behind his approach to the former NAMA official. He described how he was hired by McKillen in October 2013 to look into the source of leaks about the developer to third parties and newspapers 'that may have emanated from banks or agencies controlled by the Irish government'. From publicly available information he knew about Enda Farrell he said that he was aware that Farrell had 'previously contacted the Paddy McKillen organisation offering his help'. He confirmed that he had first called Farrell in Brussels on 3 December 2013 and he provided the gardaí with written notes of several of their conversations held in person and by phone. Some of these were written contemporaneously and others from memory 'as soon as practicable' after their conversations, which took place between 3 December and 20 December 2013. He categorically denied that he had disclosed the contents of the notes to politicians or the media. 'I gave them to Liam Cunningham at Mr McKillen's office in Hume Street [Dublin],' O'Sullivan told the detectives on 19 January 2014.

*(The pitch book was not released publicly by the PAC due to its commercial sensitivity)

Chapter 17 ～

THE THREE-HEADED DOG

In early May 2014 the staff of the Department of Finance in Merrion Street were jolted from their normal duties when an email from the secretary general popped up on their computer screens. John Moran was less than two years in the second most senior position (after the secretary general in the Department of the Taoiseach) in the civil service and his sudden resignation was almost as big a shock as his appointment to the job in March 2012. Before his accession to the post, courtesy of finance minister Michael Noonan, he had worked in the banking division of the department since April 2011, having been seconded from the Central Bank, which he joined in 2010. He replaced Kevin Cardiff, who resigned to take up his appointment to the European Court of Auditors amid significant controversy at the time.

Moran had previously worked for Swiss insurance company Zurich Capital Markets (ZCM) in Dublin, Sydney and London before he became its chief executive in 1997. A qualified solicitor, he had spent time with law firm McCann Fitzgerald in New York, GE Capital Aviation Services Group/GPA, and was an associate attorney with corporate lawyers Sullivan & Cromwell, also in New York, in the late 1980s. Noonan said that he had accepted the resignation of his fellow Limerick man with 'great regret' and said that Moran had 'been involved in every significant decision taken by me throughout the bailout programme, including those decisions which saw Ireland successfully exiting the programme. I valued his counsel during those very difficult times and I wish John every success in the future.'

Ireland had successfully emerged from the EU/ECB/IMF bailout programme six months earlier, in December 2013. Moran had also been involved in negotiating the deal on Anglo Irish promissory notes, which the government said had resulted in significant reductions in the country's debt repayments.

Not everyone was a fan of Moran, who had ruffled feathers in his own department with his unique style and unorthodox approach in the most conservative of environments in the so-called 'permanent government'. Unlike many of his predecessors, Moran was not averse to engaging with private business and financial interests. He was second secretary general in the department for only six months, responsible for banking policy, managing the state's shareholding in banks and re-organising the distressed and dysfunctional Irish banking sector following the traumatic collapse in 2008, before he secured the top job in the department. His appointment had also raised hackles in the Dáil. Sinn Féin finance spokesman Pearse Doherty was expelled when he tried to question aspects of Moran's previous career two days after his appointment in March 2012. The Ceann Comhairle accused Doherty of attempted character assassination when the Donegal TD sought to explore aspects of Moran's corporate career, in particular an adverse finding by the US Securities and Exchange Commission (SEC) against his former employer, ZCM, of which he was chief executive from 1997 to 2005.

In May 2007, ZCM was fined a massive $16 million as the SEC found that it had

provided financing, aided and abetted four hedge funds that were carrying out schemes to defraud mutual funds that prohibited market timing. Specifically, ZCM provided financing to four market-timing hedge funds that employed various deceptive tactics to invest in mutual funds. ZCM and these hedge funds knew that many mutual funds in which they invested imposed restrictions on market timing activity. In order to buy, exchange and redeem shares in these mutual funds, these hedge funds employed deceptive techniques designed to avoid detection by these mutual funds. ZCM came to learn that the hedge funds were utilizing deceptive practices to market time mutual funds, and nonetheless ZCM provided financing to them and took administrative steps that substantially assisted them.

During the relevant period, ZCM was an affiliate of Zurich Global Assets LLC (subsequently reorganised and re-named Crown Management Services Ltd), and an indirect subsidiary of Zurich Financial Services, its Swiss holding company.

Following his departure from ZCM, two years before the SEC ruling, Moran ran a juice bar in the French Languedoc region and it was this occupation and his restoration of a large property in the area that attracted most media attention following his appointment as secretary general of the Department of Finance rather than his corporate affairs in the US. As a board member of Zurich, Moran lobbied for and achieved a significant change to Irish banking rules which, for the first time, allowed a bank to operate within an insurance group and to engage in very lucrative hedge fund lending in Dublin. Ironically, Doherty's expulsion from the Dáil meant that he could not, as he intended, introduce legislation to bring NAMA under the remit of the Freedom of Information Act 1997.

Not yet in his fifties, Moran left the department in August 2014 with no indication of what position he would take up on his return to the private sector, but no one was left in any doubt that the man from Patrickswell would land on his feet.

With Noonan, he had encouraged NAMA to increase its disposal rate and actively encouraged international investors to purchase Irish property, attending frequent meetings with visiting heads from various global asset funds, along with the minister, and talking up the tax efficiencies available to the corporates through the QIF and other incentives. NAMA was moving from its acquisition and management phase into rapid sales mode with the C&AG reporting in May that the agency had sold €3.7 billion, including €1.4 billion in Ireland, in the year to the end of February 2014, compared to just €900 million in the first three years of operation. This did not include the Project Eagle sale and several other major disposals which followed in quick succession. The C&AG review indicated that NAMA intended to raise a mind-boggling €19.2 billion, including €11 billion in Ireland, over the next two years to the end of 2016, confirming its dubious status as the world's largest property disposal company. To achieve its target the agency would be required to intensify its disposal rate by almost five times that of 2013 when much of its revenues were raised from the sale of UK, US and other valuable portfolios abroad.

During this period, the agency confirmed that Noonan had appointed accountant Mari Hurley to its board of directors. The chief financial officer of Web Reservations International, she had previously worked as finance director of Sherry FitzGerald Group and also at Bear Stearns Bank PLC. She had also been on the board of Bord Gáis Éireann since 2013. A long-time activist with Fine Gael, and a former youth officer and member of its national executive council, Hurley was a trustee of the party when she was appointed to NAMA. She joined another Fine Gael supporter and a constituency organiser for Noonan in Limerick, Brian McEnery, on the board of the agency. Board members received an annual fee of €50,000 plus an extra €10,000 for chairing one of its committees.

When the sale of Project Eagle was completed in June, its largest sale by NAMA to date with a par value of €5.6 billion, Cerberus Capital Management immediately set about identifying the borrowers who were most likely to yield the quickest return on its investment. Equally, the distressed debtors who were keen to ensure that their personal guarantees over their bank loans would not be called in by Cerberus and that they would be enabled to refinance their debts, were seeking assurances from their political allies that they would be treated favourably. Peter Robinson was eager to assist those who had provided his party organisation with political and financial support over the years; others were not so fortunate. Cerberus was not called after the three-headed dog of Greek mythology for nothing and its executives were keen to ensure that those it employed were not reluctant to turn the screw on those it deemed un-cooperative. Ranald Coggle, a former investigator in Scotland Yard's Fraud Squad, and his team set up offices on Donegall Square in Belfast before moving to Harvester House on Adelaide Street in the city, from where they set about sweating out the loan portfolio it purchased from NAMA. In less than a year, by the end of May 2015, it had worked through 87 per cent of the loan book, with some 13 per cent subjected to enforcement proceedings. Many of the meetings they had with developers took place in the office of its loan administrators, Capita, in the Metro building in Donegall Square. One debtor said the rough rule of thumb was repayment in full plus 20 per cent in three months. If they wanted longer then it was more than 20 per cent.

Among the first to cut a deal with Cerberus was Newry developer Gerard O'Hare, whose company Parker Green refinanced its loans with the backing of New York-based Garrison Investment Group and venture partners Earlsfort Capital in Dublin. Garrison was formed in 2007 by Joseph Tansey, a former managing director of Fortress Investment Group, while Earlsfort Capital was formed in March 2014 by Fergus Feeney and Paul Brophy, two former officials of Anglo Irish Bank.

According to O'Hare, the arrangement allowed Parker Green to expand its shopping centre complex in Newry, and to complete extensions to the Fairgreen Shopping Centre in Carlow and its buildings on Merrion Street in Dublin, close to the Cerberus offices in the capital.

'The past number of years working with Nama have been difficult and in reality we needed the injection of a commercial player like Cerberus into the market to bring their reputation and expertise to the table. Ultimately it's business that best understands business,' said O'Hare, after the refinancing deal was confirmed in January 2015.

The developer, who was worth €171 million in 2013, according to the *Sunday Times* 'rich list', was reportedly unhappy with the engagement he had with NAMA when his loans were first transferred to the agency. It was suggested that he had complained to agency executives over his treatment and the behaviour of some NAMA representatives in the North with whom he had met. Former Taoiseach Bertie Ahern joined the international advisory board of Parker Green International following his retirement from politics in 2008.

Coggle was joined by Dublin man Brian Berg in the challenge to wind down the 850 property assets it had acquired from NAMA, and to do so rapidly.

Berg left Shelbourne Development when the company fell into the hands of NAMA in 2009 and went on to join Pepper Asset Servicing in January 2013 as its head of commercial real estate in Dublin. Pepper was chosen by giant US fund

CarVal to manage the €380 million Irish loan book acquired from Lloyds in late 2012, as well as other property portfolios it had purchased. With a degree in property economics from the Dublin Institute of Technology in Bolton Street, Berg was set to handle the wind-down of the Project Eagle portfolio and was expected to take no prisoners in the process of making a serious return for Cerberus. Like Coggle, he was no soft touch and the pair went on to earn reputations as tough and ruthless dealers when it came to debtors. Cerberus was already a global force which could bring powerful political and financial influence to bear on government ministers and civil servants in the many countries in which it operated. Through its subsidiary, DynCorp International, it provided aviation, transport, security and intelligence back-up to the US military in several theatres of war including Serbia, Afghanistan and Iraq, where the behaviour of its contractors generated significant controversy. Cerberus also owned the Freedom Group, one the world's largest gun manufacturers.

As Berg took on the task of dealing with the Project Eagle debtors in the North and acquiring other distressed loans across the country, his former mentor and boss, Garrett Kelleher, was in deep water.

At NAMA's request, Garrett Kelleher had sold assets in 2012 and 2013 in Dublin city centre as well as properties in Ranelagh in Dublin 6. In March 2013 Jones Lang LaSalle, New York, commenced the sales process of the US Anglo Irish loans for the Chicago Spire on behalf of NAMA. Kelleher had been dealing with Kevin Nowlan and John Mulcahy, among others, in NAMA. The loans had been transferred to NAMA from Anglo IBRC in June 2013.

In July 2014, NAMA sought an order for €46.8 million against the developer arising from personal guarantees he had provided on loans he received from Anglo Irish for projects in Ireland. The agency claimed in the Dublin court that some €350 million was outstanding on his various loans and he was liable under guarantee for over €40 million. The other €6.8 million arose from loan facilities advanced on one of his companies, CWD, for a development in Cratloe Woods in Limerick from 2000. His lawyer, Michael Cush SC, argued that Kelleher had been assured by NAMA that he would not be pursued given his 'extensive co-operation' with the agency. From his early dealings with NAMA, and his meeting with Mulcahy in the Schoolhouse Hotel in 2009, Kelleher had decided to assist the agency, but he was also determined that he was not going to fold his tent under the weight of its demands and that he would fight to rescue the Spire project in Chicago.

At the time of the subsequent hearing of the action before Judge Raymond Fullam in November 2014, Kelleher was in the US seeking to restructure the loans underlying the Spire acquisition. In March 2013, NAMA had commenced the sale of the Spire loans in breach of an understanding which Kelleher claimed he had with the agency. Kelleher claimed that it had been agreed that he would cooperate in Dublin, Chicago and elsewhere and NAMA would not sell the Spire loans or assets until the existing foreclosure process in the US was concluded. He insisted that the Spire site and completed substructure works was still valued at over $300 million, yet NAMA sold on the loan for $35 million. The New York office of Jones Lang LaSalle had an information pack or memo on the loan portfolio compiled, with which they were already familiar. The same JLL had previously examined the Spire data on behalf of Anglo Irish Bank in Boston and had spent several months in discussions with Shelbourne in the summer of 2010 examining the scheme. They knew the contracts, the sales achieved, the planning permission and all agreements Kelleher had with the various city, state and federal bodies for his 609-metre-high tower.

After it put the loans up for sale, NAMA was insisting that no prospective purchaser could gain access to the information memo without confirming that they would not engage with the borrower, Shelbourne, or any of the consultants or advisors who had acted for it. Kelleher submitted that it had no legal right to impose such a restriction as the NAMA Act, under which it was made, had no jurisdiction in the US. Kelleher claimed that NAMA had agreed that it would not sell until the foreclosure process over the Spire was complete, which would have enabled him as a potential creditor to recover some of his considerable personal investment in the project and simultaneously enable NAMA to recover its loan in full.

Kelleher informed the agency that he could find a purchaser willing to redeem the Spire-related loan at par. He had convinced the developer Andy Ruhan, a Galway man who was developing apartment and hotel schemes in Manhattan, New York, that the Spire dream was still attainable and the site had a real value of $300 million. NAMA did not respond to his overtures and Ruhan was denied access to the data room and sight of the various loan documents involved. Ruhan was prohibited from seeing the documents relating to the loans he wished to pay for at their par value. However, Ruhan insisted that he was not seeking to buy the loans but was offering to fund Kelleher's redemption of the loans at par value and was prepared to offer over $90 million (almost €70 million) for them.

'It was explained to us by NAMA that we would be unable to access the data room if we had discussions with Garrett Kelleher,' Ruhan said in July 2013 after the sale. NAMA insisted that the 'confidentiality conditions preclude a potential purchaser from engaging with a debtor once the formal sales process has begun and for the duration of that process'.

Ruhan said that he had to consult with Kelleher in advance as it was only through Kelleher that the loans could be redeemed. Kelleher, he was advised, had a right of redemption of his loans and 'he had knowledge of other matters which would have a bearing on the loan and so we felt we needed his input.' He said that he 'openly confirmed to NAMA that we had discussions with Garrett Kelleher'. While respecting the concerns of NAMA over borrower involvement in any purchase, Ruhan said that he could 'understand that certain rules need to be maintained but what hasn't been explained to me is why the rule means less value in a resulting sale'.

Instead, the agency sold the loan to Related Midwest, a Chicago-based real estate company, in March 2013 for $30 million, although no details of the deal were disclosed on the NAMA website at the time. Related Midwest was a unit of Related Cos, a New York-based firm. For four years after its acquisition of the loans, Related did not progress any proposals.

Throughout 2014, and as NAMA was launching its legal action against him for payment of the personal guarantees over his loans, Kelleher was still battling furiously to save the Chicago project. In March, he confirmed that he had access to up to $135 million from Illinois real estate firm, Atlas Apartment Holdings, with a view to repaying creditors of the Spire project, including Related Midwest. Atlas said it could complete and control the project with Kelleher as developer and based on the original Calatrava design. By October 2014, however, Atlas had failed to make the required payment and Related Midwest filed its petition for the deeds to the 2.2 acre site secured by the loan.

In early November 2014, attorney Joseph Frank, who represented Kelleher and Shelbourne, delivered the deeds of the Spire site to Related Midwest, which in turn withdrew a motion it had filed against the Irish developer in the US Bankruptcy Court compelling him to hand over the documentation. As Related only got deeds to 2.2 acres of the seven-acre site, it was unable to complete the development without the cooperation of Shelbourne. As of late September 2017, there has been no development on the site other than the planting of trees to placate local residents.

The loan valuations for the Spire site at 400 N. Lakeshore Drive on the shores of Lake Michigan in the 'windy city' had been circulating for some years in the US. Enda Farrell had sent the entire US portfolio to Barden Gale before he left the agency. He had worked with Gale, who served with Mulcahy on the powerful property advisory committee of the NPRF. Up to the crash in 2008, property investments by the NPRF had risen to €1.3 billion and Farrell and the committee members were familiar with a range of international banks and investment managers who helped manage and expand the portfolio. Gale worked as chief investment officer for real estate for ABP Investments US Inc., a subsidiary of Dutch pension firm Stichting Pensioenfonds ABP (later APG) when Farrell first knew him at the NPRF. Gale left the firm to join Starwood Capital as its vice chairman of real estate before being appointed as CEO of JER Partners (JE Roberts) in 2009. Farrell sent the file to Gale by email to JER Partners in New York.

In July 2013, Starwood Capital financed the purchase of the Spire loans from NAMA. In October 2013, Gale moved on to become a vice chairman of the New York-based Mack Real Estate group (MREG) founded earlier that year by William, Richard and Stephen Mack. Before setting up MREG, William and Richard Mack had established and led AREA Property Partners (formerly Apollo Real Estate Advisors) where they built investment funds totalling $70 billion in real estate ventures across 25 countries.

Farrell had also sent details of the entire US loan book held by NAMA, including the Spire, to Lee Neibart at AREA before he left the agency in early 2012. JE Roberts and Related Midwest were the original owners of the site at 400 N. Lakeshore Drive before it was acquired by Kelleher in 2006.

The NPRF had, on the recommendation of Mulcahy and Gale, invested in AREA over the years and it was that relationship which prompted Farrell to forward the valuation report relating to the Chicago Spire to Neibart at the New York investment firm, as he later informed the Garda. Neibart was global CEO of AREA Property Partners from 1993 to July 2013, when he left to join the Ares Real Estate Group immediately after its parent, Ares Management LLC, acquired AREA.

If there was any doubt of NAMA's entanglement with the intricate world of global property managers and funds, the saga of the Chicago Spire loan sale illustrated just how embedded its senior executives were with the largest and wealthiest real estate corporations on both sides of the Atlantic.

Chapter 18 ~

OF CHARITY AND TRUSTS

In late September 2014 NAMA announced the departure of Ronnie Hanna, almost six months to the day after the final bid was lodged by Cerberus to secure the Project Eagle deal. The agency said that he would serve a six-month period before joining any other company, although Hanna did not indicate what plans he had for the future. There were suggestions from NAMA executives that his leaving had something to do with the caps on remuneration in the public sector, but there was no evidence that Hanna was being offered a more highly paid position anywhere else. Instead he set up his own private consultancy company registered at his home in Saintfield, Belfast.

Hanna joined a list of 40 people who had left NAMA over previous months and was replaced by Michael Moriarty as head of asset recovery. Others to depart during the year were Hugh Linehan, a portfolio manager, who moved to Lisney, and Mark Carlin, who left for Kennedy Wilson. Marcus Wren left the agency to join Bannon. By this time, John Mulcahy had joined the board of IPUT, which was buying up office blocks in Dublin and was the fastest-growing property pension fund in the country. In early 2014 it had paid €50 million for the European headquarters of social media giant Facebook in the south Dublin Docklands, before the US company moved to larger offices at Grand Canal Square, while it also paid €13 million for a high-profile modern building at the junction of St Stephen's Green and Hume Street, Dublin 2.

Just over six months after his departure from NAMA and in line with its newly introduced rules for executives leaving for the private sector, Mulcahy took up a role as an advisor to telecoms billionaire Denis O'Brien on his extensive overseas property portfolio. This stretched from Portugal and Malta, where he was tax resident, to the Caribbean, where O'Brien's company Digicel had invested heavily since he first controversially won the tender for Ireland's second mobile phone licence in the mid-1990s. O'Brien did not have any loans in NAMA, although he had over €800 million in loans from Anglo before the crash, some of which transferred to the IBRC. He had known Mulcahy for several decades, while they both owned homes at the luxury Mount Juliet golf course in County Kilkenny.

If Mulcahy was finding lucrative employment in the reviving property sector, another former associate from the real estate business was enjoying some equally beneficial rewards from the largest residential deal in the city during 2014. Bill Nowlan acted as agent in the sale of 8.11 acres of land with permission for up to 280 homes, including apartments and houses, on Orwell Road in the highly desirable Rathgar area of Dublin 6. The lands and a monastery on the site, known as the Marianella seminary, were sold by the Redemptorist religious order to Cairn Homes for over €40 million in June 2015. At the time of the purchase, Cairn founders Alan McIntosh and Michael Stanley, previously of Shannon Homes, had just raised €400 million from a London stock market flotation.

The Redemptorists said that they intended to use the proceeds from the sale, for over €10 million above the guide price, to ensure that the work of the order in Ireland and overseas, including at their new mission in Mozambique, could continue. What was intriguing about the sale of Marianella were the advisors the Redemptorists had gathered under their wing in the years prior to the sale, which was first flagged in 2007. Among the directors of Ciorani, a charitable company formed by members of the order, were NAMA chairman Frank Daly and former NIAC member Frank Cushnahan. Cushnahan had invited Daly to join the Ciorani board in June 2010, just weeks after the Belfast man had first been appointed to the NIAC. According to company registration documents, Cushnahan resigned from the board of Ciorani in November 2013, when he also unexpectedly stood down from the NIAC, while Daly remained as a member of the charity's board. The charity was established to advance 'the Catholic religion through the care, education and evangelisation within the Roman Catholic tradition of people throughout the world, especially those who are most deprived'. Among the other directors of Ciorani were Patrick O'Keefe, who was based at the Redemptorist community house in Esker, Athenry in County Galway, and other members of the order. O'Keefe declined to answer a series of questions about the role of Ciorani and whether it had any involvement in the Marianella sale or the proceeds from it when asked by this writer in November 2015.

In its directors' report and financial statements to the end of December 2014, signed off by O'Keefe, total funds for the charity amounted to a staggering €23.14 million, up from €16.44 million the previous year. This did not include any return from the sale of Marianella, which was recorded in different accounts of the religous order. The bulk of the Ciorani income came from healthy investment fund revenues, with most of it managed by J O Hambro Investment. The Ciorani accounts for 2015, published in June 2016, showed total assets of €24.73 million. Frank Daly refused to comment on his role with the charity, telling the *Sunday Independent* that it was a private matter. Asked by the newspaper in July 2015, a month after the sale, what had led Daly to become a director and what level of engagement he had had with Cushnahan during their three years together on the Ciorani board, a NAMA spokesperson replied: 'Frank's charitable activities are a private matter for himself and it is not appropriate for NAMA to comment on them.'

Daly had his term as chairman of NAMA extended for a further five years from December 2014, but he could not have predicted the hurricane he was about to encounter as the agency entered its sixth year. It had redeemed a further €7.6 billion in 2014, bringing the total since it was established to €15.1 billion, or almost 50 per cent of its entire debt – a target it had originally planned to meet by 2016.

One of Daly's close colleagues in NAMA, and chairman of the minister's advisory group supervising the work of the agency, Michael Geoghegan found himself in the media spotlight after another scandal involving his former employer, HSBC, washed ashore. This time it involved the bank's Swiss operations after it was discovered that data removed by a former employee, Hervé Falciani, revealed a massive tax evasion scheme involving more than 100,000 account holders and billions of euro across several jurisdictions, including France, Belgium and Argentina. The bank was facing over €1 billion in fines, which was a small portion of its annual profits, and followed the $1 billion imposed on the bank in the US in 2012 after it was found to have assisted money laundering by drug dealers and other criminal operators who were moving illicit funds into the US banking system.

In February 2015, Sinn Féin leader Gerry Adams again criticised the appointment of Geoghegan to the advisory group on NAMA, given that he was chief executive of HSBC when its Swiss operations 'facilitated tax evasion'. Taoiseach Enda Kenny replied that Geoghegan did not advise the minister on taxation issues 'but in respect of the remuneration of senior executives and other issues on the strategy proposed by NAMA'. The approach contrasted with the controversy which erupted in England when Stephen Green, another former HSBC chief executive and Geoghegan's predecessor at the bank, was appointed as trade minister in the UK government, where he served from 2011 until December 2013. When the Swiss scandal broke, Green, a Tory peer, immediately stepped down as chair of TheCityUK's advisory council, a financial services industry body. Geoghegan took over as group chief executive of HSBC in 2006 after Green left, and remained until 2010, during which time much of the illegal activity uncovered by US investigators at the bank in 2012 and in its Swiss subsidiary took place. After the brief fuss in the Dáil, Geoghegan remained in his advisory role with NAMA.

Commenting on the different approaches by the UK and Irish governments, the *Irish Times* column Cantillon noted: 'the different tack being taken by politicians on the two sides of the Irish Sea says something about the difference in what passes for politics in the two jurisdictions. But it's not quite clear what.'

In March 2015, Enda Farrell appeared at the Dublin Circuit Criminal Court to face 13 charges contrary to the NAMA Act. A trial date was set for the following January. He had previously appeared before the court after he made an arrangement with the GBFI to travel to Dublin from his home in Belgium. As he travelled from Kilmainham Garda station to the courthouse in Islandbridge, near Heuston Station, in late July 2014, Farrell asked whether he would be made do the 'perp walk' and was assured that he would not be greeted by a phalanx of photographers. As they approached the court complex, he noticed the assembled media and cameras and believed that a fresh humiliation was about to be visited on him. It transpired that the media attention that day was focused on former Fianna Fáil junior minister and TD Ivor Callely, who was sentenced to five months in jail for fraudulently claiming mobile phone expenses at Leinster House while he was a senator.

The charges against Farrell centred on his leaking of what NAMA claimed was confidential information, but only to some recipients and only in relation to material he distributed after he left the agency. The reason he was not charged with the leaking of information while he was with NAMA was presumably because the files he distributed were to people outside the Irish jurisdiction, including England, France and the US, where it would have been difficult for the Garda to collect evidence or compel recipients to attend a criminal trial in Ireland. Thus, figures such as Barden Gale of Mack and Lee Neibart of Apollo, to whom Farrell sent data on the US loan books controlled by NAMA, or NewRiver, which had advised PIMCO and later Cerberus on their Project Eagle bids a year earlier, would not be asked to account for their role in the receipt of NAMA material. This despite the fact that NewRiver was affiliated to Forum Partners, for whom Farrell went to work when he left NAMA in early 2012. These had all been named in the civil case brought by the agency against Farrell in late 2012, as had another significant player, the Canadian holding company Fairfax Financial Holdings.

Farrell had sent Wade Burton, an employee of Hamblin Watsa, a subsidiary of Fairfax, a case study of the Dundrum Shopping Centre in July 2011, while he was working in NAMA. Fairfax, founded by Canadian billionaire Prem Watsa along with New York billionaire Wilbur Ross, had invested €1.1 billion in Bank of Ireland shares in 2011, securing a 35 per cent stake at just 10 cent a share in the distressed institution, to help it avert nationalisation following the banking collapse.

Farrell insisted, at all times, that he did not receive any remuneration or favour from the distribution of some 29 files from the 700,000 or more emails he had processed through the NTMA IT system during his three years with NAMA. It came as some surprise to him that Paul Hennigan, the former colleague who had provided Farrell with the details of the Avestus loan book after he left the agency in March 2012, was only subjected to an internal disciplinary procedure following this lapse.

As the NAMA sales process intensified and property prices were continuing to rise, its former portfolio manager, Kevin Nowlan, and his company Hibernia REIT made one of the more bizarre acquisitions when it purchased the Garda's main office building in Dublin, on Harcourt Street, in early 2015. The Garda offices were sold by Gangkhar, an entity controlled by Starwood Capital, for a reported €70 million in an off-market transaction. Starwood had acquired it as part of the Project Aspen portfolio of loans it bought from NAMA in 2013. The sale of the building raised considerable controversy given that the force had no alternative location in the event that the new owners wanted them to vacate the building, which was home to some of the organisation's most sensitive and elite units. For many commentators, it confirmed a growing suspicion that there was nothing sacred when it came to 'the globalisation of Irish property assets'.

The name of another former NAMA official surfaced with the sudden and shocking closure of the iconic Clerys department store in O'Connell Street in Dublin on 12 June 2015. Staff, including 130 who were directly employed and 330 who worked in franchises at the shop, were told just hours before the closure that their jobs had gone, that they were to be let go with immediate effect and that money was not available for redundancy payments by their employer. They would only be entitled to statutory redundancy payments provided by the state. In the early hours of that morning Clerys was sold in a most unusual transaction by the US-based Gordon Brothers group to Natrium, a joint venture between Cheyne Capital Management and D2 Private. The Gordons had previously separated the property assets from the trading company, which was immediately placed into liquidation following the overnight transaction. Among the executives of London asset managers Cheyne was Graham Emmett, who was one of the early senior staff departures from NAMA, while D2 was owned by Dubliner Deirdre Foley, a former employee of Quinlan Private. In 2005, she left Quinlan to set up D2 with developer David Arnold and led the acquisition of a significant property portfolio, mainly in London, valued at €1.8 billion before the crash. Investors in D2 included Anglo chairman Seán FitzPatrick, and former attorney general and AIB chairman Dermot Gleeson, who lost heavily when the company was forced to sell off assets, some in partnership with NAMA, and before an associated company, D2 Property Management Ltd, was placed into receivership. The resilient Foley resurfaced as sole owner of D2 Private in 2013 and two years later was the centre of unwelcome media attention over her role in the early-morning purchase of the valuable Clerys building and the summary dismissal of its staff.

The decision by NAMA in March 2015 to allow the 'routine destruction' of emails by its staff would have raised quite a storm, given the scale of public monies under its control, if it had been known at the time. While NAMA decided to keep certain records, including board minutes, correspondence with state bodies and key documents concerning loan sales, it permitted senior staff to destroy emails which were not considered to have long-term business, operational, legal or historic value. This extraordinary remit to destroy work done by the public service applied to the emails of staff or board members who had left the agency for over a year.

The decision was taken just before the agency came under the scope of FOI legislation. In late June 2015, the Supreme Court ruled that NAMA was a public authority exercising public administrative functions and was therefore subject to freedom of environmental information requests. The court unanimously rejected an appeal by the agency against a High Court ruling in September 2011 in a case brought by the information commissioner, Emily O'Reilly, who won her argument that NAMA was a public authority within the meaning of the 2007 European (Access to Information on the Environment) Regulations (EIR). The case originated in a dispute which arose when journalist and campaigner Gavin Sheridan was refused information by NAMA which he had sought in 2010 under EIR. Although the Supreme Court ruled against NAMA in its judgment of June 2015, it was on different grounds than those relied upon by the High Court.

As a result of the case, NAMA became subject to FOI requests under the Freedom of Information Act that had come into effect on 14 October 2014. However, there were repeated criticisms at the number of restrictions placed on those seeking information, particularly in relation to transactions by the agency and any other material or records which the agency deemed commercially sensitive.

Chapter 19 ~

THE ITALIAN JOB

In early 2015, Mick Wallace heard some disturbing stories from developers and others across the border in relation to the circumstances surrounding the sale of Project Eagle to Cerberus. In December 2014, rumours had been circulating in Belfast that large payments had been promised to certain influential business and legal people in the city in connection with the deal and that some of those involved had serious political associations within the Stormont executive. One source informed Wallace that a sum of £7 million had been placed in an Isle of Man account and that the money was intended for a number of people associated with the Project Eagle loan book deal.

The private investigator Denis O'Sullivan had also learned of some unusual financial activity surrounding the purchase of the portfolio by Cerberus. He was working for a boutique law firm in London run by Peter Griffin, who also had roots in County Kerry. A youthful 32, Griffin had qualified as a lawyer in both New York and Paris and was one of the youngest ever admitted to the partnership of the Wall Street firm of Shearman & Sterling.

He and O'Sullivan had first met when they were both working on the shareholder dispute between McKillen and the Barclays involving the ownership of the luxury London hotels.

By April 2015, they had assembled considerable and disturbing information about the deal, and O'Sullivan made contact with Wallace, with whom they exchanged information.

The bones of the story, if true, were sensational. O'Sullivan had first established from former members of the RUC in Belfast, with whom he had worked while chasing hidden assets abroad, that there were apparent irregularities with the disposal of the Northern Ireland loan book of NAMA. He also obtained confirmation from a bank official who worked in the NAMA unit of one of the main Irish banks that had lent huge amounts to developers in the North, which formed part of the Project Eagle portfolio. He told O'Sullivan that there was 'something wrong' surrounding the sale. By early 2015, O'Sullivan learned of a row at the Tughans Christmas party, which took place in Belfast in early December

2014. Ian Coulter and some of his legal partners at the firm had a serious disagreement during the party, the detective was told. He established that the row centred on the distribution of fees from the Cerberus deal. Coulter had transferred some £7 million, or almost a half portion of the £15 million in fees which Cerberus paid in the fee arrangement agreed with Brown Rudnick in March 2014, into an Isle of Man account in his own name. Tughans' finance and audit departments had raised questions about the distribution of the £7.5 million in fees as proposed by Coulter. His legal partners in Tughans demanded that the entire amount be frozen until the differences were resolved and they eventually secured control of the funds. They also reported the matter to the Law Society. Coulter resigned in late 2014 and took up a position with the Lagan Group. His wife, Vicky, left the solicitor's firm soon after to set up her own legal consultancy.

O'Sullivan and Wallace established that Coulter planned to distribute monies from the Cerberus deal to a number of parties, including Cushnahan, David Watters, Andrew Creighton and a senior politician or party. There was also a wider and more ambitious plan, devised by Cushnahan, Watters and others, which concerned the refinancing of the loans of a number of major NAMA debtors in the North. The proposal involved the purchase of the loans from Cerberus by Jefferies LoanCore at a sharp discount and their refinancing over a number of months. The organisers of the refinancing scheme would charge a commission to distressed developers which they estimated could yield up to £45 million, if successful. It would involve co-operation from well-placed people in business, financial and political circles in the North. The preparations were at an advanced stage until the row erupted in Tughans over the fees from the Cerberus deal transferred by Coulter to the Isle of Man account. Cushnahan later claimed he was due some £5 million from the transferred funds, while Watters, in a letter to Tughans, insisted that he was the intended beneficiary of the offshore monies. The details uncovered were nothing short of extraordinary, if true, and Wallace set about confirming what he had learned before he went public on the potential scandal surrounding the sale by NAMA of its £4.5 billion of distressed assets in the North.

Through his US legal contacts, Griffin alerted the SEC in New York about potential wrong-doing by US-based companies in the Project Eagle purchase. He and O'Sullivan made detailed submissions about Brown Rudnick and Cerberus, both of which had their corporate offices within sight of the SEC headquarters in downtown Manhattan. Their motive was simple. Anyone who assists the SEC in establishing illegal activities, including a breach of the US foreign corrupt practices legislation, can claim up to 20 per cent of any financial penalties subsequently levied against the wrongdoers. Griffin and O'Sullivan were keen to collect any such reward.

Peter Curistan, the businessman who believed that he was the victim of a scurrilous political and media campaign to destroy him and wrest control of the successful Odyssey centre, also heard of a dormant bank account used by Tughans into which there had been a recent lodgement of some £7 million which had raised hackles in the law firm.

In the South, Wallace checked the information he had received from his contact, but it was not complete enough to bring to the floor of the Dáil, much as he was tempted to do so. In mid-June, he raised questions about what he termed NAMA fire sales of assets for greatly less than their real value in what was now an improving property market. 'Something is the matter with how NAMA has operated,' he claimed before providing some examples of the profits being made by third parties on the sales of distressed assets following their disposal by NAMA.

Enda Kenny replied that the agency was monitored by the C&AG and the public accounts and finance committees of the Dáil and that Wallace should bring his complaints to those bodies. Wallace mentioned deals where he believed there was a failure to maximise the potential return to the exchequer. He cited properties such as the Forum building in the IFSC, which, he claimed, was sold by NAMA to US firm Atlas Capital for €28 million in 2012 and sold on less than two years later for €37.8 million. An office block on Mount Street was sold by NAMA to US fund Northwood in 2012 for €27 million and sold on, again within two years, for €42 million, he said. Wallace reminded Kenny that while in opposition the Fine Gael leader had described NAMA as a 'secret society' that 'needed an injection of competence, openness and transparency'. Wallace asked why NAMA 'for some strange reason' was in such a 'hurry to fire sale assets for less than their real value' in a rising property market. Referring to the global funds that were swooping on Irish property assets, he added: 'It's frightening how quickly these vulture funds turned them over and the extent of the profits involved. This means that foreign vulture funds have won and the Irish people are losing out.'

Calling for a commission of inquiry into NAMA, Wallace said that the 'drip-feed of questionable deals has begun' and 'the sale of large blocks of apartments for less than it cost to build them is one of the reasons the private sector has not resumed building'. If this exchange was uncomfortable for those on the government benches who had defended the work of the agency from every criticism, it was nothing compared to the bombshell that hit them a few weeks later when Wallace unleashed the mother of all allegations concerning 'fee arrangements' relating to the Project Eagle sale. On 2 July Wallace told the Dáil that monies connected to the sale of NAMA's Northern Ireland portfolio and held by Belfast solicitors Tughans were 'reportedly earmarked for a politician'. He said that Tughans had acted for Cerberus in its purchase of the Project Eagle portfolio and that 'a routine audit showed that £7 million ended up in an Isle of Man bank account'. Wallace continued:

> The legal firm acting for Cerberus Capital Management, which purchased the Northern Ireland loan portfolio for €1.5 billion, was Tughans of Belfast. Does the Tánaiste have any concerns that a routine audit of a solicitor's firm that looked after the deal where €4.5 billion of assets were sold for €1.5 billion, with a massive loss for the Irish taxpayer … showed that £7 million sterling ended up in an Isle of Man bank account? It was reportedly earmarked for a Northern Ireland politician or political party. Does the Tánaiste not think the matter should be looked at?

Wallace also told the Dáil that Frank Cushnahan had previously resigned from the NIHE following alleged breaches in at least 27 land sales. He said that the executive board of the housing agency had been given wrong or no information relating to key property deals, favoured property speculators were allowed to buy land well under market value, and interest from other parties had not been considered. Despite the report, Wallace said that Cushnahan and another former executive at NIHE, Brian Rowntree, remained as external members of the NIAC, one of them until 2014. Attempting to close him down, Ceann Comhairle Sean Barrett said it was not practice to name people who were not present in the Dáil to defend themselves and that 'this is not an inquisition'.

Tánaiste Joan Burton advised Wallace to bring his claims to the Garda. Within hours, his unexpected intervention provoked a confirmation from Tughans that 'a former partner diverted … professional fees due to the firm, without the knowledge of the partners'. In its statement to the media, the solicitors' firm said: 'The practice is not linked to any political party nor has [Tughans] ever made party political donations.' It went on:

> We can confirm that a former partner diverted to an account of which he was the sole beneficiary professional fees due to the firm, without the knowledge of the partners. We have since retrieved the money and he has left the practice. Tughans reported the circumstances of the departure of the former partner to the Law Society.

A spokesperson for the company said that it and Coulter had been engaged by a 'major US law firm' which was acting for Cerberus. It later added that no part of its professional fee would be payable to or would be paid to any third party, politician or advisor. It also confirmed that Frank Cushnahan, a member of the NIAC, had offices in its Belfast building and that NAMA had held its committee meetings there. The confirmation by Tughans that the sensational allegations made earlier in the Dáil by Wallace were largely accurate unleashed a full-scale media investigation, North and South.

Cerberus was also compelled to issue a forceful response, declaring in a statement to the BBC that it was 'deeply troubled by Mr Wallace's allegations'. It further insisted: 'Cerberus has never paid Tughans. We want to make it clear that no improper or illegal fees were paid by us or on our behalf and we take any allegation to the contrary extremely seriously.'

For its part, NAMA said it was 'fully satisfied' that the sales process for the Northern Ireland loan portfolio 'delivered the best possible return', that investment bank Lazard had overseen the sales process and that 'nine major global investment groups' had participated in a competitive sale process from which Cerberus emerged as the highest bidder. The calm reply from the agency disguised the panic that erupted internally when the Wallace allegations were confirmed by Tughans. The response also considerably misrepresented the sales process and the oversight role played by Lazard, which had been excluded from much of the negotiation surrounding the PIMCO and Cerberus bids. The claim by NAMA that nine global investment groups were engaged was seriously misleading. Only six firms were invited to bid, while major players such as Goldman Sachs and Fortress had to request entry. One potential bidder was not included in the Project Eagle 'invitation list' and when it tried to gain access after the news of the sale broke publicly the same firm was again refused the opportunity to participate.

The deputy first minister in the North, Martin McGuinness, called for an immediate inquiry and called on Wallace to speak to the Garda and the PSNI as 'a matter of urgency'. After several days of silence, Ian Coulter stated that no politician was to receive any money from the Project Eagle deal. Coulter said that neither he nor any third party had received any part of the £7.5 million fees and that 'no politician, nor any relative of any politician in Northern Ireland, was ever to receive any monies in any way' in connection with the Project Eagle purchase. His prepared statement continued:

> The fees payable were paid into a Tughans company account supervised by the firm's finance team. In September 2014, a portion of the fees was retained by Tughans and I instructed Tughans' Finance Director to transfer the remaining portion into an external account which was controlled only by me. Not a penny of this money was touched.

He said he transferred the money back to Tughans in early December 2014 and brought the matter to their attention.

Peter Robinson finally came out a week after the allegations were first aired by Wallace and insisted that neither his family nor his party were to get 'one penny' out of the Project Eagle deal, telling the BBC:

Not one penny was coming to anybody in my family or in the party as a result of this deal. All of the Ministers who were involved, whether they were in my party or not, the only thing that they were ever going to get out of this was to see on the skyline that the building cranes were moving again.

He defended his role in meeting various interests in advance of the sale and said that ministers would have been 'derelict in their duty' if they had not sought the best deal for Northern Ireland. He also denied that there was any conflict of interest between his position as first minister and his son's work for Ian Coulter and Tughans. Gareth Robinson was principal of the public relations firm Verbatim, which had helped to manage an event hosted by Tughans in 2012. Gareth Robinson also denied any involvement in the sale of NAMA assets in the North. He said that no representatives of Verbatim had 'facilitated or were in any way involved in the sale of NAMA assets to Cerberus'.

Gareth Robinson would not have been aware that Cushnahan had mentioned him favourably and as someone who could provide great assistance in the conversation taped by developer John Miskelly three weeks before the Tughans event when the consultant and NIAC member accepted a bag containing £40,000 in a car park of the Belfast City Hospital.

Peter Robinson said that this son was the target of a witch hunt by people wishing to damage him as first minister and went on to describe Coulter, 'a renowned lawyer', and Cushnahan, 'a significant financier', as 'two pretty major players in the Northern Ireland business world' with whom he enjoyed a 'good relationship'. Cushnahan was a 'significant supporter of the Executive' who had devoted 'quite a lot of his time' and had done 'a lot of good to public service … Anything that I saw, I have to say, was very much in the interests of Northern Ireland in terms of what he was doing.'

By this time, Frank Daly had confirmed at a hearing of the PAC in Dublin on 7 July that Cushnahan was to get a £5 million acquisition fee from PIMCO if it had been successful in its bid for Project Eagle. He claimed that NAMA had forced PIMCO to withdraw from the tender process after the US fund revealed the fee arrangement with Cushnahan and others. The NAMA chairman and chief executive faced a barrage of questions from committee members who wanted to know what they knew of the Wallace allegations and the £7 million held offshore.

Daly said that 'wherever that £7 million came from, it did not come from NAMA and it did not come, in any way, from the proceeds of this sale that should have been due to NAMA.'

He defended the decision to proceed with the Project Eagle sale after PIMCO withdrew on the basis of assurances from Cerberus that there would be no fee payments to Cushnahan. He told Labour Party member Joe Costello that it was 'probably' Ronnie Hanna who came up with the name 'Project Eagle' for the loan portfolio. Daly insisted that the first time he became aware that Cushnahan had an office in Tughans solicitors was in September 2013, when a meeting of the NIAC was held there.

Replying to Mary Lou McDonald, he said: 'I was never aware of Mr. Cushnahan's close connection to Tughans until this matter emerged in March 2014 when PIMCO told us about the sharing of the fee.'

With the PAC of the Oireachtas and the Stormont finance committee announcing that they were to hold separate inquiries into the Project Eagle sale and purchase, and the PSNI launching its own investigation, it was certain that the Eagle story was going to continue to fly, on both sides of the border. By this time the PSNI had called in the National Crime Agency (NCA), the UK equivalent of the FBI, which had agreed to lead the investigation into the fee payment allegations.

In the Dáil, the Taoiseach was forced to field opposition questions concerning Daly's claim at the PAC hearing that NAMA had forced PIMCO out of the bidding process for Project Eagle once it admitted to the promised fee payment to Cushnahan. Mary Lou McDonald accused Daly of misleading the committee after PIMCO had refuted his claim, insisting that it had left the sales process voluntarily subsequent to its compliance officers querying the legality of the fee arrangements. The Sinn Féin deputy also pressed Kenny on the role of Michael Noonan in the affair, saying that the finance minister had pressed on even after the proposed fee payments had been disclosed to him by NAMA and had failed to alert the North's executive of significant developments or halt the sales process because of them. Fianna Fáil leader Micheál Martin threw his party's weight behind the call for a commission of investigation into Project Eagle: 'By any definition, it was a serious issue that such a senior advisor to NAMA on the Northern Ireland loan book, and who was on NAMA's Northern Ireland's advisory committee, was subsequently playing a central role in doing the deal.'

Just as the Dáil prepared to enter summer recess and a period of calm for a government beleaguered by the constant flow of allegations concerning NAMA's largest deal to date, Mick Wallace threw more fuel on the fire. He stunned quite a few people inside and outside politics with a claim that a former NAMA official had received a bribe of €15,000 in cash in exchange for assisting a borrower whose loans were under the control of the agency. He claimed that the former portfolio manager with the agency had sought two payments of €15,000 'in cash and in a bag' from a construction company and that 'they duly obliged and all was sorted'. Again the wrath of the Ceann Comhairle descended and the Wexford TD was accused by Sean Barrett of treating the Dáil like a 'star chamber'.

The allegation had been floating in business circles in Dublin for some time. It concerned a company that wanted to speed its exit from the claws of the agency by conceding the demand for a cash payment from the portfolio manager. Wallace had been informed that cash was handed over in a north Dublin hotel some years earlier and that the portfolio manager had since left NAMA. Before he sat down, Wallace also asked:

Does the Taoiseach know how many barristers, judges, solicitors, top four accountancy firm partners and bankers are in syndicates set up by Goodman [sic] Stockbrokers, Anglo Private, Bank of Ireland Private, AIB Private, Davy, Warren and Quinlan which have transferred to NAMA but which NAMA have not enforced, despite personal guarantees being attached? NAMA is responsible for some people being tossed out of their homes but it looks like some of the great and good of Irish society are blessed with NAMA's good will.

Wallace also raised the thorny issue of the role of the former secretary general of the Department of Finance, John Moran, in relation to a particular property portfolio in which, Wallace claimed, the former civil servant was 'unnaturally interested in playing a significant role'. He was referring to the email exchange between Moran and the senior executive of Barclays during the company's battle with Paddy McKillen over control of Coroin and the luxury hotels in London.

In late July, Wallace confirmed that he had met with members of the GBFI to provide details of the allegations he had made regarding the cash payment by a builder of €15,000 to a former NAMA portfolio manager. His meeting with the Garda followed a formal request to the Garda Commissioner by NAMA for an investigation into the detailed allegations made earlier in the Dáil by the Wexford TD.

Wallace also called on the finance minister Michael Noonan to suspend the sale of Project Arrow, the largest loan portfolio disposal undertaken by NAMA to date. The non-performing loans, with an estimated par value of more than €6.3 billion, were marketed by estate agents Cushman & Wakefield earlier in 2015 and only 'a US vulture fund', he said, would be able to afford to purchase such a large loan portfolio. Sinn Féin also called for a suspension of all NAMA sales, including Arrow, and a review of the agency's operations.

There was not much rest for Wallace as he was consumed over the following months with his personal battle for financial survival with Cerberus. In late summer, the *Sunday Business Post* reported that the US fund had taken over loans of more than €2 million associated with his riverside restaurant in Dublin when it purchased the Project Aran portfolio through its Dublin-registered vehicle Promontoria (Aran). Cerberus had sent a letter to Wallace in late August calling in the loan. It was known in some business circles that Cerberus was deeply unhappy at the unfavourable media and political comment in relation to its Project Eagle purchase and Wallace was a major thorn in its side in this regard. Wallace, however, had not been made aware that the loans attached to Taverna di Bacco in the Italian Quarter of the city had been purchased by Cerberus until contacted by this writer. As I was preparing an article for a Sunday newspaper on the company's purchase of the loans, including personal guarantees, I was informed by a spokesperson for Cerberus that it had written to the politician's construction firm in the spring of 2015 to inform him that it had acquired them as part of the loan book purchased by Promontoria (Aran).

In the spring of 2015, the letter was sent to M&J Wallace Ltd by Arthur Cox, acting for Promontoria (Aran), informing the construction company that it had a new owner. The popular Taverna di Bacco restaurant in the Italian quarter on Ormond Quay in Dublin developed by Wallace, and his personal guarantee of €2 million given to Ulster Bank when he borrowed from it several years earlier, were now owned by Cerberus, of which Promontoria (Aran) was a subsidiary. Wallace only became aware of the correspondence months later in late August 2015, two months after he had made his sensational allegations in the Dáil relating to the US fund and its purchase of Project Eagle.

The Ulster Bank loan book, called Project Aran, was purchased in late 2014 by Cerberus for €1.4 billion from a par value of €6 billion. It included 1,300 borrowers and over 6,200 loans covering some 5,400 properties, mainly in the Republic and Northern Ireland. Cerberus acquired the portfolio from Ulster Bank and its parent, Royal Bank of Scotland, for an estimated discount of 76 cent in the euro. Included in the portfolio were the loans and personal guarantee Wallace had secured from Ulster Bank. Wallace had cooperated with the bank, helping it to sell 39 of the 40 properties he had developed and over which it had security. The other property was included in the bundle of distressed assets sold to Cerberus along with the personal guarantee of €2 million which Wallace had obtained in connection with a development he built in Inchicore, Dublin, in 2005.

When he claimed that £7 million had been lodged in an Isle of Man account in connection with the sale, he was not aware that Ceberus had a hold on the restaurant loan and the personal guarantee.

Meanwhile, authorities on both sides of the Atlantic were investigating the Project Eagle purchase following various complaints to the SEC, a division of the Department of Justice in the US. Among those who alerted the SEC were staff in the department who were concerned over the visits to Ireland on behalf of Cerberus by former vice-president Quayle and former treasury secretary John Snow in the spring of 2014. Official engagements scheduled for Quayle in his official diary, usually arranged several months in advance, were reportedly cancelled when he made his unscheduled trip to Ireland to meet politicians in the North and other influential people in Dublin shortly before the Cerberus bid for Project Eagle was submitted. The SEC contacted the FBI in relation to the fee payments associated with the deal; the Bureau is responsible for investigating potential criminality involving US citizens and companies in foreign jurisdictions under US foreign corrupt practices laws.

Chapter 20 ~

THE SECRET TAPES

Also engaged in battle with Cerberus was bookmaker Gareth Graham, whose property loans had been taken over by the US fund as part of its Project Eagle purchase. In late June 2015 the High Court in Belfast granted him access to £75,000 (€105,000) in funds from two companies in receivership, STH 500 Ltd and Lehill Properties Ltd, which had been taken over by Cerberus, in order to allow him to pursue legal action against the fund and challenge its foreclosure on the NAMA loans. He was soon followed down the legal route by County Down developer John Miskelly, who challenged the seizure of his assets by Promontoria Eagle, which in early 2015 had taken over his Ten Square hotel in Belfast and six other properties he owned. It then appointed receivers over Miskelly's company Applecroft Investments, which owed in excess of £80 million to lenders. Miskelly, who once sought to form a consortium to take over Liverpool FC in Britain during the boom years, was not someone to take matters lying down, despite his suffering a debilitating illness at the time.

Graham and Miskelly shared an absolute distrust of Frank Cushnahan, with whom they both had dealings over previous years. Graham had forced the consultant out of his business back in 2008 after he discovered that Cushnahan was seeking to sell off lucrative aspects of the bookmaker's operation and was making life difficult for his elderly mother when she objected to his plans. Miskelly had contracted Cushnahan to help him out of his financial difficulties after his loans were transferred to NAMA but had been careful to make tape recordings of their conversations.

Graham, in a remarkable development that resonated across three jurisdictions, discovered during the summer of 2015 that he was also sitting on taped evidence concerning Cushnahan's dealings with several prominent politicians and business people in the North when he worked out of the bookmaker's offices in Belfast city centre up to 2008. Cushnahan had first worked at the King Street office of Graham before the company relocated to Oyster House at Wellington Place in the city.

Under regulations, bookmakers are obliged to independently verify every bet made by telephone and the Grahams complied with this requirement by recording all calls into and out of the firm's head office in Belfast, where all phone bets were received. Cushnahan was aware of this requirement as he had written the staff handbook informing all employees of the taping procedure. For some reason, which the Grahams put down to arrogance, Cushnahan appeared to believe that he was somehow immune to having his calls monitored in this fashion.

Graham discovered that he had dozens of tapes which recorded hundreds of hours of conversations Cushnahan had with people during the years he worked at the business. The tapes helped to identify the circle of business and political associates Cushnahan had nurtured and who would later emerge as key players during his time as a member of the NIAC and in the Project Eagle saga.

When he engaged KRW Law LLP, the Belfast solicitors run by Kevin Winters, to help him in his legal action against Cerberus, the tapes formed part of the context in which the ensuing court cases and negotiations with Cerberus took place. Because of his association with NAMA through his membership of NIAC, Cushnahan was in a position where he claimed he could influence the fortunes of those developers, including his clients, who were now under the control of Cerberus. Given their falling out, he certainly could not be relied upon to assist the bookmakers through their difficulties, and Graham feared that he would be one of the 'bodies on the street' left after the massive disposal of distressed loans in the North was complete. When he listened to conversations on the hours of tape recordings, he was more than convinced that Cushnahan was well prepared to use every trick in the book to gain advantage for those interests he favoured, including the leading political and business associates and senior Stormont officials with whom he had frequent contact while working for the Grahams.

Graham handed over the sensitive and explosive recordings to Niall Murphy of KRW Law LLP and from there they engaged with the NCA/PSNI investigators and with the SEC and FBI in the US to assist with their inquiries into the Project Eagle deal. The information uncovered ranged from Cushnahan's secret dealings with others in relation to the disposal of the more lucrative properties in the Graham business to discussions with members of the DUP on how to reorganise constituency boundaries in order to maximise the party's vote in forthcoming electoral contests. There were also unkind references to other political and business figures, including to the director of governance who worked in the office of the powerful New York State Comptroller. Irish American Pat Doherty was seeking to direct pension and other public funds under his control to assist poorer parts of the North as part of US input to the fragile peace process following the IRA ceasefires. Cushnahan had made unsuccessful efforts to set up a fund intended to attract US investment in the North, including the New York pension monies. He was displeased with Doherty's connection with Sinn Féin and other nationalist and republican supporters who were promoting an Emerald Fund for the purpose of supporting the peace process with investment by Irish American and other US financiers. Extensive discussions he had with Brendan McGinn, among others, were taped and revealed deep suspicions and dislike felt by Cushnahan towards his perceived political and business opponents.

Cushnahan and McGinn were promoting a fund they called New Ireland Capital Partners, which was seeking to raise $250 million for projects in the North and was in competition with the Emerald Fund for the support of Irish American and other US investment. In one of the many conversations at Graham's bookmakers preserved on tape, they discussed a forthcoming visit to the US by senior politicians and civil servants from the North.

On the tape recorded on 2 September 2008, Cushnahan asked McGinn to meet with John McMillen, a senior civil servant in the Office of the First and Deputy First Minister. McMillen had a supervisory role in the Washington-based Northern Ireland Bureau and worked directly for Bruce Robinson, the head of the civil service in the North (with whom Cushnahan also enjoyed good relations). The bureau was the official representative of the government of Northern Ireland in the US. Cushnahan described speaking to McMillen about Lorraine Turner, the head of the bureau's New York office. He suggested she 'may have an agenda of her own' which, he said, 'may not be best for Northern Ireland from time to time'. He then referred to Pat Doherty and his 'green gold collar scheme, which goes the wrong way from time to time'.

McGinn replied that Doherty's scheme (the Emerald Fund) goes past 'little green people on the streets'. Cushnahan then said, 'No, sure I know that, sure I said to him [McMillen], he [Doherty] might have been out with a Kalashnikov from time to time, if he was let loose.' McGinn then referred to Doherty's 'linkages with the paper guy, O'Muilleoir'. At the time, Máirtín Ó Muilleoir was publisher of the *Andersonstown News*, a popular newspaper in nationalist areas of Belfast. As they ended the conversation, Cushnahan said that McMillen had agreed to meet with him and McGinn, possibly that evening. He explained that McMillen had 'taken my advice in a variety of other things, between you and me, a pile of things'. 'The issue, Brendan, we have to get across to John, is basically, what is the message that has to come down the pipe, which is conducive,' Cushnahan said before he was interrupted by another call. When they resumed their conversation, McGinn refers to Doherty as a 'major blockage'.

McGinn also described how he was hoping to attract support from 'the crème de la crème of the business community' in the US. Cushnahan considered the meeting with McMillen urgent because McMillen was due to travel to the US in the near future as part of the trade delegation and Cushnahan wanted McGinn to travel to the US at the same time. Cushnahan said, 'He will be going out there [to the US]. You try to make sure that your plans fit in and then make sure that you can wheel him in to some of the people you know'.

In early September 2015 Graham issued a statement through Niall Murphy of KRW Law LLP after he had met with the Committee for Finance and Personnel at Stormont during its review of the Project Eagle sale and offered to hand it the tape recordings in his possession. The solicitor said:

> Mr Graham has listened to hundreds of hours of recordings, with more to consider, and it is quite clear that there was an ingrained culture of inappropriate and quite possibly illegal business conduct, which stretched across political, legal, banking and accountancy sectors.

He confirmed that Graham had spoken to the NCA and was planning to make a complaint to the PSNI regarding alleged criminal offences.

> We have also complained on Mr Graham's behalf to the Security and Exchange Commission in Washington DC as to the inappropriate political relationships and potentially unlawful banking relationships which are disclosed in the recordings, which it is considered merits SEC investigation in respect of potential breaches of the Foreign Corrupt Practices Act 1977 in the purchase by Cerberus of his assets which were retained in the portfolio of Project Eagle.

The treatment by Cerberus of the Graham and Miskelly loan books were in stark contrast to those of other developers, including Paddy Kearney of Kilmona, who it was reported got close to a £250 million debt write-off from the US fund. Lagan and MAR Properties were also getting their loans refinanced at a rapid rate. Lagan, controlled by Kevin and Michael Lagan, and MAR, owned by Noel Murphy, had their loans refinanced by Jefferies LoanCore, the joint venture of New York-based Jefferies Bank and Singapore state-owned property investor GIC Real Estate. Lagan had recently attracted media attention after Ian Coulter was appointed to several of its boards following his sudden departure as managing partner of Tughans solicitors. A report by Susan Thompson in the Belfast newspaper the *Irish News* in early August said that Peter Robinson had met with Jefferies LoanCore at a hotel in Carrickfergus, County Down, just days before it acquired Kearney's loans on generous terms for the Gibraltar-based former Maple 10 developer.

In early September, officers from the NCA seized documents relating to its investigation from the offices of Tughans, with its prior agreement, including correspondence between Coulter and Cushnahan and some of their associates. A committee of inquiry, chaired by Sinn Féin MLA Daithí McKay, had started hearings in Stormont and was preparing to question the developers, along with senior politicians and civil servants, about their role in the Project Eagle saga, generating much anxiety and excitement in business, political and media circles. The inquiry had a rocky start when one of its first witnesses, the head of the North's Department of Finance, David Sterling, was criticised by members for refusing to answer certain questions and for providing incomplete and heavily redacted documentation on Project Eagle to the committee.

Sinn Féin MLA Máirtín Ó Muilleoir put it to Sterling that the sale of the NAMA NI portfolio was a mess. 'It would be wrong for me to offer a comment on something for which I have no accountability and no particular knowledge,' the civil servant replied.

Was it 'a good deal, a bad deal, a scandal, [or] a mess?', asked Ó Muilleoir, who accused Sterling of 'washing his hands' of the issue and of the appointments to the NIAC of Frank Cushnahan and Brian Rowntree in 2010. Ó Muilleoir said:

In my view what is happening is that we are being told that the DFP [Department of Finance and Personnel] is washing its hands of the entire NAMA sale. At the same time appointments were made to the NAMA advisory committee which is at the very heart of what is being described as a dirty scheme, the very heart of it. You can't wash your hands of that either.

Sterling replied: 'You can only wash your hands of something for which you are responsible. DFP, the department and the Minister, were not responsible for the sale of the NAMA [portfolio].'

The refusal of finance minister Michael Noonan and senior NAMA officials to attend inquiry hearings across the border at Stormont was also heavily criticised by committee members. The ongoing criminal investigations were cited by Cushnahan and Hanna, as well as a number of senior politicians and civil servants, as reasons why they could not participate in the hearings. This threatened to derail proceedings before they got into their stride. However, the committee managed to hear significant evidence from, among others, Deputy First Minister Martin McGuinness and loyalist blogger and flags protestor Jamie Bryson, which added to its understanding of events. McGuinness countered a charge made by DUP member Jim Wells that he was fully aware of what was going on within the Office of First and Deputy First Minister in relation to the Project Eagle sale, including the visit by Dan Quayle to Belfast in March 2014, just days before Cerberus made its bid. McGuinness said that he had no knowledge of the meeting Quayle had with Peter Robinson and only met the former US vice-president in an official engagement in September 2014, several months after the sale to Cerberus had been completed.

Bryson appeared on the same day, 23 September, and made the sensational claim that Robinson was to be a beneficiary of the so-called success fee that, he said, was to be paid to Tughans. He also described how he believed the money was channelled.

That success fee was paid into a dormant Danske Bank account in the Donegall Square West branch [in Belfast] and from there it was transferred to an offshore account. There were to be a number of beneficiaries to that fee. I will refer to them as Person A, Person B, Person C, Person D and Person E. I can tell the committee, without fear of contradiction, that Person A is Mr Peter Robinson MLA; Person B is Mr Andrew Creighton; Person C is Mr David Watters; Person D is Mr Frank Cushnahan; and Person E is Ian Coulter.

Coming at the end of his opening statement, Bryson's remarks were carefully calculated to cause the maximum impact and he was not disappointed by the reaction. He had been in discussions over several months with various people with assorted motivations for damaging some, if not all, of those he so sensationally named. He was frequently in touch with Peter Curistan, who blamed Robinson for the loss of his Odyssey empire, and with other members of the DUP who held grudges against the first minister. He had been in contact with Mick Wallace over previous months and had used his blog to publish details which he claimed to have gleaned from his sources about the role of the DUP leader and his business associates in the Project Eagle saga.

He was also agitated about the role in the complex affair of Alan Mains, a former RUC officer, and now an advisor to Paddy Kearney, who also gave evidence to the committee. Bryson claimed that Mains was close to Robinson and also to Ranald Coggle of Cerberus and that Kearney had managed to obtain a 'sweetheart deal' from the US fund which involved a refinancing of his loans and a write-down of in excess of £224 million in the developer's debt. Bryson claimed that Robinson attended the celebration in the Carrickfergus hotel organised by Kearney to celebrate his successful debt write-down.

Robinson confirmed to the inquiry on 14 October that he had attended the celebration in Carrickfergus organised by Kearney for a senior executive of Jefferies LoanCore, Chris Wilson, who had travelled from New York for the event. Robinson said that he had been asked to make a presentation of a 'picture or painting' at the social occasion and dinner with the 'American investor'.

Asked by chairman Daithí McKay about the dinner, Robinson said:

It was a social occasion for one of the successes of the sale of the portfolio to
Cerberus. This was a company that had been unable to get out from under,
when it was under the control of NAMA. When Cerberus took over, they did
a deal with Cerberus, though they felt that they paid too much for it, and are
now employing more people.

McKay: It has been reported that the loans of Paddy Kearney were sold to
Jefferies a number of days later. Is that the company to which you referred?

Robinson: That was what the event was about. It was by way of a celebration
at the buying out of the portfolio from Cerberus.

However, Robinson did not disclose to the inquiry that he had assisted Kearney
in the developer's dealings with NAMA, and had written to the agency on the
developer's behalf. He had also had extensive dealings with Frank Cushnahan and
Ian Coulter over the years, although he could not recall details of many of the
conversations or calls with the two men. He did not wish to comment on whether
Cushnahan displayed a blatant conflict of interest when he arranged the meeting
between PIMCO and Robinson and Sammy Wilson in May 2013, while he was a
member of the NIAC and without informing the advisory committee of his role
in hawking assets while acting as an advisor to NAMA. Robinson also disputed
the claim by Martin McGuinness that he was left out of the loop in relation to a
number of engagements, including the meeting with Dan Quayle in March 2014.
Robinson rejected the dramatic claim by loyalist blogger Jamie Bryson at an
earlier hearing that he was in line for a payment from the Project Eagle sale.

'I neither received, expected to receive, sought nor was offered a single penny
as a result of the NAMA sale,' he said.

Committee members were surprised when Kearney told the inquiry, a few weeks
later, of his meetings with Robinson and the first minister's involvement in writing
to NAMA on the developer's behalf. Kearney said that there had been 'an unfounded
accusation of improper behaviour and influence exerted on my behalf by First
Minister Peter Robinson. The relationship with the First Minister has been falsely
projected in testimony to the Committee as a cosy friendship with favours arranged
and it blatantly states that I was involved in some form of corrupt behaviour.'

Confirming that he had met Robinson on a number of occasions in his
capacity as first minister, Kearney said that 'to describe the relationship as
friendship is, at best, a gross exaggeration of the truth.'

He said that he had turned to Robinson after a particularly difficult meeting
with NAMA executives in May 2013 when he concluded that the agency intended

'to collapse my company'. He said that he found it insulting to be described as a retired boxer trying to return to the ring during a meeting with NAMA head and assistant head of asset recovery, Ronnie Hanna and Michael Moriarty. The meeting with the first minister was set up by his friend and former senior RUC officer, Alan Mains, who intervened during the Stormont hearing to confirm that he was a long-time business associate of Frank Cushnahan. Speaking of the meeting with Robinson, Kearney recalled

> I found him to be a helpful, compassionate and understanding person who wrote to NAMA on my behalf, requesting that it meet me in person to discuss its reasons for wanting to enforce on the loans, given, by its own admission, the exemplary performance of my company. He did not do anything for me that could be deemed improper or inappropriate, and it is a grossly unfair and twisted misrepresentation of the truth to say otherwise.

Kearney described how, in order to escape from Cerberus which had purchased his loans, he had to refinance his portfolio.

> I had to refinance my portfolio, which I did with another American Company, Jefferies LoanCore (JLC), a highly respected global financial institution. Just prior to the closing of my refinancing with Jefferies LoanCore, I invited the First Minister to attend a dinner that I was hosting to thank JLC, which had invested in my company and was interested in doing more potential business in Northern Ireland.

Kearney said that he had known Frank Cushnahan for years, but they only met occasionally. He was in Spain in January 2014 when he received a call from Ian Coulter. Kearney said:

> I was in Spain and got a call from Ian Coulter to ask if I would come home to meet him and Frank Cushnahan. Ian Coulter was the managing partner of Tughans, who are our lawyers. They wanted some information on my portfolio. They were acting for one of the bidders for the Northern Ireland portfolio and asked me if I would come home to give them some information because the people that they were acting for wanted to be in a position to make a proper bid. They needed some private information on the portfolio that was not public. It was private company information. I agreed to go home to meet him.

He confirmed that his engagement with Cerberus had commenced almost as soon as the US fund purchased Project Eagle in June 2014 and had concluded less than four months later, at the end of October 2014. After legal clearance, the refinancing deal through Jefferies LoanCore was completed by late January 2015. He did not wish to say by how much, but Kearney confirmed that his assets were substantially written down in the new deal. 'What I paid for the assets or the loans was more than the assets were worth on the day,' he said.

Kearney confirmed that he knew Andrew Creighton and David Watters, two of those named by Bryson as planned recipients of large amounts of money from the Project Eagle sale during his explosive evidence to the inquiry. Kearney said:

Davy Watters of McClure Watters were the NAMA auditors when we were with NAMA. They audited our accounts twice a month to reconcile everything that was going before NAMA swept the account, as I said earlier. Andrew Creighton is a well-known property developer. I have had lunch with Andrew on a number of occasions over the years.

Claiming to be a victim of faceless people, he attacked the earlier evidence of Jamie Bryson.

Over the past months, I have been on the sidelines, monitoring the proceedings of the Committee and its witnesses. I am at a loss to understand why those ridiculous, unfounded allegations have been made against me. The person responsible for the ludicrous allegations [Bryson] has never met me and does not know me. Having read the content of his blogs and so on, I view him to be a commercially naive individual who is allowing himself to be manipulated by faceless individuals who wish to remain anonymous and are feeding him with misinformation relating to some factual events that are already in the public domain. Those people have agendas driven by envy, malintent, resentment and a sick need for revenge.

Kearney told the vice-chairman of the committee, SDLP member Dominic Bradley, that the faceless people were involved in a 'personal grudge' against him 'because of history and things like that'. Kearney had reason to be concerned about the source of the allegations made by Bryson as the loyalist blogger was in contact with a range of people inside and outside the DUP, where powerful elements were conspiring against Robinson, as well as with some disgruntled businessmen. Among those who claimed to this writer that he had briefed Bryson before his sensational evidence at the inquiry was Peter Curistan, who was among those with reason to dislike Robinson and some of his business associates.

Asked by Máirtín Ó Muilleoir about his acquisition of the loans of John Miskelly from Cerberus, Kearney confirmed that he had bought the assets.

Ó Muilleoir suggested that some developers, including Kearney, were treated better than others, such as Miskelly and Gareth Graham, by Cerberus when it came to refinancing their loans and other arrangements.

Kearney confirmed that he went to see John Miskelly to see whether he could buy his loans as opposed to the assets. He said that Miskelly was 'in the middle of a battle with Cerberus', so nothing emerged from their discussion. He said that he then went ahead and bought Miskelly's assets. He denied that his more favourable treatment was due to Robinson's intervention with NAMA on his behalf. Kearney said:

> Did John Miskelly go and ask him to write? I do not know. As I said, I paddle my own canoe. I have a reputation for keeping my own counsel. I do not do joint ventures; I have been my own man for a long, long time. Everybody out there had the same opportunity as I did, and I am not going to apologise for getting an opportunity and making the most of it.

A special advisor to Robinson confirmed that Cushnahan represented a number of developer clients while he was a member of the NIAC, the first time the extent of his conflicts of interest was publicly exposed. Richard Bullick told the inquiry that he could not recall the names of those clients who stood to benefit from a memorandum of understanding prepared by the first minister's office and passed on to NAMA in January 2014 before the Project Eagle sale. It was dismissed at the time by Frank Daly as a 'debtors' charter' but subsequently proved to be a reasonably accurate forecast of how the most politically connected developers emerged from their subsequent dealings with Cerberus through their loan refinancing arrangements.

Describing Cushnahan's relationship with debtor clients that represented up to 58 per cent of the entire NI loan book, McKay said: 'Here you effectively had a double agent, who was supposed to be working in the interests of NAMA, who appears to have a litany of conflicts of interest.'

Robinson had resigned as first minister in early September in response to an allegation that the IRA was involved in the killing of Belfast man Kevin McGuigan some weeks earlier, which followed an earlier killing of former IRA member Jock Davison in the city. He stepped aside after his failed attempt to have the assembly at Stormont adjourned because of the killings. Finance minister Arlene Foster replaced Robinson as first minister while the other DUP ministers resigned from the power sharing executive, plunging the political institutions into crisis. Gerry Adams said that Robinson had serious questions to answer relating to the rapidly evolving Project Eagle controversy and over his refusal to re-enter all-party talks to rescue the political institutions. Speaking at a public meeting in Drogheda on the issue, Adams said:

The unionist parties' attitude to the two murders in Belfast and to the recent revelations about the sell-off of NAMA's northern loan book shows their ad hoc attitude to the political institutions. In July, serious concerns arose around the sell-off by NAMA of its northern loan book – valued at £4.5 billion – for a third of that amount, amid allegations that a senior politician in the North was to benefit from this. Sinn Féin could have decided at that point to walk away from the Executive. We didn't. We asserted the primacy of due process and the need for these very serious allegations of political corruption to be fully investigated properly by the relevant Assembly and policing agencies.

In a comment that went largely unmentioned in the Dublin media, he continued:

The sell-off of NAMA's northern loan book involves both the Minister for Finance in Dublin as well as senior ministers in the north. The allegations of wrong doing are very serious.

Resumed political talks ended six weeks later with the restoration of the executive, a deal on welfare and spending as well as policing issues, and the unexpected announcement by Robinson that he planned to leave the stage and retire from politics in May 2016 before the assembly elections. In late September, during a trip to the US, Adams also met with officials at the offices of the New York State Comptroller, including Pat Doherty, which had $50 million invested in Cerberus, to brief it on the controversy surrounding Project Eagle. It is understood that Doherty then raised the issue with senior executives of Cerberus, who were apparently not impressed by the Sinn Féin leader's intervention. According to one source familiar with the sometimes-heated discussion, the Cerberus representative complained about Adam's access to the New York State Comptroller's office, given the Sinn Féin leader's reputed links to the IRA. In reply, Doherty and his team pointed out that the Comptroller had $50 million invested with Cerberus. The Comptroller was thus concerned at reports that the US fund had possibly breached federal corrupt practice laws by making payments to a foreign official. Doherty was referring to the £5 million fee arrangement made for Frank Cushnahan during Cerberus' acquisition of Project Eagle. In response the Cerberus representative insisted that Cushnahan was not a foreign official but 'only a member of an advisory board'.

'We're home free', the Cerberus official is reported to have said while explaining that Cushnahan's role as a member of the 'Northern Ireland Advisory Committee of

NAMA' did not make him a government employee. As the meeting concluded, Doherty said that it would not be possible to invest more public funds in Cerberus in light of the controversy and claims surrounding the Project Eagle purchase. The State Comptroller's office was also aware of the ongoing SEC and FBI investigations into the deal. New York State Comptroller Tom DiNapoli was not present at the meeting with Cerberus; on 24 September 2015 he was part of the official delegation that met with Pope Francis on the pontiff's first official visit to New York. The New York State Comptroller manages a pension fund of more than $100 billion.

The Drogheda speech and the trip to the New York State Comptroller's office by Adams during this period were clearly intended to telegraph to Robinson that Sinn Féin would not look kindly on Robinson's alleged NAMA-related delinquencies if he did not move expeditiously to get the executive back on track.

Just days after the Fresh Start Agreement to restore the power sharing executive was successfully negotiated in mid-October, Robinson announced his retirement from politics, to take effect within months. Although he had suffered a heart attack earlier in the year, he said that his decision to step down as DUP leader and first minister was not for health reasons.

Right back from the Westminster election in May, I indicated to party officers that they had to factor into their calculations that I would not be standing at the next assembly elections, so they could do their forward planning. But the assembly was in some disarray at that time, and the view was I should remain and attempt to stabilise the assembly and executive. We've done that successfully, so now it seems to me the appropriate time to announce the departure and allow the party to take it forward.

Another visitor to New York during this period was Gareth Graham, who was invited to meet with the FBI, the SEC and the Department of Justice to discuss his complaints against Cerberus and to reveal information he had discovered on the tapes recorded in the Belfast offices of his bookmaking firm. At Adams' request, he also met with the New York Comptroller and Doherty during his visit. Graham subsequently met with Mick Wallace and revealed some extraordinary information about Cushnahan's behaviour when he was working for the bookmaker and about the consultant's dealings with other NAMA debtors from whom the former NIAC member had allegedly tried to financially benefit through his links with the agency. He did not release copies of the tapes to any of the enforcement agencies he met in the North or in the US.

Chapter 21 ~

CONTRASTING FORTUNES

A s events in the North were unfolding, the pressure that was placed on several of the leading property developers whose loans had been transferred to NAMA since 2010 was aired at hearings of the banking inquiry during the summer and autumn of 2015. Among those to arrive at the inquiry were developers Michael O'Flynn, Joe O'Reilly and Sean Mulryan, while former Treasury Holdings director Johnny Ronan sent detailed documentation on his relationship and dealings with NAMA since its formation. Cork developer O'Flynn, who had built homes, offices and apartments across the city and the country during the boom years, was scathing in his assessment of how the agency treated debtors and how it had rejected a detailed business plan he had submitted 'without explanation or discussion'. He told the inquiry, chaired by Labour Party TD Ciarán Lynch, that he had never been shown a report into his company's affairs by an external reviewer appointed by NAMA to the O'Flynn Group, which had €1.8 billion in distressed loans transferred to the agency. The loans were later sold to US investor Blackstone for a reported €1.1 billion. O'Flynn said he was fighting a protracted legal battle with the fund over the manner in which it called in the loans. He was followed by some less critical voices, with O'Reilly and Mulryan making clear their intention to continue cooperation with the agency, which was paying them up to €200,000 a year to manage the winding down of their distressed assets. O'Flynn had also been receiving a similar payment when he was working with NAMA on the winding down of his debt before his loans were sold to Blackstone. O'Reilly told the inquiry that he expected that the agency would make a multiple of what it paid for his loans when it sold them as part of the Project Jewel loan sale. He said that he expected the €2 billion in his personal and corporate loans to be fully repaid from the sale.

Sean Mulryan of Ballymore was less apologetic over his role in the banking and property collapse than some of the other developers and claimed that he had paid a 'huge price' in his efforts to repay his €2.2 billion bank debts to NAMA, telling the inquiry:

All of my executives took a 25 to 30 per cent reduction in their wages. They rolled up their sleeves for seven years and sacrificed everything in time to get through this. To get our mountain of debt taken down and paid back, which was huge at €2.2 billion. We all sacrificed our lives. No social lives, no holidays. We just worked around the clock for the last seven years.

Mulryan claimed Ballymore was a 'victim' of the crash, given that most of its assets were held outside Ireland, although they were financed with loans from the Irish banks. Ballymore had substantial assets in London and other foreign countries, which had helped it to recover more quickly through the 'tight' business plan he was executing in full cooperation with NAMA. He said:

While it was a most painful and costly process for Ballymore, our strong asset base especially in London has allowed us to stay in our core business and raise new finance and regroup and ensure the future viability of the business. ... The business ... is looking forward to paying its debt relating to the Irish banks, exiting [NAMA] soon and returning to a normal market model.

Mulryan was asked by Socialist Party TD Joe Higgins about the ongoing controversy in County Wicklow over lands he and Sean Dunne and their company Zapi Ltd had acquired from Wicklow County Council in 2003 in order to gain road access to the site at Charlesland near Greystones where they were building 1,800 houses and apartments, the largest residential development in the country at the time. Local auctioneer and former voluntary fundraiser for Fianna Fáil, Gabriel Dooley had claimed that he worked as an estate agent and lobbyist for Zapi, which developed Charlesland, and had witnessed discussions between Mulryan, Dunne and an influential councillor who helped broker the land deal. Lands worth tens of millions were part of an 'exchange of easements' with Zapi which allowed it to obtain road access to the site in a deal agreed with then county manager Eddie Sheehy. There is no evidence that anything other than the €10 cost of the administrative paperwork was paid by the developers or that any land was exchanged in the deal with the council. Asked by Higgins how he sought permission from the local authority to build roads through landlocked sites owned by Wicklow County Council, Mulryan replied: 'By doing a master plan and hiring the master planners to master plan all the area for the infrastructure of the area and the roads to service it.'

On the sensitive subject of a contract signed by Mulryan, Dunne and senior council officials including Sheehy on 17 July 2003, which secured the 'road easements that the developer needs from Wicklow County Council', Higgins asserted that 'according to Section 183 of the Local Government Act 2001, that is a reserved function of the elected members but it was never brought to the elected members'. Mulryan first replied that he was unaware of the contract and then added, 'I think it's the county manager that you should be talking to. I have no idea. I think it's the county manager who is the boss.'

Following his appearance, Mulryan was challenged by Dooley, who claimed, in a letter to the inquiry, that the developer's evidence was 'incorrect and misleading'. He said he was 'astonished' that Mulryan claimed he had no knowledge of a 'secret contract' the developers had with Wicklow County Council in relation to the project. 'I acted for him as both his land agent and lobbyist, and Mr Mulryan lobbied politicians privately with me and members of Wicklow County Council ... especially on the rezoning of Charlesland,' said Dooley.

Dooley was in a dispute with Mulryan over monies the auctioneer claimed he was owed by the developer in relation to a planned development at Florentine in Bray, County Wicklow. Dooley helped Mulryan assemble the lands in Bray town centre over a fifteen-year period up to 2004 for a retail and residential development and was a shareholder in the company that acquired the sites. He claimed he was promised €4 million in the event that the development was completed or sold off. The lands were acquired from a receiver for €1 million by the local authority in 2014, but Mulryan had resisted all attempts by the auctioneer to recoup any of the monies he claimed to be owed. When the lands were acquired by the council, Mulryan and his companies were still within NAMA. The agency had built a strong relationship with Mulryan and had agreed a memorandum of understanding that allowed him to continue managing his asset portfolio while seeking to repay his €2.2 billion debt pile, valued at €1.1 billion when it came into NAMA. Mulryan was loaned significant funds by the agency to help him to complete construction projects in London and elsewhere, and he was chosen by NAMA as its partner in a major residential development in the Dublin Docklands.

During his appearance before the inquiry Mulryan was also the subject of unfavourable criticism from UK developer James Woolf, who alleged that his company was wrongly excluded from the purchase of Savarin Palace, a major retail development in Wenceslas Square in the heart of Prague in the Czech Republic. Flow East, the Czech-registered property company founded by Woolf, claimed that it had signed a legally binding agreement with Ballymore to enter exclusive discussions to purchase the property for over €81 million in April 2015. The company said it was promised financial backing for its bid by private equity firm HIG Capital. According to a letter written by Woolf to a consultant overseeing the sale, a Ballymore executive allegedly telephoned HIG shortly before second-round bids were due and 'effectively asked them not to participate in the bid with us'. HIG withdrew its backing for Flow East's bid and the Czech group was excluded from the tender process because it allegedly could not fulfil the financing requirements. The property was sold by Ballymore to another Czech company, Crestyl. Among the senior management of Crestyl at the time of the sale was a former Ballymore executive. A request by Mulryan to the banking inquiry to respond to the allegations by Woolf published in the *Irish Times* during the week of his evidence was rejected. Flow East said that NAMA, which ultimately controlled the Savarin Palace asset, had a responsibility to ensure that the sales process was transparent and above board but, in a letter to Woolf in June 2015, the agency responded that it was 'a stranger to your dealings with Ballymore'.

Once again asking NAMA to reopen the bidding process, Woolf replied: 'It is pertinent to ask whether NAMA will sell its loan to the highest bidder? As we have repeated many times, we are willing to pay a price higher than the winning bidder.'

Flow East took an action against Ballymore and NAMA in the Czech courts. In response to the *Irish Times* report and the inquiry's refusal to allow him to address the allegations, Mulryan expressed his annoyance at Woolf's attack on him and NAMA and released the statement he had planned to have read at the inquiry. 'It is becoming more frequent that a disgruntled underbidder in a property deal tries to use the media and mention of NAMA to stop a transaction happening,' Mulryan said.

Mulryan insisted that Ballymore, not NAMA, was the seller of the asset and explained that the tender process, run for it by estate agents Cushman & Wakefield, was in order. Mulryan said Flow East was excluded from the bidding process because it could not provide 'proof of funding' and because it wanted exclusivity in the process: 'We are confident that the Czech courts will find in our favour ... and expose the claim for what it is – a disgruntled underbidder ... trying to inflict damage on Ballymore and NAMA.'

In contrast to Mulryan, who had only good things to say about NAMA, Johnny Ronan let loose both barrels on the agency and its executive in a detailed letter he submitted to the inquiry. He wrote that his company Ronan Group Real Estate had recently exited the agency having repaid '100% of the debt that it owed to the relevant financial institutions'. He described how NAMA had made a regrettable decision which would prove costly to the Irish taxpayer when, in 2011, it sold the Battersea Power Station in London – which was owned by Treasury Holdings (TH), in which he was a 50% shareholder.

Unfortunately, despite the best efforts of the shareholders and the TH executive team, NAMA moved on Battersea Power Station (which regrettably from our and the taxpayer's point of view, will make our former JV [joint venture] partners SP Setia billions of pounds). There is little doubt that if NAMA had not enforced, calling in its loans on Battersea … TH would still be operating and would have repaid all of its debts. That is the commercial reality of it.

He said that Treasury Holdings had consistently projected a €4.2 billion profit on Battersea in business plans submitted to NAMA, which never disagreed with the forecast, and that the figure was, if anything, a conservative estimate, given the recovery in the UK property market. 'The decision to enforce by NAMA was one of the costliest decisions in the history of the Irish state,' he contended. Outlining his 'grave reservations' in relation to the operation of the agency, he said that it was

granted such wide reaching and potentially unconstitutional powers that, unless it came under constant and careful scrutiny, it was always open to abuse. In addition, it seemed to me, NAMA was granted an endless financial budget to engage legal, public relations and other professionals to ensure that it would always have the financial muscle to win every argument. I firmly believe that certain individuals within NAMA decided that they did not want to work with TH … and that they would take it down, regardless of the cost to the Irish taxpayer.

Ronan went on to recount how a former NAMA official, who had handled the Treasury portfolio and that of Ballymore, had treated the two companies differently by enforcing its debts against Treasury Holdings but not against Mulryan's company. 'As far as I understand it, it was only when that individual advised NAMA of his decision to take up the position as CEO [of Ballymore Properties in London] that NAMA sought to block his appointment,' Ronan said. He also raised conflict of interest issues in relation to dealings between his former solicitors McCann Fitzgerald and NAMA and accused the agency of 'leaking selective, often un-true [sic] and one-sided confidential information to the press', including one press release that contained untruths about certain demands that Treasury Holdings allegedly made of NAMA in relation to the Battersea Power Station.

It is now almost six years since NAMA was established. In my view, it would be a mistake to look back over that time and consider NAMA to be a success. It was widely referred to as the biggest property company in the world. Yet it was led by former civil servants with no proper real estate experience. That was akin to asking an accountant to fly an airplane or a butcher to perform heart surgery. In my experience, they made decisions based on personal likes and dis-likes [*sic*], which gave little or no consideration to the ultimate return to the taxpayer.

In conclusion he claimed that in his view and experience 'no borrower/developer who has debts in NAMA will challenge NAMA or disclose the truth about how they operate, for fear that NAMA will immediately enforce their debts'.

In a number of paragraphs redacted from the statement, Ronan made reference to leaks of confidential information from the agency and alleged that NAMA had asked Treasury Holdings to 'sign term sheets that would blatantly breach company law'.

If there was little sympathy for the sore feelings of a developer widely portrayed over the years as the poster boy for the excess and hubris associated with the property bubble, there was even less when he made the unfortunate choice of ending his statement with a German phrase associated with the Nazi-run Auschwitz concentration camp in Poland. Ronan signed off with the words 'Arbeit Macht Frei' ('work sets you free'), which was then posted on the committee of inquiry website. He attracted more attention and criticism for this one line than for his entire 21-page submission.

Chapter 22 ~

A JEWEL IN THE CROWN

As soon as the Dáil resumed in late September 2015, the questions for the government over Project Eagle came thick and fast and led to some very acrimonious exchanges across the chamber. Once again there were calls from the opposition for a commission of investigation, with Sinn Féin leader Gerry Adams calling on Noonan to come before the Dáil to answer questions on what he described as the 'growing scandal' around the revelations that an illegal £15 million 'fixer's fee' was to be paid as part of the sell-off of the Northern loan book. Responding for the government, Labour leader and Tánaiste Joan Burton said she was advised that 'the loan sale was executed in a proper manner' and that the 'portfolio was sold for €1.5 billion because that is what the properties securing the loans were worth'. Burton repeated the government mantra that NAMA had answered questions, as it was obliged to do, at the relevant Oireachtas committees and she referred to the controversy over the Project Eagle loan sale as 'a highly complicated Northern tale'. NAMA, she said,

> had no relationship with any party on the loan sale against whom allegations of wrongdoing now are being made. The loan portfolio was sold after an open process to the highest bidder for what it was worth. … attempting to put NAMA into what is a highly complicated Northern tale is not necessarily, I suggest to Deputy Adams, giving the full picture.

Adams reminded Burton that Cushnahan was a former member of the NIAC who was to be the recipient of a fixer's fee and that this would 'constitute a clear conflict of interest and would cause reputational damage to all involved'. Already, he said, the finance committee of the assembly in Belfast, the police in the North and the UK and the US Department of Justice were involved in investigations into the purchase of Project Eagle by Cerberus, and yet 'the Irish government is defending it despite the move by all these agencies to address these matters'.

Mick Wallace weighed in to claim that Cerberus had been able to sell the loans which it had acquired from NAMA for approximately 27 pence in the pound for double that amount. 'The missing 73 pence has been picked up by the Irish taxpayer, those in the South, not the North, this is not just a Northern problem,' he said.

He told Burton that he had 'marked her card' before the summer recess that all was not well with NAMA and that the deal did not make commercial sense despite the agency's insistence that it was the best outcome. He claimed that a total of £45 million had been paid to fixers in respect of the Northern Ireland loan deal and that some 'big developers' were allowed to buy back their loans for 50 pence in the pound. Wallace continued:

> Given that Cerberus is under criminal investigation in two countries for Project Eagle why has that company not been disqualified from Project Arrow? How, in God's name, can the Government tolerate that? This is a portfolio with a par value of €7.2 billion which NAMA is threatening to sell off for something in the region of €1 billion. Some 50% of the portfolio is residential in Ireland, in the South, and we have a housing crisis. It looks like Cerberus is going to buy it.

Wallace finally asked: 'What role did NAMA's Ronnie Hanna, head of asset recovery, play in the sale and purchase of Project Eagle?'

Without addressing the question, which went to the heart of the issue as to the involvement of NAMA and the authorities in the South in the ongoing controversy, Burton again advised Wallace to bring his complaints and allegations to the police in the North and the UK. The government repeated this view ad nauseam during each debate on the subject of NAMA, usually adding that the agency was under the scrutiny of the Oireachtas finance and public accounts committees and subject to annual audit by the C&AG.

When the debate resumed a few days later Wallace once again launched into a tirade against NAMA in the Dáil, this time over its sale of three properties from Project Platinum to US fund Blackstone, which, he said, paid €100 million and was now offloading them for €170 million. 'That is a profit of 70% not 7%. Despite the fact the buildings were yielding approximately 6% per annum in rents, while NAMA's cost of money was less than 1%, there was still a panic to sell them,' he said.

Wallace was again particularly exercised by the impending sale of Project Arrow, which he said should not be handed to Cerberus given the ongoing investigations. In the Dáil on 29 September he went a step further in his criticism of the fund when he claimed that he had been 'recently summoned to a meeting by a public figure and a message was passed on to me from a leading member of Cerberus Ireland that I was going to get sorted'.

It was hard for opposition TDs to get anything of substance in reply to their questions but repeated suggestions from the Taoiseach and other ministers that they refer their complaints to various authorities north and south, east and west. The chairman of the PAC, John McGuinness, was also getting frustrated at the lack of clear information from the NAMA executives. At a meeting of the PAC on 1 October, Frank Daly was accused of arrogance in the responses he and McDonagh gave to the committee.

'There is sometimes an arrogance in the responses you and Mr McDonagh give, when all we are trying to do here, sometimes from an uninformed or poorly informed position, is to extract information on what you are doing within NAMA on an issue,' McGuinness said.

When Daly replied that he 'will certainly look at that', the exasperated PAC chairman interrupted with: 'There you go again.'

Other Fianna Fáil TDs were flexing their muscles on the NAMA issue, mindful of the fact, perhaps, that a general election was expected in the new year and the alleged corruption surrounding the Project Eagle sale was certain to provoke a response from voters. The party's Cork North Central TD, Billy Kelleher, insisted that the 'integrity of the State is coming into question as allegations are being made on a continual basis'. Rejecting the government line that it was a Northern Ireland problem, Kelleher told the Dáil on the same day as the PAC hearing that

this goes beyond Northern Ireland. NAMA was established by the Houses of the Oireachtas and it is the credibility and integrity of this House that is being brought into disrepute, because we are unable or unwilling to set up some form of investigation or to facilitate NAMA to co-operate with investigations in the north, in Belfast.

Responding, Joan Burton recalled that the Labour Party did not support Fianna Fáil's establishment of NAMA when in opposition but that two principles were clear at the time, including 'that developers ... would not be allowed buy back their loans at heavily discounted prices through the back door'. The second principle was that politicians would not be directly involved in NAMA, for the reason 'in the history of the bubble, and its development, of overly close connections between some political parties, developers and banks'.

Her effort to remind Fianna Fáil that it was responsible not just for creating NAMA but for the banking and property collapse that inspired it did not go down well with Kelleher, who responded: 'The Tánaiste's reply reminds me of the light brigade. It started out very well but ended very badly.'

Kelleher's party leader Micheál Martin rowed in with a suggestion that Michael Noonan wanted to sell the NAMA loan book and close the agency down for political reasons 'so that he could declare before the general election' that the agency was gone. He claimed that there had been 'an acceleration of [the sale of] many of the loans on NAMA's book.'

Martin added that a new twist had emerged in the Project Eagle saga with the recent revelation in the *Irish News* that David Watters had written to Tughans to 'lay claim to the acquisition fee of £7.5 million your firm currently holds'. Watters had claimed in the letter to Tughans that the fee payment was to go to an entity called Cadogan Futures LLP, set up in November 2010. Martin asked: 'Why is the Government ignoring this issue and essentially giving comfort to NAMA to put up a wall and not to engage fully in the investigation in Northern Ireland?'

In response to a series of questions Wallace put directly to NAMA in early October 2015, including in relation to the upcoming decision regarding the sale of Project Arrow, the agency said that it was not true for the TD to claim that 'Cerberus is under investigation in two jurisdictions' and should be excluded from the purchase. Frank Daly wrote, in a detailed response to Wallace on 8 October:

> I am not aware that Cerberus is under criminal investigation in any jurisdiction and no relevant authority, including the NCA, has advised NAMA of that to be the case [*sic*]. Accordingly, the question of disqualification from the Project Arrow sales process does not arise at present.

Daly also disagreed with Wallace's characterisation of the fee payments to Cushnahan, Brown Rudnick and Tughans, which were associated with Project Eagle, as 'illegal'. In respect of Ronnie Hanna and his role in the sale, Daly wrote that 'all key decisions in relation to the sale of Project Eagle were made by the NAMA board and not by Mr Hanna or any other executive'.

Later that month, Wallace asked NAMA about the role played by David Watters, who was closely associated with Cushnahan and attended crucial meetings with various players in the North's loan book sale saga over a number of years. On behalf of the agency, Martin Whelan, its head of public affairs, confirmed that McClure Watters, of which David Watters was a partner, was a member of the NAMA panel of enforcement and insolvency practitioners established in 2013, and had earned fees of about €60,000 over a five-year period arising from work it did for the agency. It later transpired that the firm earned €1.038 million between 2011 and 2015, or €978,306 more than Wallace was told. The larger amount included fees earned from NAMA-appointed receivers and agents not included in Whelan's response. Asked whether Hanna, along with

Cushnahan and Watters, had met with 'any US investment personnel' in connection with the Northern Ireland loan book sale, Whelan replied: 'No, Mr Hanna had no such meetings with these individuals.'

This was contradicted by Wallace in the House some weeks later when he claimed that Hanna had met 'at least one of the US investment firms'. Wallace continued:

> An executive of NAMA, Ronnie Hanna, was part of a cabal to seek payment for effecting the biggest property deal in the history of the State. The three individuals, Ronnie Hanna, David Watters and Frank Cushnahan, had information above and beyond what was available in the data room. David Watters had reviewed the business plan for many of the debtors.

Wallace then submitted that 'Frank Cushnahan was looking after the political side in the North and Ronnie Hanna was looking after matters inside NAMA in Dublin. We are not talking about Belfast; this is Dublin.'

The pressure on the government to hold a commission of investigation had risen, and while a motion calling for one was unsuccessfully moved by Fianna Fáil finance spokesman Michael McGrath in late October, the issue was not going away. McGrath had claimed that Cushnahan was privy to confidential information on Project Eagle which he received at a NAMA meeting in October 2013, less than a month before he stepped down from the NIAC. Cushnahan, he said, had arranged a secret meeting with the North's first minister and PIMCO while still an advisor to NAMA, and the agency was fully responsible for this and other questionable activities as it had made the decision to proceed with the sale in Dublin. 'Unless NAMA is exonerated by an independent commission of investigation, a shadow will be cast over the agency and its entire approach to asset disposals,' McGrath said.

During the debate on the Fianna Fáil motion, which was defeated by the government, Gerry Adams claimed that the NIAC had discussed potential purchasers on at least two occasions before the loan book was sold 'at a huge loss to Irish taxpayers'. He recounted how Watters had devised the concept of selling all of NAMA's Northern loans in a single portfolio in a proposal called 'Project Armani, which we know now became Project Eagle. He brought in Frank Cushnahan, then a member of the NIAC to work with him on the concept.' Adams described how Cushnahan was present at a meeting with PIMCO, Robinson, Coulter, Tughans and Brown Rudnick in July 2013 while an active member of the NIAC and did not declare any conflict of interest.

The constant drip-feed of often remarkably detailed information caused evident discomfort on the government benches and must have contributed in no small way to the move by a number of senior Fine Gael figures to call the general election earlier than planned. Only the hostile reaction of Labour leader Joan Burton to the prospect forced Enda Kenny to drop the idea. Within weeks of the Dáil debates and the letter of reply from Daly to Wallace, NAMA confirmed that Project Arrow had been sold 'to Promontoria Holding 176 B.V., an affiliate of Cerberus Global Investors'. The agency announced:

> The NAMA Board decision was based on the strong and clear recommendation of Cushman & Wakefield (C&W), the loan sale adviser appointed by NAMA in February 2015 to oversee the sales process for Project Arrow. The Arrow portfolio comprises loans with par debt balances of €6.25 billion. The loans in the Arrow portfolio, which were acquired by NAMA in 2010 and 2011, had been advanced to 302 debtor connections and secured against 1,906 assets. There has been a significant deterioration in the value of these assets since acquisition.

NAMA also confirmed that 90 per cent of the assets were located in Ireland, with 67 per cent outside and 23 per cent in Dublin. Another 6 per cent of the portfolio was in the UK and the remainder in other countries. It was reported that Cerberus had secured the deal after intense competition from Apollo Real Estate. The sale of Project Arrow to Cerberus, for a reported €800 million, was the latest in a string of such large-scale disposals over the previous ten months by NAMA. Six non-performing loan portfolios, with an aggregate balance or par value of €10.8 billion, were sold by NAMA for €3.16 billion, according to property industry publication *CoStar News*.

The news service reported that of these loans, Project Jewel accounted for 58 per cent of the total cash proceeds obtained by NAMA during 2015. It said that the six massive sales were: the €287 million Project Boyne, sold to Deutsche Bank for €95 million in January; the €785 million Project Maeve, sold to Deutsche Bank for around €97 million in July, on loans secured by property developer Gerry Barrett's assets; the £226 million Project Albion, sold to Oaktree Capital Management in July for circa £115 million, secured by predominantly UK commercial properties; the €608 million Project Arch, sold to Deutsche Bank in July for €164 million, with the bulk of real estate value formerly owned by property developers Jerry O'Reilly and Terry Sweeney as well as investor Ronan O'Caoimh; and Joe O'Reilly's €2.57 billion Project Jewel, anchored by Dundrum Town Centre and sold to a Hammerson and Allianz Real Estate joint venture for €1.85 billion in September.

Chapter 23 ✌

THE GOOD INVESTOR

On 17 November 2015 it was reported that the former secretary general of the Department of Finance, John Moran, had taken up a position with Japanese bank Nomura. Nomura had lent Cerberus some €750 million to complete the purchase of Project Eagle and had since been repaid. The Japanese bank had been involved with Cushnahan on the North's NAMA portfolio as far back as 2011–12, following approaches by Barry Lloyd on behalf of the NIAC member. When Nomura announced that he had been appointed as a senior advisor at its London office, Moran clarified that he would not be an employee of the bank. He would continue in his other roles: advising the online car booking service Uber, and as a director of the European Investment Bank, to which he was appointed by Michael Noonan when he worked in the finance department. US-based Uber had set up a European service centre in Limerick, hiring up to 300 staff, earlier in 2015.

In December, Cerberus agreed to enter mediation with Gareth Graham after the bookmaker appeared in the Belfast High Court challenging the attempts by the US fund to put his companies into administration. Graham argued that his businesses were performing strongly and that he had repaid £19 million in capital and interest on his property debts. His legal team argued that if it emerged that fixer fees were paid in the purchase by Cerberus of Project Eagle from NAMA, which had acquired his loans, the sale could be rescinded. Graham had earlier told the Stormont inquiry into the deal that recordings he held showed an 'ingrained culture of inappropriate and possibly illegal conduct' across political, banking, legal and accountancy sectors.

Graham's lawyers and Cerberus legal representatives entered discussions in order to separate the allegations of illegal conduct from the challenge to the firms being put into administration, with Stephen Shaw QC for Promontoria Eagle Ltd arguing that any 'fixers' had nothing to do with his client.

'They are strangers to us,' he emphasised, before adding that his client 'will go into mediation'. Three months later, Graham took out advertisements in the Belfast newspapers in which he expressed regret over any harm he may have caused over the legal action he had taken against Cerberus and the allegations that he had made in relation to its purchase of the Project Eagle portfolio from NAMA.

Following a full and frank dialogue with Cerberus I wish to make plain that the legal proceedings between Cerberus, my business and me have been resolved to the full satisfaction of all parties. I wish to distance myself from the grave and serious allegations made against Cerberus and its affiliates regarding alleged illegal payments to 'fixers' since, to the extent that it is possible for me to be, I am content that Cerberus is not (and was not) involved in any illegal conduct. I have agreed to meet Cerberus' legal costs in this matter.

Some days later it was confirmed that Graham had regained control of his property firms STH 500 and Lehill from the administrator appointed by Cerberus.

While Graham may have emerged from his battle with his shirt on, there would be no such quick result for Wallace in his ongoing fight for financial survival. In October 2015 he was served with a demand by Arthur Cox solicitors, acting for Promontoria (Aran), seeking payment of the guarantee totalling €2 million, including interest, which he owed in relation to the Taverna in Dublin's Italian Quarter. The letter said that legal proceedings would ensue unless the sum was paid within seven days. Although the Oireachtas had passed legislation in 2014 which meant that any member made bankrupt would not automatically lose their Dáil or Seanad seat, as was previously the case, the pressure on Wallace was immense. But that did not sway him from maintaining pressure on the government to set up a commission of investigation into Project Eagle and a host of other NAMA-related issues.

When the election was called in February 2016, the results were a disaster for Joan Burton and the Labour Party, whose representation in the Dáil dropped from 37 in 2011 to just seven after the votes were counted. Although the party had sought to defend its traditional core working-class and trade union vote by sponsoring legislative protections for workers, bringing up the minimum wage and protecting core social welfare rates, it had become associated with unpopular austerity measures including property and water charges and, inevitably, with the growing scandal surrounding NAMA. The result was also a potential disaster for Fine Gael, which lost 26 seats, although it still remained the largest party. The recovery of Fianna Fáil from 20 to 40 seats meant that neither it nor Fine Gael could form a stable administration with a Dáil majority. Sinn Féin grew from 14 to 23 seats to become the third largest party, while smaller parties and independent politicians took the remaining 34 seats.

After weeks of turgid and often ill-tempered negotiations, the two large parties agreed that a minority government led by Fine Gael and supported by a group of independents would survive on the basis that it honoured the terms of a 'confidence and supply' arrangement with Fianna Fáil. The agreement would allow the new government to pass three annual budgets once certain commitments to the main opposition party were honoured.

This arrangement, whereby Fianna Fáil controlled the fate of the government and influenced its decisions on a range of matters while avoiding political responsibility for them, made for slow progress in the new parliament. The arrival of an increased number of left-wing deputies across the opposition, notwithstanding the implosion of Labour, provided them the opportunity to progress legislation once Fianna Fáil came on board and votes did not threaten the government's survival. When it came to NAMA, and the Project Eagle saga in particular, there was no shortage of controversial material and revelations, which suggested that it was only a matter of time before the necessity of a full commission of investigation into the sale of its Northern Ireland loan book and a range of other disturbing matters of public interest would be conceded by the new government.

In late January 2016, Wallace claimed that the NAMA executive had given misleading evidence to the PAC at a hearing the previous July when members were informed that Lazard, the investment bank which advised on the Project Eagle sale, had identified nine potential buyers for the portfolio, including Fortress, in early 2014. In fact, Fortress only heard about the sale 'on the grapevine' and contacted the Taoiseach's office in its effort to get access to the bidding process. When only Fortress and Cerberus were left standing in the bidding by mid-March 2014, Lazard advised that there was still 'competitive tension' in the sales process and that it could continue. However, Fortress bid just over £1 billion compared to the Cerberus bid of £1.24 billion. Fortress later claimed that it was not aware that it was to be just a 'one stage process' and that it believed it had time to make a further offer. It also claimed that it had not enjoyed the same access to the data room as Cerberus and was therefore not in as favourable a position to assess the true value of the loan book.

Some weeks earlier US financial news organisation Bloomberg described as 'friendly' the relationship between the chief executive of Cerberus, Stephen Feinberg, and Frank Savage, a senior advisor of Lazard, although there was no suggestion that this influenced the Project Eagle sales process in any way.

The NAMA executives had also told the PAC on 9 July 2015 that 'there was a three month bid process from January to the end of March' 2014 for the sale, when in fact it was only six weeks, according to NWL. Cerberus only entered the race in early February while Fortress did not participate until the middle of that month, with the sales process ending on 1 April. Other contradictions in NAMA evidence were picked up as politicians and media pored over the statements emerging from various hearings, North and South, into the Project Eagle sale. At one point Frank Daly insisted that he had only joined the board of Ciorani in the autumn of 2010, whereas the company registration documents showed that he became a director in June, a month after Cushnahan, who was also on the board of the religious charity, joined the NIAC. While these could be dismissed as relatively trivial errors, there were more setbacks for the agency in the courts, both in Ireland and in the US.

In Dublin, one of the agency's portfolio asset managers, Peter Malbasha, was accused by Judge Brian Cregan of giving 'not only incorrect but positively misleading evidence' in a case involving NAMA and Garrett Kelleher. Malbasha had claimed that a NAMA receivership of one of Kelleher's companies, Middleview Ltd, had become effective in 2015, when it had actually commenced a year earlier. The difference was significant as Kelleher was claiming that he was not responsible for company filings after the receivership and was therefore not liable to pay for them. After a request from NAMA to change his judgment which, it said, had caused 'reputational damage' to Malbasha, Judge Cregan said that he accepted 'that Mr Malbasha did not intend to mislead'. It was not the first time the judge had been critical of NAMA; in 2014, Cregan had accused the agency of being 'untruthful' in its demand for repayment of loans which was served on the Florida-based Irish developer John Flynn, and awarded judgment against it. Cregan was appointed during 2015 to head a commission of investigation into 38 transactions by the IBRC, including the purchase of a company called Siteserv by billionaire Denis O'Brien.

In the US, the agency's efforts to chase down John McCann and his company, Castleway Group, which had debts of €114 million with NAMA, ran into difficulty in the courts. McCann was the previous owner of Kilcooley Abbey Estate in Tipperary, a property which had transferred to the agency, along with other distressed loans he had with the banks. McCann, from Crossmaglen, County Armagh, had purchased the estate from the Ponsonby family for €6 million in 2008. The Kilcooley property was put up for sale through sales agents Colliers in 2011. Mary and Jim Redmond, an Irish couple based in London, visited the estate, close to the Kilkenny border in County Tipperary, in 2012 and said they were prepared to offer up to €1.8 million for the 1,200-acre estate, which included 220 acres of farmland and 950 acres of forestry leased to Coillte.

It also included an eighteenth-century mansion, five staff houses, courtyard buildings, a Cistercian abbey and chapel, a lake and a boathouse. After they were informed by Colliers representative Marcus Magnier that another buyer was willing to pay €2.8 million, the Redmonds presumed that they had been outbid but asked the estate agent to keep them informed in the event that the sale fell through.

In June 2013, they discovered that the estate was up for sale and they submitted a bid for €1.9 million. In August 2013, Mary Redmond was informed by Magnier that the property had gone into receivership and was due to be sold within days. She was informed that Bannon, which is based in the same office block as Colliers in Dublin's Pembroke Street, had been appointed as receivers.

Redmond complained that she had not been given an opportunity to bid in an open sales process. Some weeks later Colliers contacted the couple and said that the receivers were obliged to view all offers and the Redmonds offered the asking price of €2.1 million. They were then informed that their offer had been rejected and a contract signed with another party at 'an acceptable level'.

The Redmonds contacted NAMA about their treatment, which passed their complaint to Bannon to deal with. The receivers and Colliers denied their allegation of a lack of integrity and honesty in the sale and that they had breached code of practice procedures. The Redmonds also complained to the finance minister, Michael Noonan.

In April 2014, the *Irish Examiner* reported that Thomas O'Gorman, a 62-year-old businessman from Newry, had purchased Kilcooley Abbey Estate in late 2013 for some €2.1 million and that he had also purchased the freehold on the adjoining forestry land from Coillte for a further €1.5 million. O'Gorman, who was described as an energy exploration entrepreneur, told the newspaper that he had also purchased, 'sight unseen', the Blarney Golf Resort in Cork for €2.5 million in early 2014, for which Colliers were also the sales agent.

The Redmonds sought further information about the sale of the Kilcooley Abbey property and found that the price paid was far less than the sum reported in the newspaper. Documents lodged with the Property Services Regulatory Authority (PRSA) recorded that the mansion, not including surrounding land and other properties, had been purchased for €700,000 and the sale completed in December 2013. It appeared from property registration and other documents that O'Gorman had purchased the freehold on the forestry land for €700,000. In May 2014, Martin Whelan of NAMA wrote to Mary Redmond informing her that he was 'advised that the information contained in the Property Price Register relating to Kilcooley Abbey Estate is incorrect.' He said that the agency had notified the purchaser's solicitor of the inaccuracy. According to Marcus Magnier of Colliers, the estate was purchased by O'Gorman and Kilcooley Estates Ltd for €2.25 million. In July 2016, the Land Registry recorded that the property was owned by Kilcooley Estates Ltd, Mill Street, Dundalk, where O'Gorman is based. The directors were named as Gerald and Sean McGreevy.

A complaint by the Redmonds to the PRSA over the manner in which the property was advertised and sold failed to yield any satisfactory explanation or outcome, in their view. They claimed that they were not informed that the forestry might be included in any purchase. Attempts to seek information from Coillte about its handling of the sale, through requests under freedom of environmental information laws, and Dáil questions by Pearse Doherty, were unsuccessful.

NAMA's efforts to obtain a judgment against McCann and his company Castleway Group in the US, including the proceeds of his $30 million sale of a 134-acre industrial complex near Philadelphia airport, suffered a setback in December 2015, when a court refused its application to have the Armagh man held in contempt over his failure to comply with orders to produce documents on his financial affairs.

The Flattery family made serious allegations of political interference in relation to the sale of NAMA-controlled properties in the High Court in a case they brought against the agency. Builder Martin Flattery claimed that auctioneer Arthur French had used his high-level 'political connections' to secure favourable treatment from NAMA in a dispute between the two men over development lands at Straffan in County Kildare.

Flattery, who was from Leixlip, sought to quash the sale of 35 acres of land and force the agency to complete their sale to him in an 'off market' deal to which he said NAMA had agreed in early 2016. He had jointly owned the lands with French before their business partnership collapsed. In a trenchant affidavit prepared for a court hearing in October 2016, Flattery claimed that he was told by the auctioneer that he 'had connections in high places' and a 'close relationship with many high ranking politicians in Fine Gael'.

He said that French had claimed that he had used his 'connections' to frustrate efforts by Flattery and his son to agree a business plan with NAMA to develop houses on the lands. Flattery's son Fergal unsuccessfully sought to buy the lands for €3.5 million from NAMA in November 2014, through his housebuilding firm, Mulberry Properties.

The case was settled in November 2016 before the allegations were tested in open court. The assets in dispute included the valuable development lands in Straffan and a four-bedroom property in the exclusive K Club which were transferred to NAMA in 2011 from the Irish Nationwide Building Society. French was a prominent member of the K Club, where he owned a property and rubbed shoulders with many prominent politicians and business people, including club owners Michael Smurfit and Gerry Gannon, Sean Mulryan, Sean Dunne and many more. His distressed loans were also transferred to NAMA following the property crash.

Paddy McKillen continued separate legal actions against NAMA and the office of the Minister of Finance, with Paul Hennigan and John Moran also named in the latter case, which involved the leaking of information relating to his business affairs.

The report of the banking inquiry proved to be something of a damp squib when it came to its 18-page (out of 476) section on NAMA. It failed to refer in any way to the more dramatic allegations levelled by Johnny Ronan against the agency in relation to the sale of the Battersea Power Station. Its recommendation that when 'NAMA completes its work it should be the subject of a further comprehensive and final review' could have been accompanied by the soundtrack of a stable door closing firmly after the horse had bolted, at least according to some sceptics.

More exciting by far was the first BBC *Spotlight* exposé on Project Eagle, which was broadcast in February 2016. Secretly recorded by the *Spotlight* team, Cushnahan was filmed speaking to Miskelly and accountant David Gray about the monies he was due from the deal. He also explained how his role in the sale of the portfolio to Cerberus was deliberately hidden.

On the tape, Cushnahan was recorded as stating that Ian Coulter of Tughans had placed £6 million (€7.7 million) into an account from which he was to benefit. During the programme, its presenter Mandy McAuley suggested that the transfer was discovered during an audit of the Tughans accounts. Coulter resigned following the discovery and the National Crime Agency began an investigation, *Spotlight* recounted.

'He actually moved £6 million of it into an escrow account,' Cushnahan said. He was asked by one of those present: 'Do you know his biggest mistake? He put it into an account in his own name.'

Cushnahan replied: 'He did that because he was then able to say, "There's this, Cushnahan's done all this work, therefore, he's entitled to his fee".'

The former NIAC member told Miskelly and Gray that he secretly worked on the Cerberus deal in a way that was hidden from NAMA.

'You know when I worked on that Cerberus thing to get that thing out, he worked with me to get that and basically all the work was done by me and him,' Cushnahan said during the secretly filmed hotel meeting.

During the exchanges, Cushnahan reminded Miskelly how they were first introduced to each other by Gareth Robinson.

On tape, Miskelly said to Cushnahan: 'You remember when Gareth Robinson phoned me that morning and told me to go to your office, and you phoned Ronnie [Ronnie Hanna, then a senior executive in Nama]?'

Gray was a partner in the large Belfast accountancy firm RSM McClure Watters. When the allegations first surfaced months earlier, Cushnahan had denied working on the deal or that he was an intended beneficiary of the money in the Isle of Man account. Miskelly told the BBC that he had made a complaint to the US Securities and Exchange Commission in relation to wrongdoing he had uncovered surrounding the Project Eagle sale. In a statement to the programme makers in advance of the broadcast, Miskelly said that he had gathered extensive evidence and records of his business meetings and dealings and, defending his practice of secretly taping them, said:

I realised that, in view of the continual suppression of my complaints to financial institutions, that this would be the only way to expose their financial misconduct and their corrupt dealings.

Describing the programme as an accurate account of the meeting, Miskelly said that Gareth Robinson, Cushnahan and Hanna had promised to help him from having his 'lights put out' by NAMA.

The dramatic footage of the three men was made by the BBC in co-operation with Miskelly in the Malmaison Hotel in Belfast in April 2015. Miskelly had made contact with McAuley with his extraordinary story after he saw her present a well-made documentary for *Spotlight* on the Red Sky controversy involving Cushnahan. Miskelly had been receiving treatment for a serious medical condition in Belfast hospitals over several years. He secretly recorded other conversations with Cushnahan in the car park of the Belfast City Hospital and in the canteen of the Royal Victoria Hospital, including in 2012 when he handed £40,000 in cash to the NAMA advisor.

Miskelly shared some of the taped discussions with McAuley following the move by Cerberus to appoint administrators over the Ten Square Hotel he had developed in Belfast in January 2015, and to place other offices and development sites he had owned into receivership a month later. The properties in Belfast, Armagh and Down were held by Applecroft Investments, which owed creditors some £80 million while its assets amounted to £36 million. With an estimated personal wealth of some £71 million in 2013, John Patrick Miskelly had successfully built developments in the UK and other countries and was once a prospective buyer of Liverpool FC, of which he is a life-long supporter. He sought to form a consortium and raise £250 million in an unsuccessful attempt to purchase the club in 2007.

In a revealing correspondence with the Northern Ireland assembly committee on enterprise, trade and investment, Cerberus confirmed that it had written off €4.6 billion of the €12.5 billion in Irish property debt it bought over the previous two years. According to Liam Strong, its European chief executive, the US fund had purchased €12.5 billion worth of property debt between mid-2014 and 2015 in three deals that included the controversial Project Eagle purchase from NAMA. By February 2016, Strong wrote, it had written off €4.6 billion from the total due on the loans, including €1.6 billion from borrowers involved in the Project Eagle portfolio. The figures did not include its purchase of Project Arrow from NAMA. The letter was in response to claims made to the committee that Cerberus had made unrealistic and unreasonable demands of borrowers and often threatened them with receivers.

Among those the fund had vigorously pursued over his debts was Mick Wallace, who had told the Dáil a few months earlier that Cerberus intended to go after him. Hot on the heels of winning its High Court judgment for €2 million against M&J Wallace, Cerberus subsidiary Promontoria (Aran) filed a petition to have the company wound up. It was the first such action taken by Cerberus against any of its Irish creditors and followed an unsuccessful challenge by Wallace to stop the US fund from calling in the personal guarantee he had provided to Ulster Bank. M&J Wallace was already in the hands of receivers appointed by ACC Bank over outstanding debts of €20 million. It was a time of mixed fortunes for Wallace, who was re-elected in the week of the successful court action by Promontoria (Aran) in February 2016, but this did not stop him making critical comments about Cerberus when the new Dáil resumed several weeks later. He also chased his seasoned adversary, Michael Noonan, the reappointed finance minister, about the revelations in the *Spotlight* programme concerning Cushnahan and the consultant's claim that he was entitled to a £6 million fee arising from his 'hidden' work on Project Eagle.

Noonan replied that the programme made no allegation of wrongdoing by NAMA but related to 'individuals on the margins of the buyer side' of the loan sale which, he said 'fall within the jurisdiction of the Northern Ireland authorities'. He advised Wallace to await the outcome of a review by the C&AG into the Project Eagle sales process. The new Dáil was barely in session before Wallace returned to the familiar theme of the disposal of public assets by NAMA in large bundles at knock-down prices which only global funds, including Cerberus, could afford to buy.

Anyone who has had the money to buy property from NAMA has made a fortune. Cerberus, for example, has spent approximately €4 billion on the purchase of assets on the island of Ireland with a par value of over €20 billion. It beggars belief that it got them so cheaply. I suggest we need to look to the future as well. We need to take back some of this property. The vulture funds have bought huge chunks of residential units and development lands that are needed. Even though we have been looking at a housing crisis for a long time, the State has allowed NAMA to sell so much of what is needed to vulture funds for peanuts.

Referring to the sale in late 2015 of Project Arrow, one that he fought bitterly to prevent, Wallace said:

It does not stack up. Before Christmas, NAMA signed off on Project Arrow, which involved a portfolio with a par value of €6.3 billion. It is reported that NAMA sold this portfolio for €800 million. This relates mostly to property in the Republic of Ireland. Where is the logic in that? We are aware that houses cannot be built overnight. We have sold houses and apartments that have already been built to these operators for peanuts. It is time for the State to take serious action, for example by introducing a system of compulsory purchase to take back what we need to deal with the crisis.

Referring to reports that Paddy Kearney had received a write-down of £250 million on his property debt from Cerberus, following the refinancing arrangement with Jefferies LoanCore, Wallace said that the US fund 'could well afford to do so because it is hammering many others and will hammer many more in the future'. He said:

The manner in which NAMA has operated is the biggest economic scandal in the history of this State. We should start by stopping it from operating, establishing an independent inquiry into what it has done and introducing compulsory purchase to take back from the vulture funds what belongs to the people of Ireland.

His impassioned pleas were ignored by the government side of the House but they set the tone for the continuing debate on the operations of NAMA over the coming months.

The findings of the inquiry of the Stormont Finance and Personnel Committee into Project Eagle were published in mid-March, after the general election in the South but before the new Dáil convened and before fresh Assembly elections in the North. Among the key questions raised was why Michael Noonan and NAMA did not 'suspend the sales process' in March 2014 when they became aware of the fee arrangements promised to Cushnahan and Coulter by PIMCO. The committee expressed disappointment that Noonan had not prevailed on NAMA executives to participate in the inquiry and said that their refusal to attend was 'particularly unhelpful'. The report expressed members' concern over NAMA's lack of knowledge of the activities of Cushnahan and his engagement with 'prospective buyers' of its NI loan book. It also said that the inquiry was frustrated by the absence of key witnesses including Cushnahan, former head of asset recovery at NAMA Ronnie Hanna, and former NI finance minister Simon Hamilton. Finance committee members hoped the inquiry could continue after the election of a new Assembly in the North in May. Commenting after the report was published, the committee chair, Daithí McKay said:

> It found that Executive ministers had 'insufficient professional advice' to fully assess the strategic considerations in relation to the Project Eagle bidding process. The committee was rightly critical of the Irish government's finance minister, Michael Noonan, and NAMA for the way they handled the sale. It also found that when issues came to light relating to the sale of the portfolio to PIMCO, Michael Noonan did not inform the power sharing executive in the North. NAMA stated that the northern advisory committee had no access to commercially sensitive information even though members of the committee said they did. So, further questions remain.

Returning to the theme in June, Wallace quoted from a letter sent by Cerberus to Peter Robinson a week before the closure of the sale of Project Eagle in which the fund promised that 'Cerberus will release personal and corporate guarantees as a key part of consensual workout plans with co-operative borrowers'. Speaking in the Dáil, he said:

> When Cerberus paid 27 pence in the pound for Project Eagle with the other 73 pence picked up by the Irish people in the South, it knew what it would get for the assets because the whole thing was sorted well in advance. It stinks to high heaven. It could offer a cosy deal like this because it was not in a competitive process. It had people working for it in Dublin and the North to make sure this was one of the great deals of all time.

This did not prevent Noonan delivering a positive progress report on the agency which, he said, had reached its end-of-year target for 2016 of redeeming 80 per cent of debt nine months ahead of schedule. Following the redemption in late June of a further €1 billion in senior bonds, NAMA had just €4.6 billion to repay out of the original €32.2 billion and was firmly on track to repay all senior debt by 2018, Noonan said. The finance minister was sticking like glue to the NAMA project and its rapid disposal of assets, despite the kicking he and the agency got in the report of the Stormont committee. Noonan continued to resist calls by Wallace, Sinn Féin leader Gerry Adams and a growing number of other

TDs for a commission of investigation into the Project Eagle sale and the myriad other issues surfacing from under the wall of silence that surrounded the workings of NAMA to date.

The arrest of Hanna and Cushnahan by the NCA in late May raised the stakes for both men and NAMA as the prospect dawned of a criminal investigation and conviction of one of the agency's most senior executives.

Wallace asked about the arrests in early June and about the significance of Hanna's role in other engagements with borrowers as head of asset recovery with the agency. Addressing the Dáil on 23 June, the day that another former NAMA official, Paul Pugh, was charged in Dublin with leaking confidential information from the agency, Wallace said:

> I have gone to the authorities in both the South and the North of Ireland before now with information on the gentleman who was arrested today [Paul Pugh]. These guys worked in Dublin. They did not work in Northern Ireland. Had Hanna stayed in the South he probably never would have been arrested, but he happened to be up there. The authorities there are only meant to be investigating the purchase side of Project Eagle. Why is the Irish State outsourcing its responsibility (to the SEC, FBI and NCA) and not investigating what is going on in NAMA?

Noonan responded that Pugh had been arrested earlier that day in respect of an alleged disclosure of confidential information in 2012 and that NAMA had reported the matter to the Garda in February 2013. 'This case', the minister said, 'is unrelated to the questions being investigated by the NCA in Northern Ireland regarding the buyer's side' of the Project Eagle sale. 'Members should not conflate these distinct cases which are being investigated separately by the appropriate authorities in the appropriate jurisdictions.'

Paul Pugh, 56, from Clontarf Road in Dublin, was charged with intentionally disclosing confidential information about McCabe Builders UK. The company owned by John McCabe had built, among other projects, the Abington development in Malahide before his loans were transferred to NAMA. His wife, Mary McCabe, had previously been pursued by NAMA for the proceeds of valuable jewellery she had sold in the US. Pugh was accused of sending the information by email to Gehane Tewfik, of London-based investment company Connaught & Whitehall Capital UK, in June 2012. Wallace told the Dáil that the former NAMA official had come 'on the radar' previously in NAMA-related allegations.

Wallace was determined to get his point across that the actions of those former NAMA officials who had been arrested had implications on both sides of

the border and warranted a commission of investigation which would be asked
to examine much more than the Project Eagle deal. He asked:

> During his employment at NAMA as Head of Asset Recovery, how many
> connections [borrowers] did Mr Hanna approve enforcement against? If it
> has been found that he has not behaved quite how he should have, it has huge
> repercussions for all the transactions in which he was involved with NAMA.
> It is important that we look at this sooner rather than later.

Wallace further asked what would happen to other deals Cerberus had done
in the South if it was found to have 'behaved badly in Project Eagle'. Once again
he asked Noonan why he did not stop the sale when PIMCO informed NAMA
that it was going to withdraw from the process after its compliance officers
warned that it could be in breach of US law over 'fixer fee' arrangements for
Cushnahan, among others. Once more the minister replied that he had 'no legal
authority to interfere with the legal authority of the NAMA board to make
commercial decisions'.

Responding, Wallace claimed that Noonan had

> no problem interfering with NAMA in May 2010, March 2012 and July 2015,
> when it suited him. The truth be told, the Minister has the power to tell
> NAMA what to do in all areas, so long as the direction or order under Section
> 14 is to do with achieving the purposes of the Act which are set out in section
> 2. He could tell NAMA to do anything in this context. He could even hold it to
> honour a social mandate. However he chose not to … He has not wanted to
> hold NAMA to account. He is happy with its commercial mandate and happy
> we have taken a completely neoliberal position. We have sold assets for half
> what it cost to build them. We have sold assets in Project Eagle to Cerberus
> for a song.

Referring in mid-July to the complaint about Cushnahan made by NAMA to
the Standards in Public Office (SIPO) Commission in March 2016, soon after the
secret recording of his remarks about the £5 million fixer's fee due to him was
broadcast by the BBC, Wallace said that the agency had known since March 2014
about the promised payment. Yet, he said, the NAMA chairman had only written
to SIPO on 2 March 2016, complaining that Cushnahan 'may have contravened
section 17' of the Ethics in Public Office Act 1995.

The section of the Act states that a person who holds a directorship in a public
body must tell SIPO of any interests they have that could materially influence
them in relation to the performance of their duties as a director. SIPO confirmed

the complaint in a letter sent to Wallace in early July 2016. The complaint centred on the failure of Cushnahan to reveal that he held shares in the Graham Group of companies which, the letter said, 'were obligors in respect of loans acquired by NAMA from participating institutions'. Daly also suggested that Cushnahan may have breached the Ethics Act in his dealings with PIMCO. SIPO confirmed that it had appointed Simon Noone as its investigating officer in the matter. Wallace asked:

> Given that Ronnie Hanna was arrested in May 2016, can we expect NAMA to complain about him in May 2018? Aside from Frank Cushnahan, the arrest of Ronnie Hanna has brought Project Eagle back home to Dublin, yet the government wants to bury its head in the sand. It is more than a year since I first gave the Garda the name of an individual who paid €15,000 in a bag in order to get favourable treatment from NAMA as well as the name of the NAMA employee who was taking the money. There was denial all around as usual. However, the man receiving the money has since been arrested on a different charge. Meanwhile, the guy who paid the bribe is doing well for himself; there is not a bother on him. Such is business in Ireland.

Wallace referred to the court action taken by Hibernia REIT to secure possession of the large Garda-leased command and control facility on Harcourt Street in Dublin 2 and said that the force would be undermined by

> scattering this technical centre to the four winds … Will the Taoiseach explain why NAMA was allowed to sell this site to a vulture fund rather than keep it in State ownership? Hibernia REIT, which now owns the site, was set up by a guy who was a big player in NAMA where he was a portfolio manager for three years. When he joined the agency, he moved his 30% shareholding in his father's company to an offshore trust. Did he declare that to NAMA? The same company then benefited from some lucrative work from the agency. He left NAMA in December 2012 and used his insider knowledge regarding the agency's assets to line up investment funds that would provide the finance for the new company, Hibernia REIT, which he manages. It would not require forensic examination to discover that Hibernia REIT did remarkably well in purchasing former NAMA assets, many of which this gentleman was involved with, but then that is how we do business in Ireland. Does the Taoiseach not think that the public interest would be best served if we examined the complete workings of NAMA? At this stage the majority of people in Ireland believe NAMA is rotten to the core.

Enda Kenny replied that criminal investigations into the activities of those arrested in the North were continuing and should be allowed take their course, while the C&AG was the appropriate authority to examine the Project Eagle sale by NAMA. In relation to the acquisition by Hibernia REIT of the Garda building, he said that there had been objections to the move. Once again, he did not think a commission of investigation was the way to go, given the different inquiries under way in various jurisdictions. To which Wallace replied:

> It is blatantly obvious that the one jurisdiction where some investigation of a serious nature should be going on is the one that does not have one, and that is us. We do not want to know, or the Taoiseach does not want to know. I can understand why he does not want to know. As a matter of interest, how come no one can ever answer the question as to why NAMA never reported the fact this individual [Cushnahan] was in line for a €5 million backhander? Why, under section 19 of the Criminal Justice Act, did it not report it? Why did the Minister for Finance not report it?

As the debates in the Oireachtas over Project Eagle and NAMA continued, the agency was busy with other problems while preparing to wind down its operations completely, earlier than its original expiry date of 2020. One of its clients turned adversary, Cork developer Michael O'Flynn, joined with four other companies in a challenge to the plans by the agency to build 20,000 houses in partnership with some of its 'favoured' developers, mainly in Dublin.

While NAMA was criticised heavily by housing charities and left-wing parties and independents for failing to make any significant contribution towards meeting the needs of homeless people and the almost 100,000 people on local authority waiting lists, it was now facing litigation at the European Court over its plans to build homes for the private market. Unlike other developers, O'Flynn had not provided personal guarantees to the banks, but his own loans of some €25 million were also transferred to the agency. Initially, the house builder, who had also constructed Ireland's largest apartment block, the Elysian Tower in Cork, cooperated with the NAMA officials, including John Mulcahy and Ronnie Hanna, with whom he was dealing before he lost faith in the ability of the agency to develop an appropriate business plan. By 2012, he was in deep disagreement with the bad bank and quickly came to the conclusion that the project was not going to work. Instead, he believed, by taking over performing loans with the bad ones, it was likely to destroy any prospects for recovery of the property industry and to contribute to a crisis in the supply of housing down the road.

O'Flynn argued that he could pay his entire debt if his business plan was endorsed, and that his debts were serviceable given the rental income coming in from various developments in Ireland and the UK. The response from NAMA was hostile and relations broke down. His plan to pay off the entire par value of his debt over a five- to ten-year period was rejected by the agency, which wanted him to dispose of assets more rapidly. O'Flynn accepted that he had the responsibility to wind down his debts but he was not prepared to concede what he considered to be the planned destruction of his business, and had a series of sometimes heated disagreements with NAMA executives including McDonagh, Mulcahy and Hanna. According to some of those in whom he confided during this tense period, relations with the NAMA executives reached such a low at one point that O'Flynn was called in following publication of an interview he gave to Ronald Quinlan of the *Sunday Independent* and instructed not to talk to the media and to desist from such public utterances.

He also took legal action against former Fine Gael minister and founder of the less than successful Renua party, Lucinda Creighton, over comments she made when he was filmed by RTÉ *Prime Time* arriving by helicopter at a race meeting at Down Royal in Lisburn, County Down, in 2010. The Cork developer had flown from his 90-acre dairy farm in Ovens in Cork to watch his horse perform, as he had when attending business meetings across Ireland and the UK for several years. In his view, he was wrongly portrayed as one of the playboys of the boom, when he had deliberately spent years avoiding publicity as he went about building his construction company.

'The helicopter was a very useful business tool at the time when I had businesses all over the UK and living out of Cork made it difficult. But it became too much of a hassle for me and I didn't want that kind of attention,' he told the *Irish Times* following the brief controversy which led to him taking defamation proceedings against Creighton for her critical remarks about his lifestyle. He realised that 'it was no longer acceptable' for developers to be seen to display trappings of wealth in the eye of the storm of austerity and hardship that hit so many householders and working people in the wake of the crash. He got rid of the chopper and took to travelling by road and rail.

'Once it came up I sold it. I never used it for personal use without paying for it and it was a business tool that I had no intention of replacing,' he told Ciarán Hancock during the frank February 2016 interview. O'Flynn had already made his mark through his open and severe criticism of NAMA in his statement to the banking inquiry a year earlier and unlike most of his contemporaries, many of whom were subject to non-disclosure agreements as a condition of their exit from the agency, he was not willing to hold his tongue. His warning about the impending housing crisis proved true, if somewhat understated, while his assessment that the depression of property prices by the agency would invite the global vultures to swoop on the carcass of the distressed assets was also prescient. In a strange alliance of the sort which only emerges in a society traumatised by extreme economic circumstances, the analysis of the root cause of the crisis was shared by the much disdained, still wealthy developer elite and the parties and people of the left when it came to the perceived failure of the 'bad bank' solution. Indeed, had not Nobel Prize-winning economist Joseph Stiglitz, among others, warned of exactly such an outcome when the agency was hurriedly established in 2009?

O'Flynn freed himself from the clutches of NAMA after it sold his loans for a reported €1.1 billion in 2014 to US fund Blackstone, which immediately called them in. Turning to Michael Cush SC for assistance, he challenged the appointment of receivers and the placing of his trading companies under High Court protection. In early 2015 he reached an agreement with Blackstone subsidiary Carbon Finance that involved him paying some €400 million to the US fund, which he obtained through a joint venture deal with New York investors Avenue Capital Group and regained control of his housebuilding business. In an added twist to the arrangement, he reached agreement with Blackstone to take over the management of his former assets, including the completion of the Elysian Tower in Cork city. Blackstone was among the vulture funds to have successfully flipped valuable assets it had acquired from NAMA at bargain basement prices, including Hume House in Ballsbridge, which had been purchased by Sean Dunne for €130 million at the height of the property bubble in 2006. Just over a year after buying it from NAMA, Blackstone put it on the market, through estate agents CBRE, for just €40 million, and it was sold to Hibernia REIT for just over €50 million in February 2016. In the UK, O'Flynn entered into a joint venture with another US investment group, BlackRock, to develop a property portfolio worth some €500 million.

Back on his feet, O'Flynn then joined with a number of other developers to challenge NAMA's proposal to construct 20,000 homes in a complaint to the EU competition directorate over what they claimed was illegal state aid. With builders David Daly, Paddy McKillen, Sean McKeon of MKN Properties and Greg Kavanagh and Pat Crean of New Generation Homes, he lodged the complaint that argued that NAMA had gone beyond the remit the government had agreed with the EU and ECB when the agency was first established in 2009 to restore the Irish banks. The builders claimed that NAMA was effectively providing state aid to certain developers who were given a competitive advantage by the agency, providing finance at lower interest than was available to others in the property market. They argued that NAMA's involvement in housebuilding would limit the number of sites available to private builders and delay the provision of new homes to meet growing demand. As it was not going to remain in the business after its termination date of 2020, NAMA also did not have to bear other costs including the replacement of sites and housing stock, unlike the complainants, who also challenged the involvement of the agency in commercial development.

Among the schemes which NAMA proposed to co-develop was a major housing development in the Dublin Docklands with Ballymore Properties and Singapore-based Oxley Holdings. The first phase of Project Wave, the NAMA-backed proposal to build office and commercial space as well as 250 apartments on 10 per cent of available development land in the Dublin Docklands Strategic Development Zone was granted planning permission in late 2015. As it came under the city council's recently introduced fast track planning scheme, the application could not be appealed to An Bord Pleanála. NAMA's choice of Sean Mulryan's Ballymore Properties confirmed his status as a favoured developer of the agency, which selected the company ahead of separate bids backed by Johnny Ronan and Denis O'Brien. The NTMA announced that it planned to move its headquarters from the Treasury Building on Grand Canal Street, developed and owned by Ronan, to the new Project Wave site, which meant that NAMA would also be rehoused there on completion of the multi-billion-euro scheme in 2018. The 2.2-hectare site on North Wall Quay lay adjacent to the shell of the planned headquarters of Anglo Irish Bank before its collapse and which was now being completed as the new location for the Central Bank.

It was the sort of plan which the six complainants to the EU competition directorate had in mind when it came to their objections to NAMA's move into commercial and residential development. That the agency chose Mulryan and his partner in the project, the former Singapore police officer and multi-millionaire founder of Oxley, Ching Chiat Kwong, only rubbed salt in their wounds, given the latter's reputation as the 'Shoebox King', a moniker he earned as the builder of what were politely called 'compact apartments' in his native city. Mulryan, along with developer Ray Grehan, were among the Irish people identified among the many thousands of wealthy people worldwide who used the offshore banking services of Panama-based legal firm Mossack Fonseca when its client details were leaked anonymously to the world's media in May 2016. Also named in the Panama Papers was Michael Geoghegan, the head of the ministerial advisory group of NAMA and former chief executive of HSBC.

A number of others in the real estate business, including another former associate of Kelleher's, pocketed a large fortune when they sold properties they had assembled through their company Argentum to Cairn Homes, the listed firm that had purchased the Redemptorist-owned site on Orwell Road in Rathgar a year earlier. In April 2016 it was reported that Argentum had sold six sites on 164.5 acres of land in Dublin for €105 million. Argentum was a joint venture between Australian-based Anchorage Capital and Dublin building firm Newlyn.

A successful house builder and commercial developer during the boom years, Newlyn had its distressed bank loans transferred to the agency following the crash. Its directors established the successful Arrow Asset Management in 2009 with Richard Moyles, a former employee of Shelbourne.

Arrow built a successful partnership with Pepper Asset Servicing, which was set up by the Pepper Group when it arrived in Ireland in 2012 with the acquisition of GE Capital Woodchester and its 3,500 mortgage accounts. Pepper expanded its operations when it was appointed by US fund CarVal to manage its €380 million portfolio of Irish loans. In January 2013, another former Shelbourne staffer, Brian Berg, was appointed head of commercial real estate for Pepper before he moved on to head the Irish operation of Cerberus. Arrow shared offices in Herbert Street with Newlyn Developments and property surveyors Kelly Walsh, one of the companies chosen by NAMA for its panel of real estate advisors.

Former NAMA employee Enda Farrell was handed a two-year suspended sentence after pleading guilty to eight counts of unlawfully disclosing confidential NAMA information after he left the agency in 2012. Before Judge Karen O'Connor in the Circuit Criminal Court in Dublin in May 2016, lawyers for Farrell said that he had not benefited from his actions and that the prosecution had not alleged that he had done so. Judge O'Connor said that in considering the sentence, she had taken into account the breach of trust involved and that Farrell had bypassed the IT security system at the agency. However, in mitigation, he had admitted his wrongdoing and voluntarily returned to Ireland from Belgium to face charges. He had suffered a loss to his personal and professional reputation, she added. Speaking at an earlier hearing, his barrister, Michael Bowman SC, said that when the offences were uncovered, Farrell lost his job and was left destitute by civil proceedings, and that his poor judgement had compromised his future employment prospects. He described how Farrell had worked 12-hour days in a highly pressurised environment and thought that his actions in sending hundreds of files to various companies was going to 'further the objectives of the agency'.

'Pressure built up, he was getting it from both ends,' Bowman said. The banks complained that he was undervaluing their portfolios and his bosses at NAMA were complaining he was overvaluing them and they would not be able to sell them to the market and make a profit, the lawyer added.

Farrell's wife, Alice Kramer, gave evidence that her husband was a broken man who had little, if any, self-worth. He was now the sole carer for their three small children, she said. He had been on a salary of just over €100,000 with NAMA and was now effectively unemployable, the court heard.

Not doing so badly was his former employer, which stated in its annual report for 2015 that NAMA had returned a profit of €1.8 billion for the year, or four times the amount for 2014. Published in June 2016, the report also claimed that it had reduced its debt to one-fifth of its original size. The agency said it had generated €9.1 billion in cash, with €8.5 billion coming from asset disposals. It was also on course to deliver 20,000 new homes, including in the Dublin Docklands. Frank Daly predicted that the agency would deliver a surplus of €2.3 billion by the time its work was complete. Notwithstanding the positive news, it was engaged in a difficult exchange of correspondence with the C&AG over his review of the Project Eagle sale and facing continuing attacks from several quarters, including from politicians who had used the loan sale as an opportunity to beat up on NAMA during the February election campaign and since.

There were bitter exchanges in the Dáil in late June when Mick Wallace put down a motion calling for a commission of investigation into the Project Eagle sale. Fianna Fáil was accused by Clare Daly and Pearse Doherty of Sinn Féin of reversing its previously stated position by proposing that the establishment of a commission should await the outcome of the NCA investigation in the North. Michael McGrath, the finance spokesperson for Fianna Fáil, denied a charge by Doherty that his party had been 'got at' and said that a commission of investigation 'would run into the sand and very quickly indeed because of arrests in Northern Ireland' and the ongoing criminal investigation there. Clare Daly rounded on Michael Noonan, who, she said, 'had resisted an investigation because you are the one who had the power to stop it but rather than stopping it you chose to insist that it go ahead'.

Referring to the fixer's fee which PIMCO had agreed to pay and of which it informed NAMA in March 2014, Daly added, 'NAMA told you and you insisted that the deal would go ahead.' She asked Noonan: 'What did you know, what should you have known? What do you know now? What action did you take?' In response, the finance minister said that Daly wanted a commission established as a 'trawling exercise'. He said he was reminded of the Mad Hatter or the dormouse in *Alice in Wonderland*, who said 'verdict first, trial afterwards'. Challenging the independents, he said they should make their allegations outside the House and without the protection of Dáil privilege if they were so sure of their ground. Mick Wallace said that the government might have thrown Frank Cushnahan 'under the bus' but that it could not do the same to Ronnie Hanna. The Fianna Fáil amendment calling for the establishment of a commission after the conclusion of criminal investigations was carried by 105 votes to 38 following the defeat of the government's motion. It had sought 'respect for the integrity of the ongoing UK National Crime Agency criminal investigation', and to allow the Committee of Public Accounts to exercise its oversight role of NAMA. The government TDs supported the successful Fianna Fáil amendment, while both major parties blocked the motion put down by the Independents4Change TD and supported by Sinn Féin.

Wallace intensified his campaign against NAMA with the launch of a website, Namaleaks, through which people with information about the agency could post it online and anonymously. He advised potential users:

Take your personal computer and go to a network that isn't associated with you or your employer, such as at a coffee shop. Ideally, you should go to one that you don't already frequent. Leave your phone at home, and buy your coffee with cash. Choose a coffee shop without security cameras, or a spot within the shop where cameras aren't recording. Be aware of your surroundings, turn your screen away from curious neighbours.

He told *Village* magazine in September 2016 that he had already received some useful information since the launch a month previous. 'We have received some really interesting correspondence but obviously we require hard evidence and we are very measured as to how we approach it.'

Among those who responded early to the Namaleaks invitation was the Asian-based businessman Barry Lloyd, who revealed the work he had done for Frank Cushnahan from 2010 to 2012, when he sought prospective buyers, including Japanese bank Nomura, for the Northern Ireland loan book held by NAMA. Earlier in 2016, it was reported that former finance department secretary general, John Moran, had lobbied Noonan during recent months on behalf of Nomura. The lobbying register showed that at meetings between September and December 2015, Moran had asked Noonan and Des Carville, who worked under him when he was head of the department, for state contracts for the Japanese bank from 'the government or government-supported banks'.

Lloyd claimed that Nomura ended contact with him after he had introduced the bank to Cushnahan and Coulter. He asserted that Nomura, a specialist in distressed assets, remained central to the discussion with PIMCO and Cerberus and emerged as the key financial backer for the Project Eagle purchase. He signed an affidavit in Dublin recounting his role soon after he made contact with Wallace.

In August Daithí McKay resigned as Sinn Féin MLA for North Antrim after it emerged that he had a role in the coaching of witness Jamie Bryson before the loyalist blogger gave his provocative evidence at the inquiry in September 2015. It emerged that McKay was aware that a party colleague, Thomas O'Hara, was in contact with Bryson in advance of his appearance and had made suggestions about how he should deliver his statement. McKay was replaced as chair of the committee by Emma Pengelly, wife of senior civil servant Richard Pengelly, who served in the departments of finance and health and was one of those nominated, unsuccessfully, to become a member of the NIAC along with Cushnahan in 2010. Media in the North recorded that Emma Pengelly was a daughter of loyalist Noel Little, co-founder of Ulster Resistance, a paramilitary group which imported a large shipment of weapons from South Africa during the 1980s. Little appeared alongside Peter Robinson in photographs of Ulster Resistance rallies from the time.

Following elections to a new assembly in the North, the finance committee resumed its inquiries into the sale of Project Eagle, although it soon became evident that the new chair was not as eager as her predecessor to rush matters along. In the wake of the arrests of Hanna and Cushnahan in late May, Emma Pengelly advised the committee that it would be wise for it to do nothing that might prejudice the NCA investigation and that it might be worthwhile to ask the police about the progress of their inquiry and get some advice from them. The new finance minister, Máirtín Ó Muilleoir, one of the more inquisitive members of the committee before his appointment following the assembly elections, was likely to be more amenable than Simon Hamilton, whom he replaced, when it came to any request to provide relevant files and documentation on Project Eagle. Committee member Jim Allister of the Traditional Unionist Voice (TUV), who had campaigned long and hard for hidden details of Project Eagle sale to be disclosed by Robinson and his DUP colleagues, suggested that Ó Muilleoir 'was an enthusiast' when it came to extracting information from the department which he now headed.

'Now would be an opportune time to invite the department to again consider the distribution of papers to the committee in respect of NAMA,' Allister told the committee, before adding that the investigation could not be 'long fingered' but addressed with 'vigour and with some expedition'. Taking issue with Pengelly, SDLP member Claire Hanna said, in comments supported by Sinn Féin and UUP members, that a 'rigorous investigation' around the deal was required in parallel with criminal inquiries.

The calls for a committee of investigation into NAMA came hot and heavy when the Dáil resumed in early September to debate the dramatic ruling by the EU competition commissioner on the potential €13 billion in unpaid back taxes due to the Irish state by giant US corporation Apple. The debate came just a day after BBC *Spotlight* broadcast yet another of the secret tape recordings by developer John Miskelly of Frank Cushnahan. The tape of the conversation in the car park of the Belfast City Hospital in August 2012 included the reference to the payment of £40,000 in cash to Cushnahan by the developer, who was trying to get out of NAMA, or at least escape with some of his assets and wealth intact.

'There's £40,000 in that and it's in bundles of two, Frank,' Miskelly is heard saying on the tape. Cushnahan then gives the developer a page containing details of the current value of each of Miskelly's properties transferred to NAMA. It was implied that the valuations on the page given by Cushnahan to Miskelly and shown by *Spotlight* were an accurate reflection of what the agency considered at least some of the developer's distressed assets to be worth.

During the taped conversation, Cushnahan referred to the fact that he had influence over Ronnie Hanna and that they were 'thick as thieves', a claim that was immediately and forcefully denied by the former NAMA head of asset recovery, who insisted that he had no improper dealings with the former member of the NIAC. It was suggested by the programme makers that a further £10,000 was paid to Cushnahan by Miskelly after the car park handover. It was claimed that Cushnahan assured the developer that he could help him to refinance his properties out of NAMA and regain control of them. The BBC programme claimed that Cushnahan told Miskelly to tell the National Crime Agency (NCA) he had never given Cushnahan any payment. Cushnahan spoke to Miskelly of his fears of ending up in prison. He told Miskelly to tell Stormont's finance committee, which was probing the NAMA sale, that he was simply acting for the developer 'in an advisory capacity'. Miskelly alleged that Cushnahan said that he was working with Sammy Wilson and that Peter Robinson could put pressure on NAMA to allow properties to be sold 'at a discount' to help developers. Robinson told the programme that the claims were 'risible'.

Just in case anyone suspected that Miskelly might have been involved in some illicit exercise in the car park of the hospital, he issued a statement to the programme in which he said that he had consistently reported financial crime and corruption to the relevant authorities. It said:

Since 2007/8 I have consistently and truthfully reported financial crime and corruption with the relevant authorities ... My overriding aim has always been to highlight wrongdoing and corruption and have all of these matters fully investigated by the appropriate authorities. I have at all times made clear that payments made by me to any persons have been lawful and legitimate. As a witness, I am participating in the ongoing investigations by the NCA and authorities in the United States and in the interest of integrity of the judicial process I am unable to make any further comment.

Given that other former NAMA officials had been convicted or charged with leaking confidential information from the agency, the tapes and document were potentially evidence of a criminal offence, at least in the Republic.

During the Dáil debate Wallace put it to the Taoiseach that further weight, if it was ever needed, had now been added to the demand for a commission of investigation into NAMA by the broadcast on 6 September. He said:

Last night's BBC *Spotlight* programme adds further weight to the need for a truly independent commission investigation into NAMA. What a contrast between the BBC *Spotlight* programme and our own State broadcaster, RTÉ, which is afraid of its life to go near the subject. What is going on? It is unbelievable. For anybody looking at the video last night, it was mind-boggling to see these bundles of cash passing hands. It was kind of scary. This person takes cash from a developer and prevails on his friend Ronnie, one of his best mates, not to enforce. Given that he had just got to know Miskelly, how many others had he done deals with? Republic of Ireland developers were enforced upon four times more than developers in Northern Ireland. Why does NAMA not tell us why? If he was arranging refinance, he must have known what the NAMA number was for the loan – a number which is supposed to be confidential and commercially sensitive. Who gave him these numbers? NAMA claimed he had no access to any commercially sensitive information … I assure the House that the Project Eagle portfolio was probably sold for approximately €500 million too little.

In strong rebuttal some days later, NAMA said that the document purportedly containing its valuations of Miskelly's properties was false.

BBC *Spotlight* claimed the source of the information may have originated from within NAMA and been illegally leaked. NAMA confirms that valuations contained in the document broadcast by BBC *Spotlight* are not the actual NAMA valuations. The factual position is that valuations in the BBC document are significantly lower than NAMA's actual valuations – in some cases up to 30pc lower.

Notwithstanding its dismissal of the significance of Cushnahan's behaviour, within days of the programme NAMA lodged another complaint against him with SIPO in Dublin and sent a report to the Garda. The questioning by gardaí of yet another, as yet unnamed, former member of its staff alleged by Enda Farrell to have leaked confidential agency information to third parties did not help the case of NAMA executives seeking to avoid an inquiry into its activities. The man was accused of leaking material of a NAMA debtor to commercial interests overseas.

Although it had refused to support the motion to this effect put down by the Independents4Change before the summer recess, and supported by Sinn Féin,

Fianna Fáil was now finding it difficult to resist calls for a commission of investigation, even if it meant upsetting the confidence and supply agreement it had forged with the government in the protracted post-election negotiations.

For Fine Gael, and despite the reticence of the finance minister, it was also clear that the writing was on the wall and its procrastination on the issue was no longer sustainable. In mid-September Enda Kenny said he would not rule out an inquiry into Project Eagle but that if one were to go ahead it would need to be very focused. The Taoiseach was speaking after the cabinet discussed the report of the C&AG into the sale of Project Eagle, which, if anything, made an independent inquiry inevitable.

Kenny said a commission of investigation or a tribunal of inquiry would 'commit the taxpayer to many millions of euro', but if an investigation was found to be necessary, 'then so be it'. For Michael Noonan, the C&AG report contained nothing 'that suggested anything illegal, nothing improper or any irregularities in the way that NAMA behaved', adding that NAMA would strongly rebut its findings. He also said that the PAC would hold hearings on the report. 'I wouldn't rule out an inquiry after that, but let's see what comes out of it,' Noonan said.

Three months earlier, Noonan had indicated there was nothing in the Project Eagle saga that could be 'usefully pursued by a commission of investigation', so his concession that there might be some purpose in an inquiry being held after PAC hearings was a slight move in that direction. However, there was a distinct sound of cans getting kicked down the road in the wake of the publication of the C&AG report. It was evident that there was some disagreement on the issue at the highest levels in government as political correspondents had been briefed in the days before its release that a judicial inquiry into the sale of NAMA's loan book in the North was to be discussed and agreed at cabinet.

The C&AG, Seamus McCarthy, did not pull any punches in his forensic and comprehensive review of the Project Eagle sales process, publication of which was delayed by several months due to the political uncertainty following the general election and other factors arising from the private responses from relevant agencies, including NAMA and the Department of Finance, which were heavily critical of its findings. Released on 13 September 2016 the report found that NAMA had incurred a loss of a potential £190 million (€223 million) from the sale of Project Eagle. Although it was essentially a 'value for money' report and did not cover all of the allegations and revelations concerning fixer's fees, political interference and corruption that had dominated public discourse for over a year, it did identify significant conflicts of interest in the process, not least relating to Frank Cushnahan. Among the other findings by the C&AG were that NAMA valuations underestimated the value of the loans; the discount applied to the sale by the agency was too high; and there were serious questions surrounding the success fees promised by PIMCO to Brown Rudnick, Tughans and Frank Cushnahan, before it withdrew from the sale in March 2014. The involvement of Cushnahan in discussions on the sales process in the NIAC should have been 'considered' by the agency, given that he was an advisor to six NAMA debtors, representing over 50 per cent of the entire loan book, among other potential conflicts of interest. On the proposed success fee, the C&AG said that NAMA should have been more proactive when it discovered the arrangement of a £15 million or £16 million payment. The report argued:

> Given the joint agreement between the parties to the success fee arrangement with Pimco, all of the payment – not just the payment to Mr Cushnahan – should have raised concerns for Nama. The board subsequently learned of the existence of a success fee arrangement involving Cerberus, on the one hand, and Brown Rudnick and Tughans on the other. The understanding that Brown Rudnick and Tughans had allegedly been in an arrangement with a member of the NIAC at any stage of the process should have raised concerns for NAMA about potential impacts of such arrangements on the sale process, unless convincing explanations could be produced.

The C&AG said that NAMA departed from its normal loan sale process in the sale and implemented restrictions which 'relative to its standard process, reduced both the level of competition and the opportunity for potential bidders to assess the value of the portfolio. They acted as a deterrent for a number of bidders and had the potential to affect the price achievable.' The report highlighted flaws in the manner in which NAMA legal dealt with the information provided by Cerberus, after its bid was submitted, that it had taken on Brown Rudnick and Tughans as advisors.

The report was met with an immediate barrage of criticism from NAMA, which claimed its findings were not supported by 'convincing, formidable and sufficient evidence' and that McCarthy was not up to the job of scrutinising such a complex deal. Even before NAMA got stuck into the C&AG, Noonan had made it clear from day one that the agency would be disputing the findings of the report. The hostile, even vicious, and relentless response to the independent report of the body charged with constitutional responsibility to audit spending by government departments and agencies was unprecedented. Much media noise was made about a spat between two state agencies, which was an inaccurate portrayal, given that the report was thorough and well argued, while NAMA had, over successive years, cited the annual audit of its affairs by the C&AG as evidence that it was doing its job diligently and with great financial expertise.

The pressure piled on the C&AG, Seamus McCarthy, was immense, coming as it did from the finance minister, senior department officials and the NAMA executive and board. The clear intent of at least some of these parties was to force him to withdraw his report or resign. He did neither, although some of those close to him believed that he had considered both options before deciding to defend the integrity of his office and its investigation into the largest single sale of public assets in the history of the Irish state. According to informed sources, NAMA had threatened to injunct the C&AG from publishing the report and McCarthy and his colleagues were informed of the deep displeasure of members of the agency's board, some of whom had indicated that they might take legal action on a personal basis against his findings which, it was hinted, could be considered defamatory. NAMA executives claimed that the C&AG's office was not equipped to carry out a forensic analysis of the Project Eagle deal and wrongly suggested that McCarthy had unsuccessfully sought to hire additional forensic accountancy staff for the inquiry. While he had sought extra staff to deal with its onerous workload, the C&AG's request to government in this regard had nothing to do with his investigation into the sale of the Northern Ireland loan book.

The report went to the PAC, which commenced hearings in late September 2016, and over several weeks took evidence from NAMA executives and current and former board members, Noonan and his officials at the Department of Finance, the C&AG, representatives of various bidders for Project Eagle, including Cerberus, the North's deputy first minister, Martin McGuinness, and former NIAC member Brian Rowntree. Chaired by Fianna Fáil TD Sean Fleming, the committee included several of those who were critical of NAMA and of the Project Eagle sales process at PAC hearings and during Dáil debates over several years, including Sinn Féin deputy leader Mary Lou McDonald, her party colleague David Cullinane, Social Democrat TD Catherine Murphy and independent TD Catherine Connolly. The main government party was represented by Fine Gael TDs Josepha Madigan, Noel Rock and Alan Farrell. Among the other opposition party representatives were Bobby Aylward, Shane Cassells and Marc MacSharry of Fianna Fáil and Alan Kelly of the Labour Party.

Over the following two months the committee and backroom staff pored over thousands of documents as well as correspondence from witnesses and others involved in the controversial loan sale, and engaged in lengthy debates over the veracity of the evidence they heard at public hearings. The absence of key individuals who declined invitations made the task more difficult, particularly when it came to drawing any conclusions about the motivations of some of those involved. Peter Robinson and Sammy Wilson were among those who refused to attend, while Cushnahan and Hanna cited the ongoing criminal investigation by the NCA as a reason for their absence from the hearings. Ian Coulter did not show up either, while others, including David Watters and Andrew Creighton, from the small group of business people in the North who allegedly stood to benefit from the loan sale, were notably absent.

Nevertheless, witnesses were put through some intense questioning, not least Daly and McDonagh, who were pressed by committee members Madigan, McDonald, Cullinane and Connolly as to how Cushnahan could have been approaching purchasers for the Project Eagle loans as far back as November 2012 without any senior executives in NAMA knowing about his activities. In his evidence to the hearings in November 2016, Daly insisted that the first he and the NAMA board knew of Cushnahan's engagement with PIMCO for two years before the sale was in March 2014, when he learned of the €15 million fee arrangements, after which the US fund withdrew from the sale. Asked by Cullinane about the circumstances leading to the PIMCO withdrawal and the late entry of Cerberus to the competition, Daly told the PAC:

What was our focus at that time in March 2014? We were in the final stages of the competition for Project Eagle. The main point was that PIMCO was gone or exiting at that stage. The main point was that we were making sure Cushnahan did not get any money. The main point was that in respect of Cerberus we were ensuring, by means of a declaration, that Cerberus was not paying any fee to anyone connected with NAMA.

At the heart of the exchanges was the insistence by Daly that NAMA was never informed by PIMCO, or anyone else, of Cushnahan's significant role in pushing the sale of the NI portfolio since late 2012. PIMCO said that it provided the agency with details of meetings it held with Cushnahan, Coulter and others starting in April 2013. Attempts by NAMA since April 2014 to find out from Cushnahan the extent of any conflict of interest arising from the deal or the fee arrangement had met with silence, Daly said. Daly and McDonagh disputed the C&AG's suggestion that NAMA could have obtained €220 million more from the sale, and claimed that there was sufficient competitive tension in the bidding even after the withdrawal of PIMCO, in March 2014, to justify pushing ahead. They also insisted that the particular conditions in Northern Ireland, and the reluctance of debtors to engage, made it more realistic to have a quicker than normal sale of the entire bundle of assets at a discount rather than a piecemeal disposal over a number of years. However, their early bullish hostility towards the C&AG and his report was somewhat muted when they were asked about the absence of detailed minutes from NAMA board meetings and other discussions pertaining to Project Eagle, in possible breach of company law. They were also forced to explain how they failed to act on the blatant conflicts of interest surrounding Cushnahan, who was advising major debtors of the agency while a member of the NIAC. In gruelling exchanges, Daly and McDonagh defended their decision not to approach Cushnahan when it emerged that he, along with Brown Rudnick and Tughans, was due a success fee from PIMCO. When PIMCO withdrew on the advice of its compliance officers, the NAMA executives did not discover that the two solicitors' firms moved over to work on the Cerberus bid until after it was submitted. When they got an assurance from Cerberus that no current or former member of NAMA staff or of any committee was in line for any fee, it did not seek to check this out with Cushnahan. Although Daly had attended meetings of the NIAC in the Tughans office in Belfast, where Cushnahan had an office, it did not dawn on him to investigate whether there was any conflict between his role as an advisor to several NAMA debtors and his membership of the NIAC. Daly said that he knew Cushnahan in a professional capacity and was also on the board of the charity Ciorani with him, but did not pick up the phone to inquire what, if any, role he had in the Project Eagle sale following the withdrawal of PIMCO in March 2014. Daly simply accepted the assurance by Cerberus that it was not involved in fee arrangements with anyone associated with NAMA. Asked by Catherine Connolly whether the bells did not ring loudly when he learned that Brown Rudnick and Tughans were 'strategic advisors' to Cerberus, Daly said 'No'. Connolly also raised the proposition that PIMCO and Cerberus could have been working together rather than as competitors in the bidding process. Daly said that the NAMA board had considered this possibility at the time it was making the final decision on the sale but that the discussion was not recorded in the minutes.

The absence of minutes of this and other vital matters meant that the PAC was expected to take much of the explanation for NAMA's behaviour during the Project Eagle sales process from the recollections of its executives, and, at one particularly contentious hearing, of board member Brian McEnery. In contrast, the C&AG had ploughed through 40,000 documents provided by NAMA before coming to his critical conclusions and was able to draw on the detail of extensive correspondence in his answers to the committee members. During one exchange with Daly, Mary Lou McDonald asked why the agency was so quick to condemn the C&AG audit for making a 'fair observation' in describing the Project Eagle sale process as unusual, or in the words of the NAMA chairman, a 'bespoke arrangement'. Accusing Daly of 'bluster', she said that it was a matter of fact that the agency had 'changed its sales process or stepped outside its established practice'.

Moving on to the conflict of interest involving Cushnahan, McDonald asked about the circumstances surrounding the disclosure to NAMA of the proposed success fee to the former member of the NIAC. Daly said he did not know when it was agreed, although he accepted that PIMCO was in discussions with Cushnahan from April 2013. Daly said his concern was that PIMCO left the process when the fee payment was disclosed and he did not ask at what stage it had first been discussed or agreed with Cushnahan.

McDonald went on to question apparently contradictory evidence given by Daly at an earlier NAMA hearing when he insisted that the agency forced PIMCO to withdraw when it revealed its fee arrangement with Cushnahan. She said there was a suggestion in the phone conversations between 11 and 13 March between PIMCO and Hanna that there was an attempt to keep their bid alive 'if the fee arrangement could be moved out of the picture'. Daly insisted that PIMCO 'withdrew because it knew we could not let it continue'.

When he appeared before the PAC in early October, Noonan defended his decision not to intervene or halt the sales when he was informed of the extraordinary withdrawal of PIMCO in March 2014 after it disclosed the finder's fee arrangements. During heated exchanges in which he was accused by a number of TDs of 'running down the clock', Noonan said that he did not have the legal power to halt the Project Eagle sales process when he learned from Daly about the fee arrangements and PIMCO's withdrawal.

'I am excluded from giving any direction to NAMA on commercial matters. That is where the line is drawn,' Noonan argued. Asked whether he had ever given a direction to NAMA to speed up the sale of assets, the finance minister said that 'the last direction I issued to NAMA was when negative interest rates came in across Europe and NAMA was unable to carry out its business as originally intended'. Noonan said that he had the power to direct but that it would be illegal under the terms of the NAMA Act for him to 'trespass on the commercial decisions of NAMA'. He insisted that once PIMCO withdrew, the issue of a payment to Cushnahan was not relevant to the sale. Accused by McDonald of talking down the clock, Noonan repeated what Daly had said, that there was still competitive tension in the process, as advised by Lazard. Noonan claimed the problem of a 'corrupted process', as McDonald described it, was 'on the purchaser side', not with NAMA. Noonan was not prepared to concede that the payment was a problem for NAMA and had been acknowledged as such due to Cushnahan's role on the NIAC.

The minister went on to suggest that McDonald's party colleague and deputy first minister, Martin McGuinness, had not dissented from the Project Eagle sale and must have agreed to the appointment of Cushnahan to the NIAC on the recommendation of the North's former finance minister, Sammy Wilson. Accusing him of 'filibustering at its most classic', McDonald said that when it became apparent, as a matter of fact, that a fixer fee was to be payable to a former member of the Northern committee of NAMA, this was an issue – not just on the purchaser's side – but was an issue for NAMA and that was the moment when the Minister should have, and had the authority, to intervene and call a halt to the sales process.

Noonan replied:

At the time of the withdrawal of PIMCO, and the subsequent assurance from Cerberus, NAMA thought this was sufficient to ensure that no former or current NAMA officials were associated with the buyer, and it decided for good and sufficient reason to proceed with the sale.

Accusing the Sinn Féin deputy of 'contorting questions into allegations' and engaging in monologues, he added: 'The decision not to proceed with the sale to PIMCO, and the decision that there was sufficient competitive tension still in the process to allow the process to proceed with a sale to the remaining interested parties, was a commercial decision by the board of NAMA.'

In an apparent row-back from his resistance to a commission of investigation into the sale, Noonan told Catherine Murphy that he expected that there would be 'one at this point because the issue is so confused and there are so many allegations flying around. We have seen BBC programmes, Garda inquiries, inquiries by criminal bureaux in the United Kingdom, the inquiry by the Committee of Public Accounts, the Comptroller and Auditor General's report and the SIPO inquiry.'

'If the matter must be clarified, there is provision under the law for the establishment of judicial inquiries. Let it commence and let the chips fall where they will,' Noonan said.

The appearance of Martin McGuinness the following week put paid to any suggestion that he was privy to any of the private meetings which the former First Minister Peter Robinson had with various parties involved in the Project Eagle sale, including former US vice president Dan Quayle and, with the exception of one phone discussion, Michael Noonan, among others. McGuinness said:

We have all become aware that a number of other meetings and engagements took place involving various combinations of the Minister, Deputy Noonan, Northern Ministers from the Democratic Unionist Party, DUP, and representatives of NAMA, Cerberus and PIMCO. I was not aware of any of these engagements. I learned in the media that Dan Quayle had met with Mr. Peter Robinson, Mr. Simon Hamilton, MLA, Mr. Ian Coulter and others at

Stormont Castle on 25 March 2014. I was also concerned to learn that Deputy Noonan had met with Mr. Robinson and Mr. Hamilton on 27 September 2013 at Stormont, again without my knowledge. The meeting, which PIMCO confirmed to the committee just last week, involving PIMCO, Mr. Robinson and Mr. Sammy Wilson, MP, in May 2013, also happened without my knowledge or approval.

In response to Fine Gael TD Alan Farrell, the North's deputy first minister said that until the revelations made in the Dáil by Mick Wallace in July 2015 he had not suspected any wrongdoing in relation to the purchase or sale of the portfolio. Relations with his DUP colleagues in the Northern Ireland executive were at a low ebb in 2013 and 2014 due to disagreements with Robinson on a number of key issues, including the future of the former Long Kesh prison site, he said, and continued:

There was nothing in my head that suggested that there was wrongdoing by anybody regarding what has since transpired – the allegation that £16 million was demanded of PIMCO or indeed the £7 million that ended up in a bank account in the Isle of Man. All of this was as much of a surprise to me as it was to anybody else. There were no bad thoughts in my head at the time of this business other than I thought it was highly irregular that the meetings that had taken place were handled in the fashion they were. I understood it from the DUP's point of view. Relationships were appalling, which presented a massive difficulty that lasted for quite some time until we reached the achievement of the Fresh Start agreement at the end of last year.

McGuinness was not informed of Quayle's meeting with Robinson on 25 March, 2014, even though he met the first minister soon after.

Even more important, on 25th March, Peter Robinson met Cerberus. An hour and a half later, he and I were at a job announcement in west Belfast. He never mentioned to me that the former Vice President of the United States, Dan Quayle, had met him earlier that morning.

Accused by Labour TD and vice chairman of the PAC, Alan Kelly, of letting his DUP partners in government deal with the toxic issue of the NAMA property sale so that Sinn Féin would not be politically contaminated, McGuinness responded:

That is total and absolute rubbish. In regard to Peter Robinson, how people cannot come to the conclusion that his attendance at a meeting with PIMCO and at a meeting with the former Vice President of the United States of America, without my presence, without any paper trail whatsoever back to my Department – or my senior officials ... Peter Robinson said during the course of his contribution on all this that there was a paper trail. I challenged him to produce the paper trail. He has not produced anything.

He further suggested that Kelly was engaged in political point-scoring and 'looking for a headline'.

Asked by McDonald about the relationship between Robinson and Cushnahan, McGuinness said: 'I think they were very close. That is my view ... He was described during the course of Mr. Peter Robinson's testimony to the finance committee, along with Mr. Ian Coulter, I think, as a pillar of society.'

NIAC member Brian Rowntree told the inquiry that the committee had access to 'commercially sensitive' information which would be of value to any bidder for Project Eagle. Contradicting the repeated claims by NAMA executives that the NIAC was not privy to such material, Rowntree said that one report on NAMA-controlled land banks presented to the committee 'not only had the location and types of property, this data also had details of planning permissions, current and about to expire and potential for renewal. It also had details of housing and residential needs overlaying on top of it.'

In late October, the *Belfast Telegraph* reported that Kilmona Property Ltd, owned by developer Paddy Kearney, had refused to confirm that Robinson had taken up a position as a consultant to the firm. The newspaper claimed that Robinson, who left political office in January 2016, had represented the company in relation to a number of major property developments and had attended at least one council meeting on its behalf. It was just a year since he and Kearney had appeared at the Stormont inquiry during which Robinson had failed to disclose representations he had made to NAMA on behalf of the developer. Robinson declined an invitation to appear before the PAC.

Earlier in the year he had registered as sole director of Rock Global Services Group Ltd (RGSG) which he said was 'to cover any business arrangements I may undertake in the future. I am, as I said when leaving office, taking time to consider my options. I have not entered into any business undertakings yet ...' His comments followed the public disclosure of details in the company registration office.

His son, Gareth, followed in his father's footsteps when he set up a new real estate company called NI KSD which was registered in July 2016 at High Street, Belfast.

It came as little surprise that former NAMA board members, including John Mulcahy, were enthusiastic cheerleaders for the Project Eagle sale, with the former head of asset management and now chairman of IPUT describing it to the PAC as

a superb deal from NAMA's perspective. To shift the whole Northern Ireland portfolio in one go, for £1.3 billion, was an inspired transaction. My fear was that something would go wrong and that the possibility would go away and we would revert to dealing with the portfolio piecemeal. That would have been very slow.

Asked by Catherine Murphy whether it would not have been wiser to value all the loans individually in order to assess whether it would have been more advantageous to sell them off in smaller bundles, Mulcahy replied:

It might be instructive to look down the other end of the telescope. We had £1.3 billion on the table. If we had said 'no' to that the chances are that it would be worth 20% less with the currency difference. Second, the Northern Ireland property market has performed badly. ... Looking at the result of taking the £1.3 billion, as opposed to not taking it, the answer is clear. That is why it was a superb transaction.

Reminded that some 50 per cent of the assets of Project Eagle were not in Northern Ireland and that they included shopping centres in England and commercial properties in Germany and other EU locations, Mulcahy pointed to the poor state of the retail market in the UK. He claimed that NAMA was

seen with some hostility in the North and the borrowers were not repentant borrowers. Rather, they felt their troubles had been caused by a failure of the banking system in the South and through no fault of their own. They were most unlikely to be co-operative. What reception we would get working the assets out asset by asset in the courts of Northern Ireland was a concern.

Neither was it a shock that the representative from Cerberus would have any concerns over the efficacy of the Project Eagle sale process. Mark Neporent, the US-based chief operating officer of Cerberus Capital Management, told the PAC that he did not observe any conflicts of interest or wrongdoing with regard to his firm's involvement in the purchase. He described how Tuvi Keinan of Brown Rudnick made an unsolicited approach to Cerberus in mid-March 2014 in relation to Project Eagle at a time when the US fund was engaged in the bidding process. Neporent did not know how Keinan became aware that his firm was planning a bid. Cerberus already had two law firms, Linklaters and A&L Goodbody, providing legal services in relation to the bid, so, asked McDonald, 'what was it that Brown Rudnick brought to the table that was so special and that merited a fee of €15 million?'

Neporent said that Brown Rudnick had been involved for over a year with the NI portfolio, before and after its engagement with PIMCO, and 'it explained to us that it had been doing this work and that, through its association with Tughans, it had developed a very good understanding of the Northern Ireland portfolio and a number of the borrowers'.

It emerged at the hearings that neither Brown Rudnick nor Tughans was given access to the data room for Project Eagle and would have been subject to a non-disclosure agreement which would prevent them from discussing what they knew of the loan portfolio. This did not prevent Cerberus from hiring the two firms and agreeing the very same fee arrangements as had applied with PIMCO. Neporent said that Brown Rudnick was familiar with Project Eagle and

> had an understanding of their business plans, the quality of their businesses and the quality of the borrowers. It understood, or purported to understand, the local economy and we regarded that information, as well as the ability to access stakeholders through its affiliation with Tughans, as potentially very valuable. Of course, one has to look at this in the context of the very condensed bidding process. We were thinking this information could be very valuable commercially to us in seeing whether we could get to the reserve price and actually participate in the bid.

He said the two law firms hired as strategic advisors

> provided quite a bit of post-acquisition work in helping us get the transaction closed with NAMA because there was a great deal of information that was not in the data room with regard to loans we acquired, information that was difficult to assemble and was the subject of some controversy between NAMA and ourselves.

This was the first public confirmation that the information in the data room was incomplete and that Brown Rudnick, Tughans and Cushnahan held key knowledge of the portfolio that was not available to other bidders.

Neporent said Cerberus was not made aware of the fixer's fee that Frank Cushnahan was to receive from PIMCO in the event that it made a successful bid and could not confirm why it withdrew from the process.

> Mr. Keinan advised us that they, Brown Rudnick, had been acting with PIMCO and that PIMCO had withdrawn. They told us there were a number

of reasons [why] PIMCO had withdrawn. One reason was there was a lot of turmoil going on at PIMCO at the time. The deputy may or may not know that around that time Bill Gross, the PIMCO chief executive officer, was in the middle of some controversy and was in the midst of leaving PIMCO. This was big news in the financial sector. Mr. Keinan told us that NAMA had a concern with PIMCO because PIMCO had disclosed to NAMA that it had a relationship, or that it intended to have a future relationship, with Frank Cushnahan, if PIMCO was to win the bid. We were told that Mr. Cushnahan would be an adviser to PIMCO post bid. We were not told that Mr. Cushnahan was working – had been working – with Brown Rudnick or Tughans before that. We were not told that he was intended to be paid.

Referring to the meeting attended by Cerberus chairman and former us treasury secretary John Snow, Neporent said that he believed it was attended by NAMA executives Daly, McDonagh and Ronnie Hanna. It was not disclosed at this meeting that Cerberus had taken on Brown Rudnick and Tughans as advisors on the bid. He suggested that there was nothing unusual about this as the law firms 'were not on our list of disclosed advisors and we did not give them access to the data room'. Neporent denied that the access to the debtor and other information assembled by Brown Rudnick and Tughans over many months conferred any advantage to Cerberus over the underbidder, Fortress. He told McDonald that his company 'had a contractual obligation to pay £15 million if we won the bid, which we did' and 'that is a completely different issue as to how much value that information actually provided to us'.

Following a dozen public hearings, with witnesses travelling from as far as the US to attend, the committee went into private session to discuss its findings and whatever recommendations it would make. Unfortunately, the refusal of Robinson, Wilson, Cushnahan and other key players in the North to attend the PAC hearings made it something of a lopsided affair, while their status as government or opposition deputies was reflected in the tone and substance of their questioning by committee members.

John Miskelly was unable to attend, while another whose evidence might have assisted the PAC, Belfast developer Paddy Kearney, was also absent from proceedings. He was otherwise occupied as, in December 2016, he said he intended to 'vigorously pursue' a legal case for damages against former Stormont inquiry chairman Daithi McKay. Solicitor Paul Tweed, acting for Kearney, claimed in a statement on behalf of the developer that McKay had conspired with loyalist blogger Jamie Bryson to make 'unfounded and unjustified personal attacks' on his client.

The stakes were high for so many players in the North in relation to Project Eagle, not least given the ongoing criminal investigation by the NCA. In October its recently appointed director general, Lynne Owens, confirmed to the Policing Board in the North that six people were under criminal investigation in relation to the controversial transaction. She confirmed that two people had been arrested 'under caution' and that no inference should be drawn from the decision to their release on 'police bail'. Owens said that more than 40 witnesses had been interviewed by her officers as part of 'Operation Pumpless'. The NCA, she said, was investigating potential bribery, corruption and fraud, and that the investigation was 'one of our highest priority operations in our serious and organised crime grid'.

The two men arrested by the NCA were Frank Cushnahan and Ronnie Hanna, while Ian Coulter was among those questioned by the agency. It is understood that Coulter gave extensive interviews 'under caution' to NCA officers following a pre-arranged meeting in early November 2015. According to the NCA director general, seven people were interviewed under 'criminal caution' while six remained 'criminal suspects'. There was no reason given as to why one person had been dropped from the list of suspects, although there was much speculation as to whether one of those arrested may have cooperated with the NCA as an 'assisting offender'. Eight properties were searched as part of 'Operation Pumpless' while court orders were granted to allow the NCA to obtain materials from 'public and private institutions'. Among the specific matters it was investigating, Owens said, was the purchase of the NAMA loan book, the 'dispersal of fees offshore' and the 'nature, extent and probity of the relationships and roles of persons involved in the process, including allegations of corruption'.

The NCA also expressed its concern to media organisations in the North, including the BBC *Spotlight* team, about publishing or broadcasting any material which could affect its criminal investigation. The Law Society of Northern Ireland, which examined Coulter's role on foot of a complaint by Tughans solicitors, told the Stormont finance committee that it had been advised by the NCA not to discuss its inquiry into the complaint as it could compromise the police investigation. Among the witnesses interviewed by the NCA in the Republic was Mick Wallace, who gained the impression after his first of two interviews that the officers were as interested in the source of his information as they were in its content. Barry Lloyd was also questioned a number of times on his detailed claims about Cushnahan and NCA officers travelled to his home in Thailand to meet him. In one interview that continued over three days, NCA officers told him they had also met with senior executives of Nomura as part of their inquiries.

Another voice missing at the PAC hearings was that of Mick Wallace, who attended daily hearings, but not as a witness. He was also going through some torrid experiences at the hands of Cerberus as one of its subsidiaries continued to chase him for the €2 million he owed from personal guarantees he provided to Ulster Bank. He was also fighting to save his family home in Dublin.

After a High Court hearing in late 2016, in which Promontoria (Aran) applied to have the politician made bankrupt, Wallace claimed that the US fund was seeking to 'settle scores' with him.

Promontoria (Aran) had secured a judgment against Wallace earlier in the year in respect of the debt. In relation to this, Wallace said:

They are liquidating the construction company, which is going to cost them €100,000, and they are not going to get anything, because there is nothing there. This is just them settling scores for me highlighting their involvement in Project Eagle. I don't like the idea of them riding roughshod over me, but even if I end up begging on the Ha'penny Bridge, it won't stop me.

Wallace said that he only discovered that Cerberus had bought his company's loan from Ulster Bank, giving the US company the right to seek its repayment, in late August 2015, almost two months after he first raised questions about Project Eagle in the Dáil. The case was adjourned after Wallace said he wished to engage an insolvency practitioner. Wallace told Judge Caroline Costello that he was seeking alternatives to bankruptcy and was trying to save his family home, over which AIB held a mortgage. His solicitor, Keith Farry, said that a personal insolvency practitioner had written to Cerberus and AIB seeking to have his family home retained while he was preparing a statement of his financial affairs. Another adjournment was granted by the judge.

Days after the hearing, it was revealed that Promontoria (Aran) had earned €54 million in profits in 2015 from income of €214 million after paying tax of €18 million. It was also announced that Cerberus was chosen as the preferred bidder for Project Gem, a portfolio with a par value of €3.05 billion in loans associated with commercial properties across the country transferred to NAMA from 38 borrowers. Oaktree Capital and Goldman Sachs were among the unsuccessful bidders. The court declared Wallace bankrupt just a week before Christmas 2016 over the €2 million personal guarantees, after Judge Costello was told that his total debts exceeded €30 million. The decision did not temper the TD's resolve to expose what he believed to be the corrupt activities behind some of the property transactions in which his tormentors were involved. If anything, his claims made under Dáil privilege became more pronounced as the Project Eagle inquiries deepened across three jurisdictions.

In January 2017, it was reported that the Wexford Youth football club, which was founded and funded for many years by Wallace, was in financial difficulty due to his bankruptcy. The club owed over €200,000 to M&J Wallace, which was now in receivership and in the hands of a liquidator.

NAMA also came under pressure in late 2016 from Michael O'Flynn and his brother, John, and their company O'Flynn Construction, when they lodged a legal action against the agency and Enda Farrell for damages over the leaking of their confidential information. As Christmas approached a group of homeless people and political activists occupied a NAMA-controlled building in Dublin to raise awareness of the numbers living on the streets in the middle of winter. Garrett Kelleher, the former owner of Apollo House, the occupied building adjoining the offices of the Department of Health in Hawkins House on Poolbeg Street, said he supported the aims of the Home Sweet Home group which took over the vacant office block to provide sleeping accommodation to rough sleepers.

'The receivers for Apollo and NAMA should seek to immediately do what they can to help, not allow this to become a political football but actually help, have their lawyers down tools and do the right thing,' Kelleher said.

While the media focus was on Apollo House and Wallace and his court battle, the significance of another news item also went largely unnoticed when it was reported that Promontoria Eagle, the company used by Cerberus to buy Project Eagle, had cleared a loan of £729.2 million (€859 million) to make the controversial purchase in 2014. The loan was used to pay most of the money NAMA sought from the sale and was provided by Nomura. According to documents lodged with the Companies Registration Office in Dublin, the debt was secured through six charges against assets acquired as part of the deal and these were settled or satisfied by Promontoria Eagle between May and September 2016 and before its due date of June 2017. Part of the debt was secured against the Savoy Shopping Centre and other premises in Glasgow, Scotland owned by the MAR Group, the Northern Ireland business run by developers Noel Murphy, Adam Armstrong and William Rush. Cerberus loaned Promontoria Eagle the balance of the purchase price through another, Dutch-registered subsidiary, Promontoria Holding 83 BV, which charged high interest rates on the loan, which in turn minimised the tax liability on the returns generated on the Project Eagle transaction.

By this time the former secretary general of the Department of Finance John Moran had been working for over a year as a consultant for Nomura. One of Japan's largest financial institutions, with offices in London, Nomura managed, among other assets, the remains of the European and Asian units of the former Lehman Brothers bank, which it purchased after the global crash in 2008 for just $2. The bank specialises in wholesale banking and financing, of which Moran had some knowledge and experience, and in the acquisition of distressed property assets across the globe.

As the PAC prepared its report into Project Eagle for publication, the Dáil once again, in early February 2017, debated the case for and against a commission of investigation, with Noonan appearing to resile from the view he expressed at the PAC hearings just three months earlier when he accepted that such a judicial inquiry was now inevitable. 'Let it commence and let the chips fall where they will,' he had told the PAC.

However, during the debate on the terms of reference of a commission of investigation on 1 February, and before the publication of the PAC report, Noonan said that he did 'not believe that sufficient grounds have been established on which to progress a commission of investigation without first taking the views of the Committee of Public Accounts into account'.

While he did not rule it out, Noonan said that the opinions of the PAC should be heard in advance of taking any such action to set up a commission. He was immediately accused by Fianna Fáil finance spokesperson Michael McGrath of 'muddying the waters' and of a 'row back' on his statement to the PAC in October 2016 and of ignoring an agreement among party and group leaders in the Dáil to set up a commission.

In a bizarre intervention, McGrath party colleague and PAC chairman Sean Fleming appeared to disagree, claiming that the Oireachtas should first debate the committee's report before deciding whether a commission was required. Fleming said, to the bemusement of many on the opposition benches:

After that, let us see what issues that could have been addressed by a commission will have been addressed by the Committee of Public Accounts and what issues are still not addressed. Many of the issues leading to the call for this commission are the result of a television programme in Northern Ireland on incidents in that jurisdiction that are beyond the remit of any commission. A commission would have no jurisdiction to investigate any events in the North.

Referring to the PAC hearings, he pointed out that witnesses from the North and the US who attended on a voluntary basis could not be compelled to appear before a commission chaired by a High Court judge. Fleming added that he was expressing a personal opinion as PAC chair, rather than a party position.

Pearse Doherty reminded Noonan as the minister headed out the door of the Dáil chamber that he had raised improprieties in relation to the Project Eagle sale in 2015, and that it was now evident that 'a deeply corrupted process was in place'. He also accused the finance minister of rowing back on the commitment made by Taoiseach Enda Kenny the previous September to establish a commission, before turning on Fianna Fáil:

Thankfully, Deputy Michael McGrath is now saying that a commission needs to be established. … Within minutes, however, Deputy Fleming said that there should be no commission of investigation. Indeed, we should not even be discussing the terms of reference until both Houses of the Oireachtas finish their scrutiny of the report of the Committee of Public Accounts. Which position does Fianna Fáil support today?

Rounding on the minister, Doherty described Noonan's insistence that he could not direct NAMA to take specific action as 'the height of bull'. He went on:

The reason we know that is because the Minister has directed NAMA on numerous occasions and not on minor issues. Let me remind the Minister, although he does not need reminding, that he issued NAMA with a direction to purchase the IBRC promissory note for more than €3 billion. … He also issued directions, for example, in terms of the winding up of IBRC, providing short-term finance to IBRC, directing it to bid for the assets of IBRC and numerous other directions so why, when he knew there was a corrupted process in the sale of billions of euro of Irish taxpayers [sic] money, did he not direct NAMA to stop that sale?

Doherty described how he had received information from the minister in recent days which showed that many developers had left NAMA without paying more than a fraction of their bank debt.

It is transferring that debt to vulture funds so it is the vulture funds that will benefit from an upturn in the property market. As bad as that is, we now know or at least we have enough evidence to tell us that the process in Project Eagle was corrupt, and there may be other sales that are corrupt also.

When he rose to speak, Mick Wallace had a list of no less than seven proposed modules for a commission of investigation, which unlike the C&AG and PAC would have power to access NAMA documents and hold the agency to account.

I agree that the commission should begin by examining Project Eagle as its first module, but the problems in NAMA are sadly not unique to NAMA's Northern Ireland loan portfolio. The allegations made by Enda Farrell, a former NAMA staff member, should be the second module. It seems NAMA may have internally investigated some of the NAMA officials named by Mr. Farrell in his affidavit who may have leaked confidential information or engaged in malpractice. The third module should examine the establishment of Hibernia REIT. It was set up in 2013, following a three year stint at NAMA by one of its founders, but it seems the company was in planning for a long time before that. Some businessmen on the east coast of the United States were briefed on Hibernia REIT's arrival as early as 2011. Kevin Nowlan is on the record as stating: 'We know enough people in Dublin to be able and go buy [sic] properties in Dublin without having to go to auction, of having to go on to the market.'

If one looks at some of the assets it has purchased, the links back to NAMA begin to appear – the Forum Building, the Dublin Observatory Building, the Harcourt Street building, Windmill Lane, New Century House and Central Quay. All those assets were in NAMA and are now in the hands of Hibernia REIT, either through direct purchases or secondary deals. A fourth module should consist of an examination of any internal NAMA investigations into NAMA officials regarding the leaking of confidential information or alleged malpractice and, if the judge sees fit, to investigate any other allegations of unauthorised leaking. The commission of investigation should provide its initial report on Project Eagle within six months and the remaining modules within 12 months. Importantly, any report should be made public.

Wallace confirmed that Barry Lloyd had signed an affidavit in the past week in Dublin, and had met the NCA in relation to his dealings with Cushnahan since 2010. He continued:

Frank Daly told the Committee of Public Accounts last September that NAMA's key decision was to set a minimum price of £1.3 billion for the portfolio, but it did not do so as PIMCO set the price. Dave Watters did the business plans, Frank Cushnahan pulled the strings and Ronnie Hanna fixed the price in Dublin. Did Ronnie Hanna declare any conflict he might have with Northern Ireland connections from his days with Ulster Bank in Northern Ireland? Why did NAMA treat business people in the Republic of Ireland almost four times less favourably than those in Northern Ireland? ... In the BBC Northern Ireland *Spotlight* programme, Frank Cushnahan clearly stated that he went to Ronnie Hanna to make sure that John Miskelly's lights would not be put out. Mr. Cushnahan said he and Ronnie Hanna were as thick as thieves. The entire Miskelly file needs to be investigated... In October 2015, I asked NAMA whether Ronnie Hanna, along with Frank Cushnahan or Dave Watters, ever met any investment fund personnel. NAMA stated that Mr. Hanna had no such meetings with these individuals. This is not true. I know for a fact he did.

Wallace asked how NAMA did not know of the £7 million stashed in the Isle of Man before he made his statement about it in early July 2015, when it was known that Cerberus was informed about the Northern Ireland Law Society investigation into it three months earlier, in April.

I have met an individual who was asked to look into the same matter in January 2015 on behalf of NAMA. The British National Crime Agency knew that all was not well so it commenced an investigation. The Securities and Exchange Commission in the US knew that all was not well. It too started an investigation. It was exercised by the possibility that Cerberus personnel John Snow and Dan Quayle may have abused their former office. It was looking at any possible bribing or inducing anyone for gain. All the while NAMA was in denial, stating that everything was grand and it was doing a great job, and the Government and Department of Finance were the cheerleaders. ...

Back in 2015, I mentioned the payment of €15,000 in a bag by an individual to a NAMA employee to garner favour. I am not sure where the Garda is with its investigation into this, but I can tell the House I am more certain than ever about what happened. They got their memorandum of understanding and were out the gap and away and they are doing very well for themselves. The new-found fortunes of these new kids on the block are built on the proceeds of crime. One of them is working in the higher echelons of Cerberus...

There are problems right through the workings of NAMA. The dogs on the street know it. Will the Government pretend forever it has done a great job and lie to the people? The people are tired of being lied to. This is why politics are changing. This is why the Americans elected an eejit called Trump, because they were tired of being lied to by the likes of Obama, Clinton and Bush. They will get tired of the Government lying to them too.

Wallace might have mentioned that Trump had also considered the appointment of the head of Cerberus Capital Management to his cabinet following the inauguration of the new US president in January. Three weeks later, NBC News in the US reported that Trump had asked Cerberus chief executive officer Steve Feinberg 'to conduct a review of US intelligence agencies and other aspects of the federal government'.

Quoting unnamed former intelligence officials, NBC said that 'Trump's expected appointment of Steve Feinberg, co-founder and chief executive of Cerberus Capital Management, is causing consternation inside the intelligence agencies'. Asked if Feinberg would conduct an intelligence review, Trump said, 'I think that we are going to be able to straighten it out very easily on its own.'

The president described his friend Feinberg as 'a very talented man, very successful man. He's offered his services and you know, it's something we may take advantage of.'

Feinberg has been a major Republican donor and, according to *Forbes* magazine, is worth $1.27 billion. In 2016, he gave nearly $1.5 million to a pro-Trump group, Rebuilding America Now, according to the Center for Responsive Politics, described as a non-partisan group that tracks political donations.

The NBC report described how Feinberg came under scrutiny in 2012 when a mentally disturbed man shot and killed 20 children and six adults at Sandy Hook Elementary School in Newtown, Connecticut, using a Bushmaster rifle made by Freedom Group Inc., a company owned by Cerberus. It continued

After complaints by investors, Feinberg tried to sell Freedom Group, but could not fetch the $1 billion price tag he sought. ... Instead, Feinberg came up with a way that individual Cerberus fund investors could sell their stakes in Freedom Group. Cerberus continues to own the arms maker. Cerberus also owns DynCorp, which is a major national security contractor with the u.s. government, charging billions for overseas military and police training, among other things.

Closer to home, Feinberg's executives were enjoying an income boost with eight staff of Cerberus European Capital Advisors sharing a pay dividend of £39.56 million (€45.7 million) for the year ending December 2015, an average of £4.9 million each and an increase of 49 per cent over the previous 12 months, according to documents filed with the UK Companies Office. Operating out of Belfast and from behind the black door of a building with no nameplate on Merrion Street in Dublin, across the road from government buildings, the Irish-based executives of Cerberus were among those to benefit from the windfall, much of which derived from the sale of the Project Eagle and other assets acquired from NAMA.

The global reach of the vulture funds from the White House to the streets of Dublin were well captured when details of their massive tax avoidance schemes were revealed by Social Democrat, later independent and then Fianna Fáil TD Stephen Donnelly, who estimated that over €1 billion in potential revenue was lost every year to the exchequer. He described how the funds avoided tax on property investments through their use of SPVs designed to exploit loopholes in the tax code. By placing the loans in SPVs known as Section 110 companies, established by leading Ireland-based law firms including Matheson, the funds could write off charitable donations against tax. Many of the so-called loopholes were closed in the October budget in 2016, despite intense lobbying by the funds and their legal firms against the changes. Among those who lobbied against the loophole closures were Oaktree, Kennedy Wilson, and CarVal. Despite their efforts, new legislation was enacted in

December 2016, allowing for profits from Irish property loans in SPVs to be taxed at a 25 per cent rate. There were exemptions, however, including where another company in the vulture fund's empire, which is financing the SPV, is based in Ireland or the wider EU for tax purposes.

Among the other investors who met with the Department of Finance to 'air their concerns regarding potential changes to the funds regime in Ireland', as described in an FOI obtained by the *Irish Times*, was Hammerson, the UK company which led the purchase of the NAMA-held loans of developer Joe O'Reilly, including those related to the Dundrum Shopping Centre and the Carlton site on O'Connell Street where a major retail centre was planned. UK-based Hammerson and German insurer Allianz agreed to buy €1.85 billion worth of loans attached to the Dundrum Town Centre and 50 per cent stakes in the Ilac and Pavilions shopping centres in Dublin. It had lobbied for existing transactions to be exempted from the new legislation, but due to the intense resistance of Donnelly, Pearse Doherty and others the government had no choice but to proceed.

'[This] is disappointing and significantly impacts the value of historic transactions, and undermines one of the cornerstones of Ireland's offering to international investors, being certainty of regime and stability,' Hammerson's chief financial officer Timon Drakesmith said after the finance bill was published in October 2016.

That was not the only controversy Hammerson landed in when it invested in Dublin; it also became embroiled, during the centenary year of the Easter Rising, in the battle over the future of Moore Street where the leaders of the rebellion against British rule in Ireland had spent their final days before surrender. According to Simon Betty, the head of Hammerson's Irish operation, the company had no idea when it purchased O'Reilly's distressed loans that part of the site it had acquired off O'Connell Street contained the houses where Pearse, Connolly and other signatories of the Proclamation retreated after they left the heavily bombarded GPO during Easter Week, and which their relatives and other campaigners wanted protected as a national monument and battlefield site. Clearly, NAMA did not see it as part of its remit to ring-fence what another state agency, the National Museum, argued was Ireland's most important heritage site. The campaigners for the protection of the monument won a significant victory when they took their case to the High Court and Judge Max Barrett ruled in May 2016 that the lanes and houses of Moore Street comprised an important battlefield site and should be preserved in their entirety. It was a matter of some irony that the leading counsel for the state, which opposed the idea of protecting the area from commercial development, was Michael McDowell SC, grandson of Eoin MacNeill, the leader of the Volunteers who had issued the countermanding order to prevent the Rising taking place and which contributed to its failure. McDowell had been proposed for the chairmanship of NAMA by Brian Lenihan in 2009, but the idea was dismissed out of hand by then Taoiseach Brian Cowen.

Donnelly said that some companies, including Cerberus, would continue to reap enormous rewards from investments made when property prices were at rock bottom. He said that Cerberus believed its recent activities in Ireland would yield 'the highest returns ever achieved' in the company's history.

He was speaking following the broadcast by RTÉ of *The Great Irish Sell Off* documentary in January 2017, which reported that giant US investment funds with hardly any Irish employees had minimised their tax bills to just a few hundred euros a year.

The programme, presented by *Sunday Business Post* editor Ian Kehoe, estimated that the state could be foregoing up to €350 million a year due to the use of tax loopholes exploited by the hugely profitable investment funds. Donnelly estimated the true figure at between €1 billion and €1.4 billion a year, given the value of assets held by the funds and the length of time they held them.

In 2014, over €30 billion of Irish property loans were sold to foreign investors, which accounted for more than a third of all European loan sales, according to PricewaterhouseCoopers.

Cerberus was among the main beneficiaries of the generous tax incentives which former secretary general of the finance department, John Moran, told the RTÉ programme were necessary in order to attract global investors into the Irish property market. Cerberus, it emerged, paid less than €1,900 in tax on the €77 million profit it earned from the Project Eagle purchase and was clearly unphased by the new tax laws, or the negative publicity it was attracting in the Oireachtas and the media as it continued to hoover distressed assets from NAMA and other institutions. In late 2016 it was declared by NAMA as the preferred bidder for Project Gem, a portfolio of loans and assets with a par value of €3 billion. In October, it acquired the Project Oyster loan portfolio from Ulster Bank with a par value of €2.5 billion, including €2.15 billion of loans based in the Republic of Ireland and distressed mortgages held by 900 borrowers. Among those who appeared on the programme was economist and housing analyst Peter Bacon, one of the original architects of NAMA. In 2009 Bacon was asked by the finance minister, Brian Lenihan, to prepare a report for the NTMA on the proposed 'bad bank' solution. In the report Bacon set out the parameters for the asset management agency. He told RTÉ that he was disappointed NAMA had prioritised the rapid disposal of assets over their management. Bacon served for several years on the board of Ballymore International Developments Ltd and also provided consultancy services to Treasury Holdings and Bovale Developments.

Michael Smurfit was also a board member of the international unit of the Ballymore Group before resigning from his position in May 2015. The RTÉ programme described how vulture funds had swooped on €200 billion of property assets and up to 90,000 mortgages at huge discounts while paying minimum tax. The role of NAMA in hampering the availability of affordable homes for people in the midst of the deep housing crisis was raised when the programme was discussed in the Dáil. RTÉ had highlighted the spiralling cost of rents in apartment blocks now controlled by corporate landlords, including IRES. The shortage of affordable private as well as social and affordable public housing meant that tens of thousands of people were unable to afford a home in a seller's market.

'Getting NAMA to do deals with Cairn Homes, Hines and those fellows means we are looking at units coming in at more than €300,000. With affordable private [housing] where the State is involved directly they will be supplied at €200,000 per unit on State land,' Wallace told the Dáil in late February.

Noonan argued that NAMA had an objective to deliver 20,000 residential units by 2020, primarily in the greater Dublin area, 'on a commercial and value maximising basis'. It was not involved in building houses but was providing 'funding on commercial terms to its debtors and receivers to facilitate their delivery of residential units on sites securing NAMA's loans'.

Wallace complained to the minister during an exchange on 28 February 2017: 'If the truth is told and a proper investigation carried out, I reckon we will find that NAMA has cost the State approximately €20 billion as a result of the manner in which it has operated.'

Pearse Doherty said that what was clearly presented in the RTÉ documentary was that 'not only was Ireland for sale but it was for sale tax-free as a result of policies pursued by this Government and its predecessor'. He also accused the minister of allowing the banks to sell people's homes to vulture funds and of failing to use his power to direct NAMA to change course in relation to the provision of housing.

Noonan rejected the arguments put by both opposition TDs, repeating his position that he had no power to interfere in the commercial decisions of NAMA. Turning to Wallace, he said that the deputy had made similar assertions previously in relation to Cerberus. 'I think he has a problem with Cerberus and that he should declare an interest rather than act here as a neutral observer commenting for the public good. Let us be fair. The deputy is a great man to make assertions under privilege,' Noonan said.

The bitter exchanges between the pair continued in early March when Wallace sought to introduce legislation that would reduce the lifetime of High Court and

Civil Court judgments from 12 years to two years, in line with recent bankruptcy legislation, and the statute of limitations from six to two years 'where the collection and enforcement of civil debt by banks and vulture funds are concerned'.

He said that state and partially state-owned banks were holding back civil claims over debtors in mortgage and debt difficulty for years before initiating them at the last minute. 'The manner in which the last ounce of blood is being extracted from these people means they are suffering to a much greater extent,' he said.

Quoting a previous statement by the minister in the Dáil, Wallace said that Noonan had described the term 'vulture fund' as a 'compliment' because 'vultures provide a very good service in the ecology through cleaning up dead animals that are littered across the landscape'. Wallace continued:

It is not surprising that the Minister has become their cheerleader, particularly in view of the number of times he has had meetings with vulture funds. He would do well to remember that the dead animals the vultures are cleaning up are the Irish people, some of whom are well into the 70s and 80s.

Chapter 24 ∿

THE FINAL COUNTDOWN

T he long-anticipated PAC report was produced in mid-March 2017, and it largely vindicated the earlier value for money analysis of the C&AG. The PAC determined that the meeting between the finance minister and the lead bidder on the day before the Project Eagle bidding closed was inappropriate and called on the government to set up a commission of inquiry into the loan sale. The support by Fianna Fáil members for this demand, which was opposed by the Fine Gael members, was driven, according to committee members, by Sligo TD Marc MacSharry, who had deployed his skills as a property valuer and sometime developer to good effect with several witnesses during the public hearings. The government members on the committee, along with Labour's Alan Kelly, strongly resisted the proposed criticism of Michael Noonan over his meeting with the Cerberus chairman and executives on the day before bids closed. Only after a last-minute compromise and a rewording of the finding, hatched by David Cullinane of Sinn Féin, was the report allowed to proceed to publication.

In its conclusion, the PAC determined that the meeting between the finance minister and the lead bidder was 'not procedurally appropriate': 'The committee considers it was not procedurally appropriate for the Minister for Finance to meet with senior Cerberus representatives on the day before the Project Eagle bid closing date.'

Fine Gael members had sought to use the wording 'not procedurally advisable', but this was considered too light, and by a vote of eight to five the committee decided to adopt the wording suggested by Cullinane.

An arguably more serious criticism of Noonan was his failure to inform the committee during his five hours of evidence on 6 October 2016 about his meeting with the Cerberus executives, including former US treasury secretary John Snow, in late March 2014. While the PAC was informed in correspondence sent by the finance department after the public hearings of the committee, its members were incensed that the information was not provided during his evidence when it could have been subjected to more forensic cross-examination. When the department did provide details of the meeting to the committee it confirmed Noonan's attendance along with Ann Nolan, the second secretary of the department; Neil Ryan, assistant secretary; and Ryan's advisor, Eoin Dorgan. Cerberus chairman John Snow was accompanied by company executives Liam Strong, CEO of Cerberus European Capital Advisors, and managing director Billy Cooper; and one of Ireland's better known corporate figures, former managing partner at KPMG, Ron Bolger. Bolger was also former chairman of Telecom Éireann, former vice chairman of EBS building society and vice-chairman of one of Ireland largest waste operators, Greenstar, which Cerberus purchased just weeks before the high-level meeting with Noonan. Bolger had worked as a consultant for Cerberus since 2009, according to the briefing notes, an indication of how long the US investor had been interested in acquisitions and commercial activities in Ireland.

The briefing notes mentioned the Greenstar purchase as a topic likely to come up in the discussion and stated that 'the firm is also known to have some interest in NAMA's Project Eagle'. The note stated that 'this project, being run by Lazard, is for the €4 billion Northern Ireland Irish portfolio and was prompted by a reverse inquiry from PIMCO in late December 2013'. (A reverse inquiry is where the potential purchaser approaches NAMA in advance of a portfolio going out to tender by the agency.)

In the days and hours before the meeting emails were exchanged between various department officials, including secretary general John Moran, about the most suitable team to accompany the minister at the meeting with Cerberus. In the final exchange, less than an hour before the meeting, Ryan suggested that he, Dorgan and senior department official Des Carville, along with the minister, 'would make a good quartet'. Instead, Ann Nolan went along, while neither Carville nor Moran was present. An email discovered to the committee following the hearings made another mention of John Snow, who was planning to travel to Ireland almost a year later in March 2015, for a courtesy visit with Noonan and for meetings with the first and deputy first minister and the finance minister in the North. In an email to Alex Lalor of the Department of Finance, NAMA chairman Frank Daly wrote on 25 February 2015 that he was due to meet Snow and that while here the former US treasury secretary would like 'to pay courtesy calls on Minister Noonan in Dublin' as well as to the North. In what was surely an overly optimistic note, Daly wrote that NAMA had sold the Northern Ireland portfolio 'to Cerberus last year' and that 'as far as I'm aware there are no issues around the Northern Ireland portfolio – the transition has gone very well – so the proposed calls are in the nature of courtesy ones. Cerberus remains interested in the Irish market and continues to do business here.'

At the time, in late February 2015, the dogs in the business streets in Belfast were loudly barking about the fee arrangements associated with the sale, the offshore account containing £7 million, and the resignation of Ian Coulter from Tughans solicitors.

The PAC report comprehensively recorded all the details surrounding the history of Project Eagle and made scathing criticisms of the manner in which NAMA organised the sale process, applying an incorrect discount and ignoring blatant conflicts of interest along the way. The committee said that Noonan's meeting with Snow and the Cerberus team could have given the perception that the US fund was benefiting from preferential treatment and said that the deal it obtained resulted in a possible loss to NAMA of €800 million on its Northern Ireland loans. It found that the sales strategy was 'seriously deficient' and that there was a failure of corporate governance by NAMA in not removing Cushnahan from the NIAC after he declared that he was advising debtors comprising over 50 per cent of the value of the loan book.

NAMA rejected the findings of the PAC report, including its 42 recommendations. Asked whether McDonagh or Frank Daly might consider their positions following the committee's criticisms of the agency, a spokesman for NAMA said: 'The issue does not arise. NAMA considers that it acted appropriately in the conduct of this transaction.'

If some of the exchanges during the hearings and following the publication of the report were bruising, they were nothing to the one in the Oireachtas restaurant in Leinster House, soon before its release, between Noonan and committee chairman Sean Fleming. According to the Fianna Fáil TD, Noonan had threatened to take legal action and injunct the report if it included criticism of his actions, or inactions, in relation to the Project Eagle sale, a confrontation which some committee members believed was a deliberate effort to interfere politically with its work and role as an independent watchdog of the Oireachtas. Most committee members knew nothing about the restaurant row until it emerged during the Dáil debate on the report on 29 March 2017 when confrontation between the minister and the chairman led to some harsh comments across the floor of the House.

Noonan opened proceedings with a strong defence of his own actions and revealed that he had written to Fleming before the report was published to object to a finding against him or his officials: 'I remain shocked that the Committee of Public Accounts disregarded due process and did not offer me or my officials the opportunity to discuss the committee's concerns even after I requested such an opportunity prior to the report's finalisation.'

Noonan argued that the minutes of his meeting with Cerberus were 'available on the Department of Finance website. It is there to read for all who are interested,' and argued that it was entirely appropriate for him to meet 'the chairman of a major international investment fund, a former US Secretary of the Treasury, at his request, while he was in Dublin on business'. He said he had previously disclosed details of the meeting with Cerberus to Fianna Fáil deputy Michael McGrath in July and September 2015, over a year before he attended the PAC; had supplied the details to the media following an FOI request; and the C&AG was provided with information and documents pertaining to the Cerberus meetings in November 2015. He accused Fleming of making 'false allegations' against him in relation to the controversial meeting during a radio interview on the day the PAC report was published, and asked him to withdraw them.

His aggressive attack on the committee chairman and almost exclusive focus on his own actions during his opening remarks were described as defensive by Cullinane. Noonan responded by accusing Cullinane's party of making 'a profession of not telling the truth'.

In relation to the commission of investigation proposed by the PAC, Noonan asked what it would investigate and how it would add to the work already done by the C&AG and PAC, or the ongoing criminal investigations, or how it could ensure witnesses from other jurisdictions would give evidence. Not to mention the cost of the exercise.

If the debate had started off on a sour note, it was only going to get worse. Michael McGrath asserted that the minister had made an 'ill-judged' speech and 'an unprecedented attack on the PAC', spending most of his time 'defending his own personal position and that of his department'.

McGrath said the sale of Project Eagle was 'marked by inadequate record-keeping, weaknesses in the management of conflicts of interest, a seriously deficient sales process and, ultimately, an inability by NAMA to demonstrate it had obtained the best value for money for the State'.

When Fleming took to his feet he said he 'had hoped the debate would be on the NAMA report, but the Minister feels it is all about him. It was not about him at all. It was about NAMA. There are 101 pages in the report and only two paragraphs about the Minister, but he thinks it is all about him.'

Fleming singled out the fact that Noonan had not revealed his meeting with Cerberus on the eve of its bid during the minister's five-hour appearance at the PAC.

It is a little bit rich of the Minister to complain that we did not ask him about something when he was the only person in the room who knew about that meeting on that particular occasion.

Then Fleming pulled a smoking gun from his pocket in relation to the letter sent to the PAC in February and his meeting later that evening, on the day it was received, in the Oireachtas restaurant:

The Minister sent that letter to the committee on 15 February 2017. I went into the Oireachtas restaurant that evening and the Minister asked me to come over to have a chat with him. He told me that I was unfair to him by not inviting him to the committee. I told him he was unfair to the committee by keeping the information for five hours. He concluded the conversation by saying that he can injunct me. Shame on the Minister for Finance for wanting to injunct the Committee of Public Accounts for doing its job. I wrote it down. He said to me, 'I can injunct you.'

Fleming told the minister he was 'unfit for office', to which Noonan replied that the Fianna Fáil deputy was a 'disgrace' and called for him to resign as PAC chair.

Mary Lou McDonald said it was news to her that Noonan had threatened to injunct the PAC and that in his contribution to the said debate he had all but ignored the report of the committee, which had sat on 11 occasions, heard 57 hours of oral evidence, studied some 3,000 pages of written evidence and vindicated the C&AG.

After detailing some of the most serious findings about those involved in hatching the Project Eagle deal, including Cushnahan, Coulter and Keinan, McDonald repeated the call for a fully empowered and judicially led commission.

Suffice to say, having just scratched the surface of a single transaction – because bear in mind our committee was limited in its powers of investigation – what we found was very troubling. The big question is this: was Project Eagle an outlier? Was this an exception? Was it exceptionally sloppy, compromised and corrupted or was and is Project Eagle the norm? That is the issue. If the Minister, Deputy Noonan, was doing his job, beside coming in here giving us guff, that is the issue that would be sounding a big alarm bell in his head and it is the reason we absolutely need a commission of investigation.

When it was his turn, Wallace expressed his shock at the aggressive tone of the Minister for Finance and described the report as powerful. Focusing on the role of Ronnie Hanna, he described how on 12 December 2013 the former head of asset recovery presented a paper to the NAMA board which called for a closed sale and set the price at £1.3 billion. Wallace continued:

The committee found this unacceptable. The December 2013 paper presented by Ronnie Hanna was a sales pitch for PIMCO but it was not all about PIMCO. It was really a sales pitch for the developers in Northern Ireland who had

Frank as their adviser, Dave Watters as their accountant, Tughans as solicitors and their man in NAMA, Ronnie Hanna. He referred to the email from Cian Kealy on the day before Hanna presented the paper to the board and wishing Keinan the best on his 'big day' tomorrow. Keinan replied that they looked forward to it. I bet they did. ...

It was a big day all right, when the NAMA board was hoodwinked by the head of asset recovery. It has emerged from the PAC hearings that the NAMA board destroyed the handwritten notes taken at that board meeting on 12 December 2013. ... Speaking of destroying records, in March 2015, the month before NAMA records became accessible under freedom of information it became NAMA policy to delete the e-mails deemed 'non-business critical' of all former NAMA staff 12 months after they had left the agency. Even more worrying is the fact that NAMA board members' e-mails would be deleted as soon as they had left. The destruction of key records will certainly make life more difficult for the commission of investigation.

Referring to Noonan's eve of bid meeting with Cerberus, Wallace cited other occasions when the minister and department officials, including the former secretary general, John Moran, met with vulture funds before crucial decisions were made on loan book disposals. He said that in early 2014, while the Project Eagle sale was near completion, the IBRC was selling Project Sand, a portfolio of 12,700 former Irish Nationwide residential mortgages with a par value of €1.8 billion.

He said that in January Noonan met with Lone Star in Davos in the Swiss Alps during the annual global economic forum and later in the week met Moran in his Merrion Street office in Dublin. A briefing note for Moran stated that Lone Star was keen to purchase a significant portion of IBRC assets and was involved in the Project Sand sale process. On 14 March, the day before bidding closed, Oaktree Capital also sought 'a ten to fifteen' minute meeting with Moran to discuss its approach to the Project Eagle purchase, Wallace said.

There were 13 indicative bidders for Project Sand. Who were the winners? Two of them, believe it or not – Oaktree and Lone Star. They split the portfolio between them. How convenient is that? It seems it will stand a US vulture fund in good stead, if they are bidding on NAMA or IBRC loans, to meet and engage with the top officials in the Department of Finance in the months before, weeks before and even – incredibly – on the day before the bids are due. That approach worked for Cerberus, Oaktree and Lone Star, which between them have now bought nearly €50 billion of Irish loans. Is it proper policy for officials and the Minister for Finance to meet and engage with US vulture funds who are actively involved in bidding on Irish loans that are supposed to be for sale on the open market?

Arguably the row between Fleming and Noonan over what transpired in the restaurant of the Dáil when the finance minister allegedly threatened to injunct publication of the report served to divert from the gravity of its findings across a range of issues. During the subsequent debate a number of TDs including Wallace and Richard Boyd Barrett cited the publication of another report of recent days which added further to the difficulties and growing criticism of NAMA.

An investigation by economist Jim Power, commissioned by house builder David Daly, into asset sales by NAMA concluded that the agency had lost an estimated €18 billion of public monies by selling assets too quickly and in bundles too large for any entity other than a few vulture funds to afford.

The report, researched in collaboration with Lisney estate agents, found that NAMA had consistently sold assets under their real value to purchasers, who sold them on at a considerable profit. According to David Daly, he commissioned the report because he suspected properties were being undersold by NAMA and, according to the research, the agency 'has failed to realise a staggering €18 billon for the taxpayer'.

Writing in the *Sunday Business Post* on 26 March 2017, David Daly said:

Jim Power and I believe that the actual figure lost to the taxpayer is likely to be much higher, perhaps as high as €40 billion, which puts it on a scale equating to the bank bailout itself. Unfortunately, it's impossible to prove this because of the veil of secrecy around NAMA, despite NAMA being a government-created body.

The report showed that NAMA had sold sites which were flipped within months in what Daly described as 'eye-watering' mistakes by the agency. One site in Dock Mill, Barrow Street, Dublin 4 was sold by NAMA for €1.3 million and re-sold within the year for €13 million. Another at Sir John Rogerson's Quay was sold by NAMA for €7.5 million and flipped two years later for €17.5 million. New Century House in the IFSC was sold for €28 million in September 2013 and sold six months later for €47 million.

'Considering that NAMA had 12,000 loans on its books, it is staggering that on an analysis of just 11 transactions alone we have identified a cumulative loss of €317.6 million to the taxpayer,' David Daly wrote. He accused NAMA of spinning when it claimed to be heading for a surplus of €2.3 billion while it was ignoring its remit to claw back the €42 billion loss to the public from the 'haircut given to the banks'.

Daly went on to blame NAMA for the deep and ongoing housing and rental crisis in the country, where almost 100,000 were on the housing lists of local authorities while fewer than 10,000 social housing units were built over the previous five years. He was critical of the manner in which NAMA had effectively shut down established house builders, including his own firm Albany Homes, which was building 800 homes each year, when it called in their poor and performing loans. He said the agency also allowed planning permissions for new homes Albany had on lands across the greater Dublin area to lapse, thus destroying the company's best assets. He said that the agency had directly contributed to the housing crisis by cutting supply over a five-year period. He later described the transfer of billions of public assets by NAMA into the arms of vulture funds as the biggest takeover of Irish property wealth 'since the plantations of the 17th Century'.

Although NAMA did its best to discredit the findings and was accused by Daly of forcing Lisney to issue a statement withdrawing its endorsement of the report, it was unable to sustain any more than a few inaccuracies. After the Power report was published, Lisney issued the assertion that it 'did not validate the numbers in the report or verify the report'. 'The sole data source in the report provided by Lisney relates to an appendix detailing 11 properties that were sold and subsequently resold, details of which were in the public domain and reported in national newspapers,' the company said.

After this was disputed by Daly, Power and the *Sunday Business Post*, Lisney clarified the matter and said 'it did not have any editorial control over the report.'

The report had wrongly described two transactions, the sale of Riverside 11 in the Docklands and another property at Bishop's Square in Dublin as NAMA sales, when they were not.

If David Daly could be criticised for reflecting a view that was motivated by the interests of the much-maligned and unpopular developer community, it touched a nerve among those in NAMA who could find little fault in the facts the Power report had uncovered. In a hostile review of the study entitled 'NAMA response to a report on its performance commissioned by an ex debtor', the agency claimed it was 'riddled with errors'.

It rejected the claim that the agency had 'undermined the ability of the development community to adequately manage, fund and develop their property assets.' NAMA said:

Contrary to this claim, NAMA has been working well with a majority (over 66%) of cooperative residential developers. For a minority of debtors, it proved impossible to develop a business relationship either because they refused to cooperate or because they lacked the expertise to manage the properties for which they had borrowed.

The report goes on to claim that NAMA was the cause of the housing crisis allegedly 'because the actions of NAMA have resulted in a situation where there are not enough viable developers to satisfy housing demand'. This is nonsense. NAMA debtors and receivers control only about 24% of residential development land in the Greater Dublin area and accordingly NAMA's influence over new supply is limited.

NAMA added that 'the analysis of 11 properties includes two properties which never had any connection to NAMA' and which 'account for 15% by value of the sample'. NAMA claimed the report

selectively and disingenuously focuses on a small number of assets which were sold at an early stage in the cycle; it fails to point out that the bulk of the Irish assets were sold during the period 2014–2016 when market recovery was well advanced. Certain assets were sold early in the cycle to drive market recovery and to attract international capital willing to invest in Ireland.

The report contradicts itself by blaming NAMA for an alleged failure to fund housing when it was not commercially viable to do so but questions NAMA's funding of residential delivery now that it has become commercially viable.

However, as the NWL website pointed out, the NAMA response was also economical with the facts. Although Power had mistakenly included the two transactions which had nothing to do with NAMA, its inadequacy was largely due to the author's inability to get access to detailed information from the agency about specific asset disposals. Its headline finding that the agency, by selling too quickly, had allowed profits of up to €18 billion to go to vulture funds over-shadowed the other main conclusion – that NAMA had achieved a rate of return on its sales of less than 1 per cent. This, NWL argued, 'contrasts negatively with returns generated by asset managers and vultures'. The NAMA response also referred to the requirement under Section 10 of the NAMA Act 2009 to dispose of assets 'expeditiously' but did not mention another stipulation in the same section of the legislation, that it 'obtain the best achievable return for the State.'

When McDonagh, in a statement in early June, accused developers of contributing to the housing shortage, he neglected to mention that NAMA had disposed of sites over the previous years with planning for 50,000 houses in land and loan sales, yet only 3,000 were built. The agency had long emphasised its role in the provision of social and affordable housing but effectively delivered little or nothing, while those who purchased from NAMA and hoarded land were mainly investment funds incentivised to do so by capital gains legislation introduced by Michael Noonan in 2012. The legislation encouraged funds, including NAMA, to hold on to lands for seven years as sellers would be subject to a one-third windfall tax if they put them on the market any earlier.

In contrast to NAMA's insistence in late 2013 to PIMCO during the Project Eagle saga that it did not engage in off-market sales, NAMA executives were plunged into yet another controversy when its disposal of €0.5 billion in loans known as the Project Tolka portfolio came under scrutiny in June 2017. The agency had earlier confirmed that it had sold €1.2 billion of assets in 240 separate transactions since early 2014 without any of them being openly marketed. Now it appeared that the Project Tolka loan book, which included assets such as the Burlington Plaza in Dublin 2, the Clarion Hotel in Liffey Valley, an office complex at Belfield in Dublin 4 and the former Harcourt Street children's hospital, had been sold in what the agency described as a 'targeted sale' at a 70 per cent discount. While Michael Noonan said that the agency got the best return, his opposite number in Fianna Fáil, Michael McGrath, called for an investigation by the C&AG into the disposal. The portfolio included loans linked to developers Paddy Kelly, John Flynn and the McCormack family and their investment vehicle, Alanis. It was acquired in January 2017 by California-based investment firm Colony Capital, whose €450 million bid for the €1.5 billion par value loan book was chosen ahead of Lone Star and Madison International Realty. The three US funds had been chosen by NAMA to ensure there was competitive tension in the sale process but there were questions as to why debtors were given a role in selecting potential bidders. McGrath said:

> While it is possible that NAMA received the best possible price for the loans concerned, the sales process could not be described as fully open and competitive. A peculiar aspect of this sales process is that debtors and NAMA agreed on the list of credible potential bidders. I think there needs to be an explanation as to why the debtors had an involvement in the selection of potential bidders.

As the latest crisis facing NAMA emerged, one fact that could not be ignored was that a few major funds were making profits in their billions, with little or no tax paid to the Irish exchequer, while tens of thousands of Irish families faced an accommodation crisis and many were facing the loss of their homes as a result of distressed mortgages now owed to faceless vultures. In the year after the country commemorated the Easter Rising of 1916, it was further evidence that not all of its children were being cherished equally and that a new golden circle had emerged from the wreckage of Ireland's property and banking collapse.

Chapter 25 ～

THE END GAME

In early April 2017, Mick Wallace again raised the issue of the shredding of emails by NAMA; and once more the finance minister defended the agency and insisted that its 'records management policy is entirely in line with best practice among public and private organisations'.

Noonan insisted that all key records held by NAMA 'are retained and they will therefore be available, if required for any business purpose including in the event that a Commission of Investigation is established into the sale of Project Eagle'. Given the levels of mistrust that now existed across the opposition benches, in the media and among the general public about NAMA's activities and the secrecy surrounding its decisions, there was inevitable cynicism surrounding the revelation that it was 'shredding files' of potentially important commercial and other information in advance of an inquiry that would have powers of compellability and discovery that were not available to the PAC or other bodies. The fact that former staff members such as Enda Farrell claimed that he had seen emails which would support allegations he made privately to the Garda about other NAMA employees, including senior officials, only served to heighten suspicions surrounding the issue. When Wallace uncovered correspondence showing how NAMA staff were advised to avoid the scrutiny of the already restricted FOI legislation, which covered the agency since 2015, the fear that significant evidence of wrongdoing was being covered up gained further traction.

During the debate on the PAC report in late March 2017, Wallace had revealed that his Namaleaks website had received communications on the deletion of emails within the agency.

One is from an ex-NAMA employee who says that when working in NAMA staff were made aware of the protocols and procedures regarding freedom of information requests. However, there was a facility to quickly search for and recover any e-mails deleted from in-boxes. It seems that the freedom of information guys could not search this. The individual does not believe that proper searches were carried out as not all in-boxes were searched. The

Minister should immediately suspend NAMA's policy of deleting e-mails and records but he is unlikely to do that.

Among those planning to benefit from the resurgence of construction activity in Dublin, in contrast to almost anywhere else in the country, were Sean Mulryan of Ballymore Properties and Johnny Ronan. They had contrasting experiences with NAMA, with Mulryan emerging as a favoured developer of the agency. His joint development with NAMA on the Docklands, known as Dublin Landings, involving the construction of hundreds of apartments alongside office space, was among the largest proposed developments along the rapidly transforming riverside.

Mulryan described as a staggering achievement his company's final debt repayment of €3.2 billion and exit from the agency in December 2016 when 'it satisfied its obligations under the company's Connection Management Agreement with the agency'. It was unclear whether Ballymore actually repaid €3.2 billion to NAMA or had satisfied 'its obligations' for considerably less than that sum.

'We have also managed to retain one of the best development land banks in London, a significant land bank in Ireland, a significant property investment portfolio and have successfully grown our development management and construction management businesses in London, Birmingham and Dublin,' Mulryan added.

NAMA had loaned huge sums to Mulryan, was still a partner in several multi-million-euro developments and also rented office space in the Dublin Landings project, a further sign of its positive relationship with its biggest debtor. Mulryan said that his exit agreement with NAMA would also involve Ballymore completing construction projects at Piper's Hill in Kildare and Royal Canal Park in north Dublin. He was also considering further cooperation with the agency to build homes on NAMA-owned sites in Dublin, Kildare and Wicklow. On hand to celebrate Ballymore's success at the launch of the Dublin Landings project was Michael Geoghegan, the chairman of the ministerial advisory committee of NAMA and former chief executive of HSBC. His public endorsement of Mulryan's favoured relationship with NAMA was the subject of bitter criticism by some of those developers who had fought tooth and nail to get out from the grip of the agency. During his speech, Geoghegan said that Ireland was right to remain in the EU post-Brexit having argued in favour of the UK leaving the EU in the country's referendum earlier in the year.

No doubt many of those who welcomed Mulryan's achievements were also present when he returned to his hobby of horse racing and sponsored the €100,000 handicap hurdle at the Punchestown races in late April 2017. Among those who most certainly were not at the races was James Woolf, who had complained to the PAC that he was wrongly excluded from bidding for buildings in Prague previously owned by Ballymore which were on the NAMA books.

'If the members of the committee agree and have an interest in the Savarin case and the matters referred to above, then Flow East is available to discuss or attend for interview and to provide any further detail required,' Woolf said in his letter to the committee.

In a report in the *Irish Times* in May, a NAMA spokesman was quoted as stating: 'We have confirmed to the PAC that we accepted the best unconditional offer and the full par debt was recovered.' The report added that 'it is understood that Crestyl's offer was unconditional, while Flow East's was not'.

Mulryan's problems at home had not all gone away; he was still being pursued by Wicklow auctioneer Gabriel Dooley for some €4 million he claimed he was owed from a joint venture over the Florentine site in Bray, County Wicklow. Mulryan and Sean Dunne had also developed the huge Charlesland residential complex in Greystones, with the help of Dooley's site assembly work, in the early 2000s. Allegations persisted about the manner in which the two developers and their companies obtained valuable public lands, which provided them with vital road access to the site, for little or no consideration from Wicklow County Council under contracts that did not go before elected members of the local authority for their agreement.

In July 2017 the High Court ruled in favour of an elected and former member of Wicklow County Council in a defamation action the two took against the local authority and former county manager, Eddie Sheehy. Councillor Tommy Cullen and former councillor Barry Nevin claimed they were defamed when the council issued a press release in April 2013 accusing them of making unfounded and mis- conceived claims against the local authority and of wasting public money. The press release was authorised by Sheehy following publication of an investigation for the council by Seamus Woulfe SC into the CPO of land at Three Trout Stream, close to the Zapi development in Greystones. The councillors had queried the cost of the CPO, issued in November 2003, and had made a series of claims, including that the land was prone to flooding, in a complaint to the Department of Environment (which was funding the purchase). An objector to the CPO, local landowner John Nolan, told An Bord Pleanála in early 2007 that the land known as the 'bog field' was in a flood plain and that the purchase was intended to facilitate road access to the Charlesland development in favour of Zapi and developers Sean Mulryan and Sean Dunne. In her judgment, Judge Marie Baker said that the councillors had raised legitimate concerns; they had not caused the alleged financial loss to the council. She awarded damages to the plaintiffs. She said that Sheehy had exercised 'a degree of malice or an improper purpose' in the release of the press statement.

During the action, she referred to the fact that Zapi was 'in the ether' of the case. This comment and her judgment revived the allegations that the company had been given access to public lands close to the Charlesland development that multiplied Charlesland's value for little or no financial consideration. The allegations made by estate agent Gabriel Dooley, who assembled the lands for the multi-billion euro, 1800-home residential development, also resurfaced as a result of the court decision. In July 2017 local TD and health minister Simon Harris among others called for an independent inquiry into the administration of local government in the 'garden county'.

Sean Dunne was still fighting his long-distance battle with court-appointed official assignee Chris Lehane, acting for NAMA and other creditors in Ireland. Dunne left for the US in 2009 owing more than €450 million, including €185 million in loans transferred to NAMA. He was declared bankrupt in the US in 2013 after failing to honour debts of €160 million to Ulster Bank. In her latest appearance in the High Court in Dublin in May, his wife, Gayle Killilea, denied that she was the beneficiary in the sale of a house called 'Walford' on Shrewsbury Road, for which the couple had paid over €60 million at the height of the property boom and which was sold for €14 million by Cypriot-registered company Yesreb. Challenging an application by Lehane for an injunction to prevent her reducing her assets below €50 million, Killilea said that she had received no money from the house sale and that in 2010 she had separated from Dunne, who still owed her, and their children, a lot of money. According to Killilea and Dunne, the official assignee and others in the Irish establishment were engaged in a 'witchhunt' against her. Lehane was objecting to Dunne's discharge from bankruptcy while seeking to prove that property and other transfers to her were an attempt to conceal assets from debtors. Among those assisting Lehane in the pursuit of their assets was private detective Denis O'Sullivan. Meanwhile, Hibernia REIT had acquired assets from the Platinium portfolio previously owned by Dunne, including office blocks in Dublin city centre.

More fortunate in his recovery was north Dublin developer, and another member of the Maple 10, Gerry Gannon, who was assisted by NAMA in building a large residential complex of 260 homes on the site of the former Belcamp school and grounds off the Malahide Road. He also announced plans in early 2016 to develop an apartment and townhouse complex in nearby Clongriffin in north Dublin. Gannon's loans were transferred to NAMA after the crash in 2010 and in 2014 his company, Gannon Homes, still had debts of €194 million.

He had been identified as another architect of the collapse when he was filmed by RTÉ, in a post-crash feature, filling the boot of his top-of-the-range silver Range Rover with bags of shopping from Brown Thomas, the expensive Grafton

Street outlet, in December 2010 just months after his loans of €1.3 billion were transferred to NAMA. Another developer to receive favourable treatment from NAMA was Mick Bailey, who, with his brother Tom and their company Bovale Ltd, made a settlement of €22 million with the Revenue Commissioners in 2006 in taxes, interest and penalties. This arose as the result of the investigation by the planning and payments tribunal into their business dealings. In 2013, the Baileys were disqualified from acting as company directors for seven years, but a year later were planning to build luxury homes in Dublin 4 with support from the agency. The Cosgrave brothers, Joe, Peter and Michael, were also looking to a brighter future. Their loans of over €500 million were transferred to NAMA, but by 2017 they were working with the agency on the completion of major house-building projects, including the 1,800-unit upmarket residential Honeypark development on the former Dún Laoghaire golf course lands.

Among the newer developers on the block, building a major office block on City Quay on land previously owned by Sean Dunne on the south side of the river, was Targeted Investment Opportunities, backed by Oaktree Capital, Bennett Developments and NAMA. Target Investment Opportunities planned to construct over 7,000 square feet of office space in the €450 million project. Grant Thornton, the receivers appointed over Dunne's assets, signed contracts to rent the building, on completion, for its new headquarters. Among the private investors in the City Quay project was Frank Kenny of Hibernia REIT. The directors of Target Investment Opportunities included John Mulcahy, who was joined on the board by Jim Bennett of the Bennett construction group and Justin Bickle, the UK chief executive of Oaktree. In July it was announced that Mulcahy was to chair a new house-building company, which Oaktree said it planned to float on the Irish Stock Exchange. In August the *Irish Times* reported that Mulcahy and two other directors were to benefit from a multi-million-euro share incentive scheme after the flotation of the new company, Glenveagh Properties, later in 2017.

If NAMA was willing to assist some of its former debtors and staff members in their efforts to rebuild Dublin, and their fortunes, the agency executives were unlikely to welcome the return of an old adversary with grandiose plans to transform the Docklands and literally bring it to new heights. In early May Johnny Ronan revealed plans to build the tallest building in Dublin on a site adjoining Tara Street rail station including offices, a 110-bedroom hotel and an open restaurant and café terrace 'with panoramic views across the city'. Two months later, Dublin City Council rejected plans for the 22-storey tower because of the potentially detrimental visual effect on most of the historic core of the city. Ronan's company, Tanat Ltd, had sought to build the tallest building in the city at 88 metres but was forced to revisit his plans following the council's decision.

Among the other less favoured developers who refused to lie down was Garrett Kelleher, who won a significant legal action against NAMA in March 2017, which provided him with the prospect of obtaining vital documents under discovery in relation to the manner with which NAMA dealt with the Spire project in Chicago. He still had several court actions in train in Ireland and the EU while he was also embroiled in a case in the US courts relating to a business arrangement he had made several years previously in Liberia.

Paddy McKillen continued separate legal actions against NAMA and the office of the Minister of Finance, with John Moran and Paul Hennigan also named in the latter case. The O'Flynn brothers were still pursuing their High Court case for damages against Farrell and his former employer.

In the North, Paddy Kearney launched legal proceedings against former Sinn Féin finance minister Máirtín Ó Muilleoir, who, the developer claimed, had made 'a number of totally false and unfounded allegations against him at Stormont' including in the Assembly and during committee meetings which examined the Project Eagle sale and its aftermath. The PSNI was also investigating the alleged coaching of witness Jamie Bryson by a number of parties.

Belfast developer Frank Boyd, whose loans were purchased from NAMA by Cerberus as part of Project Eagle, was criticised by housing rights groups over plans to build a major retail centre on the Crumlin Road in the north of the city when over 2,000 people were on council waiting lists in the immediate area. His plans, which were endorsed by the council in August 2017, were supported by the DUP and loyalist political groupings, while Sinn Féin and local community organisations opposed the proposals, claiming social housing was a more urgent priority for the area.

Boyd, who was once owner of Belfast's Connswater shopping centre, reached an agreement with Cerberus to buy back his £0.25 billion property portfolio in 2015. It was reported that Boyd paid £100 million to regain control of his company, Killultagh Estates, and other assets which were valued at £228 when they transferred to NAMA in 2010. The refinancing was arranged by Luxembourg-based ICG Longbow and was signed off by Tughans solicitors.

An even greater success story was the reported purchase by New York private equity firm KKR of Australian group Pepper. Backed by Goldman Sachs, Pepper was among the first of the global funds to invest in Irish property assets following the banking crash and managed a commercial and residential loan portfolio of some €18 billion on behalf of investors CarVal and Lone Star, among others. Pepper chairman Seumas Dawes was reported to be in line for a Aus$195 million payment for his 30 per cent stake in the company if the sale to KKR went ahead. Among the leaders of KKR was retired US general and director of the CIA, David

Petraeus, who heads the KKR Global Institute. It identifies suitable countries for the firm to invest its $137 billion in private equity funds. In 2015 KKR joined with the Ireland Strategic Investment Fund in a €500 million initiative to support residential development.

In July, as the monthly *Irish Times* crane count in Dublin rose to 70 from less than half that a year earlier, an indication of the renewed construction levels, mainly in the south side of the city and particularly in the wider Docklands area, NAMA reported that it had less than 2 per cent of its original debt to clear. Following redemption of almost €1 billion of senior notes in early April 2017, the agency said it had less than €500 million of senior debt remaining. 'NAMA is close to achieving, three years ahead of schedule, its primary commercial objective of redeeming its senior debt and thereby eliminating this contingent liability for Irish taxpayers,' said McDonagh.

While the news was good for NAMA, it was followed by the now inevitable government decision to hold a commission of inquiry into the Project Eagle sale, including into the role of Michael Noonan. The draft terms of reference proposed an examination into the management of the loan sale by NAMA and whether it had applied the correct procedures and protocols. They also proposed an investigation of any conflict of interest involving members of the NIAC and the action, or otherwise, of the agency in relation to them. The commission was also tasked with investigating communications by Noonan and his officials with members of the Northern Ireland executive and whether such contacts were appropriate. The commission was expected to examine other transactions by NAMA, if appropriate, and to report back with an interim report within six months.

The Taoiseach told the opposition leaders he expected the work of the commission to be completed by June 2018 and the draft terms of reference would be debated in the Dáil before the establishment of the inquiry. Retired High Court judge John Cooke was chosen to lead the investigation. An announcement by Enda Kenny that he was to resign as Fine Gael leader and Taoiseach on 17 May was soon followed by the decision of Michael Noonan not to seek appointment to cabinet by the new leader of the party. Although his health, which had been poor over recent years, and his age (74) were undoubted factors in his decision, the months and years of bruising challenges as finance minister and his defence of NAMA from every criticism, however justified, took its toll. His appearance at hearings of the commission of investigation into Project Eagle will be watched with interest. His fiercest critic, Mick Wallace, continued to make trenchant criticism of the successive governments led by Kenny and his finance minister.

'Since 2013, Ireland has been up for sale,' Wallace wrote in an *Irish Times* column in May 2017.

Ireland has now been the number-one seller of distressed loans in Europe for four years in row. In 2016, loan sales by NAMA and Irish banks totalled €12.1 billion, making up almost a quarter of the total of €49.9 billion of distressed debt sales in Europe.

In 2015, Irish loan sales amounted to €23.3 billion par debt. Take Cerberus, for example. It has purchased €14.5 billion of NAMA debt since 2014, which amounts to 20 per cent of the entire NAMA loan book. Cerberus earned €77 million in profit on its Northern Ireland loan portfolio Project Eagle in 2015, which it bought from NAMA in 2014. But it paid only €1,900 tax on the €77 million.

Later in the month, he told the Dáil that Cerberus was involved in 'insider trading' when it purchased loans connected to valuable German supermarkets and linked to the purchase by the US fund of Project Eagle.

Wallace claimed that Cerberus had agreed to buy the loan book known as Project Shift for £76 million, before the wider Project Eagle portfolio was put up for sale. Only then, he said, were the assets of Project Shift included in the larger Northern Ireland loan portfolio marketed as Project Eagle, and in the price paid by Cerberus for it. Other bidders for Project Eagle, including underbidder Fortress, were unaware of the German supermarkets loan, Wallace said. He called on the PAC to investigate the sale of Project Shift, which was run by the former head of asset recovery at NAMA, Ronnie Hanna. Ron Bolger, the businessman and advisor who was among those who accompanied Cerberus chairman John Snow when he met with Noonan in late March 2014, was involved in discussions with NAMA about the Project Shift purchase, according to Wallace. The Wexford TD also claimed that former NIAC member Brian Rowntree had confirmed to him that the advisory committee had not discussed the sale of Project Shift.

'Why didn't NAMA write to all bidders for Project Eagle and inform them that a debtor was sale agreed for £76 million and this might be removed?' Wallace asked.

On 23 May Wallace told the Dáil:

Fortress was bidding on Project Eagle without the knowledge that a minimum of €76 million would be taken off the price of the portfolio. Is this not a form of insider trading? Cerberus had non-public knowledge that the price for Project Eagle would be lower. Fortress did not have this knowledge. Why did NAMA not write to all bidders who signed non-disclosure agreements at the start of Project Eagle and inform them that a debtor was sale agreed for €76 million and that it may be removed from the price? I have written to the

Committee of Public Accounts today to ask them to examine all aspects of Project Shift.

Through Noonan, NAMA confirmed that Cerberus had agreed with the agency to convert Project Shift into a loan sale after NAMA selected the US fund in April 2014 as its preferred bidder for Project Eagle.

In early June, it emerged that NAMA was not going to have the C&AG as its only auditor and had appointed accountancy firm Mazars to also examine its books annually. It was claimed that the move was in order to comply with new EU audit reforms introduced in Ireland in June 2016 which required that the C&AG could only audit 'not for profit' entities. The C&AG had responded that NAMA was never intended to make a profit when it was first established in late 2009 and that it was the only appropriate authority to carry out the annual audit.

In its annual report for 2016, published on 1 June 2017, NAMA said: 'As the NAMA group entities are 51 per cent privately owned and operate to return dividends to shareholders, the companies were deemed to be trading for gain and the C&AG is not therefore in a position to audit the statutory financial statement of the NAMA group entities after 15th June 2015.' The report also stated that the agency planned to return a surplus of €3 billion when it completed its activities in 2020.

In an interview with RTÉ on the day of the report's publication, Frank Daly said that the agency was ready to provide any information required by the commission of investigation but insisted that it would not be changing its criticism of both the C&AG and PAC findings.

Daly also criticised those who attacked the agency for selling off assets, too quickly and in excessively large bundles, to vulture funds. He said that without adopting that strategy the agency would not be in its current position where only €500 million of senior debt remained from the original €30.2 billion it paid for loans transferred from the main Irish banks in 2009 and 2010.

Asked whether more than an additional €18 billion could have been obtained from the massive sale of Irish property assets if it had been done more slowly, as the report by Jim Power argued, the NAMA chairman said that its strategy was the correct one when it came to bringing down the country's debt mountain. He said that he had rejected the approach of developers who offered to repay their debts over a five- or ten-year period based on their own business plans.

'You don't repay it by sitting on your hands and doing nothing and trusting that those who got us into this mess would get us out of it,' Frank Daly told RTÉ.

It is evident that the questions surrounding NAMA and its large-scale disposal of assets will continue to attract comment, questions and criticisms for many years to come. The most important question is whether it achieved the objectives set out on its formation in 2009, including its primary task of restoring the financial health of the main Irish banks. It manifestly failed to do so. In June 2017, the government sold off 29.9% of its 99% shareholding in AIB, worth over €3 billion. The recently installed Taoiseach, Leo Varadkar, said it would use the proceeds to pay down the national debt, a decision widely criticised by many who argued that it should be used, if permitted by EU rules, to build urgently needed social and affordable housing. During the same week as the decision to proceed with the sale was announced, the former chairman and chief executive of Anglo Irish Bank, Seán FitzPatrick, walked out of the High Court after the collapse of the case brought against him by the state over his hiding of loans from the bank's auditors. FitzPatrick, widely seen as a key architect of the excess and hubris that brought down the Irish banking system and the economy in 2008 and destroyed the lives of so many thousands of Irish people, will not be held accountable for any of the damage he caused.

NAMA was established to repair the mistakes caused by excessive greed and corruption across the Irish business, banking and political systems. Many people have been enriched in the process, not least the vulture funds and their local agents, including asset managers, real estate, surveying accountancy and legal firms. It emerged in late July that Arthur Cox had been paid almost €40 million in legal fees for its NAMA work. For most of the Irish people the work of the agency remains a mystery and many of the activities associated with it and outlined in this work are either inexplicable or inexcusable.

In late June, Frank Cushnahan dropped his legal action against the BBC over the contents of the two *Spotlight* programmes broadcast in February and September 2016. He had unsuccessfully sought to obtain an injunction to prevent broadcast of the programmes and seek damages for what his solicitor Paul Tweed claimed was defamation of his client by the BBC. Rejecting his application in the Belfast court, Judge Ben Stephens recognised that 'there could be no sensible contention' that the broadcast of the programmes was not in the public interest and that there was a 'clear public interest in publication.' The BBC made no apology and paid no damages or any of Cushnahan's legal fees. The removal of the legal threat by Cushnahan cleared the way for the BBC *Spotlight* team to broadcast any further material it had on the Project Eagle scandal, although there remained the impediment of the ongoing NCA criminal investigation and its request to the media not to publish or broadcast any material which might hinder its prospects of obtaining successful prosecutions.

With most of the leading developers whose assets went into NAMA getting back on their feet, or at least enjoying the trappings of wealth far in excess of those available to most, NAMA offered another olive branch when it agreed in late June 2017 to cut deals with certain house builders. This would allow developers to share profits on schemes in which they cooperate with the agency and have the personal guarantees given by them on their family homes dropped. The agency said that it had made such arrangements with 34 developers and was in negotiations with 20 others for profit shares and debt write-offs in return for their cooperation with NAMA. In early August 2017 it was reported that major NAMA debtors, including the Cosgrave Group, Gannon Homes, Castlethorn and Ballymore, were to benefit from a €200 million state support scheme for house-building projects. Under the Local Infrastructure Housing Activation Fund (LIHAF), developers would receive government funding to build private homes once they were sold below market rates. Global firms, including Lone Star, Hines, Kennedy Wilson and Starwood Capital, were also to benefit under the LIHAF incentive scheme as well as Irish builders, Cairn Homes. Meanwhile, funds such as Hines and Ires Reit were coming under criticism for their role in pushing up rental costs to an unprecedented high, while Cerberus was ramping up its enforcement action against buy-to-let and residential mortgage holders. The proposal did not quite match the original objective of chasing the developers to all corners of the world for every cent they owed to the Irish people.

EPILOGUE

As *NAMA-land* was going to print in late September 2017, a number of significant and fresh details emerged concerning various aspects of this investigation. Among the developments was the arrest of County Down developer, John Miskelly, who had already shocked the political establishment, north and south, with his taped disclosures concerning Frank Cushnahan, Ronnie Hanna and others involved in the sale of the Project Eagle portfolio by NAMA.

Miskelly was detained at Belfast City Airport by officers of the National Crime Agency on Thursday 24 August. He was released on police bail and, along with Cushnahan and Hanna, was the third person arrested by the NCA in relation to the investigation of Project Eagle. The media did not report the arrest until a week after Miskelly was detained at the airport and only following a brief statement by the police, which did not name the County Down developer. The media did not name Miskelly as they had no confirmation from the police of the identity of the man detained. In the statement, published on 31 August, the NCA stated:

On 24 August 2017 officers from the National Crime Agency arrested a 54-year-old man at Belfast International Airport in connection with its ongoing NAMA investigation. The man was later released on police bail. As the investigation is continuing we are unable to comment further.

The NCA officers were undoubtedly interested in Miskelly's account of his meetings with Cushnahan over several years, some of which were taped, and in his payment of £40,000 in cash to the former NAMA advisor in the car park of Belfast City Hospital in August 2012. The NCA was certainly also keen to know of any other details in Miskelly's possession concerning Cushnahan and his business and political associates. They presumably wanted to know more about those involved in the Project Eagle saga and the subsequent refinancing of their loans by a number of developers in the North. They may also have been concerned that Miskelly would not put into the public domain further details, taped or otherwise, of alleged improper or corrupt dealings by those people associated with NAMA with whom he had contact in the past.

It seemed callous, to say the least, that the NCA would detain and seek to interview a person in such ill health, particularly as he may have been in no fit state to provide answers to the questions they wanted to pose. At the time of his arrest and detention, Miskelly was returning from London, where he had been treated for a serious medical condition, and his arrest in these circumstances was hardly conducive to a constructive outcome for the police investigators.

It is understood that Miskelly may have in his possession previously undisclosed and highly sensitive information concerning direct discussions with senior figures of NAMA after his distressed bank loans were transferred to it in the wake of the property collapse.

On 26 September the director of the NCA, Lynne Owens, confirmed that eight people remained under criminal investigation in connection with the Project Eagle sale, seven of whom have been interviewed. Witness statements have been taken and 61 people have been questioned, she said:

> We have eight potential suspects under investigation. Seven of them have already been interviewed. We have taken 61 witness statements. We have applied for six court production orders and there is another one in train. We have made three international letters of request to the Isle of Man and the Republic of Ireland because this is an international investigation.

The letters are seeking 'intelligence or evidence to prove or disprove allegations of bribery, fraud etc.,' she said.

In the weeks before the publication of NAMA-land, I also learned that Tyrone businessman, Barry Lloyd, has had extensive interviews with the NCA regarding his dealings with Frank Cushnahan. During a meeting in early September, Lloyd told me that the NCA had interviewed him on two occasions in Dungannon police station near his home in Clogher, County Tyrone, and later at the British embassy in Bangkok over a number of days in May 2017. He explained the central role that the Japanese bank, Nomura, had in the purchase of Project Eagle in 2014. As recounted earlier in this book, Lloyd had introduced Cushnahan to Richard Moore of Nomura soon after he was approached by the member of the Northern Ireland Advisory Committee of NAMA in late 2010. Moore had been contacted at his office in Hong Kong by Peter Banks, a close associate of Lloyd. Moore passed on the information to the Nomura office in London, which subsequently handled the discussions with Cushnahan. As he had stated in his affidavit, details of which have been recounted in earlier chapters of NAMA-land, Lloyd described how non-disclosure and other legal documents were drawn up by Ian Coulter at Tughans and signed by Nomura representatives who had expressed an interest in the proposed sale of the NI loan portfolio.

However, the bank's interest appeared to expire in 2012 after Lloyd received a letter from Moore stating that the bank was no longer and 'would not in the future' be interested in the NAMA NI loan book. However, according to Lloyd, he later learned that Nomura executives in London maintained close contact with Cushnahan and Coulter and their NI developer clients as the sale of the loan portfolio progressed in 2013 and 2014. Eventually, the bank advanced over £700 million to Cerberus towards its £1.2 billion purchase of Project Eagle in 2014. Lloyd claims that a close relationship developed between executives of Nomura and Cerberus through their respective London offices.

Lloyd claimed that Richard Moore subsequently left the bank after he learned of its continuing interest in the purchase despite the instructions he received to inform Lloyd that it was no longer interested in the NI portfolio controlled by NAMA. Lloyd claims that he became concerned after he was asked by Cushnahan at a meeting in Tughans in 2012 to try and raise some £3 million from Chinese and other Far East investors in return for a promise of UK passports for up to 30 people at a cost of £100,000 each. The scheme, he was informed, would be facilitated by prominent Northern Ireland politicians. He advised his Chinese and other interested investors not to get involved in the 'passport for investment' scheme, which he described as 'questionable'.

Lloyd and his colleague, Peter Banks, have given detailed interviews to the NCA, which has also been in contact with Richard Moore, as part of its criminal investigation into alleged fraud and other offences in connection with Project Eagle.

Lloyd described how he had first met Cushnahan in the early 2000s while the latter was chairman of the Belfast Harbour Commissioners. They met in his commissioner's office which contained a 'gigantic desk' with barely any papers or documents on it. He said that there was 'just a phone' on the desk which was, it appeared, Cushnahan's most essential tool when it came to doing business. Lloyd said that he met Cushnahan in relation to finance he was seeking for his computer software company, Microchannel Technologies. He told Cushnahan that he needed investment of some £300,000. Following a couple of phone calls, Cushnahan said he could raise the money from Bank of Ireland on condition that he was given a 10% shareholding in the company by Lloyd, and that the legal matters were handled by Tughans and the accountancy by McClure Watters. Lloyd agreed and the facility was arranged within hours with no personal guarantee required, Lloyd recalled.

Over the years, he maintained contact with Cushnahan, visiting him on occasion at his Stormont office when he worked in the Office of the First and Deputy First Minister of the Northern Ireland executive, and where he was introduced by Cushnahan to senior politicians, including Arlene Foster and Peter Robinson. Lloyd has also given a detailed interview to the BBC *Spotlight* programme as well as with TDs Mick Wallace and Clare Daly, who travelled to Bangkok to meet him in 2016. Following their meeting, Lloyd travelled to Dublin where Wallace introduced him to solicitor, Aidan Eames. Eames assisted in the preparation of the affidavit on his involvement with Cushnahan, Nomura and the Project Eagle sale, among other matters.

In late September, I learned that Galway developer, Gerry Barrett, was in possession of some damaging information which raised uncomfortable questions for NAMA. Over recent weeks, Barrett had been engaged in a High Court battle over the control of his company, Edward Holdings, including the g Hotel in Galway, the distressed loans of which had been sold by NAMA.

It was claimed to me that he had suffered at the hands of NAMA due to the leaking of a confidential file concerning his assets and debts from the agency. He claimed that, in 2011, he gained sight of the file, which was a confidential document containing his business plans and other commercially sensitive information. He claims he was given the name of the NAMA staff member who had leaked the file. He established that the document had been discussed at a meeting of the NAMA board in September 2010. It was clear from the documents he saw that his business file was Item 11 on the agenda of the board meeting on 9 September 2010. Using his mobile phone, he took photographs of the confidential documents. Through a prominent business figure, he arranged a meeting with NAMA chairman, Frank Daly, which took place in the agency headquarters in the Treasury Building in Dublin in December 2012. He was accompanied by the conduit whom had arranged the meeting, while Daly attended with the then chief financial officer of NAMA, Donal Rooney. Further discussions took place with the NAMA executives later in December and in early February 2013. At a meeting later that month, and at Daly's request, Barrett confirmed the identity of the staff member who leaked the file. He was informed that the staff member he named had left the agency.

At a hearing of the PAC in September 2013, Daly was asked whether there had been any breaches of confidentiality at the agency other than what had emerged in the public domain involving former NAMA official, Enda Farrell.

At the PAC on 26 September 2013, concerning potential abuse of confidential information by former officials of NAMA, Daly had the following exchange with Sinn Féin TD Mary Lou McDonald:

Mr Frank Daly: I assure the Deputy that we are very conscious of the taxpayers' view and that of the Oireachtas. We are very conscious of what we can do to monitor this and prevent any abuse. We are also conscious of the fact that we are not aware of abuse to date.

Deputy Mary Lou McDonald: That is fair enough. For the record, let it be said that I am not casting any aspersions on any individual bar in respect of the case reported in the media of abuse that was uncovered. I understand there is a Garda investigation. [The TD was referring here to the case involving Enda Farrell.]

At a subsequent meeting of the PAC just days before Christmas in December 2013, Daly informed members that there was an investigation, other than into the Farrell leaks, into a complaint regarding another leak of confidential information about which the agency was informed earlier that year. According to sources close to Barrett, this was a reference to the complaint he had made to Daly in February 2013. Barrett said he was first contacted by the GBFI shortly after Christmas, in late December 2013, for the first time about the leaking of his confidential file. It is unclear when the GBFI was first informed by NAMA about Barrett's complaint.

With his solicitor, Deirdre Courtney of Ivor Fitzpatrick & Company Solicitors, Barrett met with GBFI officers on a number of occasions in 2014. In November 2014 he signed a detailed affidavit and complaint recounting his experience from the time he first gained sight of his leaked NAMA file and his subsequent engagement with the agency on the unauthorised disclosure. In late September 2017 I submitted a question to Ray Gordon of Gordon PR, advisors to NAMA, about Daly's comments to the PAC and whether they related to the leaking of Barrett's material. In reply, Gordon PR, on behalf of NAMA, said that the agency had 'nothing to add to comments by Mr Daly at the Oireachtas Committee on that matter'.

If Daly was informed in February 2013 about the leaking of confidential information by a NAMA official, the question arises why he informed the PAC in September 2013 that the agency 'was not aware of abuse to date' when asked directly whether there had been leaks other than in the Farrell case. It has also emerged that at that time the GBFI had received multiple complaints of alleged criminal behaviour by NAMA officials. To date, Enda Farrell remains the only person convicted of an offence connected with the leaking of confidential material from the agency. It has been confirmed by Garda and other sources that another former staff member is currently under investigation.

In September 2017, Gerry Barrett was fighting a battle for survival against a claim by Deutsche Bank for almost €700 million in debts. The German bank was in the process of taking over his hotels in Galway, the Meyrick Hotel and g Hotel, as well as the Eye Cinema and other assets in the city and other locations, including properties in Quinta do Lago, Portugal, and Chicago. A former owner of the luxury Ashford Castle in County Mayo, Barrett had sought assistance from

Dublin-based Cardinal Capital to provide alternative finance, but the gap between what he could raise and what Deutsche Bank would accept in settlement was too wide. With tens of millions in personal guarantees at stake, Barrett sought to have examiners appointed over his assets in order to gain time to put together an acceptable refinancing package. Deutsche Bank had purchased €735 million of his debts from NAMA for just €97 million in 2015 and two years later was pursuing Barrett for the entire amount. On 15 September, the High Court confirmed the appointment of an examiner to three companies associated with the Meyrick Hotel, but declined to offer similar protection to four related companies in the Edward Holdings Group connected to the g Hotel, the Eye Cinema and other assets.

Meanwhile, Paddy McKillen was advancing his legal action against NAMA through law firm Crowley Millar over the huge financial and other damages he claims to have incurred as a result of its actions. With solicitor Aidan Eames, he is also suing the office of the Minister of Finance, its former secretary general John Moran, as well as former NAMA official Paul Hennigan, in relation to the leaking of McKillen's confidential material and other matters.

In 2012 McKillen had successfully fought off attempts by the Barclay Brothers to gain control of the Maybourne group and its ownership vehicle, Coroin. Following his lengthy and successful legal battle in London, McKillen had secured the financial support of Qatari investors and US Colony Capital, which asked him to manage and refurbish the luxury Connacht, Claridge's and Berkeley hotels in London. His former business partner, Derek Quinlan, previously a minority shareholder in Coroin and a former tax inspector with the Irish Revenue Commissioners, was among the largest NAMA clients with total debts, including to various banks, of up to €3.5 billion in 2010. He had developed the Four Seasons Hotel in Ballsbridge in Dublin, where investors in the Nollaig Partnership he formed included a host of rich and prominent Irish legal and entertainment figures. He sided with the Barclays in their battle with McKillen. In evidence in the 2012 High Court case in London between McKillen and Frederick and David Barclay and their company Misland, it was claimed that Quinlan had sought and possibly received fees of some £50 million in connection with the sale of his shares to the knighted twins. His wife, Siobhán, also received payments in excess of £3 million from the Barclay brothers, owners of the *Telegraph* newspaper group in Britain. John Moran was dragged into the controversy over his contact with a representative of the Barclay Brothers during the dispute, while Paul Hennigan, who gave evidence in the case, was accused of providing confidential information from NAMA files, relating to McKillen, to the billionaire British twins.

Quinlan worked as a tax inspector with the Revenue Commissioners for six years from 1989 and was employed there when NAMA chairman, Frank Daly, was appointed to the role of Assistant Secretary of the service. By 2001, through his company Quinlan Private, Quinlan had become one of the country's most successful property financiers with assets of some €858 million under his management rising to more than €4.2 billion at the height of the boom in 2005. He told the banking inquiry in 2015 that he had not foreseen the crash. Quinlan left Ireland in 2009 when he was 61. He said it was a 'very painful move' as he had a young family in the country. The move was designed to maximise the return for his creditor banks and was based on advice from KPMG, he said. Remaining in Ireland would have resulted in 'substantial tax to be paid on gains', he added. Quinlan initially moved to Switzerland and then to London.

In June 2017, property industry publication, *EuroProperty*, reported that Quinlan's new property vehicle, Quinlan Real Estate, in which he and his wife are directors, was advising a consortium of European investors seeking to purchase a building in Brussels, which houses the Belgian finance ministry, for a reported €1.3 billion.

Another of NAMA's most significant debtors, Harcourt Developments, emerged as the lead partner with the agency in a planned housing development in southwest Dublin. In late August, they applied for fast-track planning to An Bord Pleanála, through property vehicle Greenacre, to build 500 housing units at Saggart, County Dublin. Founded by developer Pat Doherty and chaired by Andrew Parker Bowles, Harcourt featured earlier in *NAMA-land* in relation to its multi-billion construction of the Titanic Quarter in the Belfast harbour area. A parliamentary question was put by Mick Wallace in the Oireachtas following the planning application in which he sought details of the sale of a NAMA portfolio, Project Abbey, in 2016. It included loans linked to a property portfolio held by Harcourt Developments. Project Abbey was secured by the US investment fund, Apollo, for €300 million, discounted from its par value of €700 million, according to property news outlet, *CoStar News*.

Harcourt purchased the 105 acres of land for the Titanic Centre from the Belfast Harbour Commissioners in 2003. Three years earlier, chairman of the commissioners, Frank Cushnahan, was centrally involved in the signing of a lease and development agreement for the land with the Harland & Wolff Group. In 2001, the transaction came under intense scrutiny at an inquiry in Stormont following allegations that Cushnahan was involved in a secret land deal.

Readers of *NAMA-land* will recall that Cushnahan did not emerge unscathed from the inquiry, during which he pleaded that he only acted with the best interests of the people in mind and denied that he had made personal gain from the land transactions. Remember this:

I wish to dispel any misconceptions that material benefit or personal gain have arisen for individuals on the board or in the management team from any transaction initiated by the Belfast Harbour Commissioners. That suggestion is misleading and disingenuous to the integrity of all those concerned.

The committee concluded that the harbour commissioners 'should have been proactive in seeking to publicise the deal in the interests of public openness and accountability, as well as the significant potential benefits that the deal would bring to the Northern Ireland economy'.

It would not be the last warning, mild as it was but prescient nevertheless, to be ignored by those who created, governed and operated the NAMA project on behalf of, and at enormous cost to, the people of Ireland.

INDEX